Australian Workplace Relations

Australian Workplace Relations explains the defining themes in workplace relations in the twenty-first century. It explores issues relating to employee voice, declining trade union membership, occupational health, immigrant and other disadvantaged workers, and monitoring and surveillance in the workplace. While the focus is Australia, the treatment of each topic is placed in both a national and an international context.

The book examines the effects on Australian workplace relations of globalisation, the changing international economy and the recent Global Financial Crisis. It provides a comprehensive examination of the *Fair Work Act 2009*, covering the return to an award safety net, the movement towards a national system on industrial relations, and the evolution of collective bargaining.

Case studies provide in-depth and practical explorations of the key themes of the book. The case studies examine four important sectors of the economy: health, retail and hospitality, the public sector and motor vehicle components.

Online resources are available at **www.cambridge.edu.au/academic/work placerelations**. Student resources include additional case studies and lists of further reading to extend knowledge. Instructor resources include answers to discussion questions and PowerPoint slides consolidating the key points of each chapter.

Comprehensive and fully cross-referenced, *Australian Workplace Relations* is an invaluable resource for upper-level undergraduate students of workplace, employee or industrial relations.

Julian Teicher is Professor of Industrial Relations, Department of Management, Faculty of Business and Economics at Monash University, and Adjunct Professor, College of Business at RMIT University.

Peter Holland is Associate Professor in Management at Monash University.

Richard Gough is Senior Lecturer in Management and Information Systems at Victoria University of Technology.

Australian Workplace Relations

Edited by

JULIAN TEICHER, PETER HOLLAND and RICHARD GOUGH

CAMBRIDGE
UNIVERSITY PRESS

CAMBRIDGE
UNIVERSITY PRESS

University Printing House, Cambridge CB2 8BS, United Kingdom

One Liberty Plaza, 20th Floor, New York, NY 10006, USA

477 Williamstown Road, Port Melbourne, VIC 3207, Australia

4843/24, 2nd Floor, Ansari Road, Daryaganj, Delhi - 110002, India

79 Anson Road, #06-04/06, Singapore 079906

Cambridge University Press is part of the University of Cambridge.

It furthers the University's mission by disseminating knowledge in the pursuit of education, learning and research at the highest international levels of excellence.

www.cambridge.org
Information on this title: www.cambridge.org/9781107664852

First published 2013

Cover design by Adrian Saunders
Typeset by Integra Software Services Pvt. Ltd

A catalogue record for this publication is available from the British Library

A Cataloguing-in-Publication entry is available from the catalogue of the National Library of Australia at www.nla.gov.au

ISBN 978-1-107-66485-2 Paperback

Additional resources for this publication at
www.cambridge.edu.au/academic/workplacerelations

Contents

Contributors

Santina Bertone is Associate Dean (Research) and Professor of Diversity Management in the Faculty of Business and Enterprise, Swinburne University of Technology. She has researched in the area of immigration and work since the early 1990s, having won 50 external research grants and published extensively on immigrant women, industrial restructuring, immigrants and trade unions, and managing diversity. She has a PhD from the University of Sydney, a Master of Arts (Industrial Relations) from the University of Melbourne, a Bachelor of Arts (Honours) from Monash University, a Graduate Diploma in Ergonomics (Lincoln Institute) and Certificate of Tertiary Education (Victoria University).

Pat Brewer is a Lecturer at Victoria University. Her research focus is on public sector management with particular interest in health and education. Her other major research focus is diversity and accountability. She teaches across a range of management and workplace relations subjects in Australia and Asia. Her current teaching area of interest is strategic planning in human resource management.

Dick Bryan studied economics and politics at Monash University and Sussex University. He is currently Professor of Political Economy at the University of Sydney. He has researched and published on issues related to globalization for 30 years, with a particular focus in the past decade on finance. He is the co-author of *Capitalism with Derivatives* (Macmillan 2006). His current research is on the financial liquidity and how it pertains to households, labour markets and the conception of money.

Brian Cooper is a Senior Lecturer in the Department of Management, Monash University. His research interests include the relationship between human resource management and employee outcomes. He has published extensively in the area of employee voice and its outcomes. Brian lectures in research methods and has extensive experience in quantitative business research methodologies.

Helen De Cieri is a Professor in the Department of Management at Monash University. From 2004 to 2011, Helen was the Director of the Australian Centre for Research in Employment and Work at Monash University. She has researched and consulted with a wide range of large and small organisations in Australia and overseas. Her published work includes more than 50 academic journal articles and several books. Her current research projects investigate human resource management, workplace health and safety and organisational performance. Helen has received numerous awards for her research and contributions to education.

Richard Gough is a Senior Lecturer is in the School of Management and Information Systems, Victoria University. His research interests are in the areas of the sociology of labour markets, contemporary employment models, life transitions of employees and the welfare state, sustainable workplace change, quality of work and innovative work systems in the health sector, the future of unionism and workplace bargaining.

Peter Holland is an Associate Professor in Human Resource Management, Director of the Human Resource Management Program and Deputy Head of the Human Resource and Employee Relations Discipline in the Department of Management, Monash University and visiting Associate Professor at the University of Tasmania. He has worked in the Australian finance industry and consulted to the private and public sectors in a variety of areas related to human resource management and workplace relations. His current research interests include talent management, employee voice, and monitoring and surveillance in the workplace. He has co-authored nine books and more than 60 journal articles, monographs and book chapters on a variety of human resource management and employee relations issues.

Marjorie Jerrard is a Senior Lecturer in the Department of Management, Monash University. She holds a PhD from Monash University on trade union strategy and the Australasian Meat Industry Employees' Union. She has published articles on the Australian and New Zealand meat processing industries, trade union strategy, community unionism in Australia and diversity. Her articles have appeared in *Labour History*, the *Journal of Industrial Relations*, *Labour Studies Journal*, the *Employment Relations Record* and the *Economic and Labour Relations Review*. Her current research projects include ancient Roman industrial relations and *Collegia*, and projects with a number of Victorian and Queensland trade unions.

George Lafferty is Professor of Employment Relations at the University of Western Sydney. He was previously Professor and Director of the Industrial Relations Centre at Victoria University of Wellington, having earlier worked at Griffith University and the University of Queensland. His main areas of research and teaching include the political economy of work, service sector employment, neo-liberalism and crisis, unionism and workplace restructuring. He has also occupied various policy roles at local, state and national levels.

Stéphane Le Queux is a Senior Lecturer in Employment Relations at James Cook University and a Research Fellow with the Interuniversity Research Centre on Globalisation and Work (CRIMT, Canada). His primary body of research involves trade union revitalisation, global social justice and international solidarity. His latest work focuses on labour politics in the wake of the global financial crisis. He also regularly publishes on contemporary issues in Australian industrial relations for the *Chronique Internationale de l'IRES* (France).

Malcolm MacIntosh took up an academic career after working in policy-oriented areas in the public sector. He is currently Associate Professor and Deputy Head (Teaching and Learning) in the School of Management at RMIT University. His academic research has included investigations of work organisation in several industries, including manufacturing. He was involved in an Australian Research Council linkage research project between 2005 and 2008, examining work organisation and industrial relations in manufacturing. His current research interest is the impact of globalisation on the institutions and practices of workplace relations in Vietnam.

Devaki Monani is a researcher in the Cosmopolitan Civil Societies Research Centre at the University of Technology, Sydney. She completed her doctoral degree at the University of Melbourne in 2008. Before taking up her current position, Devaki was a research associate with Professor Santina Bertone. She has published in the fields of cultural diversity, refugees, gender and international development.

Brad Nash is a senior executive working in the Australian Public Service (APS), who lectures in human resource management at Monash University, Melbourne. In the APS over the past 10 years, he has worked across different departments/agencies, including the Australian Taxation Office and Medicare. In these roles, he has managed large-scale operational teams through to discrete business improvement and workplace relations teams. His current research interests are trust in the employment relationship, monitoring and surveillance, and offshoring.

Anne O'Rourke is a Lecturer in the Department of Business Law and Taxation at Monash University, where she teaches employment law and Australian company law. Her research interests include international human rights law, labour rights under international conventions, employment law and workplace relations, workplace privacy and corporate governance. She is currently working on a PhD at Monash University, examining international framework agreements and their impact on multinational company compliance with international labour standards.

Marilyn Pittard is Professor of Law in the Faculty of Law, and Director, International, Monash University. She teaches labour law at undergraduate and postgraduate levels and publishes extensively in labour law journals. Her co-authored books include *Australian Labour Law: Text, Commentary and Cases*; *Industrial Relations in Australia: Development, Law and Operation*; and an edited volume arising from an Australian Research Council grant, *Public Sector Employment Law in the Twenty-First Century*. Marilyn is a founding and current member of the editorial board of the *Australian Journal of Labour Law*, General Editor of LexisNexis's *Employment Law Bulletin* and Vice President of the national Australian Labour Law Association.

Amanda Pyman is Associate Professor and Director of the MBA program in the Department of Management, Faculty of Business and Economics, Monash University. She has published extensively in the fields of workplace relations and human resource management. Her current research interests include employee voice and participation, comparative trade union strategy in the retail industry, the impact of the Information and Consultation Regulations on UK workplaces, and privacy and surveillance in the workplace. Amanda is an Associate Fellow at the University of Warwick and a member of several research centres in Australia and the United Kingdom.

Cathy Sheehan is an Associate Professor in the Department of Management at Monash University and an active member of the Australian Centre for Research in Employment and Work. She coordinated major reviews of the Australian Human Resource Institute membership in 1995 and 2005. Her publications have appeared in *Human Resource Management*, the *International Journal of Human Resource Management*, the *Human Resource Management Review* and her recent co-authored text, *Contemporary Issues and Challenges in HRM*. She is currently working with the Australian Senior HR Roundtable (ASHRR) on an Australian Research Council-funded project reviewing the role of the human resources function.

Julian Teicher spent many years at Monash University where, as Professor, he held the roles of Head of Department and Director of the Graduate School of Business. In 2010, he moved to RMIT University Vietnam to lead the development of a business faculty. Julian's research covers issues including employee voice and participation, bargaining and dispute resolution, occupational health and safety, skill formation, privatisation and e-government. He has extensive practical experience, having worked in the health, maritime and power industries, and undertaken consultancy projects for governments and industry.

Elsa Underhill is a Senior Lecturer and Director of the Personal Injury Management Programs in the Deakin University Graduate School of Business. She has published journal articles and book chapters in a range of Australian and international publications encompassing the fields of industrial relations, human resource management and occupational health and safety. Her current research interests focus on precarious employment and occupational health and safety, including labour market participation and post-workplace injury, particularly among temporary agency and temporary migrant workers. Her research is predominantly applied and policy focused.

Bernadine Van Gramberg is Professor and Deputy Dean of the Faculty of Business and Enterprise at Swinburne University of Technology. Her research and publications are in the areas of workplace dispute-resolution, workplace relations and public sector management.

Acknowledgements

Julian Teicher

For my wife and collaborator Bernadine, for her support of and input into this and every other project. Special thanks to Hien Hoang Thi Minh for the tedious task of reference checking the manuscript.

Peter Holland

For Nikki, Matthew and Callum, in appreciation of their support.

Introduction: workplace relations in Australia

*Julian Teicher, Peter Holland
and Richard Gough*

Our field of study was for a long time referred as industrial relations or labour relations, and in Australia these designations remained unchallenged until the early 1980s, when employer organisations – particularly the then newly formed Business Council of Australia (BCA) and later right-wing think tanks, such as the HR Nicholls Society – challenged what they regarded as the anachronistic and obstructionist collectivist/class conflict paradigm of the 'industrial relations club' (Stone 2006). In Australia, possibly the most influential and coherent critique was that provided under the auspices of the Business Council of Australia (BCA) (1989). The BCA posited a model of employee relations that looked very much like an Australian version of strategic human resources management (SHRM) (Beer et al. 1984), and this led the BCA to advance two key propositions: first, that the key to enterprise success is in finding competitive advantage; and second, that in the relationship between employer and employees, there is no room for third parties. In other words, in employment regulation unions, industrial tribunals – and even employer associations – were a distraction, or at worst an interference. While the term 'employee relations' continues to have currency in the Australian academic litera-ture, its usage does not imply endorsement of a particular reform agenda; rather, it emphasises the shift in focus to the employment relationship. In Australia more recently, the term 'workplace relations' has emerged to describe the changing field of study to which this book is devoted – for example, issues associated with mon-itoring and surveillance and employee voice are very much workplace relations issues rather than institutional aspects of the workplace in the twenty-first century. Significantly, the term 'workplace relations' has also found favour with both of the major political parties.

A useful feature of terms such as 'employee relations' and its derivative, 'employment relations', is that they explicitly place our study in an international context, and thus open the way to a consideration of the impact of both international competition and the financial sector. Indeed, far from international political economy being peripheral to the study of workplace relations, Chapter 1 demonstrates the centrality of the global economy. Another attribute of these newer usages is that they place employment relationships at the centre of the study – though this focus increas-ingly has to be recast, as we explain a little later, and this opens the way to a consideration of the literature on the nature of work and work organisation. Such studies are truly cross-disciplinary, being informed by the disciplines of politics, sociology and even anthropology.

Returning to the issue of the employment relationship and its limitations, it has widely been acknowledged that, while most people in Australia still perform paid work under the terms of a contract of employment, self-employment – whether genuinely on 'own account' work or as a 'dependent' contractor – is an increasingly common form of paid activity in Australia and many other places. Indeed, in many developing economies, waged (time-based) work is not the dominant form of employ-ment relationship. For example, in Vietnam – a country with close connections to Australia – it is estimated that the informal economy accounts for more than 82 per cent of all jobs (Cling, Razafindrakoto & Roubaud 2010). While many people working in Vietnam are employees, they are not bound by a contract of employment and may even be unpaid workers.

Taking these considerations into account, in this book we have adopted the term 'workplace relations' in order to encompass the field of study. While it could be said that the term is somewhat controversial, as it recalls the divisiveness of the Howard Liberal-National Coalition government's *Workplace Relations Act 1996* and the later Work Choices amendments, this is precisely its value. The policies of this government represent just one phase in the evolution of the Australian workplace relations system, from what was arguably a centralist model to one focused on regulation of relationships at work. This process of decentralisation, which commenced in the 1980s and has continued through successive governments, has shaped the policies of the major participants in the Australian workplace relations system. What distinguished the period of the Howard government were the aggressive attempts to marginalise trade union influence and to erode employee rights at work. These issues recur throughout this book, but receive particular attention in Chapters 5 and 8.

In choosing to describe the field as workplace relations, it is not necessary to reject terms such as 'industrial' or 'labour relations', but it is necessary to recognise that these terms emerged in a particular historical context in countries such as the United Kingdom, the United States and Australia. At the same time, we do not reject the more recent ways of describing our field; rather, we want to build on the analytical advances they embody. The choice of workplace relations provides an anchor in the contemporary development of our field in Australia, and reinforces the policy context while providing a sense of continuity with the earlier terms. From industrial and labour relations, we are able to draw an understanding of the importance of institutions, processes and politics, as well as the role of the state. From employee and employment relations, we draw into our analysis consideration of employment regulation in its widest sense, an understanding of the international and economic contexts, and a recognition of the salience of strategy.

In this book, we have attempted to provide a comprehensive statement of the elements that constitute workplace relations in Australia. The work contained here is consciously cross-disciplinary, in order to place the study of workplace relations in the most meaningful context possible. In so doing, it is necessary to give considerable attention to the implementation of the *Fair Work Act 2009*, because in the eyes of most commentators – for better or worse – this was the most significant set of changes to the legislative framework since the enactment of the *Conciliation and Arbitration Act 1904*. Certainly, the earlier Work Choices legislation constituted a fundamental break with the historical system of conciliation and arbitration, which was premised on the centrality of unions and employer associations, in attempting to radically shift the balance of power in the employment relationship to employers and to advance market-based mechanisms in regulating the employment relationship. The still new and evolving system partly reverses this direction, implementing a national system of regulation that places tribunals and governments at the centre of the system. What makes the *Fair Work Act* stand out is the provision of a comprehensive system of minimum employment standards, as well as the attempt to entrench a form of collective bargaining as the centrepiece of employment regulation. Of course, from the outset, this model came under challenge from a variety of ideological and economic interests, and whether these interests will be able to coalesce and secure a retreat from the reforms of the *Fair Work Act* remains to be seen.

Exploring the terrain of workplace relations in the early twenty-first century

In developing this book, we invited authors to contribute chapters on some of the major defining questions and themes in Australian workplace relations. Obviously, not all of these questions are addressed in each chapter; however, by asking these questions consistently and requesting that the authors respond to them, we set out to create a connected discourse. By taking a different but related approach in the analytical case studies in the final section of the book, we then provide a space where each of the questions or themes can be revisited in the context of a series of representative Australian employment settings. We can see there how the different themes interact with each other. Accordingly, we now frame the major questions addressed by the book.

The starting point for framing these questions is the role of neo-liberal ideology and globalisation in influencing changes to the model of workplace relations in Australia. Neo-liberal ideology has three major aspects: a focus on smaller government with outsourcing and privatisation of government business activities and lower taxes; minimising government interference in individuals' decision-making; encouraging self-reliance; and reducing the level of government regulation to allow markets to operate in a more unimpeded way (see Chapter 1 for further discussion of this important issue).

Complementing the growth in neo-liberal ideas is the impact of globalisation on the Australian economy. This took the form of opening up the Australian economy under the Hawke Labor government in the 1980s by floating the currency, so that the exchange rate was driven by international market forces and not government regulation. While the dollar was floated, tariff protection for Australian businesses was cut significantly and progressively reduced. These major changes put pressure on companies to either reduce labour costs or innovate by introducing new technology in order to remain internationally competitive.

These changes had significant impacts on various aspects of the Australian employment model, which were mediated by the changing power relations between unions and employers, and the political contest between neo-liberal ideas about the respective roles of the state and the market on the one hand and Labor Party ideas about protecting employees' living standards and wages on the other. This struggle was also played out in the context of structural change in the labour market, with the growth in female employment, the shift to services and the impact of new technology on skills and job design, as we discuss in Chapter 2.

The impact of neo-liberalism and globalisation can be seen in a range of different issues covered in this book: declining union membership and, related to this, unions' role in maintaining wages and conditions, as well as their attempts to develop strategies to increase membership and retain influence over employment regulation and take part in international union bodies to offset the impacts of globalisation; the growth in precarious employment and wage inequality as a result of employers' drive to increase flexibility and reduce labour costs; the politically contested trajectory of change to employment regulation from centralisation to the workplace level, accompanied by the recent growth of minimum standards under the Rudd and then Gillard Labor governments; the impact of international employment regulation in the context of the domestic labour market; and the development of the discourse of human resource management, derived from the United States and United Kingdom, which stresses the importance of individual commitment to management goals (and not the collective of employees) to enhance productivity.

While our focus is essentially contemporary, some chapters have an historical dimension, as it is simply not possible to discuss trade unions (Chapter 3) or disadvantaged workers (Chapter 10), for example, without considering developments over time. Similarly, the nature of human resources management (Chapter 6) and its place in workplace relations cannot be separated from the development of the field in this country. However, the historical dimension has been covered in a range of other works, so in relation to human resources management we ask: *How has the field developed and in what ways?* Similarly, with trade unions, we ask questions like: *In the twenty-first century, have the issues or tactics employed by unions changed or evolved and why?*

True to the evolving nature of the field, the international economy looms large in our discussion, but debates on the nature and causes of globalisation have been well rehearsed elsewhere (e.g. Stiglitz 2002; Bhagwati 2004; Friedman 2005). Of greater interest is the way in which globalisation has played out, and here too we remain consistent in keeping our lens focused on the twenty-first century. A consideration of the Global Financial Crisis (GFC) of 2008 highlights both the intense interconnectedness of nations and the vulnerabilities of individual economies and societies to these fluctuations. As we were compiling this book, there were continuing threats of global economic crises emanating from the parlous state of government budgets and the challenges facing the financial sector in Greece, Italy and Spain. In the case of the GFC, the impact of the financial sector on the real economy was perhaps the most significant fact. As a consequence, in many developing countries the engine of growth stalled and even went backwards, due to declining investment, reduced foreign aid and a deterioration in the balance of trade. In Australia, the pace of growth slowed but did not stop, due to the continued strong natural resources demands from China and India and timely fiscal interventions by the federal government. Notwithstanding, we need to ask: *What consequences did the GFC have in Australia and were they enduring – for example, in the case of disadvantaged workers?*

Also relevant is the way the GFC underscored the need for state intervention, not just to regulate markets but to stabilise the macro-economy; however, these lessons were not learned particularly well in most cases, and there has been a resurgence of the global march of the ideology of deregulation. In the Australian context, there is a need to consider the legacy of these global disruptions for workplace regulation, particularly in the light of the contest between the competing models of employment regulation provided by the major political parties. These debates echo those that have occurred throughout the world, especially in Europe, Scandinavia, the United Kingdom and the United States. At a more fundamental level, this is part of the dynamics of capitalist society, in which advocates of freer markets – who typically are aligned with major business interests – seek to shift the operation of the political and economic system to create a more beneficial regulatory climate and to use that influence to change the pattern and level of public expenditure. In relation to this, we should consider the lengths to which the Republican Party has gone in withholding support for raising the borrowing limit of the US government. Until the Obama presidency, raising government borrowing limits was a relatively routine matter – for example, during the years of the George Bush Sr presidency, substantial increases in government borrowing were necessary in order to finance a regime of lower income taxes. In 2011, the Republican Party was determined to defend low taxes and compel expenditure reduction as a condition of its support for the passage of the budget. In terms of the political dynamics of the United States, this is likely to play out in future years in welfare reductions and the increasing vulnerability of low-wage earners. Whether this will lead to increasing US competitiveness in the global economy is doubtful, but it is a powerful manifestation of how politics and economics impact on employment. This gives rise to the question: *What has been the trajectory of employment regulation and the pattern of social expenditure in Australia in recent years?*

The focus on globalisation and the international economy gives rise to a need to inquire into the impact of international employment regulation in the context of the domestic labour market. *To what extent is international regulation a source of domestic employment regulation and does it shape that model?* Likewise, we need to consider how international regulation plays out in the context of international competition, particularly in terms of the role of international labour standards and trade agreements in regulating competition between developed and developing economies – see Chapter 4. How this plays out will impact Australian workplace relations and the employment system for a long time to come.

Understandably, and in contrast to earlier treatments of industrial relations in Australia, the issue of strikes does not loom large in this book, but we are intensely interested in what has happened to industrial conflict. As is evident in Chapter 8, the decline in the number of strikes in Australian workplaces over the past two decades hides the reality of widespread but less visible conflict. There is ample evidence of the growth of other forms of workplace conflict – for instance, in the number of complaints to the Human Rights and Equal Opportunity Commission (HREOC). Complaints rose by 80 per cent to 2517 between 2006 and 2010, and most of these disputes were from workplaces. Employment-related complaints constituted 88 per cent of all complaints under the *Sex Discrimination Act 1984*, 65 per cent of complaints under the *Age Discrimination Act 2004*, 44 per cent of complaints under the *Racial Discrimination Act 1975* and 36 per cent of complaints under the *Disability Discrimination Act 1992* (HREOC 2010). At the same time, the Australian Industrial Relations Commission (AIRC) – which became Fair Work Australia, since renamed the Fair Work Commission – reported an increase of disputes referred from failed workplace dispute-settling procedures from 851 in 2004/05 to 1243 in 2009 (AIRC 2009). So, while strikes have subsided, there are still many other forms of workplace conflict. In the Australian context, we investigate the question: *Has the decline in strikes been associated with the growth of alternative expressions of conflict? Is it associated with the decline of unions and is it related to management developing more sophisticated mechanisms for managing conflict?* This raises associated questions about the development of union and non-union voices in Australian workplaces, which is the subject of Chapter 7. The decline of visible manifestations of conflict also prompts us to ask whether the trajectory of employment regulation – particularly more vigorous enforcement of sanctions on industrial action – has driven down the incidence of strikes and other forms of organised industrial action.

Case studies of workplace relations

A distinctive feature of this book is the inclusion of integrated case studies of workplace relations in four important sectors of the economy: retail and hospitality; the public sector; motor vehicle components; and health. In some respects, inclusion of the motor vehicle sector harks back to a manufacturing past, but the continuing existence of this sector highlights the pressures to become and remain internationally competitive in an industry that increasingly is becoming dominated by Asian manufacturers employing the latest technologies and methods of work organisation combined with low labour costs. How does the new landscape of vehicle manufacture play out in the Australian industry and how do the institutions of Australian workplace relations accommodate this landscape? These are the sorts of questions that are addressed in the case studies. The other three cases reflect the decline in manufacturing in the rise in service sector industries (extensively discussed in Chapter 2), as well as the ageing of the Australian population. These are important aspects of the study of Australian workplace relations, which this book draws out.

The case studies serve another larger purpose: they are designed to complement the earlier chapters and integrate the book. Unlike standard case studies, which are added to the end of chapters for teaching purposes, or cases developed solely for the purposes of graduate teaching, these cases explicitly address the themes of the book. These analytical case studies provide in-depth considerations of how the 'topics' and themes of the chapters play out in real-life situations. Typically, cases are provided to illustrate a point, but these cases illustrate the complex interplay of ideas and so enhance the readers' understanding of the earlier chapters. Finally, it should be noted that teaching cases and questions have also been included at appropriate points in the text.

Part

Foundations of Australian Workplace Relations

Globalisation, economic policy and the labour market

Julian Teicher and Dick Bryan

■ Chapter objectives

This chapter will enable readers to understand the:
- development of neo-liberal policies in Australia and the implications for workplace relations and the employment model
- internationalisation of the Australian economy, the floating of the Australian dollar, and the growth in international trade and foreign capital investments
- impact of neo-liberalism on the opening up of Australian industry to global competition, and the privatisation and outsourcing of major elements of the public sector
- way in which the neo-liberal reforms, combined with the relaxation of controls on finance, led to heightened risks for employees and those who depend on them.

▪ Introduction

In this chapter, we discuss the development since 1980 of 'neo-liberalism', 'globalisation' and the expanding role of the financial sector in economic activity – often referred to as 'financialisation' – as well as the implications of these changes for the workplace (Kotz 2008). As we will see, these are not three discrete developments, but their evolution and interaction are important, for they reveal the sorts of pressures that are faced by employers, and that are experienced in workplaces and working lives.

Neo-liberalism, which can be cast as the over-arching development, has no single definition. As the name implies, neo-liberalism is a derivative of classical liberalism, but with the major difference that economic rather than individual freedom is a central element. It generally refers to the rise to prominence of market-based processes of deciding what gets produced and who acquires it – that is, the forces of supply and demand. Neo-liberalism therefore stands at odds with the historical role of governments in overriding market processes and outcomes (or what is generally called 'social democracy'), because the facilitation of markets requires the state to vacate all non-core functions and focus on facilitating market-oriented processes. But neo-liberalism is not about the decline of the state – it is about the changing role of the state to one of facilitating market processes (Crouch 2011).

The rise of neo-liberalism occurred in the context of the global economic crisis of the 1970s, a crisis characterised by high unemployment, rising inflation and low growth in the economies of advanced industrial countries, including Australia. The solution to these problems put forward by neo-liberals such as British Prime Minister Margaret Thatcher and US President Ronald Reagan, and eventually adopted in Australia in particular ways, was to significantly narrow the role of the state in the economy. They did this by programs of privatisation and cutting social welfare programs; removing barriers to trade and international movement of capital; lowering the taxation of high income earners; and undermining the power of unions by regulation that constrained their activities (Harvey 2005). Importantly, these developments did not occur in the same way or to the same extent in all developed countries, and what we describe as the 'neo-liberal agenda' was carried out most vigorously in Anglo-American countries such as Australia and New Zealand.

Cumulatively, the changes outlined above created an environment in which union membership diminished and the real wages of employees stagnated in the United States, and rose very slowly in Australia (see Chapter 2 for further comment on real wages movements). Especially in the United States, recourse to funding living standards via borrowings became the alternative, and this was itself facilitated by neo-liberal reforms removing controls on financial institutions' operations, such as the separation of normal commercial banking from merchant banking and the relaxation of the requirements for loan eligibility. Such changes proved critical during the Global Financial Crisis (GFC) from 2007, and we will consider them later as an aspect of 'financialisation'.

In the Australian case, neo-liberalism formed the basis of the dismantling of industry protection and centralised wage determination by industrial tribunals that had prevailed since the early 1900s. The reduction of industry protection opened the Australian economy up to global markets. It was accompanied by the floating of the currency in 1983. As we will see, it would appear that the rise of global systems of management and global pricing of productive inputs – including labour – have permanently changed the Australian labour market and the wider society.

Yet, for all the dynamism of market forces, the world economy moved into financial crisis in 2007 and 2008 in what became known as the Global Financial Crisis, and leading industrial economies remain in or close to recession. In Europe, a debt crisis is ongoing. Australia largely escaped the direct impact of this financial crisis; however, in Australia it was not financial markets in the spotlight during the GFC, but labour markets. While mortgagors were defaulting in large numbers in the United States, Australia was having a 2007 federal election fought on issues of industrial legislation and whether to restrict the power of unions and shift bargaining strength to employers in the name of flexibility in employment and making corporations in Australia more internationally competitive.

While a simple dichotomy between agendas of fairness and equity and the imperatives of international competition does not exactly capture the terms of debate that existed in 2007, these debates do signal the continuing social, political and economic importance of workplace relations and workplace policy in both the national and international contexts. Australia may not have suffered directly from the crises in global markets; nevertheless, the challenges to the roles of states and markets and the changing links between global finance and labour markets and the lives of ordinary people are certainly being felt in Australia.

In particular, there are two wider social meanings that drive our understanding of the nature of Australian workplace relations: the international setting (globalisation) and increased marketisation (including 'privatisation' and 'financialisation') of economic activity, which see both workers and managers impelled to calculate their interests in a conspicuously economic way. As will be seen below, the rise of workplace relations as a field of study (as opposed to older usages discussed in the Introduction) is linked to the liberalisation of trade in goods and services, and of capital and investment flows, and to the growing quantitative and qualitative influence of finance in the economy and wider society. This turn to neo-liberalism, and the agenda it initiated, is our focus in this chapter.

The structure of the chapter is as follows. In the second section, the advent of neo-liberalism in Australia and its connections with workplace relations are outlined briefly, particularly the shift from what might be called the criterion of fairness to one of market efficiency. This leads into a discussion of the impact of neo-liberalism on the opening up of industry in Australia to global competition, and the privatisation and outsourcing of major elements of the public sector. In the third section, we explore key elements of the internationalisation of the Australian economy, including the floating of the Australian dollar and the growth in international trade and foreign capital investments, and their impact on the labour market. Finally, we examine the way in which the neo-liberal reforms, combined with the relaxation of controls on finance, led to heightened risks for individual employees and their families – a process that has been called 'financialisation'.

A turning point in workplace relations

The clearest way to identify just how dramatic the changes in workplace relations have been is to start at the turning point: the 1970s. This was a pivotal time in the global and Australian economies, and it is often referred to as the end of the long post-war boom (also known simply as the 'long boom') – which had lasted from the end of World War II. The end of the boom saw the declining rate of corporate profit, which led to slowing capital accumulation and hence to declining investment and employment (Duménil & Lévy 2011). Both the falling profit rates and rising inflation in the early 1970s were, in significant part, attributable to the power of unions to extract wage rises higher than productivity increases in the proceeding period of full employment. It was, at least in retrospect, clear that labour markets and workplace relations would be at the centre of any long-term response to that crisis.

The response that did eventuate was not a conscious turning point, nor was it clear, quick or unidirectional. It took governments time and debate to adjust to the end of a period where economic growth and stability were simply assumed to be the norm. Indeed, it is read as a turning point only in retrospect. But the 1970s was also a period of economies and governments adjusting to a new and uncertain era; it was the start of an era when the presumed superiority of the market mechanism was being advocated increasingly in economic debate, as well as across most areas of economic and social life. In this regard, Australia was no exception – though it took its own path, in its own time. In the context of workplace relations, we note that a stable, state-centred system of determination of wages and employment was coming under increasing challenge, and the momentum of that challenge snowballed over the coming decades.

What was that stable, state-centred system? In his book aptly titled *The End of Certainty*, Paul Kelly (1992) describes the end of what was called the Federation Settlement – essentially, a tacit agreement founded at the beginning of the twentieth century in which opposed political interests in Australia were reconciled by policies that restricted exposure to the vicissitudes of the global economy. In this agreement, workers in manufacturing (where unions were strong) would receive state-determined minimum living standards and working conditions, and a state-funded social security system. Immigrant competition for jobs would also be restricted. In return, the profitability of manufacturers – who would now face higher wages – would be secured by restrictions on manufactured imports via high tariffs (taxes on imports), quotas and restrictions on foreign investment. Finally, farmers, who would suffer costs of higher wages and more expensive manufactured inputs, would be assisted via fixed exchange rates and state-backed and underwritten agricultural marketing schemes, which in effect provided guaranteed prices for their products.

In this context, issues of the role of wages in competitive corporate calculation and the impact of global finance were not strong in Australia. Employment relationships developed under the auspices of the Australian state, in which social and political evaluations of norms, fairness and equity in employment relations were prominent, and the global disciplines of competitive trade and finance were blocked by trade and capital controls. In this way, some of the risks associated with being an employee were borne by the state rather than the individual. As we will see in Chapter 2, this was one of the major characteristics of the Australian employment model.

This balance between economic interests – always somewhat fraught – came under significant pressure with the end of the 'long boom' in the early 1970s. Three factors were critical in this situation. First, the end of the boom saw losses of industry profitability and growing unemployment. Wage levels and working conditions therefore came under challenge, and there emerged a concerted argument from a variety of quarters, including the Australian Treasury, that the share of wages in overall national income was excessive – this situation was sometimes referred to artfully as the 'real wage overhang' (see also Chapter 2). Second, in Australia there was a massive growth in the mining industry – an industry that was (and is) highly internationalised and opposed to both centrally fixed wages and tariff protection of manufacturing. Third, with an economic downturn and a growing disquiet with national economic policy, there were mounting challenges to the conventional wisdom in economics – with the leading challenge coming from those who advocated the benefits of 'market forces' and argued against the capacity of the state to create economic wealth or to manage the macro-economy.

Manufacturing itself had risen and blossomed over the long boom, but only so long as government policy had sought to tax import competition (via tariffs) and to provide a range of subsidies. Indeed, it can be argued that without industry protection, Australia would never have developed a manufacturing sector and its associated skill base. As these state-driven tariffs and subsidies came under challenge (and ultimately were repealed), and market criteria came to the fore, the manufacturing sector itself went into decline. Thus employment in manufacturing declined from 24.7 per cent of the workforce in 1971/72 to 11.9 per cent in 2001/02 and 8.8 per cent in 2010/11. With it went the sector that had been the bastion of centrally fixed wages based on securing family living standards (Productivity Commission 2003: 27; ABS 2012g).

The 1970s, therefore, was in some senses a period of uncertainty and confusion, and this was the environment in which a neo-liberal agenda started to take shape. It is difficult to pinpoint when and how the shift started, but it was probably, ironically, with the Whitlam federal Labor government (1972–75). We say 'ironically' because this government, the first Labor government since 1945, held strongly to a social democratic agenda; however, it also introduced the first significant market-based reform of the Australian economy. One manifestation of this was in cutting tariffs on manufactured goods by 20 per cent (Quiggin 1996). Conceived as an anti-inflation policy (to reduce the price of imported goods and locally produced goods that competed with imports), this was nonetheless an assault on the delicate policy balance that was the Federation Settlement. The Whitlam government also removed postal services and telecommunications from the public service, and established statutory corporations that were required to operate on a 'user pays' basis (Teicher, Holland & Gough 2006).

The Fraser Liberal-National Coalition government (1975–83) replaced the Whitlam government. While not a government of radical reform (it did not advance tariff reductions or free-market agendas), Prime Minister Malcolm Fraser spoke the language of small government and the responsibility of the individual, which concurrent governments in the United States (Reagan) and United Kingdom (Thatcher) were actually putting into place. At the level of policy implementation, the period of the Fraser government was seen by neo-liberal advocates as a missed opportunity: government expenditure was not curtailed, the welfare system remained largely intact and efforts to reform the industrial relations systems were confined to a small number of initiatives, most notably the introduction of provisions into the *Trade Practices Act 1974* that outlawed union-imposed secondary boycotts and, in 1977, the establishment of a largely ineffectual regulator, the Industrial Relations Bureau. The Fraser government nonetheless initiated an ideological shift in Australian politics towards a belief in smaller government and the embrace of market calculation, and built the basis for subsequent bipartisan support for some decisive, globalising reforms (Hampson 1996; Quiggin 1996).

The neo-liberal shift

It was not until the Hawke and Keating Labor governments (1983–96) that the policy shift became substantial. And here too, the Australian process was decidedly different, for while the shift to neo-liberalism in the United States and the United Kingdom was instigated by Republicans and Conservatives respectively, in Australia it occurred largely under Labor governments. It didn't appear as 'anti-state' or 'free market' politics, in the name of a belief in individualism and market forces. Rather, it was presented as a financial and global imperative that Australia had to embrace. Pusey (1991) describes this as the rise of 'economic rationalism' in Australia, a process through which the national government and the bureaucracy 'changed its mind' about what constituted necessary, effective and ethical economic policy. The term 'economic rationalism' was Australia-specific: internationally, and now also in Australia, the common term is 'neo-liberalism'.

Strangely, the major development of a neo-liberal agenda in Australia also started under a government that came to office with an 'Accord' with the trade union movement – an agreement that gave senior union officials a conspicuous role in the formation of economic, and especially industry, policy. But the implicit deal in this Accord was that trade unions needed to embrace the need for flexibility in the economy overall: it was evident that some industries and some companies would flourish, while others – especially in manufacturing – were likely to go into decline unless they changed rapidly. This need for flexibility flowed through to requirements in the workplace. It meant that many of the workplace conventions that had evolved over the twentieth century were under challenge in the name of initiating new conditions for economic growth and full employment. There was increasing pressure for greater flexibility in working hours, job security and work practices. Accordingly, employers had increasing expectations of more and more work on casual rather than permanent contracts, with flexible and perhaps part-time working hours, and that work practices – what workers actually did in the workplace – would be driven by what was needed for company profits rather than simply on the basis of how work had been organised in the past. The effect was to overturn the Federation Settlement and the workplace relations attached to it.

In several important respects, however, it was not until the arrival of the Howard Liberal-National Coalition government in 1996 that Australia saw strong ideological battles about these developments and union power in the workplace – battles that had occurred in the United Kingdom and United States at the beginning of the 1980s. So, under the Hawke–Keating era of Labor government, the broad driver of neo-liberal reform was the pragmatic view that Australian industry – both public and private – needed to become more efficient, and that meant more responsive to market forces. Two critical expressions of the shift were 'privatisation' and 'globalisation', with direct ramifications for employment and workplace relations.

■ Privatisation

In many cases, privatisation in the form of the sale of public assets was preceded by 'corporatisation'. In effect, this meant that public organisations, which were created to provide services without charge or on a heavily subsidised basis, began to operate in the manner of private corporations with a focus on full cost recovery or profit max-imisation and the adoption of private sector management approaches and accounting standards.

Australia saw this shift in areas such as government-owned transport, specifically airlines, shipping and rail, telecommunications and infrastructure. Often implemen-tation of a 'corporatised' model (running state-owned services on the principles of profitability) was a precursor to full or partial privatisation through asset sales.

This period was significant not only for the decline in union membership and deteriorating wages and conditions of employment in the former public services, but also for the rise of human resources management across the public sector (for further discussion of this issue, see Chapters 6 and 15). Accordingly, the economic redistrib-ution mechanisms that were once built into public institutions were discarded in favour of a business mindset in terms of both internal operations and service delivery.

Once public sector organisations operated along the lines of private sector organ-isations, there could be little reason for them to remain in government ownership. As with many other issues of economic policy, there was broad consensus among the two major political groupings that privatisation was the preferred option. Among public managers, too, there was a widely held view that public ownership placed unneces-sary restraints on corporatised entities, particularly with regard to the prevalence of public sector wages and conditions. Privatisation was seen by some as the key to economic viability and competitiveness.

An initial government response was 'partial' privatisation, where the state sold off part of the ownership of public assets but retained majority ownership. This compromise, however, had opponents on both sides of the ideological battle – both those who believed in state ownership on behalf of society and those who believed in private ownership. In particular, the latter argued that private owners were being shackled, not protected, by the state. Over time, the privatisation processes became more variegated and included outsourcing of service and function provision, the use of agency labour and more recently the use of so-called public–private partnerships. In common with asset sales, these newer forms of privatisation often had the effect of relieving government of the need to fund service delivery through taxation or capital raisings, effectively moving service delivery into the marketplace and the realm of private consumption (Fairbrother, Paddon & Teicher 2002).

As in other developed capitalist nations, Australian governments became preoccupied with the sale of public assets, both because this revenue could be used to fund tax cuts and because it supported the ideological proposition that smaller government was by definition superior to larger government. John Howard, who became prime minister of a Liberal-National Party Coalition government in 1996, emphasised the philosophical desirability of privatisation, arguing that the sale of once-public enterprises to 'mum-and-dad investors' would help Australia become a 'shareholder society' in which individuals would benefit not as recipients of subsidised goods and services, but as direct equity owners, sharing in the profits (or losses) of privatised enterprises.

A further development of the privatisation process was the extension of privatisation to state governments. The process and the rate of progress and extent of privatisation have been variable, but always accompanied by an ideological battle about the merits of public ownership compared with privatisation. We have seen the notable privatisation of utilities such as water, public transport, hospitals, new road developments, electricity and gas, among others. An effect of all such privatisations on workplace relations has been to reduce the status of state enterprises as leading sites in the setting of employment conditions.

■ Globalisation

Reductions in tariff protection of Australian industry – especially manufacturing – were mentioned earlier as a policy development of the early 1970s. This was an early form of 'globalisation', as local markets opened up to competition from increasingly cheap imports. Subsequently, and more broadly, an emerging focus on the 'competitiveness' of Australian industry (Bryan & Rafferty 1999; Bryan 2000) required industry in Australia to achieve rates of profitability at least as good as global alternatives in order that corporations (local and international) would want to invest in Australia.

This competitive calculus imposed pressures on Australia for technological innovation and lower costs, including labour costs. The dilemma was that wages could not be presumed to simultaneously achieve labour costs consistent with international competitiveness and provide wage levels consistent with growing living standards. The two could grow together under some conditions, especially rapid technological change (which could include discovery of new fertile mineral deposits), but there was the possibility that national competitiveness might require falling wages and that, if wages did not fall, there would be a decline in Australian production, leading to job losses. The critical variable of the calculation here is labour productivity.

The decisive factor here was not only ongoing tariff cuts, but the decision to float the Australian dollar in December 1983, and the associated lifting of many controls on the international movement of finance and investment. The float meant that the performance of the Australian economy was being evaluated on an ongoing basis in global foreign exchange markets. Whether the dollar went up or down depended in part on market evaluations of 'Australia' as an economic entity. A consequence was that the Australian dollar price of exports and imports varied with movements in the dollar. This meant that, along with reductions in tariffs, Australian-based industry was no longer secure: to be an exporter and to compete with imports now became activities of fierce competition.

Accordingly, both exports and imports grew in response to the growing 'openness' of the Australian economy. As a proportion of gross domestic product (GDP), exports and imports combined were the equivalent of 28 per cent of GDP in the mid-1970s, rising to 34 per cent in the mid-1980s and then to over 40 per cent in the early 2000s, where they have remained fairly constant (ABS 2012a, Table 34.1). These developments impelled Australian producers to be increasingly internationally cost-competitive, with attendant consequences for workplace relations – an issue explored in Chapter 15.

Critically, as noted earlier, Australian manufacturing industry – the home of full-time, male, skilled jobs during the 'long boom' – went into decline in the name of competition and free trade. With manufacturing unions a major strength of the union movement, union influence itself was under challenge, and with growing unemployment, the influence of unions within society and on public policy was challenged further. As will be seen in Chapters 2 and 10, these developments were also associated with the growth of the service sector, and with it the rise in low-wage jobs and casual employment.

■ *Labour market implications*

Wages and employment conditions increasingly became subject to global markets and the ability of corporations in Australia to compete globally. Increasingly, the thinking of policy-makers, interest groups and the general public was cast in terms of the supremacy of market-based solutions. This was not just a reform agenda oriented to the international economy, for the pursuit of 'market efficiency' also translated to domestic policy settings, and involved state as well as federal government agendas.

Public sector employment increasingly adopted a market-based calculus and, in the private sector, global conditions of company profitability have become a major determinant of employment conditions (see Chapters 15 and 16 for examples of how this has played out in both the private and public sectors). Indeed, the overwhelming emphasis on profits underpins the rise of human resources management as a field of study and as an area of practice, which offers a literature on the techniques most conducive to maximising the value of labour's contribution to production, and a set of management tools and techniques to achieve that end (see Chapter 6 for a critical review of these developments).

In the labour market, the neo-liberal turn saw the replacement of centralised wage fixing with enterprise bargaining, and government encouragement and facilitation of individual employment agreements, which were the early manifestations of deregulation. At a national level, the main legislation introduced by the Howard Liberal-National government, the *Workplace Relations Act 1996*, was classic deregulation, with the new Act longer and more complex than the *Industrial Relations Act 1996* that it replaced, particularly in the areas of agreement-making, freedom of association and regulation of industrial action (see Chapter 8 for further details). Reflecting the reality of a neo-liberal agenda, labour market deregulation required political compromises, hence it was necessary to retain minimum wages and other safety net conditions of employment.

Moreover, the repeal of the *Workplace Relations Act 1996*, with its unpopular Work Choices amendments and its replacement by the *Fair Work Act 2009* by the incoming Rudd Labor government, while far from a retreat from the dominance of market criteria in workplace relations, showed that nothing about neo-liberalism is guaranteed. Rather, it is a set of ideas around the primacy of markets and the role of government, which is implemented opportunistically by the major political groupings. The reliance on market mechanisms is sometimes qualified by competing agendas, such as the political imperative to provide a level of social protection to the workforce and their families and dependants.

In terms of productivity, Australia had a long and sustained period of growth from the mid-1980s, and especially from the mid-1990s, which then ground to a halt. According to Productivity Commission research, 'after a record-high rate in the 1990s, growth in multifactor productivity (MFP) slumped in two steps of equal size, first to a more typical rate, and then to zero in the mid- to late 2000s' (Parham 2012: 1) (see Figure 1.1).

This slowdown in productivity growth has been difficult to explain, although there is significant support for Eslake's (2011) proposition that it can be sheeted home to a lack of workplace relations reforms. That is, the rapid economic reforms of the Hawke–Keating Labor government and the Howard Liberal-National Coalition government are thought to have demonstrated that the process of reform must be ongoing, for if the rest of the world is changing, Australia cannot stand still.

It has led employer organisations and the Productivity Commission to call for yet more flexibility in workplace arrangements, including working hours, by changing provisions of the *Fair Work Act 2009* (Productivity Commission 2011). These calls accelerated further in 2012, with a variety of industry leaders calling for further legislative reform in order to unleash new sources of labour (cost) flexibility.

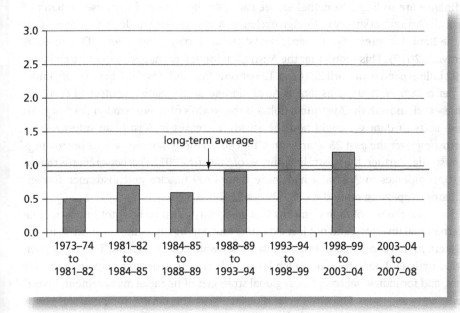

Figure 1.1: Australia's multifactor productivity growth over productivity cycles in the 12-industry resource sector (% per year) *Source:* Parham (2012).

Put simply, we can characterise this change in the labour market as a shift in the organising principles of employment from criteria of 'fairness' to 'flexibility' in the name of international competitiveness' – albeit with ongoing debate about the balance. The change is remarkable not because there were now powerful voices advocating market forces and individualism, for those voices had always had a presence, but because the state itself became the leading voice for change (Doogan 2009: 119). The basic *direction* of this change has been supported by the key political parties forming government: the Australian Labor Party on the one hand and a coalition of the Liberal and National Parties on the other (Bell 1997).

Nonetheless, while there may have been a dramatic shift in the nature of employment associated with the globalisation of economic relations, the speed and specific forms of reform remain hotly debated within Australian politics. As noted at the outset of this chapter, debates around workplace relations reforms were central to the 2007 federal election. So, as will be seen in Chapter 5, in the sphere of workplace relations what is commonly called 'deregulation' actually has required continuing and increasing amounts of regulation. 'Deregulation' – which is a superficially attractive term, with its overtone of reducing government bureaucracy – does not capture what is critical about neo-liberalism.

■ Financialisation and risk

While growth in international trade and investment shows the importance of international competition in terms of costs of production, finance presents a more pervasive discipline on economic activity within Australia. Because finance flows so rapidly, it is difficult to compare data on finance with either trade or investment, for the numbers in finance are so large. Nonetheless, we can note the results of the Reserve Bank of Australia's triennial survey of foreign exchange and derivative trade in Australia – part of the Bank for International Settlements' global survey (Nightingale, Ossolinski & Zurawski 2010). This shows that the Australian foreign exchange market turned over $192 billion per day in April 2010, up 12 per cent from 2007 and an increase of almost 75 per cent from 2004. This makes Australia one of the leading centres of currency trade – and, indeed, the Australian dollar is the world's fifth most traded currency. To these sorts of data we could add the steady increases in Australian international borrowing over the past 25 years – and, indeed, in foreign organisations borrowings in Australia. Further, the Australian Bureau of Statistics' 2012 *Yearbook* records that in 2010, companies in Australia had more than 1200 finance and insurance foreign affiliates, employing more than 75 000 staff (ABS 2012b).

In effect, the rise of finance means that all activity in Australia – not just by mobile international investors, and not just exporters and import competitors – must shape up to international conditions of profitability if they want access to credit. The implication is that national boundaries are much less of a barrier to economic activity than they were, and for individual companies, global strategies of financial management, investment, sourcing, sales and tax declaration are now the norm. Competition – be it between companies in the same industry, between companies for access to investment funds or between labour and capital – is now conducted in an international arena. It is the ideology of neo-liberalism that asserts these market forces are immutable and incapable of influence without unacceptable consequences for economic advancement.

In the context of integrated financial markets, globalisation therefore manifests in the labour market as intense competitive pressure to increase productivity via flexibility and skill enhancement, to lengthen the working day, and to accept wage increases consistent with corporate viability in internationally exposed markets. The nation-state, too, is seen to play a role in this competitiveness agenda, creating and perpetuating a set of labour market institutions and regulations that can generate competitive outcomes. These issues are examined in detail below, especially in Chapters 2 and 3.

The competitive pressures have also created new risks in the lives of employees. Although Australia never had universal welfare services, as in Scandinavian countries, in the post-war period, services provided by the government to its citizens to obviate risks – such as public health and pensions – have increasingly become partly the responsibility of individual employees and households.

As we have noted earlier, this process is described as financialisation. This term can be taken to mean simply 'the increasing role of financial motives, financial markets, financial actors and financial institutions in the operation of the domestic and international economies' (Epstein 2005: 3). In particular, the issue of financialisation addresses the 'mindset' (or mode of calculation) of risk management, and the use of financial instruments such as futures, options and swaps as tools of risk management. The growth of financial markets, in Australia and elsewhere, has been illustrated above, but the process of financialisation suggests something more pervasive.

The growing momentum for both reduced public provision or funding of services – from utilities like electricity to health care and age pensions, and also for increasing labour market flexibility – are changing the life experiences of workers and their families, and not just in the immediate workplace. The issue for workplace relations is that individuals are increasingly being required to treat themselves (and their families) as if they are financial units (or enterprises) to be risk-managed. We can note a number of critical changes associated with the rise of neo-liberalism:

- Commercialisation and privatisation of public utilities mean that, along with competition, there is increased choice for consumers. While this is lauded by some neo-liberal advocates, consumers must now choose which is the best (for them) supplier of services, like telecommunications, power and water, and which particular contract to sign. We are all aware how complex these sorts of calculations can become, and the level of computational sophistication required to evaluate the contracts of competing electricity or telecommunications providers. Wrong choices can lead to unexpected but significant impacts on family budgets.
- Diminishing government services (per head) in areas like health and education mean that individuals must now pay for many of the services once readily available via public provision. They need to take on the costs of private health insurance and private education if they are to maintain the perceived quality of their access to these services. Health insurance in particular requires individuals (households) to determine how much of their income to allocate to health and compute their best form of health cover.
- Diminishing government services and increased marketisation of service provision are leading to the purchasing power of age pensions falling behind the general rise in living standards. When universal superannuation was introduced by Labor Treasurer Paul Keating in 1992, superannuation was posed as a supplement to a publicly funded pension. In the ensuing two decades, the emphasis has been on private provision as a substitute for a government-funded pension. Each individual therefore has to decide how to invest their pension – which company, which policy, which risk profile – or indeed whether to establish a self-managed superannuation fund. And as the recent GFC and its aftermath have shown, the well-being of each individual in old age is now tied inextricably to their ability to manage their financial assets.
- Contracting out of many government jobs, particularly at state and local government levels, means that those who perform this work increasingly are self-employed contractors, not public sector employees. They are employed on contracts, not in permanent forms of employment, and they bear the risks associated with this form of employment.
- The growing casualisation of employment and growth of contracting (particularly dependent contracting) similarly involves the insecurity of contingent employment. For further consideration of this issue, see especially Chapters 2 and 10.

Each of these types of change can be posed as a consequence of the growth of competitiveness and of flexibility, and the forms of calculation that attach to them. Things that were managed by the state until the 1970s increasingly have passed to the market. Individuals are now required to be active participants in the market, not just as workers but as managers of their (family's) life risks, and at precisely the time when employment itself is less secure. Moreover, this increasing 'financialisation' of daily life has faced the massive volatility and uncertainty of an ongoing Global Financial Crisis. These sorts of changes have led Guy Standing (2011) to refer to the working class of wage and unemployed workers not as the 'proletariat' but as the 'precariat', in recognition that in the globalised world of competition and risk, the condition of ordinary people – at work and in their daily lives – has become increasingly precarious. This, it seems, is the emerging consequence of the neo-liberal reform agenda.

Conclusion

A central feature of this chapter has been to establish the nature of neo-liberalism and to demonstrate that, while this it is not a rigid political program, it is a coherent ideology that guides policy-makers. The primacy of ideas around the superiority of market-based solutions and a state that facilitates and promotes market calculation has produced recognisably similar policies in a range of countries, with the differences reflecting necessary political compromises.

In Australia, the influence of neo-liberalism beginning in the 1970s should not be under-estimated. The pervasiveness of neo-liberal ideas on both sides of politics and the active advocacy of these ideas by government departments and agencies are now convention, and have had the effect of giving neo-liberal policies an air of inevitability. This is seen most clearly in an overview of policy implementation covering issues such as privatisation, regulatory reform of labour markets, introduction of flexible exchange rates, elimination of industry protection, liberalisation of capital flows and a preoccupation with governments achieving budget surpluses.

These policy measures have been shown to have profound impacts on the labour market by exposing it to the force of international competition. An important result of the Hawke and Keating Labor governments embracing the competitiveness agenda was that the internationalisation of the Australian economy helped to undermine the existing system of labour market regulation, and provided the basis for the incoming Howard government in 1996 to radically change the system of employment regulation.

Despite the differing understandings of the competitiveness agenda outlined above, from the late 1980s onwards under both Labor and Liberal-National governments, what emerged was a number of profound changes in the labour market and in management–employee relations: the spread of enterprise or workplace bargaining, a shift from awards and collective agreements to individual work contracts and a persistent focus on increasing labour flexibility in order to cut costs and increase productivity. What these changes have in common is that they shift determination of wages and conditions of employment away from the historical and national norms that secured some notion of employment comparability across the country, and towards a focus on the capacity of individual companies to compete in internationally exposed and increasingly uncertain markets.

Discussion questions

1.1   What is meant by the term 'neo-liberalism'? Explain the rise of this perspective, both internationally and in Australia.

1.2   Identify the key turning points in Australian workplace relations.

1.3   Outline the consequences of the neo-liberalism in Australia in terms of government policies.

1.4   Explain the link between the deregulation of markets and the increasing exposure of workers and their families to risk.

1.5   Discuss the tensions between fairness and competitiveness in the context of Australian workplace relations.

2

The Australian employment model in an international context

Richard Gough

■ Chapter objectives

This chapter will enable readers to understand the:

- concept of employment models and their use in analysing the interactions between the state and markets
- development of the services sector and the links to the 'incomplete female revolution'
- growth in casual work and its links to the growth in services, female employment and low-paid work
- rising income inequality and the related growth in wage dispersion in OECD countries.

Introduction

This chapter explores the key features of the Australian 'employment model'. We deliberately use the term 'model' as distinct from 'labour market' because it is more holistic and invokes an important literature that links the welfare system and the labour market. This work originated with Esping-Andersen's (1990) delineation of three models of welfare capitalism: social democratic (Sweden); conservative (Germany); and neo-liberal (United Kingdom and United States, which we also term the Anglo-American cases). The latter model is particularly relevant, given that our focus in this book is on the implementation of neo-liberal ideas in the labour market and more widely. The three models of welfare capitalism are not, however, a static typology, and Esping-Andersen characterises the models as emerging from political and economic struggles in each of the countries where they emerged. Importantly, this approach explicitly rejects the arguments of neo-classical economics (and neo-liberalism), which view markets as predominant and welfare provision as limited, instead of viewing labour markets and welfare as interlinked.

In the discussion below, we explain the characteristics of Esping-Andersen's three models of welfare capitalism and situate Australia in this typology, which sits within the Anglo-American model. The second section explores the development of services in advanced economies, the different composition of services in these economies and the consequences. The following two sections examine the links between the 'incomplete female revolution' (the trajectory towards full-time female employment on the same terms for men and women), its impact on the family, the development of child care and the growth of services in an international and then an Australian context. A major outcome of the growth in services and female employment, the rising level of low-paid work, is then assessed in the international context. This is followed by a discussion of casual work, which has expanded over the past 30 years, along with the growth in services, female employment and low-paid work. Finally, the issues of rising income inequality and the related growth in wage dispersion in OECD countries and Australia are addressed.

Employment models

An important aspect of Esping-Andersen's analysis is the extent to which market approaches are predominant or social protections are extended to workers in relation to rights to collective bargaining, employment protection and reducing inequality in wage dispersion. In the late 1990s, Esping-Andersen (1999) expanded his analysis to include discussion of the differing nature of the family in models of welfare capitalism, examining the extent to which the welfare role of the family is outsourced or undergoes 'defamiliarisation'. More recent analysis (Hall & Soskice 2001) has added to the debate on the grouping of employment models by looking at the factors that give rise to national competitiveness, such as whether ownership of capital is concentrated or dispersed, the nature of corporate governance, the level of skills required by job roles and the nature of skill-formation and workplace relations. This led Hall and Soskice to posit two varieties of capitalism: neo-liberal market economies and coordinated market economies. In neo-liberal market economies, coordination of businesses is achieved largely through the market, although there are some constraints. In coordinated market economies, there is a greater role for the state in constraining the market. The work on varieties of capitalism complements the models of welfare capitalism.

Another feature of an employment model is the way in which it handles key life transitions such as the movement from school to work (Anxo, Bosch & Rubery 2010). This can be illustrated by comparing the German case, where about 60 per cent of those leaving school enter an apprenticeship, which enables them to fit readily into an occupational labour market, whereas in the United Kingdom and Australia, most young graduates have general education and get jobs based on relevant work experience.

As explained above, Esping-Andersen's original work established a typology which identified three main types of welfare capitalism: social democratic, conservative, and neo-liberal. The basis for this typology was the differences between the states in their extent of decommodification of labour (Esping-Andersen 1990). Decommodification means the extent to which access to support such as pensions, illness and unemployment benefits is not seen as market determined but is established by governments as rights for employees and other designated groups. The nature of these rights differs according to the type of welfare capitalism, with the neo-liberal model being based on low-level means-tested benefits, the conservative model linking benefits to work performance (e.g. employees make contributions to social insurance along with employers and the state over time) and the social democratic model premised on universal rights to adequate pensions and benefits.

Historically, in the Australian case, there has been a strong emphasis on targeted, stringent, means-tested benefits. Castles (1985) argues that strong unions had used wage negotiations and test cases in the industrial tribunals as a means to achieve social protections. The 2011 Equal Remuneration Decision of Fair Work Australia (now renamed the Fair Work Commission), which awarded social and community service employees a 19–41 per cent wage increase, is an example of this approach. In analysing the extent decommodification in the Australian case, Esping-Andersen (1990) places Australia in the neo-liberal model, reflecting the historical influence of liberalism – despite Australia's history of strong unionism.

A key use of such typologies is to contrast the different character of employment models and to see the relationships between different elements of a model. For example, in conservative states like Germany, the level of female employment is considerably lower and there is a greater proportion of part-time employment than in Sweden, and welfare benefits for families depend to a greater degree on long-term employment by male breadwinners. Lack of sufficient access to child care also restricts female employment and careers. Because of the characteristics of the German model, providing job protection to males becomes critical to keeping families out of poverty.

When restructuring occurred in German industry in the western region of the country, this resulted in male workers being retired early on generous pensions in order to maintain family living standards. By contrast, in Sweden the existence of universal benefits for all citizens, much higher levels of female employment (76 per cent in 2011) and a greater number of households with two full-time wage earners, the provision of heavily subsidised child care and extensive retraining programs for unemployed workers means that protection of jobs is not as crucial to keep families out of poverty (Esping-Andersen 1999).

Hence identifying the articulation of the elements of an employment model is important to understanding how the elements reinforce one another, and this cannot occur if the elements are looked at in isolation. Comparisons, then, are key to the discussion that follows.

The emergence of a services economy in developed nations

The process of deindustrialisation since the 1970s has been complemented by the growth in services in advanced industrial economies. In discussing services, it is necessary to restructure the ANZSIC (Australia and New Zealand Standard Industry Classification) classification to gain a better understanding of the nature of the service sector. Elfring (1988, 1989) has developed a taxonomy of services broken down into *producer services* (business and professional services, financial services, insurance services and real estate services), *distributive services* (retail trade, wholesale trade, transport services and communications), *personal services* (hotels bars and restaurants, recreation, amusements, domestic services and other personal services) and *social services* (core government, health, educational and miscellaneous social services). This taxonomy identifies who the customer is as the basis of classifying services – for example, a wide variety of services for business, from different parts of ANZSIC, are clustered together under producer services.

There has been a convergence in OECD countries in the size of the service sector to around 70 per cent of the economy, but the structure of the services sector varies in different employment models. In particular, there are differences in the level of social services and also personal services provided – for example, in 1988 social services in Sweden, with a larger welfare state, amounted to 34 per cent of employment, whereas in Australia they constituted about 22 per cent(OECD 2000). In the case of personal services, in 1998 the level of employment was low in Germany, with about 6 per cent of employment in personal services compared with 13 per cent in the United States and about 13 per cent in Australia. This is in line with Australia fitting into the neo-liberal model of welfare capitalism. Such a low level of personal services in Germany reflects the low levels of female employment (just below 50 per cent in 1998), high wages and the greater propensity for German households to provide services themselves, due to the cost of services and availability of females to undertake personal service activities at home (Esping-Andersen 1999).

Besides the varying structures of service employment in different employment models, the nature of work organisation also varies. For instance, in nursing, three different configurations have been identified by Mehaut and colleagues (2010): use mainly of qualified nurses in Germany and the Netherlands; high use of nursing assistants who have received regulated formal training in France and, to a lesser extent, in Denmark; and high use of nursing assistants who have received little or no formal training in the United Kingdom and United States. Retail work, which is seen as a low-skilled and poorly paid services dominated by females who work part-time, is another example of the differences in national employment models. Catrice and Lehndorff (2005) show that, while in Germany and the Netherlands there is extensive part-time employment in response to employers' needs for time flexibility, in France – which has a highly rationalised retail sector – there are high levels of full-time work.

The reasons for this variability in employment models arise from the differing balance between market-led deregulation and the social, political and institutional counterweights to market dominance (Bosch & Lehndorff 2005). The growth in services has led to debates about the relative increase in productivity in services compared with manufacturing. Baumol (1967) presents a formal model of the unbalanced nature of growth in what he calls the progressive (manufacturing) and non-progressive (largely services) sectors of the economy. In this model, the progressive sectors are those that experience consistent productivity growth. Baumol argues that, in a closed economy with competitive markets and with similar wage levels between the sectors, the non-progressive sector would grow and the progressive sector would decline, leading to stagnation in growth. This theory is known as the *productivity disease* of services because, given his assumption that wages are rising equally in the progressive and non-progressive sectors, wage costs in services (non-progressive sector) rise without the offsetting the productivity improvements of workers in manufacturing (progressive sector), where substitution of capital for labour allows for increases in productivity. This theory also assumes the existence of effective unions in the progressive sector, which allows workers to secure wage rises as a share of increased productivity.

Moving to a more realistic situation, relaxing the closed economy assumptions and allowing the market to set wages, can mean much lower wage costs for personal and social services. This would drive wages down, but make the cost of services more affordable, as has occurred in the US model, where 24.8 per cent of employees were low-paid in 2009 compared with 14.4 per cent in Australia (OECD 2011a). An alternative to low wages in the services sector is for social services – like health or education – to be subsidised by the state, thus making them more affordable. State subsidy of social services can lead to unskilled workers having comparable wages to workers in the progressive sector, as in Sweden, or to low-paid workers, as in the Australian case (Esping-Andersen 1999; ACOSS 2011).

In Australia, labour productivity in the retail area of distribution services equalled that of the rest of the market sector, at 2.1 per cent per year from 1988/89 to 2007/08 (Pech et al. 2009). Research by Triplett and Bosworth (2006) in the United States points to a take-off in productivity growth (both labour and multi-factor) in distribution services such as retail and wholesale trade, transport and communications after 1995. They attribute this to the impact of information technology such as automated stock tracking in these industries, and it can reasonably be expected that these developments explain much of the observed productivity growth in Australia.

Although productivity improvements have occurred in services such as retail, wages are still lower than in other industries. Since the late 1990s, wage growth (as measured by the growth in total hourly rates of pay excluding bonuses) has been lower in retail than the average of all industries. Average growth in retail wages from 1998–2008 has been just over 3 per cent, compared with 3.6 per cent across all industries (Pech et al. 2009). Also, unlike other industries, wages in collective agreements in retail are the same as the award rates.

The pattern of employment in personal services for Australia from 1994 to 2011 (see Table 2.1) does not show any major change over time; however, the slight growth in employment in the hotels and restaurants sector is in an area characterised by low productivity in line with Baumol's argument. Labour productivity increased by only 26.7 per cent in hotels and restaurants from 1990/91 to 2005/06, compared with 42.1 per cent for all market industries over the same period. Over a similar period, 1994–2007, unionisation decreased from 19.2 per cent to 6.3 per cent (ACIL Tasman and Colmar Brunton Social Research 2008). In retail (distribution), there was a slight decline in the employment share – no doubt reflecting the greater use of information technology (including online purchasing from overseas) mentioned above. From 1994 to 2011, by comparison, there was a growth from 13.2 per cent of employment to 17.7 per cent in producer services, and a growth from 26.5 per cent of employment to 31.2 per cent in social services over the same period.

The incomplete female revolution and the growth in services

Esping-Andersen (2009) describes the changing roles of women in the family, and their level of participation in education and employment, as the incomplete revolution. This concept of completeness would exist where families have both partners in full-time employment, with female earnings on average providing approximately 50 per cent of household income and where there is equal sharing of child-care and housekeeping duties between partners, as well as social support available, including affordable quality child care and paid maternity leave until the child is one year old. Esping-Andersen argues that some Scandinavian countries, such as Denmark, are beginning to approximate completeness.

The complete female revolution is in stark contrast with the male breadwinner or standard employment relationship (SER) – Bosch's (2004) model of the family, which still partly characterises countries as diverse as Germany and Australia. This is typified by a male with a full-time job with conditions such as standard hours, pay, work organisation, rest breaks, sick pay and holidays; these are regulated by collective

Table 2.1 Distribution of employment – total employment in services, 1994 and 2011 (%)		
Personal services	1994	2011
Hotels and restaurants	6.5	6.9
Recreational and cultural services	2.9	4.1
Other personal services	4.2	3.6
Sub-total	13.6	14.6
Social services		
Government	5.6	6.5
Health	7.1	9.1
Education	7.2	7.6
Miscellaneous social services	6.6	8.0
Sub-total	26.5	31.2
Distribution		
Retail	12.8	12.0
Wholesale	5.4	3.6
Transportation	2.9	5.5
Communications	1.7	1.7
Sub-total	22.8	22.8
Producer services		
Business and professional services	8.3	12.3
Financial services	2.9	2.6
Insurance	1.1	1.0
Real estate	0.9	1.8
Sub-total	13.2	17.7
Total	76.1	86.3

Source: ABS (2012f); author's calculations.

agreements, or by awards of industrial tribunals as in the Australian case. Various forms of welfare provision, such as unemployment benefits and health care, developed in conjunction with this SER in the post-war period. A segmented labour market existed, with women paid less than men with lower rates of participation in the labour market until the late 1970s. It should be noted that in the more conservative countries, such as Germany, there is a greater tendency for men to adhere to a more traditional role in relation to household and child-care responsibilities, and German women are also more likely to take longer career breaks after childbirth and to work more in part-time jobs since they have limited access to child-care facilities.

Irrespective of the extent of change in female roles in the different employment models, there has been significant growth in women's employment since 1945, and this largely has involved a shift out of industrial work into services in most advanced economies. The shift to services has broken the SER because collective regulation of employment is less common in services. Pay in low-skill service jobs has been lower than in similar jobs in industry, which can be explained by reference to the productivity disease model discussed above.

The rise in female employment has also coincided with the growth in service jobs, particularly in part-time work – which is common in some forms of service work. In Australia in 1978, 33.2 per cent of employed females worked in part-time jobs and by 2012 this had risen to 45.1 per cent (ABS 2012g). From Table 2.2, it is apparent that in 2011, in two of the major areas of personal services, hotels and restaurants, 63.9 per cent of female employees worked part-time, and in recreational and cultural services,

Table 2.2 Female employees in services: full-time and part-time, 1994–2011

	1994		2011	
	Full-time	Part-time	Full-time	Part-time
Personal services				
Hotels and restaurants	39.0	61.0	36.1	63.9
Recreational and cultural services	47.5	53.4	45.6	54.4
Other personal services	56.5	43.5	50.3	49.7
Social services				
Government	77.1	22.9	72.9	27.1
Health	53.6	46.4	51.6	48.4
Education	58.7	41.3	52.7	47.3
Miscellaneous social services	56.4	43.6	44.2	55.8
Distribution				
Retail	43.3	56.7	40.3	59.7
Wholesale	68.0	32	69.2	30.8
Transportation	68.3	32.7	67.2	38.8
Communications	74.4	35.6	69	31.0
Producer services				
Business and professional services	61.9	38.1	57.7	42.3
Financial services	71.4	29.6	69.0	31.0
Insurance	81.8	18.2	79.7	20.3
Real Estate	70.2	29.8	65.9	34.1

Source: ABS (2012f); author's calculations.

54.4 per cent of all female employees worked part-time. The increasing prevalence of part-time female workers is evident in most other services employment sectors. Gender pay inequality tends to be more pronounced in such service jobs – particularly part-time work, as we will see later.

In discussions about the three different employment models or regimes of welfare capitalism, the size of the service sector has been a factor in debates about the causes of unemployment and income inequality. The growth of low-paid service jobs in neo-liberal economies like that of the United States has been presented by some as the solution to unemployment in European Union (EU) countries. Some economists have argued that the growing income inequalities that have emerged with the growth of low-pay service jobs is the price that must be paid for lower unemployment. The fact that Nordic countries have similar employment levels to the United States, but less wage and welfare inequality, has been ignored in such low-wage service economy scenarios. However, Bosch and Lehndorff (2005) argue that the nature of the employment model is important in determining the form that service sector work may take. In effect, there can be both 'high' and 'low' road models of service work with, for example, quality public sector provision of services in Sweden, with highly trained and well paid employees, versus market-driven low-paid and variable quality service work in the United States. The issue is as much about political choice as about economic necessity arising from the nature of service work.

■ Australia and the incomplete female revolution

The extent to which the female revolution is incomplete in Australia can be seen by the following figures. In 1981, 19 per cent of mothers were working full-time and 24 per cent were working part-time, whereas in 2009, the proportions were 28 per cent and 35 per cent, respectively. The number of women in full-time and part-time work who have children has increased from 43 per cent in 1981 to 63 per cent in 2009 (ABS 2009b). Overall, women's participation has increased from 45.7 per cent in 1984/85 to 57.2 per cent in 2005/06 (ABS 2006a). In 2003, 56.2 per cent of women with children were working in Australia, compared with 68.2 per cent in the United States and 77.2 per cent in Denmark.

Esping-Andersen (2009), as indicated above, regards dual full-time working couples as the key to completing the female revolution. In Australia from 1983 to 2010, the percentage of such couples with children increased from 17 per cent to almost 25 per cent of couple families (ABS 2011c). The predominant form of couple families with children in Australia remains those with one-and-a-half jobs, followed closely by one-job families. By comparison, in Denmark in 2008, 66 per cent of couple families with dependant children were dual full-time working couples (Craig & Mullan 2011).

One result of couple families with both members working full-time is that this adds to general social inequality, a point that is considered at length in Chapter 10. Two factors explain this situation: first, the tendency of well-educated and employable women to marry partners with similar levels of education and employability, and for women with poor skills and employment prospects to marry partners with similar characteristics (Esping-Andersen 2009; De Vaus 2004); and, second, partners with poor skills and employability tending to work fewer hours than those with high skills and employability.

An important factor in supporting women's involvement in the workforce is the cost of child care. Figure 2.1 shows that there is considerable difference between social democratic and neo-liberal model countries in this regard. In 2004, in Sweden and Denmark respectively, 5 per cent and 8 per cent of the average wage was spent on full-time child care for a two-year-old compared with the neo-liberal model economies with 20 per cent in the United States and 25 per cent in the United Kingdom. Australia is clearly aligned with the neo-liberal regimes, with 22 per cent of the average wage spent on full-time child care for a two-year-old.

Low-paid work

The extent to which employees on less than two-thirds of the median wage (or in the bottom 20 per cent of the wage distribution) in a given year continue to be low-paid is a critical issue concerning the functioning of an employment model. If employees only spent a small part of their working life as low-paid, this would not be a significant social problem. For the period 2002–08, on average 52 per cent of employees at or below the federal minimum wage moved above that level, while 32 per cent remained at or close to this level and 9 per cent became unemployed (Watson 2010). Such an outcome points to many employees being trapped in low standards of living rather than just going through a life transition to better paid work.

The Australian response to Baumol's productivity disease of services has been to utilise low-paid, full-time workers in distribution services such as retail (12.2 per cent low-paid); personal services such as hotels and restaurants (19.6 per cent low-paid), cultural and recreational services (14.2 per cent low-paid), personal and other services (13.4 per cent low-paid) and social services (10.3 per cent low-paid). The incidence of low pay among part-time workers is considerably higher (Pocock 2009).

The incidence of low-paid work, using the OECD definition of two-thirds of the full-time gross median wage, varies across neo-liberal, conservative and social democratic model countries. The OECD figures in Table 2.3 only include full-time employees, and as a result, they understate the actual level of low pay in Australia, since part-time workers have higher levels of low pay. Using the Household Income and Labour Dynamics in Australia (HILDA) survey data for 2001–04, which includes juniors, students and part-time employees, Masterman-Smith and Pocock (2008) calculate that about a quarter of Australian employees are low-paid.

As Table 2.3 indicates, neo-liberal regimes such as the United Kingdom, Canada and the United States have the highest level of low-paid workers, with an anomaly in the German situation, where low-paid work has risen by 47 per cent since the mid-1990s (Kalina & Weinkopf 2008). Given the categorisation of Germany as a

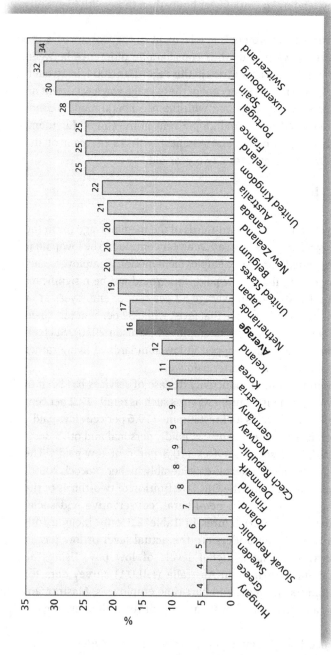

Figure 2.1: Fees charged by child-care centres (% of average wage)
Source: Immervoll & Barber (2005).

conservative model, it is important to understand the reasons for these changes. Germany does not have a minimum wage (unlike even the United States), and wages historically were maintained by the wide coverage of collective agreements. Since the early 1990s, the sharp reduction of collective agreement coverage – particularly in service industries and small firms – has contributed to increased numbers of low-paid workers. A complementary growth in service work, particularly in business, household and personal services, has accentuated the problem. Outsourcing of work to firms not covered by collective agreements has also contributed, as has the growth in part-time work, where the incidence of low-pay is 4 per cent higher than in full-time work. The growth in – largely female – marginal part-time work – the so-called 'mini jobs' where employees earn less than 440 Euros a month (compared with an average gross monthly wage of 3695 Euros in 2012) and have no access to social security payments from employers, has also contributed to low rates of pay. The low-pay route out of Baumol's productivity disease of personal services has been embraced by German governments and employers by using the escape routes provided by the decline in German labour regulation.

Australia does not fit with the neo-liberal economies like the United Kingdom and United States in terms of the levels of low pay, as can be seen in Table 2.3. In 2009, low-paid workers comprised 14.4 per cent of full-time employees compared with 24.8 per cent in the United States and 20.6 per cent in the United Kingdom. The more compressed wage structure can be explained by the setting of minimum rates of pay by the Fair Work Commission and its predecessors. Before the shift to enterprise bargaining in the early 1990s, wage rates for lower paid workers had been set in industry and occupational awards. Historically, Australia has had one of the highest levels of minimum wages – for example, in 2005, the minimum wage in Australia was 58 per cent of the median wage and was exceeded only by France and Turkey among the 21 OECD countries with a statutory minimum wage (OECD 2011). The typical

Table 2.3 Incidence of low pay of full-time employees in selected OECD countries, 1999 and 2009

	1999	2009
Australia	14.3	14.4
Germany	20.0	20.2
Norway	10.4	8.0
Denmark	8.0	13.6
Netherlands	14.8	NA
Canada	23.1	20.5
UK	20.1	20.6
US	24.5	24.8

Source: OECD (2011).

neo-liberal model countries, like the United States and United Kingdom, have considerably lower minimum wages at 39 per cent and 46 per cent of the median wage.

However, Figure 2.2 demonstrates that the Australian minimum wage has been on a downward trend since the mid-1990s, having fallen from just above 60% of the median wage to 54% in 2010. In this development we see the influence of the spread of neo-liberalism into the operations of companies and the policies of governments as we discussed in the previous chapter.

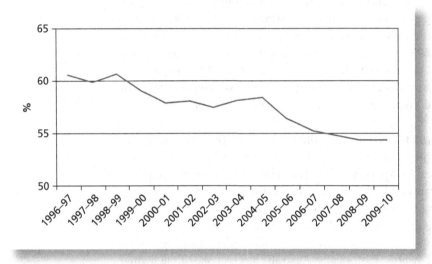

Figure 2.2: Minimum wage as a percentage of full-time median earnings
Source: ACOSS (2011).

The reason for the differences in levels of low pay between different countries can explained in terms of the national employment models (Appelbaum et al. 2010). Employment models that have extensive collective bargaining coverage and high levels of union membership have lower numbers of low-paid workers. When these conditions are complemented by high levels of minimum wages – or, as in France, low levels of unionisation and a law to extend collective agreements from the unionised to the non-unionised sector – then these labour market institutions are characterised as 'inclusive' (Bosch, Mayhew & Gautie 2010).

Casual work

The dynamics within employment models whereby employers are able to use 'exit routes' such as withdrawing from collective agreements, outsourcing to firms with lower pay and conditions, the use of non-standard employment arrangements – such as temporary contracts – and agency workers all give rise to a situation of low pay (Bosch, Mayhew & Gautie 2010).

In the Australian case, the use of casual work – particularly in services – provides an exit option that has aspects which are unique. As we have explained, in Australia casual work developed in the context of a male breadwinner model of employment with very low levels of female employment (Watson et al. 2003). Casual employment grew out of the needs of particular industries, such as the waterfront, construction, meat preserving and flour milling. Such work was either seasonal or irregular, in contrast to the ongoing standard employment of full-time male workers. While this work was usually regulated by awards, the typical definition of casual workers was broad, and in some cases tautological, with the workers described as 'casual' because they were paid in that way.

Given the importance of the income of the male breadwinner in supporting a family (as in the German case), the regulation of casual work through award clauses providing for restrictions on the number of casuals employed was also common. Often these provisions were in the form of a quota – such as the number of hours or percentage of employees. Awards gave casuals few rights and benefits beyond that of being paid by the hour; they had little or no protection against dismissal and no rights to notice of termination. By definition, casual employees do not have the right to standard working hours, as employers set the number and timing of hours of work and may vary these at short notice. They also lack rights to annual leave, sick leave and public holiday pay (Campbell, Whitehouse & Baxter 2009). Casual workers do receive a loading on the hourly wage rate paid to ongoing employees in order to compensate for the lack of benefits such as annual and sick leave. Another feature of the system of regulation was the poor enforcement of causal clauses in awards. In one survey, only 48.3 per cent of respondents agreed that they received a casual loading and 13.2 per cent said they did not know (ABS 2006a).

Table 2.4 (overleaf) shows that, overall, 19.9 per cent of employees were casual in November 2010 (ABS 2012e), with about 40 per cent of casuals aged between 15 and 24 years. Despite the history of casual employment, women are now more highly represented in this category (24.2 per cent compared with 16.3 per cent of employed men) and they were more than twice as likely to be working part-time. Another notable feature of casual employment is that female casual employees were twice as likely as men to be working part-time (19.7 per cent compared with 8.9 per cent).

Not surprisingly, high levels of casual employment are also found in the service sector, especially in personal services like hotels and restaurants, and in distributive services like retail, which between them employed almost 20 per cent of the workforce in 2011. While only 20.3 per cent of workers across the economy were employed on a casual basis in May 2008, in hotels and restaurants casual employees made up 56 per cent of the workforce in the industry (ACIL Tasman and Colmar Brunton Social Research 2008).

Until the 1980s, awards in hotels and restaurants restricted the use of part-time employees, and they were typically casual workers, due to award restrictions on the number of hours that could be worked by part-time employees and a requirement for union agreement – and even then, only if no full-time employees could be found. However, over the past 25 years, these controls have been removed as employers strive to achieve flexibility in the context of much longer opening hours and declining union membership (see Chapter 13 for a discussion of employer efforts to achieve flexibility in retail and hospitality during the Global Financial Crisis). In retail trade, 73.2 per cent of part-time employees were casual in November 2007, compared with 58.2 per cent of employees in all industries (Pech et al. 2009).

Table 2.4 Types of employment by gender, 2010 (%)

	Employees		Self-employed	
	Permanent	Casual	Owner-managers of incorporated businesses	Owner-managers of unincorporated businesses
Males				
Full-time	57.0	7.4	8.3	10.7
Part-time	3.9	8.9	1.0	3.0
Total males	60.9	16.3	9.3	11.0
Females				
Full-time	43.1	4.5	2.3	3.6
Part-time	19.6	19.7	2.2	5.0
Total females	62.7	24.2	4.5	8.6
Persons				
Full-time	50.7	6.1	5.6	7.7
Part-time	11.0	13.8	1.5	3.9
Total	61.7	19.9	7.1	11.6

Source: ABS (2012e).

■ Income inequality and widening pay dispersion

Changes in earnings inequality for seven countries, including Australia, are represented in Table 2.5, which compares the earnings of different deciles – for example, the difference between highest and lowest paid workers is the ratio of the 9th to 1st earning decile. It is notable that there has been growing inequality in gross full-time earnings for all countries except France, with the two social democratic countries – Sweden and Denmark – showing increasing inequality. However, relative to the neo-liberal regimes of the United Kingdom and the United States, the two social democratic countries still have lower levels of inequality.

However, in Germany – a conservative regime, as discussed previously – wage inequality increased due to the greater number of low-paid workers since the 1990s as we have already noted. In line with this increase in low-paid employees, between 2000 and 2010 the average gross monthly wage for the bottom 40 per cent of German workers declined by18.5 per cent, whereas the top 10 per cent only rose by 2.1 per cent (German Socio Economic Panel 2011), reflecting the very low

Table 2.5 Comparison of earnings dispersion of gross earnings of full-time employees, 1995 and 2008

| | Ratio of deciles | | | | | |
| | 9th to 1st | | 9th to 5th | | 5th to 1st | |
	1995	2008	1995	2008	1995	2008
Sweden	2.20	2.28	1.59	1.66	1.39	1.37
Denmark	2.47	2.73	1.69	1.74	1.46	1.57
Germany	2.79	3.32	1.79	1.72	1.56	1.93
France	3.08	2.91	1.93	1.98	1.59	1.47
UK	3.48	3.63	1.88	1.98	1.85	1.83
US	4.59	4.89	2.17	2.34	2.11	2.09
Australia	2.91	3.34	1.77	1.92	1.65	1.74

Sources: OECD (2007a, 2008b, 2010).

growth in real wages in Germany since the late 1990s. In the United Kingdom and even more in the United States, the top earners are pulling away – particularly from the bottom, but also from the middle. This is confirmed by a review of OECD countries over the twentieth century, which shows that recent increases in inequality are largely due to growing incomes of the top income earners (Atkinson 2008). In Australia, the top income earners are pulling away from the bottom and to a lesser extent from the middle, but the ratio of middle to the bottom has hardly shifted.

The extent of the increasing in inequality in the United States is demonstrated by Freeman (2007), who found that real median wages for all employees were 6 per cent lower in 2004 than in 1973, and that labour productivity had increased by 55 per cent over this period. Figure 2.3 (overleaf) reveals a similar situation in Australia, where average real wages have only grown by about 17 per cent over the 30 years to 2008, whereas labour productivity has grown by 80 per cent. Standard economic theory would suggest that, over time, real wages should rise in line with labour productivity growth – that is, the profit share should be relatively stable. However, after three decades of sustained neo-liberal reforms in Australia, the real wage overhang referred to in Chapter 1 arguably has been replaced by a real wage underhang. In the absence of the minimum wage decisions of the industrial tribunals, the extent of this wage inequality would be even greater.

Another way of expressing this relationship between productivity and real wages is to look at the share of GDP going to labour and capital (profits) in Australia. This is set out in Figure 2.4 (p. 43), which shows the labour share of GDP has shifted downwards from 1984, when it was 62 per cent, to just above 52 per cent in 2008.

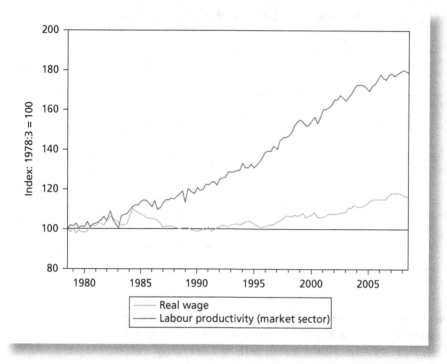

Figure 2.3: Wages and labour productivity, Australia, 1978–2008
Source: ABS (2009b).

The explanation for growing inequality in Australia and the United States varies according to the theoretical lens used. A standard economic account is that growth in inequality is related to demand for skills (Borland 1999), specifically due to a shortage of skilled workers. For example, employing university graduates increases their price, whereas low-skilled workers (e.g. those who have failed to complete high school) are at the bottom of the earnings distribution and are in less demand. Hence there is a widening in the dispersion of earnings. Although the premium paid to graduates over school leavers is a factor in wages, a range of institutional factors are relevant to wage dispersion; these include the power of unions and the coverage of collective bargaining and the level of minimum wages. Minimum wages provide a floor for low-paid workers in the service sector and other areas – for example, from 1994/95 to 2005/06 in retail, women's average real hourly wages rose by only 10.8 per cent, and in hospitality they rose by only 3.9 per cent compared with a 15.9 per cent increase for women across all industries (Austen et al. 2009).

In examining the growing inequality of wages in the United States, Freeman (2007) identifies several causes for the relative decline in the incomes of high school dropouts compared with graduates, including a low and declining real minimum wage, union decline and the influx of low-skilled migrants. Freeman also notes that very large increases in executive pay at the top end of the distribution had significantly increased the level of inequality of earnings inequality. Furthermore, when employees with similar skills in Germany or Sweden are compared with their

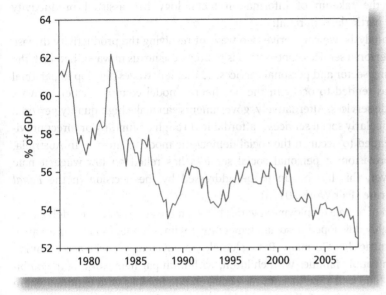

American counterparts, there is still a much greater dispersion of earnings in the United States.

Figure 2.4: Share of wages as percentage of GDP
Source: ABS (2009b).

■ Conclusion

This chapter has set the understanding of the Australian employment model in the context of deindustrialisation and the expansion of services, and the related growth in female employment. By locating the Australian employment model in relation to Esping-Andersen's (1990) three regimes of welfare capitalism, it is possible to both grasp the essential characteristics of the Australian model by comparing it with examples of other models (Sweden, Denmark, Germany, and the United Kingdom and United States) and pay special attention to the significance of the links between employment and welfare. In this way, we begin to understand how the shift of employment from goods manufacturing to services under the different models varies systematically in regard to the quality of jobs, skills required and pay levels, and we can perceive where Australia fits in terms of the three models of welfare capitalism (neo-liberal, conservative and social democratic).

A reformulated framework of services industries, derived from Elfring (1988, 1989), conceives of services in four major categories: producer services, distributive services, personal services and social services. The analysis in this chapter reveals that the growth of jobs in these four sectors varies between the countries examined, as does the nature of the jobs and pay levels. Furthermore, we see that, with the exception of producer services, slow productivity growth in service industries like retail, personal and social services – those areas involving direct interaction with customers – is consistent with Baumol's productivity disease argument. Of course, to some extent, the take-up of information technology has assisted productivity improvement, particularly in retail.

From our analysis, we can derive two ways of resolving the productivity disease dilemma for personal services. One option is to break the nexus in wages between the goods-producing sector and personal services, so that low wages develop in personal services, as has tended to occur in the neo-liberal model countries where private markets provide services. Alternatively, governments can make high-quality personal services – particularly social services – affordable through co-funding or direct provision, as has tended to occur in the social democratic model countries. In Australia, government provision of personal social services has relied on low-wage female labour; however, this has begun to be addressed by the decision in the *Equal Remuneration case* (Fair Work 2012a).

The growth of female employment varies between the employment models examined, being highly developed in social democratic regimes but less so in conservative regimes in countries like Germany. Rising female employment has been accompanied by a growth in couple families with children, with both partners working in combinations of full- and part-time jobs. In Australia, couple families with children where one partner only is working full-time and the other is working part-time comprise the largest category of couple families, whereas in social democratic countries, the majority of couple families with children have both partners working full-time. In Australia, the partner working full-time is usually male, so the male breadwinner model is still dominant; we have described this as the incomplete female revolution.

In Australia, female employment has been focused to a significant extent in retail, personal services and social services. Such industries also have significant levels of low pay, although Australia has levels of low-paid employees across all industries that are well below the neo-liberal regimes. A major reason for the existence and expansion of low-paid employment has been shown to be institutional reasons around the weakening of collective bargaining, union density and national regulation. The impact of neo-liberal ideology, which pushes for deregulation and the extension of markets, has provided a basis for the undermining of institutions that prevent low-paid work.

Bosch, Mayhew and Gautie (2010) advance the notion of the creation of in institutional frameworks. As discussed in the German case, there has been a significant increase in low-paid work since the 1980s, due to a combination of reduced employer involvement in industry collective bargaining, employers shifting to coverage by weaker industry agreements (for instance, using cleaning industry agreements instead of health), outsourcing and privatisation, and marginal part-time work. This outcome demonstrates that typologies like Esping-Andersen's (1990) are not static, but evolve. In the Australian case, an exit route is provided by the lack of appropriate regulation of casual work, a considerable proportion of which is performed by part-time female employees, who are often low-paid.

Related to the issue of low-paid employees is the growing dispersion of wages, which has affected most EU countries and the neo-liberal regimes, including the United Kingdom, United States and Australia; however, the social democratic regimes remain less unequal than neo-liberal and conservative regimes. Australia bears similarities to the United States in experiencing slower growth in real wages relative to labour productivity since the 1970s, although in the United States real wages have actually fallen.

Overall, in contrasting the elements of the Australian employment model with the social democratic, conservative and neo-liberal countries, it is evident that the alignment with the neo-liberal model is incomplete. Hence we see that, while neo-liberal policies have been implemented in Australia over a long period, political compromises have preserved some semblance of the social democratic model.

Discussion questions

2.1 What are the three variants of Esping-Andersen's (1990) employment model? Using examples, explain how they differ.

2.2 Consider which employment model best applies to Australia, and identify the associated economic and social outcomes of that model. What are the points that distinguish the Australian variant of the employment model from the Anglo-American or neo-liberal model?

2.3 How is the rise of the service sector linked with employment models, and what is the difference across the countries discussed in this chapter?

2.4 What is the link between the concept of an incomplete female revolution and the male breadwinner model that has characterised Australia?

2.5 Is the employment model analysis applicable to the developing nations of Asia? If not, could it be made applicable and useful?

3

Australian trade unions and international labour movements

Marjorie Jerrard and Stéphane Le Queux

■ Chapter objectives

This chapter will enable readers to understand the:
- role of the Australian Council of Trade Unions (ACTU)
- reasons for trade union decline in Australia
- different strategies for trade union renewal, including the organising model
- ways in which globalisation has led to the development of international union structures
- prospects for unions to operate effectively at an international level.

▪ Introduction

Trade unions are 'collective organisations of workers in the workplace that focus on improving the terms of the wage–effort bargain through creating collective leverage' (Gall 2009: 177); that is, they act as collective agents to protect and improve their members' wages and conditions through bargaining and other means. Some trade unions also have a legal, political, ethical and broadly social agenda, which means that unions are also interested in their members' welfare and rights away from work. These interests also affect wider society and include activities that fall under the label of 'community unionism'.

In Australia, in order to have legal representative rights on behalf of members, trade unions must be registered pursuant to legislation. Registration gives trade unions legal protection and enables them to carry out a range of functions, including the recruitment of new members, the provision of services to existing members, the representation of those members, and the monitoring and enforcing of labour laws on behalf of members (Fenwick & Howe 2009). Registration has granted Australian trade unions legitimacy and a recognised role in the institutional framework that shapes Australian workplace relations, thereby enabling Australian unions to make substantive gains for their members in wages and conditions pursuant to decisions of the industrial tribunals.

Viewed from the outside, unions are often considered to be an homogeneous group; however, the approximately 40 federally registered unions – most of which are voluntarily affiliated with the Australian Council of Trade Unions (ACTU) – cover different industries and different types of work, have different histories and traditions, different political and ideological views, and different structures and strategies. Thus relationships between different unions are not always harmonious, as each seeks to represent its members' interests – sometimes at the expense of the interests of the members of other unions.

This chapter draws upon these differences within the Australian trade union movement to explore the challenges facing unions today and possible solutions to these challenges. These challenges arise from the shift in the economy from the traditional industrial base of unions to the relatively poorly organised private services sector; the development by employers of human resource strategies engaging with employees as individuals rather than members of collective organisations extending beyond the workplace; the impact of the pressures of globalisation on workplace competitiveness and workplace relations with unions (see Chapter 15 on the impact of international supply chains on workplace relations); the shift of the legislative framework of bargaining from the national and industry levels to the workplace; and the constraints placed on union operations by the state. The resulting decline in union membership – particularly in the private sector – has led unions to try a range of strategies to grow membership again. These include organising strategies based in workplace-level delegate activism and also reaching out to community groups to invoke their support to protect jobs and working conditions. Examples will be given of specific campaigns of the Australian trade union movement that illustrate different strategies adopted by unions. In response to globalisation of business, trade unions have developed international confederations and industry groups since the 1940s. Since the late 1980s, these bodies have developed strategies to deal with multinational employers, and recently the need to embed unions internationally in social movements and calling for decent jobs for employees worldwide. This chapter concludes with an overview of these international developments and their potential to renew unionism.

The role of the Australian Council of Trade Unions

The ACTU was formed in 1927 and remains the national peak body for the Australian trade union movement. While affiliation is voluntary, most unions are members. ACTU officials are elected from among officials of individual trade unions and become national figures, who wield considerable political influence, and at times they are able to influence not just workplace relations policy, but also key public policies. The ACTU provides umbrella strategies for the trade union movement as a whole, as well as providing resources and training, and a national and coordinated face for the union movement. Some examples of specific national campaigns include the recent campaign on 'greening and sustainability', as well as the ongoing campaign to reduce the gender pay gap (Jerrard & Heap 2010).

Other areas of activity for the ACTU are the representation of workers in international bodies such the International Labor Organization (ILO) and the International Trade Union Confederation, of which Sharan Burrow, a former ACTU president, is currently president; conduct of test cases (e.g. technology and redundancy, parental leave) and minimum wage cases; and training and education programs for union officials to enable them to recruit and organise more effectively within their own unions (Crosby 2000). Under the current leadership of Ged Kearney and Dave Oliver, the ACTU continues its focus on the global arena and decent jobs for all workers.

The ACTU strategy of trade union amalgamations

As part of a modernisation strategy, in the late 1980s the ACTU began to promote union amalgamations to align unions with the 20 specific industry-based unions. The focus was to remove demarcation disputes between unions on multi-union worksites and to allow a more coherent national strategy aimed at moving towards a regulatory model of workplace relations more aligned with the corporatist models then in place in Sweden and Germany. Fewer, larger unions were expected to be able to maximise economies of scale for delivering services to members and to help arrest a long-term decline in membership.

One of the key difficulties with amalgamations was that the process of forcing ideologically different unions together into an industry union framework resulted

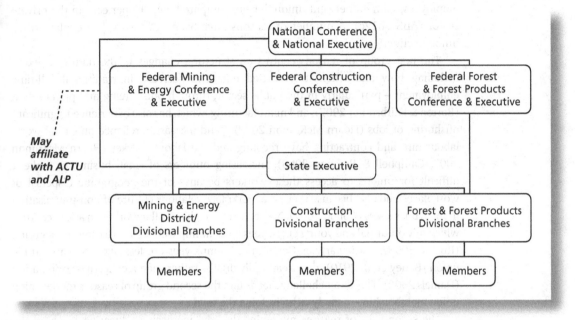

```
                    ┌──────────────────────┐
                    │  National Conference │
                    │  & National Executive│
                    └──────────────────────┘
     ┌─────────────────────┬──────────────────────┬─────────────────────┐
  ┌──────────────┐  ┌──────────────┐      ┌──────────────┐
  │ Federal Mining│  │Federal Construction│  │ Federal Forest│
  │ & Energy       │  │  Conference   │      │ & Forest Products│
  │ Conference     │  │  & Executive  │      │ Conference & Executive│
  │ & Executive    │  └──────────────┘      └──────────────┘
  └──────────────┘
    May
  affiliate
  with ACTU                    ┌──────────────┐
  and ALP                      │State Executive│
                               └──────────────┘
  ┌──────────────┐      ┌──────────────┐      ┌──────────────────┐
  │Mining & Energy│      │ Construction │      │Forest & Forest Products│
  │ District/      │      │Divisional Branches│  │Divisional Branches│
  │Divisional Branches│  └──────────────┘      └──────────────────┘
  └──────────────┘
    ┌────────┐          ┌────────┐              ┌────────┐
    │Members │          │Members │              │Members │
    └────────┘          └────────┘              └────────┘
```

Figure 3.1: Internal structure of the CFMEU

in various divisions covering different industries and having different political viewpoints and interests. One such merged union, the Construction, Forestry, Mining and Energy Union (CFMEU) (see Figure 3.1 for the internal structure of the union) demonstrates the problems, with the militant and left-wing Construction and Mining Divisions opposing the Forestry Division on a number of issues, including the environment. This was illustrated during the 2005 federal election campaign, when the Tasmanian Forestry Division aligned itself with the right-wing Liberal-National Party government's policy to continue logging in Tasmania in order to protect members' jobs; this position directly contradicted that of the remainder of the union. It also clearly illustrates the heterogeneity within large trade unions, as well as illustrating the disparity within the entire trade union movement. The actions of the CFMEU are not always looked upon favourably – even by its own members in some instances. An example is the unprotected industrial action taken by the CFMEU against the Melbourne-based construction company Grocon in late 2012, over the union's demands outside of a bargaining period to appoint safety representatives on Melbourne worksites, a dispute that did not involve CFMEU members employed by Grocon but instead involved other members.

■ Declining trade union membership

Since the 1970s, Australia's trade union membership has been in decline, from more than 50 per cent of all employees in 1974 to only 18 per cent of Australian employees in 2011 (ABS 2012c). The highest proportion of membership is among public sector employees, with 43 per cent union density compared with 13 per cent in the private sector (ABS 2012c). A number of reasons have been put forward to explain trade union decline.

The first group of reasons centres on structural changes in the nature of work, including how and when it is carried out. The decrease in traditional full-time employment – particularly in the public sector, through outsourcing and privatisation (Barton & Fairbrother 2007), and manufacturing, which has also experienced significant offshoring of jobs (Hearn McKinnon 2007) – and increasing reliance on casual work, labour hire and contracting have reconfigured the labour market (Hearn McKinnon 2007; Campbell & Brosnan 2005). Increasing numbers of small businesses make it difficult for unions to access these workers because of the geographic dispersal of workplaces and also because there is a workplace relations culture of non-unionisation in small businesses (Abbott 2007). Newer forms of white-collar work such as call centres, which rely on casual and young employees, pose multiple challenges to union organising (Russell 2008), particularly as Generation Y employees are less likely to join a trade union (Bailey et al. 2010), due to an individualist rather than a collectivist orientation (Daniels 2006). This latter challenge leads into the second group of reasons for declining union membership – namely, who is doing the work.

The second set of reasons maintains that the increasing education levels of the workforce have given rise to the belief that education equates with individual work-place power, making trade unions less necessary than they were in earlier decades and leading to changes in individual attitudes and job choices (Griffin & Svensen 1996). This particularly appears to be the case for younger employees (Daniels 2006). As we discuss in Chapter 10, Australia now has one of the most diverse populations in the world as a result of continuing high levels of migration from an increasing range of countries and cultures, many of which have little or no experience with trade unions. This increasingly diverse workforce presents a new challenge for unions when organising and servicing current and potential members (Jerrard & Heap 2010; see also Chapter 10 in this volume). Further, prolonged skills and labour shortages in Australia have seen an increase in migrants on short-term visas filling labour-market gaps; these groups are unlikely to see the need for or benefits of union membership. It has also been argued that increasing numbers of women in the workforce have proved challenging for the traditionally male-dominated unions to recruit and organise, partly because female-dominated industries are often highly casualised and more difficult to organise for the reasons discussed above (Pocock, Buchanan & Campbell 2004). However, two female-dominated unions are among those showing membership growth across the nation and countering the trend of declining union membership: the Australian Nursing Federation (ANF) and the Australian Education Union (AEU). These unions have been able to take advantage of a more direct relationship with the public when running campaigns around conditions and remuneration, and have uti-lised 'community unionism' as a successful strategy (Cockfield et al. 2009), including in enterprise bargaining rounds with the Victorian state government in 2012. It is noted that the union density for both male and female workers is now equal at 18 per cent, so the traditional stereotypes of the different propensities to unionise no longer apply.

The third group of reasons for membership decline focuses on external factors, such as increasing unemployment – which, in this era of globalisation, is affected by the state of the international economy as well as the national economy, as discussed in Chapter 1. However, in the light of Australia's relatively strong economy – albeit largely as a result of the resources boom and despite the recent Global Financial Crisis – this argument alone does not explain the continuing decline in union membership. If we also consider increased employer opposition to trade unions and improvements in human resource management techniques leading to decollectivist or union avoidance strategies by management (Peetz 1998, 2005), then there is more support for this group of reasons. Other contributing factors include community perceptions fuelled by some sections of the media, public statements of the Howard Liberal-National government (1996–2007) and campaigning by some employer groups, such as the Business Council of Australia, the Australian Chamber of Commerce and Industry and the Australian Mining and Metals Association, which together reinforced negative stereotypes of unions as too powerful and of union members frequently resorting to thuggery and violence (Woolcock & Jerrard 2009).

A fourth group of reasons consists of the impact of judicial decision-making pursuant to legislative changes that are variously anti-union or pro-employer, or that promote individualisation of the employment relationship. The most recent example of this was the Work Choices 2005 amendments to the *Workplace Relations Act 1996*, which are discussed extensively in Chapter 5; such measures can inhibit union activities, making it difficult to retain existing members and recruit new members. Specifically, the introduction of prohibited content into collective agreements under Work Choices removed benefits that unions were able to offer members – for example, paid time off from work to engage in union-provided training on a range of issues, from occupational health and safety through to negotiation and communication, was disallowed. Even though the enactment of the *Fair Work Act 2009* by the Rudd Labor government removed the contentious Australian Workplace Agreements (AWAs), some trade unions would argue that little was done to depart from the philosophy of Work Choices, as the *Fair Work Act* retained the specific restrictions on the building and construction unions that were first introduced under the *Building and Construction Improvement Act 2005*. These restrictions remained until the passing of the *Building and Construction Industry Improvement Amendment (Transition to Fair Work) Act 2012*, which incorporated the powers of the Australian Building and Construction Commission into Fair Work Australia – now the Fair Work Commission – the tribunal charged with regulating all aspects of Australian workplace relations.

The fifth group of reasons for membership decline derives from inside the trade union movement itself, and reflects the structure and internal rules of unions. In particular, the time needed to introduce changes within a union is long – often years rather than months – because of the restrictive rules placed on them as registered organisations and because of legal requirements for membership ballots and rigid hierarchical structures (Fenwick & Howe 2009). Trade unions have also proved slow to adopt technological change for organising and communicating with members (Moody 1997), and in utilising the communication media 'to put the trade union message to the public' (Manning 1998). Even strategies aimed at halting membership decline, such as amalgamations, may have hastened membership decline, because small unions with distinct membership identities disappeared into larger industrial or general unions, leaving their members as part of a large, amorphous union (Bodman 1998).

Finally, the political and legal protection that Australian unions have received for much of their history has created high levels of self-interest among senior union officials to a point where they have sometimes lost touch with their membership (Cranston 2000). The close relationship between the Labor Party and the union movement has seen many union officials move into electoral politics, perhaps suggesting to potential members that trade union leaders use their roles as a step towards gaining a seat in parliament rather than to protect members' interests – for example, Bob Hawke, former ACTU President, became prime minister in 1983; Simon Crean and Martin Ferguson, both ACTU presidents, were ministers under the Keating Labor government, and at the 2007 federal election, Greg Combet, former ACTU secretary, and Bill Shorten, former Australian Workers Union (AWU) federal and Victorian secretary, were both elected to the Australian parliament and now hold ministerial roles. While the trend for union officials to move into parliament is not new, perhaps public perceptions of such moves as self-serving may have changed over time.

Models of trade union strategy

Models of union strategy are long-standing, but declining membership has led to the development of new models. These models can be used to understand the ways in which unions operate and the goals they pursue. It must be remembered that trade unions do not necessarily adhere to only one model, and that unions may also progress from one model to another. In reality, most unions – irrespective of whether they are classified as servicing or organising – always exhibit a combination of models. In developing strategies to increase membership, Australian unions have been influenced by overseas examples, particularly from the United States, where there has also been a major decline in union membership. Within the literature on trade union strategy, six key models can be identified.

Servicing

This model relies on union activities external to the workplace, as distinct from the development of workplace-level delegate structures as occurs in the 'organising model' (see below), to achieve improvements in wages and conditions and settle disputes. In the Australian context, servicing historically has often been associated with union dependency on a centralised industrial relations system of awards, and conciliation and arbitration. As a consequence, unions have relied on employers to provide lists of workers to recruit and on industrial awards to 'rope in' other employers and their employees to award coverage.

A further development of this strategy occurred in 1987 when the ACTU adopted its 'Future Strategies' policy. As explained above, union mergers were advocated as a means to more efficient unions, which would be able to more effectively service their members' needs. The development of enterprise bargaining in the early 1990s under the Keating Labor government, and subsequent changes under the Howard Liberal-National government, removed the underpinnings of the servicing model. This change occurred because the *Workplace Relations Act 1996* curtailed the ability of the then Australian Industrial Relations Commission to conciliate and arbitrate disputes on wages and conditions through making awards. A further move to decentralised bargaining occurred under the Work Choices 2005 amendments to the *Workplace Relations Act 1996*, which prioritised individual agreements over collective ones. This shift of the locus of bargaining to workplace level required unions to support employees who were bargaining with management instead of relying on the arbitration system to set wages and conditions.

■ *Organising*

The key to the organising model is active workplace delegate structures to identify credible campaigns of concern to members at a workplace. British authors, Blyton and Turnbull (2004: 131) identify six elements of successful union organising:

- *Campaign*. Union officials seek to get members involved around an issue and in the union; the union is not just the activities of the executive and officials but of the members.
- *Credibility*. Union officials 'establish what the issues are for a particular workforce', rather than impose a 'union' agenda. This will encourage member ownership of the issue and build commitment.
- *Commitment*. The union needs a sustained organising program with expert organisers to support members in the workplace.
- *Contact*. Face-to-face contact is essential, using techniques of mapping and 'like-recruits-like' (e.g. women recruit women) to establish a positive image of the union.
- *Communicate*. Union officials need to use a variety of media to improve their internal communications and external image, including ensuring that any public print and electronic coverage is positive and informed about the union's position.
- *Collective*. Union officials emphasise collective issues at work and seek to build a strong and self-sustaining organisation of delegates and members in the workplace.

An example of a recent (2011–12) Australian organising campaign is that carried out by the Australian Licensed Aircraft Engineers Association (ALAEA) at the Australian airline Qantas, where 1800 engineers *campaigned* for job security by preventing offshoring of aircraft maintenance and also to gain a salary increase through enterprise bargaining. In addition to these two key *collective* industrial objectives for members, the union also had a third collective objective around which the *credibility* of the campaign centred: the survival of the union, because if engineers' jobs went overseas, the reason for the union's existence would be lost. This could be expected to strengthen member *commitment* to the union and to the campaign. The ALAEA is a smaller union, so it was easier to maintain direct contact between members and officials, and to build tight *communication* structures even though it was a national campaign.

When assessing the need for member involvement and activism in organising campaigns and union renewal strategies aimed at membership growth, it is important to recognise that successful campaign strategies can differ depending on particular circumstances, and that membership activism may only be one factor contributing to a successful outcome (Hickey, Kuruvilla & Lakhani 2010). However, unions with an operational delegate structure and at least some workplace activism occurring are those that are most likely to develop broader social objectives that extend beyond their membership base into the wider community (Jerrard, Cockfield & Buttigieg 2009). For example, the ANF in Victoria has a hospital-based delegate network, which has effectively used community campaigns to support retention of key employment conditions, such as nurse-to-patient ratios, in its enterprise bargaining with the state government (see Chapter 13 for further discussion of this campaign).

However, not all organising unions progress to 'community unionism', because of internal rigidities of structure and the subsequent reliance on formal and bureaucratic structures rather than looser networks. Despite this word of caution, it appears that, for many unions, community unionism is a return to the grassroots of the movement, and will provide both new opportunities and ongoing challenges.

◼ *Community unionism*

The concept of community unionism is defined by Tufts (1998: 28) as being 'characterised by the formation of coalitions between unions and non-labour groups in order to achieve common goals'. It involves unions 'campaigning on issues beyond specific concerns of workers' wages and conditions in an individual workplace, and allocating union resources to campaign on issues beyond the economic. It means seeing workers as more than just workers, but as people' (Tattersall 2004: 260). A return to community unionism has been implemented by a number of American unions, and is now being introduced by unions in other Western market economies, including Australia (Jerrard et al. 2007). In many ways, community unionism is reflective of social movements, and of social movement unionism – such as that found in trade unions in African and South American countries (Waterman 2005). However, unlike social movement unionism – which requires rank-and-file mobilisation – community unionism can be driven centrally by trade union leaders. There are a number of different types of community–union alliances that can be identified in Australia. These alliances are emerging in literature on union renewal as new strategies aimed at retaining union relevance in the workplace and in society, as we explain below.

■ *Instrumental or traditional alliances*

These alliances are formed for the life of a particular campaign, which can combine industrial objectives and strategies, such as a strike, with community or social objectives. In one notable case, the Finance Sector Union (FSU) ran enterprise bargaining campaigns in the late 1990s and early 2000s, in which the union provided information to customers about issues affecting job security, working conditions and remuneration in the major Australian banks in a successful attempt to turn bank customers into union members' allies, as customers did not want to lost face-to-face banking services (Cutcher 2004).

The Electrical Trades Union (ETU)–BHP 2002 dispute at Hastings in Victoria over the threatened outsourcing and loss of job security for ETU and Australian Manufacturing Workers Union (AMWU) members saw the unions appeal to the Hastings community for support. They were successful in achieving broad-based community support, especially from local businesses, which were also threatened with closure as a result of the decision by the management of a locally based steel fabricator, BHP, to outsource over 300 jobs. Support came in the form of donations of food and money to strikers, public meetings supporting the unions' position and informing those present of the likely negative impact of the company's decision on the community, and general respect for what the striking workers were trying to achieve (Hayes & Jerrard 2007).

A high-profile waterfront dispute in 1998 saw extensive support for the Maritime Union of Australia (MUA) by all sections of the community when Patrick Stevedores illegally terminated the employment of all MUA members across Australia and attempted to replace them with a non-unionised workforce. The MUA's objectives were industrial, but the union and its predecessors had a history of supporting community interests by applying political and 'green' bans on the handling of goods to particular countries – for example, South Africa during the apartheid years and East Timor while it was under Indonesian occupation and control. The MUA, like many other unions, had a tradition of raising funds for charities and those less fortunate in society, and this may have increased its capacity to garner community support for its campaign (Jerrard, Cockfield & Buttigieg 2009).

■ *Reciprocal alliances*

These alliances are formed for the benefit of both parties, usually over an extended period of time. One of the better known alliances was the Stop Live Exports, formerly People Against Cruelty to Animals in Transport (PACAT), which was formed specifically to campaign against the live export of livestock from

Australian ports, such as Fremantle in Western Australia. This community organisation has worked with officials and members of the Australasian Meat Industry Employees' Union (AMIEU) in campaigning against live animal transport, including ongoing petitioning of members of state and federal parliaments for legislation to restrict live export and picketing the Fremantle docks when vessels are being loaded. While both the community organisation and the AMIEU had the same objective, their reasons for forming the alliance were quite different. Stop Live Exports' reason resulted from concerns about animal cruelty, while the AMIEU's reason was that that live exports of animals in effect exported meatworkers' jobs (Jerrard 2007). The campaign gained a major boost in early 2011 with the screening by ABC TV's *Four Corners* of a program on the practices used in slaughtering cattle exported from Australia to Indonesia. This resulted in a temporary cessation of cattle exports to that country and the Australian government introduced restrictions against cruelty in overseas slaughtering with other temporary cessations in 2012.

A second example of a reciprocal alliance involving many partners is the union-initiated campaign against the James Hardie Company, which manufactured building products containing potentially lethal asbestos fibres. This alliance saw the ACTU, the AMWU and Unions NSW (the state equivalent of the ACTU), asbestos groups represented by a prominent victim of mesothelioma, Bernie Banton, and his lawyer, Jack Rush QC, and the New South Wales government cooperating to raise public awareness of the financial and legal liabilities of the company, which had failed to warn people using fibro-cement building products. After 1978, health warnings were placed on these products and finally asbestos was removed entirely from the manufacturing process, but not before many workers suffered illnesses that ultimately resulted in their deaths. Public rallies in capital cities around Australia in September 2004 followed the establishment of the New South Wales government's Special Commission of Inquiry. The Jackson Inquiry found that James Hardie had seriously under-funded its liabilities to asbestos victims when it established its Medical Research and Compensation Fund. The inquiry recommended charges against company directors and officers of James Hardie for making misleading and deceptive statements. Finally, the company negotiated a settlement and made compensation payments to victims of asbestos-related illnesses and their families. In June 2010, the ACTU, the AMWU and the Cancer Council of Australia developed a set of strategies for an asbestos-free Australia and, in October 2010, the federal Labor government established the National Asbestos Management Review to implement the strategies developed (Holland & Pyman 2011).

■ Partnership unionism

Partnership unionism has been explored in research from the United States, the United Kingdom and New Zealand (Ackers & Payne 1998; Haynes & Allen 2001; Oxenbridge & Brown 2002). Typically, unions facing management's desire to restructure an organisation are not in a strong bargaining position, and in these cases collaboration becomes an option. Consequently, partnership unionism may be interpreted as incorporating unions into management, with unions being viewed as accepting efficiency improvement programs and human resource policies that do not effectively protect members' interests. However, in countries where organisations face strong unions, such as Sweden, a strategic partnership can lead to changes that improve the organisation's competitiveness, improve the quality of working life and protect jobs (Huzzard & Nilsson 2004).

International structures of labour representation

As they have created forms of labour representation at a national level, unions have also joined together to develop international bodies to protect workers' rights and offer mutual support. The structures that have developed include umbrella bodies, which mirror the role of national trade union confederations like the ACTU, and also international trade union federations or secretariats covering particular industries. Unions at the national level have also joined representatives of national governments and employer organisations to oversee the work of the ILO, which – among other things – sets global labour standards. These standards or conventions are then ratified by member countries; see Chapter 4 for further details. The existence of these international confederations and their activities is in part a response to the increasing globalisation of capital as instanced in the development of international supply chains, which seek out cheap and exploitable labour in developing economies (see Chapter 14 for a discussion of this issue with regard to the international automobile parts industry). At a regional level, joint management and union bodies have been created – as in the case of the European social model, which we consider below.

International confederations

The International Confederation of Free Trade Unions (ICFTU) was formed in 1949 after a split with the World Federation of Trade Unions, which became the World Confederation of Labour (WCL) in 1968. The split occurred in the context of the Cold War, and concern by the US government and some unions about the extent of communist influence in the World Federation of Trade Unions. Over time, however, the ICFTU became the pre-eminent international labour organisation, mostly under the lead of Western European countries and with the United States joining in the early 1980s. In the post-Cold War era, and with growing concern about the adverse social consequences of globalisation, such as increased poverty and inequity, and also because of the lack of democracy in global governance, there has been a renewed impetus for labour internationalism (Waterman 2005). As a result, the ICFTU and the WCL merged in 2006 to form the International Trade Union Confederation (ITUC).

Apart from international trade unions themselves, organised labour has a voice within international institutions, notably at the United Nations through the ILO as well as via the Trade Union Advisory Committee (TUAC) to the Organization for Economic Cooperation and Development (OECD). To keep up with globalisation, former institutions – like the International Trade Secretariats (ITSs) – have been re-formed into Global Union Federations (GUFs) and a new body, Global Unions, has been created.

■ The International Trade Union Confederation

The ITUC represents 170 million workers in 157 countries and territories, and has 312 national affiliates. It is the largest trade union confederation in the world, apart from the All-China Federation of Trade Unions (ACFTU), which is neither independent nor free of state dominance. The ITUC's primary mission is promoting and defending workers' rights and interests through international cooperation between trade unions, global campaigning and advocacy within the major global institutions. Its main areas of activity include:

- human and trade union rights
- economic and social policy
- equality and non-discrimination
- development and cooperation, and international solidarity.

The ITUC is divided into regional structures. Australia is part of the ITUC Asia Pacific (ITUC-AP). Regional structures also include the African Regional Organization (ITUC-AF) and the American Regional Organization (TUCA). In addition, the ITUC cooperates closely with the European Trade Union Confederation (ETUC), including through the Pan-European Regional Council, created in 2007.

■ The Trade Union Advisory Committee

The TUAC was founded in 1962 as an intergovernmental policy-making body. Its main function is to provide an interface for trade unions with the OECD, and this is achieved by it having consultative status with the OECD and its various committees. It has recently evolved as a leading forum to respond to the challenges of globalisation and 'help ensure that global markets are balanced by an effective social dimension'. In practice, the TUAC is responsible for promoting the views of trade unions in industrialised countries, and for coordinating labour movement input to the G8 and G20 economic summits and employment conferences. TUAC affiliates consist of over 58 national trade union centres in the 30 OECD industrialised countries; most of these unions are also affiliated with the ITUC.

■ Global union federations and global unions

GUFs, formerly known as ITSs, represent industry sectors or occupational groups – for example, the CFMEU in Australia is affiliated with the International Federation of

Chemical, Energy, Mine and General Workers' Unions (ICEM); the MUA is affiliated with the International Transport Federation (ITF); and the National Tertiary Education Union is affiliated with Education International (EI).

Currently, 10 GUFs are active in the international arena. They include Education International; the International Federation of Building and Wood Workers; the International Federation of Journalists; the International Metalworkers' Federation; the International Transport Workers' Federation; the International Textile, Garment and Leather Workers' Federation; the International Union of Food, Agricultural, Hotel, Restaurant, and Catering, Tobacco and Allied Workers' Associations; the Public Services International; and Union Network International.

All GUFs are associated with the ITUC, but they also act independently as organisations in their own right. Unlike the ITUC, their industrial grounding gives them considerable bargaining strength. Early in the 1970s, the International Trade Secretariats sought to develop world company councils and promote international codes of conduct; however, such initiatives failed to influence international business regulation. It is only since the late 1990s, with the establishment of International Framework Agreements (IFAs), that any impact has been felt. IFAs usually involve a GUF and a transnational corporation (TNC). By 2010, around 80 IFAs had been concluded. These agreements often start as a code of conduct, but develop the scope and coverage of the provisions of the code of conduct beyond the firm level over time (Fairbrother & Hammer 2005). As a consequence of their changed scope and coverage, they carry much more weight. In contrast to codes of conduct, IFAs typically are negotiated between labour and corporate management; they recognise all core labour standards; they usually cover suppliers; unions are involved in their implementation; and they form a strong basis for dialogue between unions and management. The GUFs are linked to Global Unions (see <http://www.global-unions.org>), which is a network-based trade union platform that recently has been established to take up the challenge of globalisation. Global Unions is made up of the ITUC, the GUFs and the TUAC.

■ Labour and regional integration: the European social model

The European social model reflects the belief that, rather than being a hurdle to free market mechanisms, institution-building provides a background for better economic coordination and governance (Traxler 1995). The European social model is therefore presented as a model of 'stakeholder capitalism' geared towards a 'high road' – high-level innovation and value-added production, high investment in skill formation and high labour standards – in contrast to and in competition with a market-driven 'shareholders' capitalism based on deregulation and labour exclusion, and relying on cost reduction, where workers are reduced to the level of production factor costs and regarded as commodities to be bought and sold in the same way as inanimate commodities ('low-road') (Hoffmann & Hoffmann 1997).

The social dialogue of the European Union (EU) also reflects the corporatist models of governance already in place in most continental European countries, such as Germany and the Nordic countries, where trade unions play a central role as social partners. As a result, the EU context can be defined as labour inclusive. The European social dialogue and the European Works Council (EWC) Directive are two major expressions of the EU's political commitment to foster collective bargaining and employee representation at a transnational level.

The European social dialogue involves the European Trade Union Confederation (ETUC) and European employer associations. As a rule, if those European social partners cannot reach an agreement, it is up to the European legislator to enact an EU Directive enforcing legal provisions for all member states. Over time, growing numbers of framework agreements have been reached: on parental leave in 1996 (revised in 2009); part-time work in 1997; fixed-term contracts in 1999; teleworking in 2002, work-related stress in 2004; and preventing harassment and violence at work in 2007. Also reached was a framework of actions for the development of lifelong skills and qualifications (2002) and a framework of action on equality between men and women (2005). The European initiative has triggered an internal debate in Australia as to whether similar mechanisms for employee consultation – such as works councils – could be implemented successfully in Australia (Gollan & Patmore 2006; Gollan, Markey & Ross 2002).

Towards a new internationalism?

Recent years have witnessed the reframing of international labour structures and leadership, with the formation of Global Unions being symbolic of the new dynamism. Labour internationalism had for so long remained divided along ideological and economic lines, mostly serving the interests of the dominant trade unions in industrialised countries. The international arena was seen mainly as a locus for the extension of national trade union agendas, and therefore as primarily instrumental to the promotion or defence of national interests.

In many respects, twenty-first-century globalisation has created an impetus for change. The increasing integration of capital – including global supply chains – has challenged unions to consider whether workers' interests would best be defined and articulated across and beyond national borders. Increased capital mobility, coupled with the liberalisation of trade and finance, has created conditions where workers and their workplaces are deemed to compete with each other for jobs and investments internationally. This is more the case in a context of intensified business competition wherein the balance of power rests predominantly with multinational corporations (MNCs). As a result, internationalism has become a far more direct concern for rank-and-file unionists at the grassroots level (Moody 1997; Holland & Pyman 2011). Globalisation has also raised questions about whether national regulation remains the major level on which unions should focus. The rise of supra-national bodies such as the World Trade Organization (WTO), the World Bank and the G20 are expressions of a potentially different world order, and have prompted organised labour to secure a voice within the emerging framework for global governance.

Contemporary views on the prospects of a renewed labour internationalism are a mixture of pessimism and optimism. The pessimists highlight the daunting task of uniting a heterogeneous global workforce and the difficulty in overcoming competing interests, especially – but not exclusively – along the North–South divide. The optimists would rather emphasise concrete examples of cross-border solidarity (e.g. Gajewska 2008; Garver et al. 2007), and advocate that there are ways to challenge transnational capital through comprehensive union campaigning (Bronfenbrenner 2007; Holland & Pyman 2011). Bieler, Lindberg and Pillay (2008) identify three avenues for action: intensified transnational labour solidarity and cross-border campaigning; organising the informal sector (where the bulk of labour is often to be found in developing economies such as Vietnam, India and Brazil); and building alliances with new social movements. Although the future shape and fortune of international trade unions are subject to much speculation, if unions are to successfully face the challenges of the twenty-first century, there is no doubt that they will need to demonstrate a level of leadership, unity of purpose, and social and political awareness that has seldom been evident.

■ *Globalisation as a means to union revitalisation?*

Apart from a few exceptions where organised labour has held on to a tradition of social movement unionism – like France, South Africa, South Korea and Brazil – trade unions have devised their strategy either *from above*, by means of social partnership for the purposes of institutional consolidation, or *from below*, by organising efforts designed to improve their membership both in qualitative and quantitative terms. The former approach represents the archetype in the continental European context, and even more so within the European social dialogue; the second, is found much more in Anglo-Saxon countries, as a product of cross-dissemination and frequently, for want of an alternative, in adverse institutional contexts, as in the United States and Australia.

Yet both strategies have left behind the realm of traditional party politics. Prominent union researchers and activists on both sides of the Atlantic are urging for a 'revitalisation' of labour organisations. Turner (2005: 21) sees the activation of a social movement by and within the trade unions as the precondition for a democratic counterweight in an environment that is hostile in all respects: 'ongoing global liberalisation has weighted the odds heavily against organising, bargaining and legislative success, unless such efforts are part of rank-and-file based mobilisations that attract broad social support in campaigns framed as battles for social justice'. According to Hyman (2007), trade unions need to commit themselves once more to the battle for ideas and retake the ideological initiative by embracing the demands for global justice. Trade unions have to 'win back their legitimacy', and a major way of achieving this is by defining 'alternative ways of connecting economy and society, work and life'. They need a 'new vision, even a new utopia if they are to become subjects and not objects of history' (Hyman 2007: 207–8).

Such belief is perceptible across the ranks of Australian trade unions, and has been expressed on several occasions by some leading union activists. Leigh Hubbard, former secretary of the Victorian Trades Hall Council, stated in 2004 that there are three interrelated issues facing the Australian labour movement:

- A trade union movement must be prepared to meet the challenges of changing workplaces and industries (its core agenda).
- A union movement must be prepared to meet the challenges of wider society (its civil society and social justice agenda).
- A union movement must be prepared to meet the challenges of a changing world (its international agenda) (Hubbard 2007: 11).

Another example of this social concern is the 2009 ACTU broad policy framework entitled 'Working for a Better Life: A Vision for a Fairer Society'.

Conclusion

Trade unions have played a generally accepted role in Australian workplace relations, protected and fostered by the conciliation and arbitration system. However, over the last two decades, the role played by trade unions has changed considerably with the move to enterprise bargaining and away from the making of industrial awards as the major instrument regulating the employment relationship. Political, economic and legal changes have forced changes upon trade unions in terms of membership (declining), new strategies (the move away from servicing) and a dual focus on the workplace (internal) and on the community (external). Internationally, unions have adopted a broad external focus, looking to build alliances outside of the trade union movement in an attempt to counter the negative consequences for labour of global-isation. If unions, both nationally and internationally, are to retain their representative voice, and not be perceived as merely sectional interest groups, they need to focus their attention on retaining existing members and attracting new members while also challenging the capitalist paradigm that widens the gap between the rich and the poor.

Discussion questions

3.1   Identify the key reasons for the decline in trade union membership.

3.2   What is the difference between the servicing and organising models of trade unionism?

3.3   Using examples, illustrate how community unionism operates.

3.4   What are the limitations of nationally based unions in a globalised era, and how might they be transcended? What evidence can you find of a move to more international forms of unionism?

4

International employment regulation and labour rights

Anne O'Rourke

■ Chapter objectives

This chapter will enable readers to understand the:
- role of the International Labor Organization (ILO)
- debates surrounding the application of ILO core labour standards and the link between international trade and labour rights
- distinction between codes of conduct and international framework agreements
- difference between 'soft' and 'hard' law approaches to global regulation
- possible solutions to the problem of enforcement of core labour standards.

▪ Introduction

In Chapter 3, the decline of unions was explored in the context of structural changes to the economy – such as the shift to services and neo-liberal policies of labour market deregulation. Reference was also made to union strategies, which are employed at both the local and international levels in order to gain new members and protect workers' rights. Besides union strategies at an international level, there are a number of ways in which international labour standards have developed and become increasingly relevant in recent years.

According to Christopherson and Lillie (2005: 1919), for much of the last century, 'the question of international labour standards was of interest only to a handful of international experts and union officials'. However, facilitated by the implementation of trade and investment treaties that altered and restructured the international architecture of trade, capital and investment, wider public interest in global labour standards began to mushroom, particularly in the last quarter of the twentieth century. This period not only saw the establishment of the World Trade Organization (WTO) in 1994, but also a significant increase in bilateral trade and investment treaties. The International Centre for the Settlement of Investment Disputes (ICSID) reports that, by 2010, over 5000 bilateral trade and investment treaties had been negotiated (ICSID 2011). This proliferation of multilateral and bilateral agreements, while strongly supported by business groups and multinational corporations, as well as the majority of governments – North and South – has caused much anxiety among other groups, particularly over concerns that it will initiate a 'race to the bottom' (Tonelson 2000), namely 'a global race to the absolute minimum that would undercut hard-won employment standards' (Tsogas 1999: 352).

Much concern exists about the unequal power between employers and employees, and the ability of multinational corporations (MNCs) to undermine international labour rights in order to gain a competitive advantage in cross-border trade and investment. Many commentators – including the international trade union movement and human rights groups – have expressed disquiet that the globalisation of the world economy is increasing the inequalities between the owners of capital and labour, between the educated/skilled and less educated/less skilled, as well as between the people of the more developed/less developed world (Rosen 2005; ICFTU-APRO 1997).

These concerns have given rise to demands for the creation of a link between international trade and labour rights, or some form of legal mechanism that ensures adherence to fundamental labour standards by transnational corporations. However, even among proponents of enforceable labour standards, much disagreement exists as to how such a link should be established, which body should oversee enforcement and whether it should it be voluntary or mandatory. Some argue that such a link should be established under the remit of the WTO, others that the ILO is the appropriate body to govern compliance with international labour standards; a third group of proponents contend that national governments should play a role in the regulation of international labour standards (Kururvilla & Verma 2006).

The demand for a linkage between international trade and labour rights has been compounded by the GFC and concern by the International Trade Union Confederation (ITUC) about its impact on global trade and development, particularly in the area of work and workers' human rights (ITUC 2009). Indeed, ITUC has established a 'Global Financial Crisis watch' to monitor developments and keep the international trade union movement abreast of government responses and stabilisation strategies. National unions are also responding to the economic crisis – for example, the Australian Council of Trade Unions (ACTU) 2009 Congress passed a resolution on the Global Financial Crisis, blaming it on the 'uncritical worship' of the neo-liberal paradigm and supporting ITUC demands that G20 countries coordinate stimulus packages and develop plans that maximise job retention and protect the incomes of the most vulnerable (ACTU 2009).

This chapter examines the main institutions and mechanisms of international labour regulation that have developed over the last century in order to encourage compliance with fundamental labour rights. We begin with an historical and theoretical overview of the regulation of international labour standards. The second section provides an overview of the ILO, looking at its purpose, functions and the problematic nature of its enforcement procedures. We next turn to the campaign to establish a link between international trade and labour rights, while the fourth section casts a critical eye over the development of 'soft law' mechanisms, by which we mean quasi-legal instruments, such as codes of conduct and similar non-governmental organisation (NGO) standards that are not legally binding on nation states or on international economic actors. The fifth section looks at trade union criticisms and responses to corporate, NGO and private codes. This is followed by an examination of 'hard law' approaches to international labour regulation and, more specifically, labour rights abuses in the global economy. Finally, we look at the way in which US human rights lawyers have utilised a little-known 200-year-old law, the *Alien Tort Claims Act 1789* (ATCA), to bring MNCs to court for labour rights abuses. By providing an extensive coverage of issues pertaining to international regulation, this chapter provides both context and linkages to the ensuing chapter on national employment regulation.

◼ The regulation of international labour standards

There have been various attempts by organised labour and some governments to establish regulation at the global level to protect workers' fundamental human rights, particularly in the context of international trade and investment treaties. The first attempt was made in 1948 under the Havana Charter. The purpose of the Havana Charter was to establish the first global trade body, the International Trade Organisation (ITO). Article 7 of the Havana Charter, titled 'Fair Labour Standards', stated that:

1. The Members recognize that measures relating to employment must take fully into account the rights of workers under inter-governmental declarations, conventions

and agreements. They recognize that all countries have a common interest in the achievement and maintenance of fair labour standards related to productivity, and thus in the improvement of wages and working conditions as productivity may permit. The Members recognize that unfair labour conditions, particularly in production for export, create difficulties in international trade, and, accordingly, each Member shall take whatever action may be appropriate and feasible to eliminate such conditions within its territory.

2. Members which are also members of the International Labor Organisation shall co-operate with that organization in giving effect to this undertaking. (Havana Charter 1948: 8)

Drache (2000: 17) argues that the significance of the Havana Charter is that it 'recognized that labor standards belong in a trade agreement' and that, in contrast to more recent debates, the view of governments 'was that the articulation of workers' rights had to be an integral part of trade and commercial policy'. However, the ITO was stillborn due to the fact that the US Congress failed to ratify the Havana Charter. The ITO was the precursor to the General Agreement on Tariffs and Trade (GATT), and many of the provisions of the Havana Charter were included in the GATT; however, the labour provisions were not carried over, thus severing the link between global labour standards and international trade.

Nevertheless, the failure to establish a link between trade and labour standards in the GATT did not prevent proponents from exploring other avenues. Over the past 50 years, there have been a 'disparate range of sub-global mechanisms' developed to regulate international labour standards, ranging from international commodity agreements to regional and bilateral trade agreements, and codes of conduct (Cleveland 2004: 129). Van Wezel Stone (1996), Hepple (1997), Cleveland (2004), Sengenberger (2005), and Block and colleagues (2001) have all developed typologies or models that provide a basis for classification and analysis of the merits and problems of each approach. They use different terminology in constructing their respective typologies – for example, Van Wezel Stone (1996) describes the four approaches as: pre-emptive legislation; harmonisation of domestic legislation (EU); cross-border monitoring and enforcement (exemplified by the North American Free Trade Agreement [NAFTA]); and extra-territorial application of domestic law, while Block et al. (2001), in their examination of existing international labour regulation, classify the various approaches as the legislative model, the ILO model, the multilateral enforcement model and the most recent approach, corporate codes of conduct. Although using different descriptors, there is much commonality and overlap between all these models, classifications or typologies.

According to Block et al. (2001), the first category, the *legislative model*, is exemplified by the European Community (EC), which incorporates a multi-governmental legislative structure that derives the authority to issue directives on both economic and social policy to all member countries pursuant to various treaties. The EC has issued a number of directives covering workplace relations, such as Directive 94/45, which requires the establishment of European Works Councils (EWC) and an employee consultation procedure in all large organisations; and Directive 97/81, requiring member states to enact legislation covering part-time workers, ensuring that they are no less favourably treated than full-time workers and allowing for flexibility for workers to shift between full- and part-time work. The EU also provides for enforcement through national courts and tribunals of minimum labour standards and for participative frameworks agreed to on a cross-national basis (Hepple 1997: 362). According to Block et al. (2001), the EC model is the most viable option for establishing labour standards on a cross-national basis. However, they concede that the EC approach, which was developed within the context of a common market and integrated community, has limited application outside Europe.

The second existing model is the ILO, a tripartite United Nations (UN) body that establishes labour standards in the form of conventions and recommendations – more than 180 of which have been created since its establishment in 1919 (Hepple 1997: 268). The ILO Constitution establishes a supervisory system to oversee member states' application and compliance with conventions. The three main provisions are Articles 22, 24 and 26. Article 22 requires member states to make annual reports on the measures that they have taken to give effect to the provisions of the conventions that they have ratified. Article 24 provides an avenue by which representative worker or employee organisations can make complaints to the ILO about a member country's non-compliance with conventions. Article 26 deals with the most serious cases and complaints by members regarding non-observance by other members (Elliot 2000: 5); this can lead to the establishment of a Commission of Inquiry to investigate and report on the complaint (ILO 1919a). In the more extreme cases, under Article 33, if any member fails to carry out the recommendations contained in the report of the Commission of Inquiry, the Governing Body may recommend 'such action as it may deem wise and expedient to secure compliance'. This Article was invoked for the first time in 1999 to suspend Burma from any technical cooperation or assistance from the ILO (Cleveland 2004: 131).

The third model is *trade-related*, linking trade and labour standards. This includes regional and bilateral trade agreements, such as NAFTA, which contains a labour side-agreement, the North American Agreement on Labor Cooperation (NAALC), requiring member states to enforce their own labour laws in relation to 11 labour principles. A similar chapter on labour rights is found in the Australia–United States Free Trade Agreement (AUSFTA); however, in contrast to the provisions relating to economic and investment activity, labour clauses have proved ineffectual as they are premised primarily on cooperation between the parties rather than subject to any binding mechanism to ensure compliance.

The fourth model involves mostly *voluntary mechanisms*, such as corporate codes of conduct, independent certification schemes and social labelling mechanisms. There has been a proliferation of codes of conduct in recent years; however, they have been criticised by many labour unions and labour lawyers because they are non-binding, and therefore do not provide a strong incentive to ensure compliance with those rights deemed to be fundamental workers' rights. A second problem is that codes of conduct are often unilateral management tools with little union input, and as such signify a crucial theoretical departure from the traditional protective function of industrial relations (Blackett 2000–01). Hepple (1998–99) argues that the history of codes of conduct for regulating transnational corporations (TNCs) and labour standards is one that can be described as a 'retreat from public international law, embodied above all in the Conventions and Recommendations of the ILO, to privatised "soft" law'. This move away from international public law towards private corporate codes has seen the international trade union movement develop its own code of conduct specifically targeted to ensure corporate adherence to ILO core labour conventions. These International Framework Agreements (IFAs), which were discussed in Chapter 3, are viewed by the international union movement as providing 'a global framework for protecting trade union rights and encouraging social dialogue and collective bargaining' (IFBWW 2004). Their emergence has also been located in the 'effectiveness crisis' of traditional regulatory methods and institutions, such as the ILO, where 'moral suasion and technical assistance remain the most important tools' (Gibb 2005). Each of these models will be examined below.

▪ The International Labor Organization

The ILO is the intergovernmental tripartite body responsible for the formulation of international labour standards. It was created at the end of World War I, and became part of the short-lived League of Nations established under the Treaty of Versailles. Recognising the implicit link between world peace and social justice, the preamble to the ILO Constitution states:

> Whereas conditions of labour exist involving such injustice, hardship, and privation to large numbers of people as to produce unrest so great that the peace and harmony of the world are imperilled ... an improvement of these conditions is urgently required ... by the regulation of the hours of work, including the establishment of a maximum working day and week, the regulation of the labour supply, the prevention of unemployment, the provision of an adequate wage, the protection of the worker against sickness, disease and injury arising out of his employment. (ILO 1919b)

It can be argued that in establishing the link between peace and social justice, and the promotion of decent working standards for all people, the ILO was the first institution or body in the modern era to focus on establishing universal human rights standards. But, as Bartolomei de la Cruz, von Potobsky and Swepston (1996) point out, the ILO was created before the term 'human rights' was in common usage, and the focus was less concentrated on the struggle between the individual and the state. The concept of 'social justice', while not in contradistinction to human rights, is wider and implies a positive obligation upon the state to implement policies that improve social conditions. It is only in recent times that the 'concept of fundamental human rights' has become part of the ILO's normative speech and action, and that its character as a human rights organisation has been recognised by the broader international human rights community (Bartolomei de la Cruz, von Potobsky & Swepston 1996: 127).

The ILO, in a sense, has its own 'legal personality'. It enjoys privileges and immunities within the territory of member states necessary for it to carry out its functions. While starting out as part of the League of Nations after World War I, it became a specialised agency of the United Nations. It is the only tripartite United Nations agency to give equal representation to governments, employers and unions, thereby ensuring that all parties' views are reflected in shaping policy and programs (ILO 2011a).

The primary mission of the ILO is to promote and enhance human rights at work, and to promote opportunities for women and men to obtain decent and productive work in conditions of freedom, equity, security and human dignity (ILO 2011a). The ILO has the following four strategic objectives:

- to promote and realise standards and fundamental principles and rights at work
- to create greater opportunities for women and men to decent employment and income
- to enhance the coverage and effectiveness of social protection for all
- to strengthen tripartism and social dialogue (ILO 2011a).

In order to achieve these objectives, the ILO has developed expertise in the area of work, employment and related issues, particularly in relation to:

- formulating international policies and programmes to promote basic human rights, improve working and living conditions and enhance employment opportunities
- creating international labour standards backed by a unique system to supervise their application
- an extensive program of international technical cooperation, formulated and implemented in an active partnership with constituents, to help countries put these policies into practice in an effective manner
- training, education and research activities to help advance all of these efforts.

Three principal bodies make up the ILO: the Governing Body, the International Labour Conference and the International Labour Office. The Governing Body, which is the executive body, consists of 56 nominal members (including 28 governments, 19 employers and 19 workers) and meets three times each year. It makes decisions on ILO policy, decides the agenda of the International Labour Conference, adopts the draft programme and budget of the ILO for submission to the conference, and elects the Director-General (ILO 2011b).

The International Labour Conference is a quasi-parliamentary conference that brings together government, employer and worker delegates on an annual basis to establish and adopt labour standards and provide an international forum to discuss important social and labour questions. Government representatives are Cabinet ministers responsible for labour affairs or workplace relations in their own countries. Employer and worker delegates are nominated in agreement with the most representative national organisations of employers and workers (ILO 2011c). Delegates are free to vote as they wish, so worker and employer delegates sometimes vote against their government's representatives or against each other. This does not prevent decisions being adopted by very large majorities – or in some cases even unanimously (ILO 2011c).

The third body is the International Labour Office, which is the permanent secretariat of the ILO. It is situated in Geneva and employs more than 2500 people from over 150 nations. It organises the activities of the ILO under the scrutiny of the Governing Body and the Director-General. The International Labour Office also collects and disseminates information, as well as undertaking research and providing information and data through its research and documentation centre.

There are 189 ILO Conventions, of which eight are considered fundamental or core labour standards. These fundamental standards are:

- Convention No. 87 – Freedom of Association and the Protection of the Right to Organise 1948
- Convention No. 98 – Right to Organise and Collective Bargaining 1949
- Convention No. 29 – Forced Labour Convention 1930
- Convention No. 105 – Abolition of Forced Labor 1957
- Convention No. 100 – Equal Remuneration 1951
- Convention No. 111 – Discrimination (Employment and Occupation) 1958
- Convention No. 138 – Minimum Age 1973
- Convention No. 182 – Elimination of the Worst Forms of Child Labour 1999.

These conventions are described as fundamental because they are considered to be basic human rights. They overlap with rights found in the UN International Covenant on Civil and Political Rights; the International Covenant on Economic, Social and Cultural Rights; the 1956 Supplementary Convention on the Abolition of Slavery, the Slave Trade, and Institutions and Practices Similar to Slavery; and the Convention on the Elimination of All Forms of Discrimination Against Women.

Despite wide rates of ratification of ILO conventions across Africa, the Americas, Asia and the Pacific region, and in Europe, violations are still a regular occurrence. The problem relating to country compliance with core labour standards has often been blamed on the ILO's lack of binding enforcement mechanisms. As discussed above, Articles 26 to 34 of the ILO Constitution allow the ILO to address breaches of conventions, but these measures are limited and do not contain an enforcement procedure, which severely limits the organisation's ability to secure compliance. Even in the event of a serious breach, such as when the ILO invoked Article 33 against Burma, its only direct sanction was to suspend Burma from any technical assistance or cooperation provided by the ILO. In effect, the ILO was reliant on member governments to take more serious actions (Elliot 2000: 6). This inability of the ILO to enforce compliance with core labour standards has caused some to question its relevance and capacity to contribute to or deliver the social dimension of globalisation (Hagen 2003). According to Hagen, the ILO has three crises: identity, relevance and effectiveness. The identity crisis refers to the problem of 'representativity', which relates to the fact that the ILO shares its global space with a range of NGO actors, also promoting compliance with labour standards. The relevance crisis concerns the conventions that constitute the core labour standards, which omits other significant standards such as minimum wages and occupational health and safety. Finally, the effectiveness crisis relates to the ILO's supervisory machinery, which is viewed as too complex and inefficient, and incapable of ensuring compliance to fundamental labour standards by multinational companies and many governments.

It is the effectiveness crisis, or 'lack of teeth', of the ILO that has led to the development of other methods of soft regulation and private initiatives such as corporate codes of conduct and social or product-labelling schemes. The international trade union movement has also developed mechanisms and campaigns in an effort to institute and enforce compliance with ILO core labour standards.

These attempts include a campaign to create a link between international trade and workers' rights under the auspices of the WTO and the creation of codes of conduct and international framework agreements (see Chapter 3 for a discussion of IFAs).

■ Globalisation, international trade and labour rights: the linkage proposal

As we commented above, globalisation has caused widespread anxiety, with some groups fearing that it will initiate a 'race to the bottom' in terms of wages and conditions. This concern sparked a contentious debate between developing and developed nations, and between business groups and supporters of the labour movement over proposals to link respect for core labour standards with international trade. Essentially, proponents argued that core labour standards should be incorporated into international trade agreements and be subject to the same WTO enforcement mechanism as the trade, intellectual property and investment provisions contained in such agreements (Griffin, Nyland & O'Rourke 2003: 470). Proponents believed that a link between trade and labour rights would ensure that multinational companies and governments would not violate workers' rights in order to attract foreign investment and trade. Supporters of this position included the Clinton presidency in the United States, the EC and the ITUC, Global Union Federations (GUFs) and the majority of national trade union or workers' organisations. Those opposed included the International Employers Organization, business groups, developing country governments and some Southern unions, principally trade unions in India, who viewed the proposal as a form of Western 'protectionism' (Griffin, Nyland & O'Rourke 2003: 470). Indeed, the governments of many developing countries viewed the proposal trade and labour rights linkage as undermining their comparative advantage in providing abundant cheap labour to the global economy.

After five rounds of WTO ministerial meetings, as well as numerous mini-summits and concerted campaigns by the international trade union movement for a trade–labour linkage, the issue remains outside the WTO. This inability to bring a trade–labour linkage within the framework of the WTO has led to claims that the linkage demand was dead and buried within the WTO (Haworth, Hughes & Wilkinson 2005). However, an examination of government lobbying by the trade union movement and developments at the bilateral level suggests that significant gains have been won by linkage advocates, which may see the debate reinvigorated at the multilateral level in the future.

Despite the impasse on the linkage issue at the multilateral level, the United States and the EU increasingly are including labour clauses in bilateral trade agreements. These clauses explicitly link trade and investment to the promotion and protection of workers' rights. US agreements that have incorporated workers' rights include NAFTA and AUSFTA, as well as agreements with Jordan, Chile, Singapore and Cambodia.

Though the inclusion of labour chapters in US bilateral agreements is a step forward, the reality is that such chapters are not legally binding, and therefore do not share the same status as the economic and trade provisions within the agreements. At first glance, they appear impressive and comprehensive, but a closer examination highlights the flaws. Most agreements contain a clause allowing the parties to maintain the right 'to exercise discretion with respect to the investigatory, prosecutorial, regulatory and compliance matters' and to make decisions regarding the allocation of resources to enforcement with respect of other matters determined to have higher priorities – for example, the US–Chile Free Trade Agreement 2002, Article 18.2. In addition, the chapter is peppered with non-binding terms such as 'may' and 'shall strive', rather than 'must' or 'shall', which denote that the provisions are binding (Griffin, Nyland & O'Rourke 2004a: 50). Indeed, the Labor Advisory Committee for Trade Negotiations and Trade Policy (LAC), an advisory body to the US President, has been highly critical of the labour chapters in US trade agreements, stating that they fall short of promoting and protecting labour standards, with only one labour right obligation – the obligation of a country to enforce its own labour laws – enforceable (LAC, quoted in Griffin, Nyland O'Rourke 2004a: 50). The only exception to this general trend is the Agreement Relating to Trade in Cotton, Wool, Man-made Fiber, Non-Cotton Vegetable Fiber and Silk Blend Textiles and Textile Products Between the Government of the United States of America and the Royal Government of Cambodia, which combines oversight roles for local and international actors, and interventions by governments and international organisations that ensure compliance with ILO core labour standards.

Despite these criticisms and lobbying by the American Federation of Labor and Congress of Industrial Organizations (AFL-CIO) to have the labour chapter improved, the same provisions continue to be included in bilateral trade agreements. For example, AUSFTA replicates the model and the flaws of the Chile and Singapore bilateral trade agreements. However, an examination of the context also demonstrates that, despite the non-mandatory aspects of the labour chapter, the inclusion of labour provisions in a trade agreement was unprecedented and represented a significant step forward for the Australian labour movement (Nyland & O'Rourke 2005: 458). Before AUSFTA, in a display of neo-liberal unanimity, both major Australian political parties refused to countenance the inclusion of provisions designed to protect labour rights in international trade agreements. That the trade union movement was unsuccessful in lobbying the Labor Party was perhaps surprising, because former ACTU President Martin Ferguson reversed his position once elected to parliament. The Labor Party's reluctance to address labour issues in trade agreements was due to concerns about being labelled 'protectionist', and also its support for the ASEAN position that labour rights should remain within the province of the ILO alone (Griffin, Nyland & O'Rourke 2004b: 93). The Labor government's position on labour rights was at odds with party policy. The 2007 policy stated that Labor would play an active role to ensure that the activities of the WTO respected core labour standards (ALP 2007). The 2009 platform contained less discussion of trade and core labour standards, but made commitments to support a rules-based system underpinned by core labour standards, as well as to the incorporation of core labour standards in all international trade agreements (ALP 2009: 14–15). The 2011 Labor Party Trade Policy recognises that trade policy may be deployed to assist with the development of non-trade issues such as labour, environmental or health issues, but makes it clear that trade policy measures should not be a backdoor measure to impose trade barriers (ALP 2011: 13). The 2011 policy also notes that Australia has entered a number of agreements that contain labour and environmental standards. It states that Australia is currently involved in trade negotiations with a number of countries, including Korea, Malaysia and the Trans-Pacific Partnership, where the inclusion of labour and environmental provisions is under active consideration (ALP 2011: 14). While this represents a firmer commitment to a trade–labour linkage, it is significantly weaker than that of the US Obama administration, which committed to better enforcement of US trade laws, including workers' rights provisions (Kirk 2009). The US Special Trade Representative stated that the United States would hold its trading partners to their commitments on workers' rights by better identification and investigation of labour violations, indicating a more proactive stance than previously. Expanding on this new approach, the office of the United States Trade Representative (USTR) announced a more regular monitoring of labour standards, enabling swift bilateral consultation and resolution (USTR 2009). In addition, the USTR committed to assisting FTA nations with resources and experts, as well as individuals from the US trade union movement and interested NGOs, to help resolve labour problems and improve respect for the rights of working (USTR 2009).

By comparison, the federal Labor government approach has been timid. In 2008, the government commissioned an independent and comprehensive review of Australia's approach to international trade and investment. In its submission to the review, the ACTU stated that Australia's trade policy should demonstrate a commitment to the fundamental rights of workers and the core labour standards of the ILO (ACTU 2008). They argued that future FTAs 'must include a labour clause benchmarked against the US provisions, providing for respect of core labour standards and access to dispute mechanisms' (ACTU 2008: 3).The ACTU called for a reference to core labour standards to be included in several locations in bilateral trade agreements: in the preamble, in an operative article at the start of the agreement and in a substantive chapter based on the US model. Most importantly, it also argued for a provision on monitoring and enforcement with a panel chaired by a nominee of the ILO (ACTU 2008). Disappointingly, the review report addressed issues of labour skills and labour shortages, but not labour rights and international trade.

The precedent set by US bilateral agreements, together with the Obama Administration's more aggressive approach to enforcement of labour rights, may reinvigorate the trade–labour debate, facilitating a firmer commitment to the enforcement of labour rights in the global economy. Concern about the global economic crisis also featured prominently at the 98th International Labor Conference in June 2009. Many participants – unionists as well as presidents – called for a new approach to globalisation, including reregulation and the adoption of a more cooperative rather than competitive model. Indeed, the French President at the time, Nicolas Sarkozy, criticised the 'schizophrenic' approach under the current model of globalisation that allows for the mandatory application of WTO rules while maintaining that environmental and social standards should be voluntary.

■ Soft law: codes of conduct and international framework agreements

The demand for a trade–labour linkage was not the only mechanism being developed at the international level, however. Private companies, industry associations, international quasi-governmental bodies and NGOs were all developing codes of conduct to ensure that transnational corporations complied with international human rights and workers' rights obligations when undertaking trade and investment, particularly in developing countries. Some of the better known include the Social Compliance Audit 8000 (SA8000), RUGMARK, the Ethical Trading Initiative, the OECD Guidelines on Multinational Enterprises, the UN Global Compact and International Standards Organisation 14001 (ISO14001). There are also specific company codes such as the Levi Strauss Business Partner Terms of Engagement and Shell's Revised Statement of General Business Principles. Codes of conduct have been around since the 1970s, but it was not until the early 1990s that – after a decade of the growth of transnational corporations and the associated expansion of international trade and investment fostered by global deregulation – codes began to proliferate (Jenkins 2001). Such codes vary widely; there are many different formats and many groups involved in their creation. Some are initiated by the companies, but also by NGOs, shareholders and investors, consumers, trade unions and trade associations.

Despite the proliferation of codes of conduct, some commentators – particularly unions and labour lawyers – argue that they are deeply flawed instruments, and will not ensure the protection of and compliance with labour rights. Critics question the motivation behind codes of conduct, while others focus on their efficacy. Hepple (1998–99) argues that codes are often a response to public pressure from consumers, investors and trade unions, and the desire to enhance corporate reputation. Similarly, Bartley (2005) claims that companies adopted codes in the midst of domestic and international controversies about labour and human rights, sweatshops and child labour, when the threat of government regulation was heightened. Bartley (2005: 12) further argues that:

> the origins of codes do not lay in philanthropy or the goodwill or business, but rather in attempts to deflect growing concerns about the responsibility and legal culpability of corporations for labor conditions in 'flexible', networked supply chains, characterized by multiple layers of contracting and subcontracting.

This perspective is shared by Arthurs (2002: 447), who states that most codes do not include procedural arrangements or independent monitoring, nor do they involve any third-party enforcement. In contrast to the relatively precise and direct language of regulatory statutes, the language of most codes 'lack[s] clarity and specificity' (Murray 2004: 179). They utilise terms such as 'best practice' or require firms to provide 'reasonable' conditions, without defining what 'best practice' or 'reasonable' might mean. In some Australian codes of conduct, the language has been found to be so vague and imprecise as to offer little assistance in the practical application of the code (Murray 2004: 179).

In the scholarly literature, the adoption of codes of conduct is seen primarily as a means by which companies can appease governments, unions and consumers while at the same ensuring the maintenance of a self-regulatory regime. In this way, they are perceived by critics as disingenuous and implemented as a mechanism to avoid public regulation and public scrutiny, rather than as a genuine attempt to apply ethical standards to corporate activity. It has also been argued that codes serve to displace workers from the process of regulation:

> As voluntary codes of conduct, they remain in the sole discretion of the corporation; they are often not the product of a negotiation between employer and employees. Crucially, perhaps, corporate codes of conduct embrace company level regulation of work-related issues while often rejecting union involvement or other forms of organized worker representation. As such voluntary codes bear the danger of cutting the ties between the worker and the outside system of institutional safeguards. (Zumbansen 2005: 295, footnotes omitted)

By contrast, IFAs are viewed more favourably by the international trade union movement and labour scholars because they place the treatment of labour and workers' rights at the centre of the agreement. In addition, they are negotiated documents rather than unilateral corporate instruments, and representatives of 'independent workers' are involved from the start of the process (IFBWW 2004). The International Federation of Building and Woodworkers (IFBWW) claims that IFAs are qualitatively different from codes of conduct, as they 'constitute a formal recognition of social partnership at the global level (IFBWW 2004: 11). According to the Union Network International (UNI), the partnership model that underpins IFAs 'provide[s] the basis for future global dialogue and a framework for tackling individual problems', as well as a 'way forward in democratizing the multi-nationals' (Graham 2002: 45). The IFBWW points out that one key difference between codes and IFAs is that the latter contain a clause recognising and accepting unions in the workplace – something that is rarely included in codes or statements regarding corporate social responsibility (see Chapter 3 for more detailed discussion of IFAs).

Hard law: the *Alien Tort Claims Act 1789* and labour rights abuses

According to Collingsworth (2002: 1983), General Counsel with the US-based International Labor Rights Fund (ILRF):

> [a] fundamental inequity is at work when commercial interests and property rights are protected by enforceable agreements – such as international and bilateral trade and investment agreements – while adherence to internationally recognized human rights norms remain voluntary.

Collingsworth (2002: 185) is critical of human rights and workers' rights activists who settle for what he refers to as 'the distorted paradigm that limits their tools to reporting atrocities and debating new standards that can be the subject of yet more reports'. He strongly criticises institutions – such as the ILO – and activists who continually focus on refining standards, knowing that they are unenforceable. Indeed, Collingsworth states that the greatest challenge in international governance is overcoming the asymmetrical approach to the governance of commercial interests compared with the governance of social interests. The former are regulated by binding mechanisms such as arbitral tribunals, with the power to enforce their decisions. This hard-law approach is the preferred model in the realm of commercial and economic interests. By contrast, soft law – such as voluntary and non-binding conventions and treaties – governs the latter, with breaches most often addressed by condemnation and shame rather than any substantive penalties. This frustration with the lack of enforcement mechanisms for international human rights and workers' rights has caused US human rights lawyers to turn to a little-known 200-year-old US statute titled the *Alien Tort Claims Act 1789* (ATCA) to bring perpetrators of workers' rights abuses before the US courts. The use of the ATCA is not without controversy, and debate continues over whether it can be utilised in a modern setting to prosecute human rights violations in US courts, particularly when the alleged violator is a corporation rather than a state party.

The ATCA is an interesting one-sentence statute that remained dormant for two centuries until it was revived by human rights lawyers in a 1980s case against a Latin American former military officer who was residing in the United States and had been involved in torture and extra-judicial killing in his home country (Collingsworth 2005: 1). The ATCA is part of the *Judiciary Act 1789*, and simply states that the 'district courts shall have original jurisdiction of any civil action by an alien for a tort only, committed in violation of the law of the nations or a treaty of the United States'. Basically, the law allows 'aliens' (non-US citizens) to bring an action for damages against breaches of international law in the US courts. It essentially has an extraterritorial reach over acts committed outside the United States, provided that it can be demonstrated that such acts violate the 'law of nations' – or international law, as it is referred to today (Pagnattaro 2004: 210). This raises questions about what constitutes the law of nations, and whether international labour conventions can be considered as such. Some commentators argue that the law should be read in the context of its enactment (e.g. Dodge 1996; McGinley 1992). At that time, the principal offences against the law of nations were violations of safe conduct (security or passport granted by government to a stranger to travel within its jurisdiction); infringement of the rights of ambassadors; and piracy. However, other legal commentators have challenged this view, claiming that the law 'cannot be frozen in time' and that courts must interpret international law or the law of nations as it exists among the nations of the world today (O'Rourke & Nyland 2006: 160).

The use of this law to bring corporate defendants to court has caused much controversy, and resulted in a concerted campaign by the US National Foreign Trade Council to rein in the use of the law by human rights advocates. The Council was joined in its campaign by the former Bush administration, which argued that the courts should limit the jurisdiction of the ATCA to ensure that the Act was not misapplied. The Bush administration's attack on the jurisdiction of the ATCA was supported by the Australian, British and Swiss governments, who viewed the use of the statute as interfering with foreign relations and national sovereignty, discouraging investment and permitting suits against innocent bystander companies. Indeed, over the last 10 years, the ATCA has become a leading tool for US lawyers pursuing corporate violators of human rights. These cases have included proceedings against the Unocal Corporation in Burma for use of forced labour, rape and murder, as we discuss in the case study below; against Royal Dutch Petroleum and Chevron for alleged human rights breaches in Nigeria; against Exxon Mobil for alleged human rights violation in Aceh, Indonesia; and against Coca-Cola in Columbia for the murder of trade union leaders. As of 2011, there had been over a dozen cases filed against multinational corporations for labour rights violations, the majority brought by the ILRF.

Although many US labour lawyers view the ATCA as an emerging and useful tool to enforce international standards, they also acknowledge its limitations. First, the ATCA can only be used against defendants over which the federal courts have jurisdiction. Second, the 'law of nations' is narrow in scope, and requires international consensus on many human rights issues – for example, it is uncontentious that torture is a breach of the 'law of nations', but there is no consensus that deplorable work conditions or child labour constitute a breach (Collingsworth 2002: 202). Finally, although some of the cases have settled, none of the corporate cases has reached final hearing, leaving the applicability of the ATCA to labour rights abuses untested. To date, cases have settled due to external media exposure and embarrassment, or through fear of ongoing damage to corporate reputation, rather than a final decision and/or penalty imposed by a court. Nonetheless, though limited in scope and largely untested, the threat of litigation pursuant to the ATCA has caused one major multinational company to settle a claim brought against it for alleged breaches of international law. However, litigation based on the ATCA is fraught with uncertainty and cannot replace a comprehensive and cohesive global regulatory structure able to impose penalties for violations of the law. The real solution is 'the creation of a procedure to enforce human rights [and workers' rights] on equal footing with property rights in the World Trade Organization and other regional trade agreements' (Collingsworth 2002: 203).

Conclusion

As this chapter demonstrates, the issue of labour rights and their enforcement has been the subject of debate for more than 50 years. Various mechanisms have been created in an attempt to ensure government and transnational compliance with core labour standards; however, most of these mechanisms have been flawed and have failed to protect labour rights in the global economy. This failure is due to a number of factors, particularly the institutional limitations of the ILO, the dominance of neo-liberal economics and an asymmetrical legal approach. President Sarkozy characterised this problem as a schizophrenic approach to global governance that favours the enforcement and legal protection of economic rights while maintaining that compliance with human rights and workers' rights instruments remains voluntary.

Recognising that international civil society has pushed for respect for human rights and workers' rights in the global economy, governments and corporations have supported the development of codes of conduct – largely self-regulatory soft options that cannot be enforced in the event of breach. However, as discussed in this chapter, such codes have come under increasing scrutiny and criticism, prompting the global union movement to develop its own codes. This chapter also discussed the US *Alien Tort Claims Act*, which has been increasingly utilised by human rights lawyers in the United States in an effort to force transnational companies to adhere to international human rights and workers' rights standards. Drawing together the threads of this discussion, it is clear that there is a general lack of commitment on behalf of the world's governments to ensure that workers are protected in the global economy, and Australian governments are no exception. Instead, such rights are 'protected' by a clutter of codes of conduct, moral suasion, shaming and media exposure, and the remote possibility of legal action in the US courts.

■ Discussion questions

4.1 What are the arguments for a link between international trade and labour rights?

4.2 What are the major alternative mechanisms for providing a link between trade and labour rights?

4.3 Evaluate the relative efficacy of codes of conduct and international framework agreements as mechanisms for linking trade and labour rights.

4.4 Should countries enact laws similar to the ATCA to ensure that citizens have redress for human rights violations?

4.5 The Bush administration and the former Australian Howard Liberal-National Party Coalition government argued against the use of the ATCA for breaches of human rights on the grounds that such matters should be left to diplomatic measures. Do you agree with them? Is this a better option than bringing actions in the courts?

CASE STUDY

Unocal Burma

The Unocal cases involved allegations of human rights violations that occurred in Burma (Myanmar) during the construction of the Yadana gas pipeline through the Tenasserim region. There were parallel state and federal cases brought in the United States, which are referred to here collectively as the Unocal case.

The case began in 1996 when the ILRF filed a complaint against Unocal, which was the first case to utilise the ATCA to sue a corporation for human rights violations. The plaintiffs in the case were villagers from the Tenasserim region of Burma. They sued Unocal for its alleged complicity in human rights violations committed by the Burmese government and the military during the construction of the Yadana pipeline. The Burmese military provided security and other services for the construction project, including the building of helipads and roads along the proposed pipeline for the benefit of the project. The plaintiffs claimed that Unocal, through the military, had used force, violence and intimidation to relocate whole villages, enslaved villagers living along the pipeline and engaged in assault, rape, torture, forced labour and murder. Unocal disputed that it had hired the military for the security of the project, but in the first hearing in the US District Court for the Central District of California – in which Unocal attempted to have the case dismissed – the court found that Unocal could be held liable, and as such compensatory relief could be granted. This first hearing was significant in that the court effectively found that the ATCA provided jurisdiction to hear cases of human rights violations against corporate defendants.

At the next hearing, three years later, the plaintiffs were able to provide evidence suggesting that Unocal knew forced labour was being used and that the project had benefited from the practice. However, the case was dismissed on the grounds that Unocal could not be held liable unless it could be shown that Unocal engaged in state action and controlled the military. The plaintiffs appealed the decision, and in 2002 the US Court of Appeals for the Ninth Circuit reversed the earlier decision, allowing the action against Unocal to proceed. The Ninth Circuit held that the District Court was wrong in its interpretation and that all the plaintiffs were required to demonstrate was that Unocal knowingly assisted the military in perpetrating the abuses to be held liable. The Ninth Circuit also held that there existed enough evidence for the matter to go to trial.

In 2001, Unocal again filed a motion for dismissal, but this was again rejected. This was followed by a request by Unocal for summary judgment, which was also rejected, and the court ruled that the matter should go to trial as there were material issues of fact concerning whether Unocal could be held vicariously liable for the human rights abuses committed by the military. In addition, the Ninth Circuit found that forced labour was a modern variant of slavery, to which the 'law of nations' attributes individual liability and does not require state action to give rise to liability under the ATCA. The court also found that Unocal may be liable under the ATCA for aiding and abetting the Burmese military in subjecting plaintiffs to forced labour as the evidence supported the conclusion that Unocal gave practical assistance to the military in subjecting the plaintiffs to forced labour. According to the court, the practical assistance took the form of hiring the military to provide security and build infrastructure along the pipeline in exchange for food or money. It also took the form of using photos, surveys and maps in daily meetings to show the military where to provide security and build infrastructure. This assistance, the court said, had a substantial effect on the perpetration of forced labour, which may not have occurred in the way it did had the military not be hired to provide security. Therefore, the court found that a reasonable fact-finder could conclude that Unocal's conduct met the *mens rea* (intention) requirement of aiding and abetting in the commission of a crime. The court then reversed the lower court decision and required Unocal to stand trial (see *Doe v Unocal Corporation* 2002).

However, the court did not have the opportunity to make a final decision in the case because, on 13 December 2004, the parties in *Doe v Unocal* announced that they had reached a settlement. On 21 March 2005, the following joint statement was issued by the plaintiffs and Unocal:

The parties to several lawsuits related to Unocal's energy investment in the Yadana gas pipeline project in Myanmar/ Burma announced today that they have settled their suits. Although the terms are confidential, the settlement will compensate plaintiffs and provide funds enabling plaintiffs and their representatives to develop programs to improve living conditions, health care and education and protect the rights of people from the pipeline region. These initiatives will provide substantial assistance to people who may have suffered hardships in the region. Unocal reaffirms its principle that the company respects human rights in all of its activities and commits to enhance its educational programs to further this principle. Plaintiffs and their representatives reaffirm their commitment to protecting human rights. (Unocal 2005)

As a result of the settlement, the court was not required to deliver a judgment for an action brought under the ATCA, and consequently its scope in corporate breaches of human rights remains untested. However, the initial findings in the Ninth Circuit and the ongoing publicity surrounding the case not only brought the issue of corporate conduct in developing countries to public attention, but possibly facilitated or perhaps forced the company to settle.

Case study discussion questions

1. What is the significance of the Unocal case?
2. Why do you think that the parties reached a settlement before the court had the opportunity to determine the plaintiffs' claims?
3. Does this case suggest that the *Alien Torts Crimes Act* is a mechanism that could be widely used for protection of labour rights in international trade?

5

Australian employment regulation

Marilyn Pittard

■ Chapter objectives

This chapter will enable readers to understand the

- development of Australian employment regulation from the inception of the system of conciliation and arbitration
- system of bargaining and agreements implemented under the *Fair Work Act 2009* and the role of the Fair Work Commission
- nature of the National Employment Standards and Modern Awards in providing a safety net
- protections for employees from unfair dismissal, unlawful dismissal and discrimination under the *Fair Work Act*
- protections under the Act for casual and temporary employees and contractors, and the shortcomings of those protections.

Introduction

Legal regulation of Australian employment has undergone massive changes since the mid-2000s. The legislative regime introduced under the Work Choices policy by the Howard Liberal-National Coalition government in 2005 was revolutionary – it dismantled arbitrated awards, ensured that individual agreements prevailed over collective agreements, removed unfair dismissal protection from most Australian employees, introduced secret strike ballots and greatly diminished the independent industrial tribunal's role. In a dramatic policy contrast enshrined in the *Fair Work Act 2009*, operative from 1 January 2010, the federal Labor government significantly reversed most of these changes, emphasising enterprise-based collective bargaining underpinned by a safety net of modernised awards and legislated conditions, eliminating individual bargaining and reintroducing job security through unfair dismissal laws. The common law employee–contractor distinction importantly underpins the new national system, together with employment anti-discrimination and occupational health and safety legislation. This chapter analyses these features, critiquing the new national system, which largely has moved away from reliance on market forces to a system of collective bargaining supported by protections for weaker groups and a new good-faith bargaining concept.

Overview: state intervention and the push for 'deregulation'

The Australian employment system has been characterised by a high level of state legislative intervention from the time of its inception in 1904 to the present day. This legislative intervention established the first formal system of conciliation and arbitration to prevent and settle interstate industrial disputes, borrowing conciliation from the approach in Britain which then utilised mediation councils (which had worked in some colonies of Australia) as well as New Zealand's compulsory arbitration system. Indeed, the Commonwealth parliament relied primarily on section 51(35) of the Constitution, which enabled parliament to make laws with respect to 'conciliation and arbitration for the prevention and settlement of industrial disputes extending beyond the limits of any one state'. The terms of this power in large part determined the process of dispute settlement – conciliation and arbitration – that was enacted in the *Conciliation and Arbitration Act 1904*. Thus the interstate disputes between labour and capital could be resolved compulsorily by the intervention of the independent third party (initially the Commonwealth Court of Conciliation and Arbitration), and with the compulsory enforcement of arbitrated awards that set terms and conditions of employment. Collective agreements could be struck between unions and employers, and their legal status was assured under this legislation when they were registered. The contract of employment underpinned this system.

Although originally conceived as a system that would provide a mechanism for resolving disputes that were beyond the capacity of any single state to settle, the federal system became dominant, facilitated by interpretations of the High Court, so that it was easy to seek and obtain federal awards and to come under the protective umbrella of federal regulation. The system of conciliation and arbitration remained intact for 90 years, with tinkering and amendments to the governing legislation, including amending the powers and nature of the bodies and so on, but the essential aspects of the system remained the same and there was little impetus for radical change (for further discussion, see Creighton & Stewart 2010: 198–218; Owens, Riley & Murray 2011; Pittard & Naughton 2010: 421–88).

The beginnings of change occurred in 1991 when there was a push, through the national wage system, for greater collective bargaining (AIRC 1991). In 1993 (following minor legislative change in 1992), the Keating Labor government, committed to greater flexibility and deregulation of the centralised system and to bringing Australian labour law into line with international standards and obligations, introduced significant reforms. Though maintaining conciliation and arbitration, the *Industrial Relations Reform Act 1993* essentially facilitated the making of collective agreements, either between employers and unions or, radically for a Labor government, between employers and groups of employees (non-union collective agreements) underpinned by mechanisms for tribunal approval and ensuring that employees were not disadvantaged compared with the terms and conditions that would have been applicable under the award system. Collective bargaining was supported for the first time by a measure of a right to strike in the course of bargaining as well as freedom of association protection. In addition, the reform legislation conferred for the first time at federal level the statutory right of employees not to be dismissed unfairly, protection from discriminatory dismissal and provision for equal-pay determinations. The operation and development of the unfair dismissal jurisdiction are discussed further in Chapter 8.

In a short space of time, the next period of change occurred with the enactment of legislation introduced into parliament by the Howard Liberal-National Coalition government – the *Workplace Relations Act 1996* – which gave further encouragement to collective bargaining largely through decreasing the subject-matter of awards. However, there was a novel statutory individual agreement, the Australian Workplace Agreement (AWA), introduced as a mechanism for avoiding the operation of the award minima through agreement by individual employee and employer. While the Howard government had preferred to introduce a more radical model of encouraging bargaining supported by statutory minimum conditions without awards and for unfair dismissal to be pared back so as not to apply to small businesses, it did not have the political power to legislate for this in 1995. The 1996 Act was then something of a compromise in terms of wishing to introduce a more flexible, less protected system of labour regulation (Fetter & Mitchell 2004).

▪ Deregulating through massive regulation

Such an opportunity came in 2005, when the Howard Liberal-National Coalition government was returned with a majority in both houses of parliament and was able to enact dramatic industrial relations law changes at the federal level. The legislative regime introduced under this Work Choices policy was revolutionary while in 1996 award content was reduced to 20 'allowable matters' with other content to be contained in agreements; Work Choices virtually dismantled awards, as no new awards could be made. Work Choices ensured that individual agreements (AWAs) prevailed over collective agreements; removed the protective 'no disadvantage' test as a safeguard for enterprise agreements, relying instead on a new legislated standard covering a few core conditions (the Australian Fair Pay and Conditions Standard or AFPCS); took away from most Australian employees the right to fair dismissal; introduced secret strike ballots as an essential precondition (and hurdle) to unions taking lawful industrial action; and diminished greatly the independent industrial tribunal's role, including removing effective third-party review and approval of enterprise agreements (Owens, Riley & Murray 2011; Stewart 2009; Pittard & Naughton 2010; Teicher, Lambert & O'Rourke 2009). Essentially, the system of conciliation and arbitration was finished. Relying largely on the power in section 51(20) of the Constitution to make laws with respect to corporations, Work Choices introduced a national system. Under the guise of promoting deregulation, the system was highly regulated, with a complex set of matters that enterprise agreements were permitted to address (or prohibited from addressing), with provision for considerable penalty for parties not heeding these requirements (Pittard 2005). The 'Work Choices' label suggested a promise of choice, which was echoed in the objects of the Act, but the reality was that AWAs were the dominant form of agreement, and would take priority over collective agreements – whether they were union or non-union agreements. In many instances, such was the power imbalance that employees exercised no real choice over the type of agreement that regulated their employment.

While the *Workplace Relations (Work Choices) Act 2005* became operative in March 2006, the full extent of its impact emerged slowly. Various studies have documented the impact of Work Choices (Peetz 2007; Peetz & Preston 2007) on the drastic diminution and loss of terms and conditions of employment benefiting employees (Owens 2006), and the plummeting of job security caused by the application of unfair dismissal laws to employees in larger organisations only (those engaging 101 or more employees) (Pittard 2006a, 2006b). The predicted erosion of basic terms and conditions – particularly of groups with weak bargaining power – occurred, and only 15 months after the inception of Work Choices, the government was forced to reintroduce a form of no-disadvantage test protection (the fairness test) to safeguard employees' rights. The political damage was already done, though.

Forward with Fairness

In opposition, the Labor Party formulated its 'Forward with Fairness' policy, a blueprint for a return to fairness in labour standards and an improved balance between employer and employee interests (Rudd & Gillard 2007a, 2007b).The policy was formulated by the parliamentarians who were to later become the Prime Minister (Kevin Rudd) and the Deputy Prime Minister (Julia Gillard) of the incoming Labor government in 2007 – fairness in industrial relations and labour standards seemed to win the day when the Howard government was voted out of office.

The first legislative acts of the Labor government in the workplace relations area were to abolish AWAs and to reinstate unfair dismissal protection to a majority of workers. Step by step, the new Forward with Fairness system was introduced legislatively, culminating in the enactment of the *Fair Work Act 2009*. The new system was fully operational from 1 January 2010.

Nonetheless, Forward with Fairness never contemplated a return to the days of traditional conciliation and arbitration. The clock could never be turned back; instead, a form of collective bargaining at the enterprise level was the main method of determining employment conditions – enterprise agreements were to be under-pinned by a safety net of awards (with 10 matters), together with legislated standards (again another 10 matters) encompassed in the National Employment Standards (NES). The industrial action provisions of the Act were largely unchanged and secret strike ballots introduced by the Howard Liberal-National government remained. Although Work Choices was abandoned, its legacy in the removal of the more fully fledged conciliation and arbitration system that we had known before 2005 remained.

Legal framework of bargaining under the *Fair Work Act 2009*

Enterprise agreements

The bargaining regime in the *Fair Work Act* continues aspects of bargaining that were implemented under the *Workplace Relations Act* 1996. It permits agreements generally to be made between employers and groups of employees, thus retaining the non-union stream of bargaining first introduced in 1993 with the *Industrial Relations Reform Act 1993*. Non-union bargaining remained in both the *Workplace Relations Act 1996* and the 2005 Work Choices legislation, and this issue was not one that the Forward with Fairness policy sought to address; it simply was not in contention. However, agreements with unions were not reintroduced in the *Fair Work Act*. As a result of the 2009 reforms, there are currently several different types of collective agreement. Single-enterprise agreements – that is, agreements between an employer and the employees within the enterprise who will be covered by the enterprise agreement – are the most common form of agreement.

Under the *Fair Work Act*, agreements with more than one employer are generally not permissible within the scheme except in two instances. First, agreements can be made with two or more employers where they are regarded as 'single-interest' employers – this takes account of employers that are engaged in a joint venture or a common enterprise, or that are related bodies corporate (s. 172(2)(a)). The Fair Work Commission (formerly Fair Work Australia) can make a 'single interest employer authorisation' to permit more than one employer to enter into an enterprise agreement. Second, multi-enterprise agreements may be made; these involve employers that are not single-interest employers, enabling them to negotiate the agreement with employees who will be covered by the agreement. All these agreements – single-enterprise and multi-enterprise agreements – may cover the trade union where it applies for coverage, but the union will not be the party to the agreement in the way a union could be a party previously under the *Industrial Relations Reform Act 1993* or the *Workplace Relations Act 1996*. Significantly, this was Labor government policy and generally was not contested. However, a union may be a party to a greenfields agreement – which is an agreement with an employer (or employers) that plans to establish a 'genuinely new business' and to employ persons who will be covered by the agreement (s.172(4)). A significant change was the abolition of the widely opposed individual statutory agreements – AWAs. The system then was returned to a true collective basis with no AWAs, but union involvement – at least as a party – was diminished and, as we have noted above, unusually there can be collective agreements without union involvement. The employers that may be parties to the agreement are corporate bodies (trading, financial or foreign corporations), the federal government, maritime and flight crew employers, territory employers and non-corporate employers in all states except Western Australia.

Collective agreements at the enterprise level, as opposed to agreements at an industry or sectoral level, have been the subject of criticism and debate. While the Act fosters such disaggregation and continues the practice of not permitting pattern bargaining, attention is now being focused on the costs and inefficiencies of forcing agreements to be made at the enterprise level.

■ *Content of enterprise agreements*

The *Fair Work Act* retains prescriptions about agreement content, but the restrictive notion of 'prohibited content' under Work Choices was discontinued. First, agreements may contain 'permitted matters' (s. 172 (1)), which are matters 'pertaining' to the employment relationship or authorised deductions from wages. This limit to employment-related matters is a legacy from previous Acts, which were reliant on section 51 (35) of the Constitution, but the policy-makers today have retained it as a concept despite moving to use the broader corporations power to underpin the *Fair Work Act*. Although the expression 'pertaining to employment matters' has been interpreted liberally, it is not without its limits and does act as a check on what is within the range of bargaining matters (see, for example, *Re The Manufacturing Grocers' Employees Federation of Australia & Another; Ex parte The Australian*

Chamber of Manufactures & Another 1986 and *Electrolux Home Products Pty Ltd v Australian Workers' Union & Others* 2004). For example, environmental matters may not be included as the subject-matter of collective agreements – thus innovations at work inspired by better practices from an environmental viewpoint, but not necessarily conferring benefit on the workplace, are beyond the scope of enterprise agreements.

Second, the legislation utilises the concept of 'unlawful' matters – those matters that cannot be introduced into a collective agreement. These include:

- terms that are 'discriminatory'; those that are 'objectionable' in being contrary to freedom of association; those relating to bargaining services fees; those dealing with absences of a temporary nature from work because of illness or injury; terms that contravene Part 3–1 of the Act relating to prohibiting employees from inter- ference in workplace rights, etc.
- provisions that are not consistent with legislative provisions about industrial action
- terms that deal with right of entry that are not consistent with the statutory right of entry, and
- terms that change unfair dismissal provisions in the Act.

The device of unlawful matters in some instances preserves statutory standards, and ensures that these are not altered by agreement. However, it also takes some matters out of the negotiating territory – such as bargaining services fees. An agreement cannot be approved and is therefore enforceable if it contains unlawful content.

A third category embraces the mandatory terms – those that must be in every enterprise agreement. These terms relate to dispute-settlement clauses (discussed in Chapter 8) about matters arising under the agreement; terms providing for consulta- tion where there are major changes proposed at the workplace; and terms that provide for individual flexibility agreements (discussed further below). Failure to include consultation and individual flexibility clauses will result in the respective model clauses being included as prescribed by the Regulations (ss. 202 and 205). Finally, those legislated standards in the NES must not be excluded by the enterprise agreement.

◼ *Yardstick for agreement approval*

In addition to the content requirements necessary for the Fair Work Commission to approve an agreement, the agreement must pass the 'better off overall test' (BOOT). Significantly, the need for third-party approval of the agreement and the requirement that the employees must be better off are features of the *Fair Work Act* that safeguard employees' interests – something that was noticeably lacking in the original concep- tion of the Work Choices legislation. The essence of applying the BOOT involves the relevant modern award (discussed below) as the yardstick for determining whether the employee is better off overall. The test is not whether a *majority* of employees are better off or whether each employee who is covered by an award would not be not worse off. The bar has been raised from the previous 'no disadvantage' test so that employees *must* be better off than under the applicable award. As with the previous test, there are problems in that many matters cannot be quantified and accurately assessed in terms of whether employees are better off.

The Fair Work Commission has discretion to approve the agreement where it considers that it is not contrary to the public interest and may approve an agreement that does not pass the BOOT. As with the 'no disadvantage' test under the *Workplace Relations Act*, an agreement that fails the BOOT test may be approved where it forms 'part of a reasonable strategy to deal with a short term crisis in, and to assist in the renewal of the enterprise of an employer covered by the agreement' (s. 89(3)).

Awards generally will not be applicable while an enterprise agreement operates, but once the enterprise agreement is lawfully terminated, the award will govern the employment relationship. However, should award rates or wages under a National Minimum Wage order exceed wages in the enterprise agreement during the life of the agreement – which may be up to four years – the higher rate must apply (s. 206).

■ *The bargaining process: the good-faith approach*

Unlike earlier legislation, the *Fair Work Act* prescribes the bargaining process. The major change is the introduction of 'good-faith bargaining' – a concept probably borrowed from New Zealand and the United States (Forsyth 2010). It relates to procedural matters and does not require an agreement to be reached or concessions made. Indeed, it is possible for the parties to be unable to reach agreement and still have satisfied the good-faith bargaining provisions. Essentially, the bargaining requirements specified in the Act can be grouped together as follows:

- *meetings* – both attending at and participating in meetings held at reasonable times
- *bargaining representatives* – recognising the bargaining representative(s) nominated by the employees (which will be the union if no other nomination is made) and employers, and bargaining with all representatives
- *information* – providing relevant information (but not information that is confidential or commercially sensitive) in a timely manner
- *proposals of parties* – responding to negotiating parties' proposals, genuinely considering them and giving reasons for the response to the proposals
- *specific conduct* – no conduct of a capricious or unfair nature that undermines the goals of freedom of association and collective bargaining.

Admittedly, these provisions are largely procedural and might be weak in that they cannot force parties to agree; they proscribe simply refusing to bargain and sticking to one position; bargaining agents must all be present at the bargaining table, and they cannot be 'picked off'; some unfair conduct is banned; and negotiations cannot be stalled by refusal to attend meetings. Sometimes it may be hard to establish whether 'genuine' consideration has been given to a proposal or whether there is simply 'hard bargaining'.

The Fair Work Commission has interpreted provisions so that it may be permissible for employers to communicate directly with employees, even where they have a bargaining agent, or to put agreements for approval directly to employees, even where the employees' bargaining representative may think that the negotiations are still proceeding (*Construction, Forestry, Mining and Energy Union – Mining and Energy Division v Tahmoor Coal Pty Ltd* 2010).

■ *The role of the Fair Work Commission*

The role of the Fair Work Commission – the body originally established as Fair Work Australia under the *Fair Work Act 2009* – includes approval of agreements. Its discretion is proscribed by the statutory criteria that have been discussed above. However, it is significant that this body was given a supervisory role over agreements and their variation, whereas its predecessor had been stripped of such a role.

The Fair Work Commission also has a supervisory role over the process of negotiating to ensure that bargaining has taken place in good faith – the Commission can grant 'bargaining orders' to ensure the good-faith requirements are met and that agreements apply to the appropriate group of employees through a scope order, and can make a 'majority support determination' if a majority of employees wish to bargain and the employer does not agree to enter into negotiations. The Commission also has a role in relation to industrial action, which is discussed below.

■ *Industrial action and secret ballots*

In essence, the provisions relating to industrial action are the same as those under Work Choices. Parties can engage in direct industrial action provided the action falls within the definition of 'protected industrial action'. This means that the industrial action must be for the purpose of negotiating a new agreement, as no industrial action is permitted during the nominal life of the agreement, and a proposed action ballot must be authorised by the Fair Work Commission – that is, a secret ballot must be ordered by the Commission and held to support the industrial action with a majority of employees participating in the ballot approving it. In deciding to authorise a ballot, the Commission must in turn ascertain that the parties have been 'genuinely trying to reach agreement'. In 2010, Fair Work Australia dealt with 926 applications in respect of protected action ballots, compared with 981 in the previous year (Fair Work Australia 2011). These included applications for protected action ballot orders, applications to vary protected action ballot orders and applications to revoke protected action ballot orders.

When secret ballots were introduced in Work Choices, it was argued that the ballot would prove a difficult hurdle for unions. This does not appear to have been the case, partly because the tribunal has taken a fairly realistic view of the process of ballot approval.

The Fair Work Commission has the power to suspend or terminate protected industrial action that imposes significant economic harm on the parties, or significantly affects the economy or the health and safety of the population or a part of it. In 2010/11, Fair Work Australia dealt with 39 such applications. This power can be exercised by the Fair Work Commission on its own motion, or on the application of parties or the relevant government minister. However, it is acknowledged that a purpose of taking industrial action is to put economic pressure on the party with whom the union is negotiating so there must be harm inflicted that is more than the harm industrial action would normally cause (e.g. see *Construction, Forestry, Mining and Energy Union v Woodside Burrup Pty Ltd and Kentz E & C Pty Ltd* 2010). Significantly, industrial action also includes lockouts by employers and recently in *Re Minister for Tertiary Education, Skills, Jobs and Workplace Relations* 2011, brought to an end the airline employer's (quite dramatic) lockout of employees.

■ The remnant of arbitration

Arbitration prevailed for a century in Australia. Although it has largely been abolished, there are still some remnants. Arbitrated outcomes or 'workplace determinations' are possible in some instances: where protracted industrial action causes 'serious harm' to the economy or to the parties in dispute; where there is low-paid bargaining in progress; and following a serious breach declaration. The Fair Work Commission can make a serious breach declaration if it determines that there has been 'serious and sustained' breaches of good faith bargaining provisions and that there is no likelihood of agreement in the foreseeable future, and that all the avenues to try to agree essentially have been followed.

■ The legislated safety net and the award safety net

A feature of the *Fair Work Act* is the continuation of the legislated safety net. This commenced under Work Choices in a radical departure from the previous practice, where awards generally served that purpose. Under Work Choices, the AFPCS – with some other standards located elsewhere in the Act – replaced the safety net. The inadequacy of these protections soon emerged, and Labor's Forward with Fairness policy flagged a change to have a double safety net of awards and legislation. The NES – the *Fair Work Act*'s legislated standards – scooped up provisions already legislated under Work Choices, such as standard hours of work, leave provisions and so on, made some slight modifications to these and reduced their complexity in some instances. Many of these provisions had in turn been the subject of test cases before the Australian Industrial Relations Commission (AIRC), and the standards had not been changed greatly since these cases (Pittard 2011). So, while the standards were not particularly innovative in themselves, the fact that they were legislated was novel. Significantly, the 'right to request flexible work' was added; however, as is demonstrated in this chapter, while this right is novel, it provides a very limited protection because while an employer may not unreasonably refuse a request, there is no mechanism for an employee to challenge such refusals. Moreover, there is a limited category of employees entitled to make the request – parents of under-school-age children or children under 18 years with a disability.

While a legislated safety net is a step forward in Australian employment regulation, there remain questions, particularly as to whether they will be subject to the political processes and altered by governments of different political persuasion; and whether the rather minimalist and cautious approach to what is included in these standards will remain unchallenged.

After a period of relative stability over nearly a century of conciliation and arbitration, where awards laid down comprehensive set of employment conditions, two major changes occurred to the role of arbitrated awards. First, in 1996 the very wide range of employment matters that traditionally were combined in awards was reduced to 20 allowable award matters under the *Workplace Relations Act*. The policy was to encourage bargaining, leave a limited number of specific core matters in awards and place the rest to be negotiated in agreements. Exceptionally, and for a limited duration, other matters could be included in awards. Awards could be updated and new awards made in settlement of industrial disputes.

Second, in 2005 Work Choices all but eliminated awards. No new awards could be made, and existing awards would not be updated so eventually their relevance would be reduced and fall away altogether (Teicher, Lambert & O'Rourke 2011). The safety net was shifted from awards to the small core of conditions in the AFPCS and other legislated standards (meal breaks, etc.). However, some of these legislated standards could be altered (diminished) through negotiation. The underlying policy of Work Choices was to promote determination of conditions by the parties without the perceived rigidity and inflexibility of awards. Moreover, the bargaining regime introduced by Work Choices abolished the approval process of agreements in relation to the no disadvantage test and awards were not relevant to agreements. If an agreement did not meet the AFPCS, there was breach of that standard but no mechanism to reject the agreement.

The third and current approach is that awards, revived in importance and function, again perform the role of safety net for minimum conditions, together with the NES and the yardstick for enterprise agreement approval, as discussed above. Awards were modernised by the AIRC – an enormously challenging task in which more than 4000 awards were reduced to 122 and their terms were also streamlined (Pittard & Naughton 2010). The new modern awards, covering industries or occupational groups, came into force from 1 January 2010. They contain 10 core conditions, and they are kept up to date by a legislative mandate requiring the Fair Work Commission to review them every four years, except in the case of wages, which are subject to annual reviews.

▪ Unfair dismissal and the prohibition on unlawful dismissal

Unfair dismissal protection, in the federal legislation since 1993, operated to protect employees from 'harsh, unjust or unreasonable' dismissal, providing reinstatement as the primary remedy, or compensation if reinstatement was not practicable. The effectiveness of unfair dismissal protection was profoundly diminished under Work Choices when employers who engaged 100 or fewer employees were excluded from the provisions. This resulted in a two-tiered system where larger employers, as defined by the total number of employees engaged (full-time or part-time) were obliged to dismiss fairly while others were not. The research data showed that this threat to job security for the unprotected employees resulted in employees being fearful of complaining about occupational health and safety issues or other rights at work. Moreover, the impact in bargaining was subtle but real, as employees could not bargain hard if they were at risk of arbitrary loss of their jobs (Peetz 2007).

Unfair dismissal protection was reinstated under the *Fair Work Act*. Debate had always existed about whether the unfair dismissal laws should apply to small business employers, and Forward with Fairness proposed concessions for small business employers, with some safeguards. While the law applies to them, compliance with the Small Business Fair Dismissal Code, including setting out a checklist of what the employer must consider in dismissal decisions, generally insulates the small business employer from a claim (*Narong Khammaneechan v Nanakhon Pty Ltd ATF, Nanakhon Trading Trust T/A Banana Tree Café* 2010). The panel established to review the Act in 2011 will address, among other matters, the needs of small businesses.

Unlawful termination of employment – dismissal on prohibited grounds ranging from personal characteristics of race, sex, political opinion and so on to temporary absence from work on account of illness or injury or involvement in union activities – which was introduced in 1993 is retained in the 2009 Act.

■ General protections and adverse action and other protections

In addition to unfair and unlawful termination of employment, the *Fair Work Act* made a notable addition to the repertoire of protection at the workplace. 'Adverse action' taken by employers against employees, prospective employees and independent contractors is prohibited in respect of interference with a 'workplace right' and interference with industrial activities. It is early days, and the scope and operation of these novel provisions have yet to be determined by the courts. However, the Full Court of the Federal Court in *Barclay v Bendigo TAFE* (2011) provided relief against suspension and possible dismissal of an employee who was a union official in respect of what the majority regarded as 'union activities', but the High Court overturned this decision in 2012. Reverse onus of proof provisions mean that employers who are respondents to an adverse action claim must establish the reason for the action taken. These provisions link with discrimination law, as discriminatory conduct is embraced within the notion of adverse action. It is not certain whether adverse action extends to both 'direct' and 'indirect' discrimination, as this language is not employed in the legislation and no definitive ruling has been made. The provisions also scoop up some of the long-established legislative protection for victimisation of unionists provisions.

While specific legislation at the federal and state levels prohibits and proscribes remedies for discrimination in employment, equality of opportunity, harassment and workplace bullying, the *Fair Work Act* deals with this field in three respects:

- Unlawful termination of employment on specified grounds, including attributes of the employee – race, sex, marital status and so on – remains in the Act since its introduction in 1993.
- Adverse action provisions protect against 'discrimination' by an employer, including discrimination among employees. While the full scope of these provisions is yet to be the subject of jurisprudence in the superior courts, this is the first meaningful foray of workplace relations legislation into the field of discrimination.
- Adverse action provisions protect against interference with a 'workplace right'. This enables possible protection against 'bullying', as it might interfere with health and safety obligations, for example. As with the previous point, the full scope of these provisions has not yet been subject to full judicial consideration.

The role of individual agreements and the contractor–employee distinction in the collective system

One of the radical developments in the framework for Australian industrial relations enacted in the *Workplace Relations Act* was the introduction of the statutory form of individual agreement between an employer and employee, the AWA. It enabled parties to avoid the obligations of a federal award so long as the agreement did not disadvantage the employee overall. While take-up by employers of the AWA as an industrial instrument was initially very slow, full encouragement was given to the AWA in the Work Choices changes of 2005. The main features of the AWA which were introduced to ensure full utilisation of individual agreements were that the AWA would override a collective enterprise agreement and the award and that the no-disadvantage test was abolished (although it was reinstated in May 2007) so that tribunal scrutiny of AWAs did not take place to ensure no disadvantage (except for administrative scrutiny to ensure compliance with the small core of conditions in the Australian Fair Pay and Conditions Standard) (Creighton & Stewart 2010).

The public hostility to AWAs and the documented exploitation of workers who lost basic award conditions through both individual and collective agreements (Peetz 2007; Peetz & Preston 2007) led to a return to a form of the 'no-disadvantage' test in May 2007. With the election of the Rudd Labor government in 2007, the parliament legislated initially to eliminate AWAs and as a transitional feature to roll existing individual agreements in Individual Transitional Employment Agreements (ITEAs). When the *Fair Work Act* was enacted, there was a return to full emphasis on collective enterprise agreements underpinned by the safety net of modernised awards and legislated standards, as explained above (see also Creighton & Stewart 2010; Pittard & Naughton 2010).

However, while AWAs were abolished, the door was left open for there to be an individualisation of arrangements in the *Fair Work Act* in two respects: first, individual flexibility agreements could be entered into to enable the operation of awards or enterprise agreements in a limited range of matters; and second, the NES permitted the right to request flexible work, subject to the agreement of the employer and employee. The operation of these provisions in the retail and hospitality sector is considered in Chapter 12.

Critics warned that these windows of opportunity for individualisation might prove too tempting for employers and be open to abuse by employers, particularly in those industries where employees did not have bargaining strength. Moreover, a complaint to the ILO Committee on Freedom of Association in respect of certain aspects of the *Fair Work Act* identified IFAs as an area of concern. The committee concluded that it 'requests the Government to keep it informed of the application of individual flexibility arrangements in practice' (ILO 2010: 10).

Of course, the common law contract remains at the heart of the system of regulation. It is open to parties to negotiate contracts of employment that equal or exceed the provisions in any applicable award and enterprise agreement. Any clause negotiated that provided less favourable conditions than these industrial instruments would result in their contravention (s. 145(3)). Similarly, negotiated terms that do not meet the minimum of the legislated standards in the NES would contravene the NES and expose the employee to civil proceedings and the possibility of imposition of monetary penalties for breach (s. 44).

■ *Individual flexibility arrangements (IFAs)*

Individual flexibility arrangements (IFAs) can be made pursuant to the relevant term in an award or enterprise agreement. A model flexibility clause in modern awards was developed by the AIRC, the predecessor to Fair Work Australia and the Fair Work Commission, as part of the award-modernisation process. This clause permits a varia-tion of award conditions by agreement of the employer and employee; however, there are many safeguards. Significantly, the matters that can be varied by agreement are limited to five: overtime rates, penalty rates, allowances, leave loading and arrange-ments for when work is performed. Thus the parties do not have carte blanche to vary the award conditions. It is mandatory that the employee must be better off overall under the individual arrangement than he or she would be under the award. Moreover, there must be genuine agreement between employer and employee as to the variation; this provision was recently tested in the Federal Court and is discussed below.

Procedural safeguards are that the agreement must be in writing, it must be signed by both parties and a copy must be given to the employee. A written proposal must first be made by the employer to the employee – and, as with collective enterprise agreements, an employer is obliged to make sure that an employee whose first language is not English understands what is being proposed. Termination by either party can end the agreement with 28 days' notice. Unlike awards and enterprise agreement, IFAs are not subject to scrutiny and approval by a third party or the Fair Work Commission.

Each enterprise agreement must contain an individual flexibility clause. The Act's specifications of the provisions are similar to those in the model award clause – namely that the parties must genuinely agree, the employee must be better off overall under the IFA, the agreement must be in writing, signed by the parties, and the employee must be given a copy. A similar ability of either party to terminate the agreement on 28 days notice is also set out. The Regulations set out a model flexibility form term for use in enterprise agreements.

In its report, *Fair Work Act, Bargaining Provisions and the First 100 days*, the Australian Industry Group (AIG) (2009) was critical of the ability of the employee to give 28 days' notice to terminate a flexibility term 'which was considered far too short for business planning'. It also referred to the data released by the Deputy Prime Minister about the nature of flexibility terms in the first 81 enterprise agreements that had been approved:

- Seventy-five per cent of the agreements used the model flexibility term in the Regulations.
- A further 15 per cent used the flexibility term but omitted leave loading as an area where flexibility would be obtained.
- The remaining 10 per cent had a flexibility term that was either more or less flexible than the model term. (AIG 2009: 21–2)

As the Act has been operative in its entirety since January 2010, with some parts operating earlier from 1 July 2009, cases are beginning to emerge that address the issue of individual agreements within the context of the collective emphasis in the *Fair Work Act*. A case decided recently in the Federal Court concerned a small business employer that entered into individual agreements with seven employees. The Federal Court in *Fair Work Ombudsman v Australian Shooting Academy Pty Ltd* (2011) fined the company $25 000 and the managing director $500 for contravening provisions of the Act that related to not forcing employees into individual arrangements. But it may be questioned whether the Act goes far enough. After all, merely presenting employees with an IFA in some industries where employees are vulnerable may be enough to obtain their agreement to the IFA.

The ILO's requirement about monitoring individual agreements must be met and the government's report is awaited. However, as explained in Chapter 4, the ILO lacks the powers to compel compliance, so any view it takes of the abuse of individual agreements must be persuasive only. The leader of the opposition, Tony Abbott, recently has affirmed opposition to the return of AWAs despite the public support for them given recently by a previous Minister for Industrial Relations ('Reith defends individual choice in IR' 2011), and this view was endorsed by the then CEO of AIG ('Employer group calls for individual contracts' 2011).

The *Fair Work Act* was designed to achieve balance in the system (Rudd & Gillard 2007a, 2007b), and arguably that goal has been met. Contracts of employment may still be entered into, but will contravene the Act if the safety net obligations are not met. Individuals can request flexible work – although there is no process for guaranteeing that the request will be met or for review of an employer's unfavourable decision. Similarly, award and enterprise agreements can be lifted by IFAs in appropriate cases. Collectively, there is scope for even greater divergence from award conditions so long as the employees are better off overall (that is, they must meet the BOOT). Even then, as explained above, where the public interest is served, an enterprise agreement can be approved that does not meet the BOOT – admittedly, this will be in exceptional circumstances. The ultimate strategic weapon is available to employers in deciding whether to engage workers as employees or contractors.

■ *Underpinning regulation: the employee–contractor distinction*

At the heart of the *Fair Work Act* remain the concepts of 'employer' and 'employee'. Persons who meet the common-law definition of employee will fall under the umbrella of the federal system. They will have rights to bargain collectively, to select another bargaining representative if they do not want their union to fulfil that role, and to receive the benefits of an award and the standards under the NES. Unfair dismissal protections are given to 'employees', as are rights – where prerequisites have been fulfilled – to take protected industrial action and to participate in industrial action secret ballots. Thus the system, as with its predecessors, takes as its starting point the distinction between contractor and employee. There are, however, some exceptions to that general proposition:

- Independent contractors are entitled to protection under the 'general protections' in Part 3–1 of the Act. Discriminating in relation to an independent contractor is prohibited.
- Sham contracting is prohibited and an employer can be liable if it misrepresents an employment relationship as that of principal and contractor.
- The *Independent Contractors Act 2006* protects the wages and conditions of contractors and enables review of contracts that are unfair.
- Sometimes awards prescribe minimum rates and conditions for independent contactors, but generally such contractors are not entitled to paid annual leave or sick leave.

The emphasis on employees, however, means that true contractors are precluded from certain rights and entitlements, including minimum standards. This can give rise to a class of dependent workers with few rights and little bargaining power to negotiate improved conditions. Outworkers were traditionally in this category, although certain reforms have meant that their conditions have improved, at least in the clothing and textile sector. Industries with a predominance of migrant workers whose first language is not English, who are predominantly women and who work outside the employer's premises – often from home – may escape the safety net of conditions. These workers' job security is virtually non-existent. Occupational health and safety concerns may also arise – see the discussion of workforce disadvantage in Chapter 10.

■ Potentially disadvantaged groups: casual and fixed-term workers and the low-paid

The extent to which casual employees and those on specific contracts, such as fixed-term contracts, are entitled to similar treatment has been the subject of debate over the years. Particular award rates, for example, were set depending on whether the employee was regarded as 'casual'. The AIRC test case relating to casual workers gave some comfort that long-term casual workers could seek permanent employment. Later, this was held to ultimately be assessable award by award – that is, on a case-by-case basis (see Pittard 2011 for further discussion). The NES, regrettably, did not address this right to convert casual to ongoing employment, but awards might include such terms. Some but not all NES apply to casual workers, thus their entitlements are uneven.

True casual workers – that is, those not engaged systematically for over a year – are not entitled to protection from unfair dismissal provisions, unlawful termination of employment or adverse action protection. Persons on fixed-term or fixed-task contracts are similarly excluded from unfair dismissal protection. This was reflected in the first legislatively enshrined protection at the federal level in the *Industrial Relations Reform Act 1993* and has remained consistent policy of both Labor and Coalition governments.

Given that approximately 27 per cent of the workforce is casual, and some estimates suggest that 70 per cent of the workforce are either employed as casual workers or on short-term contracts or performing seasonal work (ACTU 2012), the traditional application of NES and awards, and the scope of the Act, should be reconsidered. For an Act to promote fairness yet bypass – or at least be less relevant to – the bulk of the Australian workforce, despite the system of workplace regulation being a national system, calls the Forward with Fairness policy into question.

Acknowledging that negotiating their own agreements might present special challenges for the low-paid, the government also introduced provisions in the Act to assist the low-paid in various circumstances. There are some curious aspects of these provisions. 'Low-paid' is defined nowhere – the Act does not contain a definition of this category of workers. The only hint comes from the Explanatory Memorandum, which provided some examples of the workers who were anticipated to be in this category. For further discussion of these provisions see Naughton (2011).

■ Current issues and the *Fair Work Act*

■ *Union fees and bargaining fees*

Union fees were once prohibited from being the subject of federal awards insofar as employer systems of deduction of fees ('check-off') were not regarded as matters pertaining to the employment relationship, and were therefore viewed as being outside the lawful scope of federal awards. The *Fair Work Act* now permits these to be the subject of collective agreements. However, bargaining fees – whereby unions could charge employees who are not members of the union fees for their bargaining – have been regarded as being outside the domain of the subject-matter in enterprise agreements. This series of decisions has been enshrined further in the *Fair Work Act*.

■ Freedom of association

The 1993 changes introducing freedom of association remain in the legislation. Freedom of individuals to form and belong to associations was enshrined. The Howard government also introduced the right not to become a member of an association as the subject of protection, and that somewhat controversial approach to freedom of association remains in the *Fair Work Act*.

■ Compliance and enforcement

A system that confers rights and protections on employees must have adequate and sophisticated mechanisms for enforcement of these rights. Penalties under the *Fair Work Act* for breaches of the Act and civil offences increased to more realistic levels compared with previous legislation. It seems that the *Fair Work Act*, together with the Fair Work Ombudsman – which is the compliance and enforcement arm – provides the best and most effective means of enforcement that the system has seen. It is true, though, that historically unions had largely performed this role and that today many unions are weaker – and certainly union membership has declined, as we explained in Chapter 3. Thus there is a certain fading of the role of unions in enforcement (Hardy & Howe 2009), though arguably this has been redressed by the establishment and role of the Fair Work Ombudsman. The Ombudsman enforces awards and enterprise agreements as well as taking a role in adverse action claims and enforcing other civil offences under the Act. It claims to be responsible for rectifying breaches of the Act and forcing the repayment of monies owed to employees (Targeted Campaigns Unit, Fair Work Ombudsman 2011). It also enforces employer rights, so is not seen only as the champion of workers.

■ Surveillance at work

Overt and covert surveillance of employees at work or in the workplace more generally has been the subject of law reform investigations and specific legislation but, as discussed in Chapter 9, legislative coverage of this important area is piecemeal, and the courts and tribunals are filling the gaps on a case-by-case basis. Some jurisdictions prohibit covert surveillance and limit surveillance to public areas in the workplace. While employee surveillance is not the subject of workplace relations legislation, enterprise agreements might be utilised to address these matters.

■ Health and safety at work

The legislative regime in the *Fair Work Act* does not generally enter the field of workplace safety. Issues such as length of shifts, meal breaks and so on may relate to safety, and these are encompassed in awards and the Act. Generally, the duty to provide a reasonably safe workplace is the province of specific occupational health and safety legislation, as well as the contract of employment and the law of negligence.

All states have enacted their own occupational health and safety laws so that, in large part, safety issues became and were the responsibility of the states. However, a national, harmonised approach to occupational health and safety has been proposed, and it was anticipated that it would be fully operative from 1 January 2012. Five states and territories – Queensland, New South Wales, South Australia, the Australian Capital Territory and the Northern Territory – plus the Commonwealth have enacted relevant legislation. Tasmania has also enacted the legislation, but it will not apply until 2013 and the remaining states of Victoria and Western Australia have yet to enact legislation.

▪ Conclusion

In this chapter, we have addressed the nature and degree of legal regulation of the workplace relations system, particularly since the mid-2000s in Australia, against the backdrop of the fairly stable and relatively unchanging system of conciliation and arbitration that existed for approximately nine decades.

While the system is significant for its degree of regulation, there remain areas where regulation is absent or which the regulation cannot effectively reach. Relationships outside the traditional employer–employee one are not governed by the *Fair Work Act*. Although that Act has far greater coverage than its predecessor legislation, because the system is almost fully a national one – Western Australia being the only state not governed by that Act – the employment relationship remains significant and underpins the regulatory system. The legislative model does endeavour to prevent sham contracting – preventing true employment contracts from being represented as that of principal and contractor – and to provide a mechanism for reviewing the fairness of contracts with independent contractors. However, where the relationship is genuinely that of principal and contractor, the safety net of protections in the *Fair Work Act* do not apply, and this opens up problems of exploitation for certain categories of workers and in particular sectors, as we consider in this chapter and Chapter 12 in particular. The question of extending coverage of the federal Act to contractors has not seriously been debated or proposed; no doubt issues of tribunal or statutory interference into the independent businesses of true contractors would arise.

Thus the system currently in place has the following features:

- a safety net of award and legislated standards that are beneficial to the weaker, more vulnerable employees, which can be enforced
- enterprise agreements, which are collectively negotiated to enable employees to secure above-award benefits or to negotiate flexibility in the award conditions, subject to the safety net provided by the better off overall test (BOOT) and meeting the legislated standards; these are vetted by the third-party tribunal of the Fair Work Commission
- multi-employer enterprise agreements that can be negotiated but are not the standard agreement, and will not be made save for the low-paid and in exceptional circumstances.

Curiously, the system permits individual arrangements in addition to the common law contract of employment. Thus, despite the abolition of the statutory form of individual agreement, the AWA, individual agreements can be made to enable award or enterprise agreement flexibility in individual cases.

At the time of writing, a review panel had completed its review of the *Fair Work Act 2009*, and some of the perceived deficiencies discussed in this chapter are the subject of recommendations of this panel (for further details, see http://www.deewr.gov.au/WorkplaceRelations/Policies/FairWorkActReview/Pages/Home.aspx, accessed 20 November 2012).

■ Discussion questions

5.1 To what extent and in what ways has the *Fair Work Act 2009* reversed the trend towards neo-liberal reforms in workplace relations?

5.2 In Chapter 1, you were asked to consider the major turning points in Australian workplace relations. Review your response, bringing together the discussion of politics and law.

5.3 If the Work Choices laws ended the arbitral model that had been in place throughout most of the twentieth century, to what extent did the *Fair Work Act* restore it? What, if any, are the shortcomings of the new laws?

5.4 Unfair dismissal laws have proved to be a contentious area, and have been subject to continuing amendment. Review the development of these provisions and consider why the provisions contained in the *Fair Work Act* have failed to quell calls for further changes.

5.5 What are the major forms of agreements available in Australia today? Consider how well they satisfy the interests of the various stakeholders.

5.6 To what extent are employers utilising individual agreements and in what circumstances would they be desirable to both employers and employees?

5.7 What are the major features of the Australian safety net and how well do these standards conform with the conventions of the International Labour Organization?

Part II

The Evolving Workplace

6

The changing role of human resources management in the employment relationship

Cathy Sheehan, Helen De Cieri and Peter Holland

■ Chapter objectives

This chapter will enable readers to understand the:
- different perspectives of the relationship between management and employees put forward within human resources management (HRM)
- impact of workplace relations change on human resources responsibilities
- role tensions in the developing field of HRM
- directions for HRM in the twenty-first-century workplace.

Introduction

Over the last two decades, human resources management (HRM) increasingly has been seen as a strategic partner to management, and in these volatile times this can cause tension with its traditional role of employee champion. In Australia and elsewhere, the strategic promise of HRM has supported the elevation of human resources (HR) professionals to strategic, senior management positions (see Fisher, Dowling & Garnham 1999; Sheehan, Holland & De Cieri 2006). At the same time, significant changes to Australian workplace relations legislation (examined in Chapters 5 and 8) have brought additional responsibilities to the HR role that require more direct involvement in the employer–employee relationship. The progressive decentralisation of the employment relationship through enterprise bargaining, non-union agreements and individual contracts that promote direct dealings between employers and employees at the workplace level have intensified the focus on the HR professional as a key stakeholder in the successful management of the employment relationship. Consequently, those working within the HR function are expected to fulfil the role of strategic partner, as well as to attend to the traditional employee advocacy roles and remain a steward of the social contract (Buyens & De Vos 2001; Lansbury 2004).

The issue of HR role diversity has become more prominent (and will continue to do so) as Australia enters a period when organisations are dealing with major changes in the workplace relations environment. As well as maintaining strength and credibility as a strategic business partner, the increased devolution of communication between employers and employees intensifies the focus on the HR professional's role as a key negotiator in the employment relationship. The strategic trajectory of the HR function and the decentralisation of the workplace relations system have created opportunities for the HR professional to become a key architect in the employment relationship during a period when complex HR planning is needed to respond to environmental global pressures. The strategic elevation of the work of the HR professional, however, has also created potential tensions for those working in the role, with HR practitioners struggling at times to balance employee well-being priorities with business imperatives (Brown et al. 2009; Francis & Keegan 2006; Kochan 2004). In this chapter, we begin with an overview of explanations of the relationship between management and employees within strategic HRM. The changing HR role in Australia and the impact of workplace relations change on HR responsibilities are considered next. The final sections provide commentary on the resulting HR role tensions and future directions for those working within the function.

The employment relationship within strategic HRM

Schuler's (1992) definition of strategic human resources management (SHRM) acknowledges that the field is largely about the integration and adaptation of HRM with firm strategy and the strategic needs of the firm. He states that the concern of SHRM is:

> to ensure that: (1) human resources (HR) management is fully integrated with the strategy and the strategic needs of the firm; (2) HR policies cohere both across policy areas and across hierarchies; and (3) HR practices are adjusted, accepted, and used by line managers and employees as part of their everyday [work] (Schuler 1992: 18).

The positioning of HRM as a strategic priority within the HRM literature in the 1980s and 1990s came at a time of similar recognition of the people resource within the strategic management literature. Market-oriented models proposed primarily by Michael Porter (1980, 1985) were supplemented by internal resource models as argued by Barney (1991). Porter's views on competitive strategy emphasised external opportunities and threats, and the resultant criticality of decisions about which industry to enter and the appropriate competitive positioning within that industry. The Resource Based View (RBV) – or Resource Based Theory (RBT) as it is now known – provided a counter-balance to industry positioning by arguing for the importance of the internal strengths and weaknesses within an organisation (Boxall & Purcell 2011). Based on the premise that human capital formed an important source of internal strength, SHRM was seen to promise a substantial and lasting impact on sustainable competitive advantage (Barney, Ketchen & Wright 2011; Barney & Wright 1998).

With respect to the relationship between management and employees, the strategic view of HRM advanced by Beer and colleagues (1984) from the Harvard Business School aligned stakeholder needs and was supported by an underlying unitarist assumption, in which employees and management are united in their goals and where conflict is seen as aberrant behaviour. The proposed positive long-term consequences were seen to be improvements in individual well-being, organisational effectiveness and societal well-being. In its more aggressive form, however, this approach to HRM activity seeks to avoid third-party (union) intervention, and has been described by UK academics such as Legge (2005) as the 'new realism'.

Attempts to draw distinctions between the various aspects of HRM have focused on what have been described as the 'hard' and 'soft' HRM approaches, a distinction that has ramifications for employee (workplace) relations (Guest 1987; Hendry & Pettigrew 1990). The hard perspective of HRM focuses on the integration or 'fit' between short-term business strategy and HRM policies and practices. The hard approach sees human resources as a factor of production that needs to be measured and monitored systematically (Legge 2005). In the context of the employment relationship, the focus is on increasing efficiency and reducing labour costs (Wright 1995). In other words, human resources are seen as a variable cost (Bratton & Gold 1999).

The soft perspective emphasises the integrative aspect of HRM while focusing on its qualitative aspects – it is an approach that identifies employees as valued assets. This provides the firm with a competitive advantage, and the emphasis is on the retention and development of these assets (Legge 2005). The return to the organisation will be in the form of increased commitment, quality and flexibility of these resources (Guest 1987). This stresses the unitarist philosophy of behavioural commitment of employees to organisational goals (Bratton & Gold 1999). The hard and soft perspectives create tensions and contradictions in the development of HRM policies and practices. The hard perspective emphasises monitoring, outsourcing, cost-reductions and downsizing, while the soft perspective focuses on trust, development and commitment. Changes in the Australian economy, and the resultant workplace relations reforms of the last three decades, created a business environment that was focused on efficiency and effectiveness. In response, those working in HR were faced with the challenge of balancing these perspectives – that is, they were forced to weigh up demands for greater efficiency with an ongoing expectation of developing employee trust, cooperation and commitment.

The impact of workplace relations change on HR responsibilities

The Australian economy in the 1970s and 1980s experienced a decline of the export market in agricultural goods as a reliable source of national wealth. When Britain entered the European Community (now the European Union) in 1973, a traditionally secure market disappeared. At the same time, the manufacturing sector was pressured to improve efficiency and quality levels, as explained in Chapter 2. There was a growing view at the beginning of the 1980s that Australia needed to restructure its highly regulated and protected economy in response to its declining competitiveness. As well as the floating of the Australian dollar and the reduction in tariff protection, a systematic dismantling of the centralised workplace relations framework was undertaken along with the deregulation of the labour market, as discussed in Chapter 1. In conjunction with these changes, there was an increased emphasis on the development of human capital as an answer to the challenges of increasing levels of competition. This was summed up in 1991 by then Prime Minister Bob Hawke, who paraphrased the author Donald Horne to make the point that Australia had to change from the 'lucky' country to the 'clever' country (Dowling & Boxall 1994).

The changes in the Australian economy in the 1980s made it clear that the future success of organisations depended on the quality of their management of people (Collins 1987). During this period, the Hawke (and then Keating) Labor Party federal governments undertook significant labour market reforms to enhance productivity and skill development. More importantly for the field of HRM, deregulation focused on developing workplace relations at the level of the enterprise to facilitate better and more effective labour management arrangements, and in order to enhance communication, cooperation and productivity – all of which are key elements of the HRM role.

The inception of enterprise bargaining provided the framework for enterprise-specific agreements to become the main vehicle in the determination of working conditions and rates of pay (Charlesworth 1997). By enterprise bargaining, we mean a particular process – bargaining – conducted at a particular level – that of the enterprise. It can operate with any substantive issue related to collective and/or individual bargaining, and could either coexist with, or be completely independent of, the process of conciliation or arbitration. The workplace rules arising from enterprise bargaining can supplant, complement or replace those arising from other processes, including conciliation and arbitration (Fox, Howard & Pittard 1995: 615).

This move to decentralise the setting of wages and conditions initially was rejected by the Australian Industrial Relations Commission (AIRC) in 1991. The AIRC's two concerns were whether the parties were mature enough to bargain effectively and the pace of reform (Fox, Howard & Pittard 1995). However, under sustained pressure from the key participants in the national system of workplace relations (major employer organisations, the ACTU and the federal government), in the National Wage Case of October 1991, the AIRC took some cautious first steps to decentralisation by introducing an Enterprise Bargaining Principle.

The Enterprise Bargaining Principle provided a framework for enterprise-specific agreements to become the main vehicle in determining working conditions and pay rates. A key procedural reform undertaken by the AIRC under this principle was to reduce its role as arbitrator over total wage outcomes, preferring to adopt the role of conciliator between the parties. This development placed the responsibility for enterprise bargaining firmly in the hands of the negotiating parties (Fox, Howard & Pittard 1995). Thus, from an HRM perspective, productivity agreements could be negotiated with each workforce, providing a platform for new strategies to potentially develop a partnership arrangement and enhance productivity. Further reforms followed the establishment of the Enterprise Bargaining Principle; these were driven primarily by the Keating federal Labor government, which believed the pace of reform needed to increase. The key changes that followed provided for Certified Workplace Agreements in 1992, the Enterprise Award Principle in 1993 and the *Industrial Relations Reform Act 1993*, which consolidated these changes. The thrust of these changes maintained the progressive shift of responsibility for the substance of agreements firmly into the workplace, while further reducing the role of third parties to the negotiations. In this way, the reforms potentially placed greater emphasis on the role of the HR professional in the setting of pay and conditions, and aligning employee compensation with organisational strategies.

The election of the Howard Liberal-National Coalition government in 1996 provided further impetus to the decentralisation of labour regulation and workplace reform, with the focus on entrenching employee relations in the workplace. As we have explained elsewhere, the government articulated the aims and objectives of the *Workplace Relations Act 1996* as:

- developing a more direct relationship between employers and employees, with a much reduced role for third-party intervention
- simplifying the system for all participants, without the heavy regulatory burden
- encouraging international competitiveness through higher productivity and a flexible labour market
- placing primary responsibility for determining matters affecting the employment relationship with the parties at the workplace or enterprise level, and

- providing the means for wages and conditions of employment to be determined as far as possible by agreement of employers and employees at the workplace or enterprise level, upon a foundation of minimum standards (Clark 1997).

These changes were bitterly opposed by the trade union movement in particular because they represented a barely disguised effort to marginalise and undermine trade union organisation and to dramatically shift the balance of power in the workplace in favour of employers.

This continued deregulation created a substantial change in the regulatory environment of the labour market. This process was predicated on the belief that a more dynamic and competitive economic environment can best be enhanced by increasingly decentralising responsibility to the workplace, as it is the management and the workforce that understand the needs of and constraints within an enterprise (Clark 1997; Fox, Howard & Pittard 1995).

The legislative changes brought on by the *Workplace Relations Act 1996* and the Work Choices amendments, discussed at length in Chapter 5, dramatically curtailed the collective system of labour regulation (Cooper & Ellem 2008: 534). These changes were partially reversed by the *Fair Work Act 2009*, which restricts the making of individual agreement, re-establishes unions in the bargaining process (when supported by the majority of employees), and introduces 'good-faith' bargaining. Nevertheless, the sequential changes in legislation have, in one form or another, been associated with an expectation of a more consensual approach to the employment relationship embodied in the unitarist philosophy of HRM. The background decline in union membership and the move to decentralised bargaining have provided grounds for a shift from a pluralist to a unitarist perspective, in which it is assumed that the employment relationship is constructed as a partnership where everyone shares the same set of goals and therefore conflict is negligible and the areas of negotiation are relatively narrow and workplace focused. For HRM professionals in many organisations, this has meant an emerging pivotal role in the management of the employment relationship that has to be managed alongside an emerging strategic management role.

In response to the economic imperative to increase efficiency and effectiveness, the HR professional community in Australia has made several adaptations. In 1992, the Institute of Personnel Management Australia (IPMA) was renamed the Australian Human Resources Institute (AHRI) to reflect the substance of the move from Personnel to HRM and the push towards increased sophistication of HRM policy and practice. At the time, there was a growing awareness within executive management of the potential contribution of the human resources function, and HR specialists were increasingly aware of the need to closely integrate HRM with corporate strategy (Fisher & Dowling 1999; Wright 1995). In a review of the HR profession in 2005, a national study of HR managers (Sheehan, Holland & De Cieri 2006) confirmed a consolidation of the strategic role of the HR professional, with nearly half of the senior manager respondents reporting an active HR role in all strategic decisions and similar involvement at each stage of the decision-making process. The research indicated that HR was also being repositioned within the organisation to participate at the senior decision-making level, and therefore impact on both the goals of the organisation and the organisational culture and values.

Along with a more prominent HR role at the strategic management level, there was also evidence that HR was taking a more active role in workplace relations. In their research, Sheehan and colleagues asked HR managers to identify how much responsibility was being taken by HR professionals for a range of workplace relations issues. In the 1995 Australian Workplace Industrial Relations Survey (AWIRS) data-set, the analysis distinguished between respondents whose area of responsibility was employee relations and compared their involvement with professionals from other areas of management, such as finance, administration and sales (Morehead et al. 1997). Sheehan, Holland & De Cieri's (2006) research was more specific, distinguishing between the roles undertaken by HR, employee relations and industrial relations professionals. When compared with the reported involvement of these other two groups of professionals, HR professionals reported primary responsibility across a range of workplace relations tasks, including negotiating with unions, setting and negotiating wage levels and preparing for industrial tribunal hearings. Within the 'other' classification, line managers were the most commonly listed category. These results suggest that, for those working in the HR role, the ongoing changes to workplace relations laws and the resultant devolution of the management of the employment relationship to the workplace level have increased HR responsibility for workplace relations issues. At the same time, those working in HR are now more likely to be expected to take on a strategic focus and become more aligned with management. Sheehan, Holland & De Cieri (2006) suggest that HR personnel have accepted this challenge, and report positive reactions to the strategic demands of their new role. Although this is an important step towards recognising the importance of people as a source of strategic competitive advantage, it may also cause role conflict for HR specialists regarding their responsibilities as employee champions versus strategic partners. Consequently, it is important to consider the impact of spanning roles that include both employee advocacy and strategic advantage. The following section reviews potential tensions within the HR role and implications for the HR professional.

■ HR role tensions and implications

The tension between achieving efficiency and maintaining the commitment of employees is reflected in potentially competing HR roles. Ulrich and Brockbank (2005) identify a number of HR role distinctions. Classifications include 'employee advocacy' and 'human capital developer', HR roles that recognise the ongoing centrality of the employee in the delivery of successful organisational outcomes. These employee-focused roles have been contrasted with the strategic partner role, which incorporates change agent responsibility and a focus on the execution of strategy by aligning HR systems with the organisation's vision and mission. The shift to a strategic HR focus and the elevation of the strategic partnership role have been criticised for having a negative impact on the traditional HR responsibility for the stewardship of the social contract at work (Van Buren, Greenwood & Sheehan 2011). Initially, the framing of employees as valued assets offering an inimitable contribution to the firm suggested a better appreciation of, and a concomitant rationale for, investment in employees (Kamoche 2001). However, as the imperative to contribute to economic value in the firm has increased, HRM has been criticised for being concentrated almost exclusively on linking employment management to organisational performance (Paauwe 2009). Wright and colleagues (2005), for example, cite 68 refereed empirical studies examining the relationship between multiples of HRM practices and firm performance. Many have argued that this concern for performance is not necessarily compatible with a concern for people (Legge 2005). Furthermore, Kochan (2004, 2007) argues that by 'partnering' with management, the HR profession has become more inward focused and aligned with organisational goals; as a result, it faces a crisis of trust and a loss of legitimacy with both employees and society. In the US context, Kochan (2004) cites examples of longer working hours, stagnant wages and increasing job insecurity to conclude that diverging HR priorities and workforce pressure have created a widening gulf between the needs of organisations and their employees, and ultimately a breakdown in employee trust in the HR function. The issue of employee voice and trust is considered further in Chapter 7. There is also evidence from the United Kingdom that there is an amplification of the strategic partner and change agent roles and a relatively diminished focus on the employee advocacy role. Research undertaken by the Chartered Institute of Personnel and Development (CIPD) reveals that the majority of the 1200 HR respondents surveyed saw their primary role as that of strategic business partner or change agent, and very few senior people saw themselves as employee champions (CIPD 2003).

In Australian research (Sheehan, Holland & De Cieri 2006), when 1372 HR professionals described the primary emphasis of their role, just over 20 per cent identified HRM strategic development as their primary responsibility and only 7 per cent identified workplace relations as a priority. When asked to rate the level of importance of a range of HRM areas in the last five years, strategic integration of HRM policies attracted the highest score. Similarly, when asked about the next five years, this area again attracted the highest number of responses, with 60 per cent of respondents selecting the 'very important' category (Sheehan, Holland & De Cieri 2006). In view of the push to elevate HR to a strategic position, these results are not surprising, but Simmons (2003) has suggested that the benefits of strategic labelling for HR practitioners must be carefully weighed against the drawbacks for employees. Francis and Keegan (2006) agree, and make the observation that the potential marginalisation of employee needs is exacerbated by the structural changes in HR, such as the outsourcing of HR activity, that have accompanied the strategic push. The strategic rise of the HRM function has also been accompanied by an expectation that HRM activities should be devolved to, and carried primarily by, line managers (Kulik & Bainbridge 2006). Even though HRM may set up these external and internal relationships to ensure that HRM activities are being provided for the organisation, the outsourcing and devolved relationships may distance HR professionals from direct interactions with employees. Furthermore, although many line managers are proficient in dealing with employee concerns, there are some areas of human resources that are not managed closely. For example, in Australia, Kulik and Bainbridge (2006) report that although line managers are willing to take responsibility for a number of HR areas, they resist 'hot potato' activities such as workers' compensation, leadership development, culture, succession planning, career planning, coaching and performance management; however, many of these areas – specifically developmental coaching, career planning and performance management – provide important access to career opportunities. There is thus evidence that HR outsourcing and devolution to the line have distanced the HR professional from employee concerns, and potentially allowed strategic priorities to dominate employee advocacy priorities.

In a focused investigation of the strategic versus the employee advocacy roles in Australia, Brown and colleagues (2009) interviewed HR professionals to determine how they reconciled their responsibilities as a strategic partner with their responsibilities for employee well-being. They found that HR manager responsibilities do still include employee concerns. The majority of respondents reported that they dealt directly with distressed employees, but the size of the organisation and the HR department, as well as the workload of the HR manager, influenced the extent of their involvement. Acknowledgement was given to the value of outsourcing cases to other professionals when the situation required specialised knowledge. In response to questions about the conflict between the employee champion and strategic partner HRM roles, the HR professionals commented that they managed the different requirements by adopting the unitarist view that a focus on employee-centred activities was strategic, because they generated benefits for the organisation.

Clearly, there are practical difficulties in reconciling strategic and employee advocacy roles. Brown and colleagues (2009) found that in situations where employees use HR as a 'sounding board' but do not wish to lodge a formal complaint, the HR professional is put in a difficult position and stopped from actually resolving the issue. Similarly, when overseeing the performance management process, HR professionals often have access to relevant employee information that is provided outside the performance management review, and which impacts on the performance assessment. Respondents also commented on difficulties when acting as a third party in disputes between employees and management. Although the overriding objective is to resolve the situation in everyone's best interests, it was noted that this was not always straightforward.

In this discussion of the tensions within the HR roles that have emerged in response to the strategic HR imperative, it may be useful to consider the attention given by HR professionals to developing an ethical perspective that could assist in resolving competing priorities. In a review of HR manager reactions to statements on ethical issues, Martin and Woldring (2001) identified a lack of consensus between HR professionals about ethical priorities – for example, respondents differed as to whether cultural diversity should be encouraged only if it has organisational benefit and on whether the interests of society should take precedence over the interests of the company. On this issue, respondents expressed a high level of satisfaction with their employing organisation's ethics, and a reported congruence between their personal values and those of their organisation. The authors wryly observe that the HR managers were either very good at choosing employers with similar values to their own or that the managers had too readily assumed the same position as their organisation. Respondents also reported that they played an active role in fostering ethical activities, such as developing a code of ethics and auditing ethics and social responsibility activity. Despite this positive involvement, Martin and Woldring (2001) note that the lack of unanimous reactions to ethical statements from HRM professionals is a concern, and reflects a need for ongoing analysis and discussion of the importance of ethics in HRM. Sloan and Gavin (2010) similarly address the role of HR in ensuring an ethical approach to employment practices. They note that the HR function cannot create an ethical organisation on its own, and that the leadership team plays a critical role in creating an appropriate environment. When the support exists, however, HR is in a unique position to consolidate an ethical approach through policy and procedure design, and communication of an organisational commitment to ethical behaviour.

In Australia, drawing from responses from a national survey of the membership of the AHRI, Van Buren and colleagues (2011) reported that when HR professionals were asked about specific ethics-related activities, 63 per cent of the 1372 HR professionals surveyed reported the issue or revision of a code of ethics and 53 per cent stated that HR played an important role. However, fewer than 20 per cent of this group reported general structural changes for ethical accountability, 19 per cent reported an audit of ethics including the identification of ethics-related risks and the adequacy of policies and procedures for handling ethical issues and only 16 per cent reported changes to reward systems to reinforce ethical priorities. Van Buren and colleagues (2011) argue that there is scope for HRM managers to become much more conversant with the language of ethics, and that this ethics gap in the practice of HRM arises partly because much HRM education within universities is positivistic in nature. Ethics is receiving some recognition within HRM textbooks and the academic literature more generally, but there is a need for greater attention to a more critical approach and to d a consideration of the underlying philosophical frameworks.

Along with concerns that the changing role of HR has produced a shift away from its historical responsibilities towards employees, there is a debate about whether strategic HR responsibilities to the organisation are being understood and enacted effectively. In a comparative review of the perspectives of both top-level line and HR executives, Wright and colleagues (2001) found that, although both groups recognised the importance of the HR role for enabling a firm's competitive advantage, there were differences in their perceptions of the effectiveness of the HR function. Most notably, top-level line executives were less confident of HR's successful carriage of its strategic role and its ability to provide a value adding contribution. Within the practitioner writing, similar doubts are noted about HR's capacity to add value. Hammond (2005), writing from a US perspective, questions the capacity of the HR function to add value, and posits that it represents a wasted opportunity. Despite adopting structural changes within the HR role, such as outsourcing tasks to enable HR professionals to concentrate on more strategic priorities and raise the intellectual capital of the company, Hammond argues that HR is not meeting the challenge. In short, 'HR is the corporate function with the greatest potential and also the one that most consistently under delivers' (2005: 42).

In Australia, the AHRI's *HR Pulse Research Report* (2007) highlights a similar lack of appreciation for HR's role, with nearly two-thirds of HR respondents reporting a low organisational understanding of what HR does or should do. Furthermore, three-quarters of non-HR respondents believed that HR was either ineffective or they were unsure of HR's effectiveness. Among a list of reasons for HR's failure to add value, Hammond (2005) explains that in some cases the HR profession attracts the wrong sort of people – those who are committed to the promise of assisting people, rather than serving the business by creating a workforce that creates investor confidence in the future of the firm.

The preceding discussion highlights the disparate interpretations of HR functional priorities, with some commentators (e.g. Hammond 2005) suggesting that HR is too strongly aligned with the needs of individual employees and other writers (e.g. Van Buren et al. 2011; Kochan 2004; Brown et al. 2009) offering alternative criticisms that HR's bias toward the strategic management role has created a breach in employee trust. These conflicting interpretations of the evolution of the HR function are partly an inevitable product of having been forced to make enormous changes to its position within organisational processes. The following section reviews prospects for the HR function and possibilities for creating ongoing value.

▪ Future directions for the HR function

There are several directions that could be explored for the HR function to strengthen the employee–employer relationship. Potential areas include a refocus on HR policy design that specifically acknowledges the impact of HR on the employee and the need to enhance employee well-being. As well as a reassessment of HR policy content, new global networking roles for the HR professional are emerging that offer possible avenues for increased HR influence and impact on organisational culture. The evidence of an increase in the number of women entering the HR profession also potentially signals a 'softer' view of HRM.

First, within the academic literature, there is increasing criticism of the 'management-centric standpoint' that focuses on improving the efficiency and effectiveness of HR practices and largely ignores the effects of HR design on employee well-being (Kroon, van de Voorde & van Veldhoven 2009). In response, there has been a call for a refocus on the employee (Boselie, Brewster & Paauwe 2009). Guest (2002) has established that key HRM practices related to employee work satisfaction include efforts to design or make work more interesting and challenging, direct employee participation and extensive information provision. Guest (2002) also identifies the importance of a further set of employee-oriented practices that include family-friendly, equal-opportunity and anti-harassment initiatives. More recently, this has been broadened out to consider work–family/life practices that encompass issues not only related to family, but life in general (see Bardoel, De Cieri & Santos 2008). As well as the push from within the academic literature, the World Health Organization (WHO 2007) has also highlighted the impact of work on employees, and has identified work as a major determinant of health and health inequalities in both mental and physical terms.

Despite this recognition of the importance of employee well-being, there remains a need for a better understanding of the relationship between the workplace and employee health and well-being, and identification of the HR strategies that employers and managers can utilise to recognise, prevent, alleviate and manage difficulties experienced by employees in the workplace and to enhance employee well-being. Research has shown that workplace factors that are influential for employee well-being include an inclusive and positive organisational culture (Hartnell, Ou & Kinicki 2011); support from supervisors and co-workers (Rhoades & Eisenberger 2002); and work–family support (Bardoel, De Cieri & Santos 2008). On the other hand, workplace factors such as job strain and job insecurity (König et al. 2010) have strong evidence linking them to negative outcomes for employee well-being (Holden et al. 2010). For a more detailed discussion of the links between work, work organisation and management, and employee health and well-being, see Chapter 11.

Some HR strategies are becoming available to help employers enhance employee health and well-being; these include education programs, organisational culture transformation and employee assistance programs (LaMontagne, Sanderson & Cocker 2010). However, there is strong potential and opportunity for HR managers to be able to develop more understanding, resources and guidance for employers and employees on how to develop strategies to support employee well-being.

With respect to the roles of HR professionals, Ulrich and Brockbank (2005) provide some important guidance for defining key HR roles that has been strongly supported by the Australian HR professional community. The 'employee advocacy' and 'human capital developer' roles recognise the ongoing centrality of the employee and the delivery of successful organisational outcomes, and the 'functional expert' and 'strategic partner' roles highlight the contribution that HR expertise makes to the business. Exploring the roles of HR professionals in a recent large-scale study, Farndale et al. (2010) discuss the emergence of additional HRM networking roles in international operations. They note that globalisation creates pressure for new corporate HR roles, such as the 'effective political influencer' and 'guardian of culture' that are emerging alongside the traditional roles noted by Ulrich (2009). Research by Sheehan and De Cieri (2012) also found evidence in Australian companies of the networking roles for HR that recognise the increasing engagement of HR professionals in global coordination and the management of a geographically dispersed workforce. What we do not know at this stage is how these emerging roles may interact with the strategic partnership role that has already been identified. The networking roles, however, are valued within organisations that are increasingly reliant on international markets, and consequently these roles provide an opportunity for HR to make a positive impact on organisational culture.

Finally, Sheehan and De Cieri's (2012) review of the role of HR in Australia acknowledges the increase in the number of women working in HR, reflecting the trend documented in many other industrialised countries, where women now represent the majority of HR professionals. Previously, in the decade following World War II, an increase in the presence of women in the personnel function – the precursor to HR – was accompanied by a decrease in the status of that function (Roos & Manley 1996). The recent rise in the inclusion of women does not appear to have impacted the status of the area. From the organisation's point of view, Reichel, Brandl and Mayrhofer (2010) argue that there are very sound strategic diversity reasons for the inclusion of women in senior HR roles that may explain the concurrent rise of women in HR and its increased status. Reichel, Brandl and Mayrhofer (2010) also argue that female stereotypes are consistent with initiatives that support the alignment of organisational and employee interests, and increased employee commitment to the organisation. Consequently, it could be argued that the increasing prevalence of women in HR may be associated with efforts to consider employee interests and is more consistent with a softer HR approach.

Conclusion

In this chapter, we have provided an analysis of the implications for the employment relationship of the major repositioning of the HR function at the strategic level in the early twenty-first century. The elevation of the HR function has coincided with the decentralisation of the workplace relations system in Australia and the emergence of workplace relations, and has resulted in an intensified focus on HR's key strategic value in the successful management of a more direct employer–employee relationship. The transition has not been without its challenges, balancing hard and soft interpretations of HRM, managing potentially competing strategic and employee advocacy roles and addressing doubts raised about the managerial expertise of those involved in the HR area. Future directions for HR include areas where HR can make a substantial contribution to the lives of employees through health and well-being initiatives, and by identifying and developing new roles. We have also reviewed differing views on the issues that have faced the HR professional in transitioning from a reactive personnel approach to a proactive, strategic stance.

Discussion questions

6.1 What key changes in the Australian workplace have provided a catalyst for the development of HRM?

6.2 What would you identify as the major differences between HRM and personnel management?

6.3 Why has the move of HRM to a strategic management partner created increased tension in the employer–employee relationship?

6.4 How do you see the role of HRM developing in the future?

CASE STUDY

Managing a workforce during a period of high uncertainty

Holden started operations in South Australia in 1856 as a saddlery business. In 1908 it moved into the automotive field, and in 1931 became a subsidiary of the US-based company General Motors (GM). It was renamed General Motors-Holden's Ltd and later Holden Ltd in 1998. Holden is now one of seven fully integrated global General Motors operations that design, build and sell vehicles for Australia and the world. It has its headquarters in Port Melbourne, Victoria with an engine manufacturing plant on site and vehicle manufacturing operations in Adelaide, South Australia.

Exporting activity grew in the 2000s and a new product provided the opportunity for further development of exporting. Holden exported around 55 000 units in 2008. To deal with the increased production underpinning the export activity, the firm introduced three eight-hour shifts per day (around-the-clock production). In 2009, as a direct outcome of the Global Financial Crisis (GFC), exports dropped suddenly and dramatically to around 5000 units. Rather than managing a downturn with wide-scale layoffs, senior HR managers and the Holden management group decided to move car assembly at Holden's Elizabeth plant to a single shift in an effort to survive the GFC. Workers at the Elizabeth plant were told that the afternoon shift would be 'axed' in favour of a single shift worked by two teams, operating on different days. Production at the plant dropped to about 300 cars a day. This was a dramatic change from the 650 cars a day being produced when the VE Commodore was launched in 2006. Holden acknowledged that the new shift pattern at Elizabeth was in response to global economic

conditions and falling volumes across the Large Car Segment. Chairman and Managing Director Mark Reuss said the change would enable the company to preserve jobs ahead of the introduction of Holden's new small, fuel-efficient, four-cylinder car in 2010. The company said that employees would receive 50 per cent pay for the days when they were not working. At the time, Mr Reuss said: 'This is the best way to protect jobs in the current climate and keep Holden in its best possible shape leading into the opening of our second car line and an improvement in global market conditions.' He said that defining the output for the Commodore would ultimately have a beneficial effect for suppliers and employees, as the changes would provide certainty and clarity for everyone involved.

The plan focused on reduction of work hours rather than workforce downsizing. The reduction of work hours meant, in the worst case, a 43 per cent reduction in a worker's wage; in the best case, a 25 per cent wage reduction. This was negotiated with an approach of high involvement in decision-making with the seven on-site unions and the workers. It was introduced as a temporary measure but with an undefined timeframe.

Senator Carr, the federal Minister for Innovation, Industry, Science and Research, announced at the time:

The reduction in shifts is one of the several steps the company has taken to reduce costs during the global economic crisis. It has also cut pay for senior executives, frozen pay for all salary workers and withheld payment of bonuses. The critical thing is that there are no retrenchments.

Senator Carr said that the government remained positive about the future of the Australian car-making industry.

On 1 November 2010, Holden reinstated the second shift. The business that had been operating under the shared two-crew, one-shift arrangement returned to full-time employment. In mid-November 2010, following the return to two shifts, Holden hired 100 new employees for the restored afternoon shift, while a further 65 positions were created before the end of 2010. The director of vehicle operations, Richard Phillips, said that the return of the second shift was a step forward for Holden and the Australian manufacturing industry as a whole. At the time, Mr Phillips said:

Our new employees joined their new teams over the last fortnight for training in readiness for the second shift starting today and Cruze start of production next year. These new programs and increased production give everyone at Holden a renewed sense of confidence and they also create new opportunities for the local community and supplier network in Adelaide's northern suburbs.

The recommencement of the second shift was welcomed by union representatives. The Australian Manufacturing Workers' Union's (AMWU) South Australia Secretary, John Camillo, said:

It is a credit to the workers and the government's auto industry strategy that Holden has been able to hold out through this tough time, especially as the crisis forced its global parent, GM, to face bankruptcy in the US.

Since the production shift changes at the Elizabeth plant, the company has unveiled the new Cruze hatch (in November 2011), which has gone into full production at its Adelaide assembly plant alongside the Cruze sedan and the Commodore range. Despite controversial discussion about the location of the design and engineering of the Commodore, which has topped the sales charts in Australia for the past 15 years, the management of the Elizabeth site during the GFC provided security during a two-year period of uncertainty and acknowledgement for the management initiatives to maintain the workforce.

Case study discussion questions

1. How has the HR function at Holden assisted in the management of the workforce during the GFC?
2. What are the options that face an organisation such as Holden during periods of high uncertainty?
3. Has the HR function at Holden taken action from an employee perspective, an employer perspective or both? Explain your response.
4. What are the implications of the experience for future employer–employee negotiations at Holden?

7

The dynamics of employee voice in Australia

*Amanda Pyman, Peter Holland,
Julian Teicher and Brian Cooper*

■ Chapter objectives

This chapter will enable readers to understand the:
- concept and varieties of employee voice and of voice channels
- development of employee voice in an Australian context
- importance of employee voice for organisations and their employees
- comparative efficacy of different employee voice channels
- importance of power and influence when analysing employee voice.

Introduction

The contemporary Australian workplace relations landscape, as in many other Anglo-American advanced market economies, is strongly influenced by neo-liberal ideologies. Related to this has been a series of important developments, including declining trade union membership and density, the emergence of sophisticated human resources management (HRM) strategies focusing on the individual and the rise of enterprise bargaining. These changes have had a significant effect on the structure and practice of workplace relations, not least on the ways in which management variously communicates, interacts with and involves the workforce or its representatives in the organisation and its processes (which we refer to here as 'employee voice'). The shift in the locus of decision-making power to the workplace level, and a focus on direct communications between employers and employees, increasingly is becoming the norm so that forms of voice involving unions are generally in decline in the English-speaking world. As unions and union voice channels in the workplace have become more marginalised, this has acted as both a cause and a catalyst for the development of alternative voice channels in many – usually larger – organisations. These fundamental changes in workplace relations have stimulated increased interest in new patterns of employee voice and employee participation in Australia, specifically in terms of establishing and utilising effective mechanisms to engage employees and manage the employment relationship.

This chapter explores developments in employee voice, with a particular focus on the Australian context. In the first section, we discuss the concept and differing approaches to employee voice that have been taken by various scholars. In the second section, we examine the evidence regarding the value of employee voice and then analyse the arguments in support of the three channels of employee voice (direct, union and hybrid). The third and major part of the chapter examines employee voice in Australia, including the important issue of the unmet demand for union membership.

What is employee voice?

From an employee perspective, voice describes how employees raise concerns, express and advance their interests, opinions and ideas, solve problems, and contribute to and participate in workplace decision-making with management. Van Dyne, Ang and Botero (2003) suggest that individual employee voice can be associated with acquiescent, defensive or pro-social behaviour, depending on whether employees' motives are passive or proactive. Proactive motives and pro-social behaviour are based on cooperation, meaning employee voice is used to express solutions to problems or suggest constructive ideas for change that have benefits for the organisation.

Bryson and colleagues (2007) take an organisational perspective on employee voice, seeing it as governance mechanisms for employment contracts that exist where institutions or processes are present to generate two-way communication between managers and employees. These two-way channels can be direct or indirect in nature, and can be delivered via a single or multiple channels. Direct voice refers to direct communication between individuals and/or small groups of employees and their immediate managers, and emphasises the enhancement of productivity and employee commitment as a consequence of these interactions. This approach is consistent with the unitarist perspective, which is deeply embedded in contemporary HRM and advocates developing direct relationships between employees and managers with minimal third-party (trade union) influence (see Chapter 6 for further discussion of these ideas). Indirect voice refers to communication and interaction between management and an employee intermediary, union representative or other representative, and typically is oriented towards the enhancement of employee participation in managerial decision-making (e.g. see Brewster et al. 2007; Bryson 2004; Wilkinson et al. 2004). Irrespective of the nature of the channel, employee voice arrangements vary widely in terms of their design, employee coverage, the scope of issues covered and their depth or embeddedness in the workplace (Dundon et al. 2004).

Freeman and Medoff (1984) first adapted the voice concept to the labour market in terms of an exit-voice strategy. They argued that where employees felt aggrieved, they would use 'voice' to seek redress, and if this was not achieved, they would 'exit' the organisation. According to this view, employee voice, in terms of direct two-way communication, was important for both employers and employees, and unions were seen as the central, independent vehicle for the collective voicing of employees' dissatisfaction. Traditionally, much of the workplace relations literature has viewed the articulation of grievances – whether on an individual or collective basis – as the sole component of voice. This emphasis on grievances and union-only voice reflects a narrow conceptualisation of the options available to employees to advance their rights and interests at work, and to contribute to and participate in organisational decision-making. It also reflects an era in which union membership was widespread – particularly in the Anglo-American world – and in which it was not uncommon for unions to be the 'single channel' for employee voice. As recognised in the HRM literature, however, the contemporary meanings of employee voice can be categorised into multiple strands, including the articulation of individual dissatisfaction, communication/exchange, collective representation and organisation, upward problem-solving, engagement and contribution to management decision-making and the demonstration of mutuality and cooperative relations (Dundon et al. 2004).

The importance of employee voice

The importance of establishing, maintaining and integrating employee voice channels in the workplace can be seen at a variety of levels in the organisation. Employee voice is often viewed as a key element of high-performance work systems, and of high-involvement and high-commitment management approaches (Bryson et al. 2007; Wood & Wall 2007), and has been linked with:

- increased organisational performance and a more favourable workplace relations climate (Boxall & Purcell 2011; Pyman et al. 2010)
- employee satisfaction, commitment and organisational citizenship behaviours through the harnessing of employees' discretionary effort (Holland et al. 2011; Boxall, Purcell & Wright 2007; Wood & Wall 2007)
- positive supervisor–subordinate relationships, through more effective due process, process control, decision control, awareness of employee rights, and justice and fairness in the employment relationship (Marchington 2007).

While these findings strongly suggest that employee voice predicts organisational performance, the research designs are typically cross-sectional and the data are perceptual. Unfortunately, there is a lack of research that utilises organisation-level data to gauge the views of employees and their managers.

The workplace relations and HRM literatures identify a number of determinants of employee voice. As Hyman (2004) argues, employee voice is only one feature of the broader regulation of the employment relationship. The relative efficacy and sustainability of voice is intertwined with other social and economic features. For example, employers' decisions to adopt, or not adopt, voice channels will be driven by their perceptions of the net benefits of voice to the firm, the costs of switching and external economic pressures (Bryson et al. 2007; Willman, Bryson & Gomez 2006, 2007). Such economic pressures will be influenced by organisational size and indus-trial sector (Brewster et al. 2007). However, employers' decisions will also be influenced by the 'internal contradictions of industrial relations' (Belanger & Edwards 2007) – that is, the regulation of cooperation and conflict within the work-place. Therefore, the attitudes and style of management towards trade unions and employee involvement and participation in the organisation in general, and the effectiveness of informal processes of conflict management and dispute resolution become critical for determining and shaping the nature, processes and operation of employee voice in the workplace (Holland et al. 2009; Saundrey & Wibberley 2012). In other words, the workplace relations climate – defined as the state and quality of workplace relations between employers, employees and unions in an organisation – will have an important influence upon employee voice. As a consequence, employee voice is a contested process that is shaped by external pressures, such as regulation, industry and sectoral pressures, and internal managerial choices (with respect to employee voice), conflict management and dispute-resolution processes within the organisation (Dundon et al. 2004; Saundrey & Wibberley 2012). The links between employee voice and dispute-resolution procedures are considered further in Chapter 8.

The advantages and disadvantages of different types of employee voice channels have also generated debate in the academic literature, particularly regarding the union system of voice versus non-union and direct voice channels. Taking a unitarist perspective, direct voice is seen to be superior to union voice for two reasons. First, barriers between employers and employees can be broken down by dealing directly with employees rather than through an intermediary (Bryson 2004). Of course, this argument does not consider the ways in which power and status differences play out in direct interactions to secure an outcome in the interest of the organisation. Second, direct voice allows managers to better respond to workers' heterogeneous interests in an increasingly diverse, complex and dynamic work environment (Holland et al. 2009; Bryson 2004). Direct voice can therefore elicit positive benefits for the organisation by promoting or instilling organisational values and a corporate culture that facilitates employee motivation and commitment. This argument sits neatly with the diversity management agendas of contemporary HRM, which view the workforce as fragmented by a wide variety of characteristics, whether innate or acquired.

These arguments receive some support from empirical research. In the United Kingdom, Bryson (2004), for example, found that non-union voice was more effective than union voice in eliciting managerial responsiveness to employee needs. In contrast, in Australia, an analysis of the Australian Worker Representation and Participation Survey (AWRPS) research found that an amalgam of different types of employee voice was most effective in eliciting managerial responsiveness to employee needs (Pyman et al. 2006).

The pluralist perspective posits that union voice is superior on the basis of 'union independence'. In the Western tradition, trade unions are independent representatives of employee interests and democratically accountable to their members (Charlwood & Terry 2007). As a consequence, unions have at their disposal collective power, resources and the availability of sanctions for non-compliance, making them less susceptible to managerial influence and control. Freeman and Medoff (1984) also argue that the provision of union voice can have a positive effect on organisational performance, by reducing grievances, which in turn promotes employee satisfaction and reduces labour turnover and absenteeism. Union voice can also provide employees with a channel to suggest improvements to working practices, and therefore potentially enhance productivity, health and safety, and job security (Freeman & Medoff 1984). Despite the intuitive appeal of these propositions, decades of empirical research have failed to generate unequivocal empirical support for union voice. For example, in Australia, an analysis of the 2007 AWRPS revealed that employees' perceptions of the workplace relations climate were more favourable where they had access to direct-only voice arrangements, whereas in unionised workplaces, the workplace relations climate was perceived to be poorer where management was opposed to unions (Pyman et al. 2010).

From a pluralist perspective, it has also been argued that joint regulation of the employment relationship leads to better wages and working conditions, and procedural fairness for union members compared with non-unionists (Charlwood & Terry 2007; Verma 2005). Enterprise or in-house unions have long been challenged on various grounds, including that they lack independence from management and that they are driven by managerial objectives specific to the enterprise (Gaffney 2002). Benson (2000), in a comparison of unionised and non-unionised workplaces in Australia, found that employees in unionised workplaces had a greater number of voice mechanisms present than their counterparts in unorganised workplaces. Delery and colleagues (2000) identified a similar pattern of voice arrangements in US workplaces.

From a Marxist or radical perspective, one of the major challenges to the effectiveness of non-union representative and direct voice channels is in their capacity to transform the power relations in an organisation. As Charlwood and Terry (2007) suggest, management may use information provision and consultation as a 'fig-leaf' cover for unilateralism and managerial prerogative. It is therefore the lack of sanctions for non-compliance, collective power or access to independent sources of advice or assistance that mean non-union voice channels are more susceptible to managerial influence and control (Wilkinson et al. 2004).

The substitution thesis is also a major theme in the workplace relations and HRM literatures, and is important to consider when examining the incidence and superiority of different employee voice channels. Research in the United States and the United Kingdom often portrays non-union employee representation as a union-avoidance strategy, suggesting that such voice regimes are more likely to be found in non-union workplaces because unitarist HRM practices act as a substitute for unionisation and collective bargaining (pluralist) practices (Fiorito 2001; Machin & Wood 2005). There is no doubt that union substitution forms part of the strategic options that are available to employers in particular regulatory and economic contexts. However, this view does not take into account the increasing tendency towards a coexistence of different voice mechanisms operating simultaneously, which is evident in the 'social partnership' literature and is prominent in European countries (Boxall & Purcell 2011; Wood & Wall 2007). Moreover, consideration of the superiority of a single union-voice channel needs to be considered against the range of issues and organisational contexts within which management may need to solicit employee voice, particularly in larger organisations. Empirical research increasingly supports the incidence and effective coexistence of a plurality of voice arrangements in both Australia and the United Kingdom (e.g. Pyman et al. 2006; Charlwood & Terry 2007).

Despite increasing evidence of alternative forms of non-union representative and direct voice channels, employee voice research has tended to focus on the two streams as mutually exclusive. One stream of research investigates the impact of union activity on the exit-voice model, including variables such as employee turnover, quit rates, retention, job tenure, job satisfaction and training. While empirical research comprehensively shows that unionisation reduces quit rates and turnover (e.g. Iverson & Currivan 2003), empirical research examining the relationship between union voice and job satisfaction has produced mixed results (e.g. Garcia-Serrano 2009; Hammer & Agvar 2007; Bryson 2004; Bryson, Cappellari & Lucifora 2004).

These mixed results on the impact of union voice may reflect what Renaud (2002) describes as reverse causation. Reverse causation theory argues that union membership has a negative impact on the workplace due to a variety of issues, including first that employees with lower job satisfaction are more likely to join a union to improve their terms and conditions (Freeman & Medoff 1984). The second and related point is that unionised workers are more likely to be dissatisfied because unions raise awareness of management inadequacies, resulting in more negative evaluations of the workplace, which in turn can adversely affect job satisfaction (Guest & Conway 1999). A third argument is that unionised jobs tend to be less attractive in both content and context – for example, the industrial location of jobs and their manual character – and workers become primed to look for improvements (Hammer & Avgar 2007). This leads to a fourth argument that unions increase the quantity of dissatisfied employees in the workplace by encouraging them to express a voice instead of quitting, and expressing dissatisfaction (voice) through unions is seen as less costly than leaving the organisation (Bryson 2004). This expression of voice may then lead to a poorer workplace relations climate because dissatisfied employees fail to exit, and their attitudes may impact on those of other workers.

A second stream of research has focused on the operation and effectiveness of different combinations of voice mechanisms in practice (e.g. Holland et al. 2009; Haynes, Boxall & Macky 2005; Dundon et al. 2004; Kim & Kim 2004; Bryson 2004), and has also produced mixed results, due to the different measures of employee voice utilised. However, there is substantial evidence that the use of multiple (dual-channel) voice arrangements is common and effective (e.g. Brewster et al. 2007; Bryson 2004; Charlwood & Terry 2007; Pyman et al. 2006).

In light of the theoretical arguments for employee voice and varied empirical evidence, it is interesting that Danford and colleagues (2009: 338) argue that the concepts of worker participation and employee voice remain highly imprecise, too often underpinned by the nebulous idea of participation in management decision-making. This sentiment is also reflected in Marchington's (2007: 142) work, in which he argues that:

> employee voice is probably the area in human resource management where tensions between the organisation and workers' goals, and between shareholders' and stakeholders' views, are most apparent, because it connects with the question of managerial prerogatives and social legitimacy.

The degree of power and influence associated with different employee voice channels therefore varies significantly, and is fundamental when considering and gauging the impact and efficacy of employee voice arrangements in the organisation from both employer and employee perspectives. Employee voice is not only a function of internal and external pressures and policies, but also a function of what workers desire, which in itself is determined by the options available and the employees' and managers' sets of needs (Bryson 2004). Where a gap exists between what workers desire and what they want, this is referred to as the *influence gap*. Freeman and Rogers (1999) found that a significant influence gap existed in the United States across a diverse group of workers and across many different issues, leading them to suggest that the system of workplace governance had failed the country. The authors went on to argue that this system had not delivered US workers the role they wanted in decision-making.

■ The changing nature of employee voice in Australia

In Australia, for historical and other reasons which we considered in Chapter 5, union voice has been the most prominent means by which workers have been organised and represented in the employment relationship. The predominance of union voice dates back to the creation of systems of compulsory conciliation and arbitration at the federal and state levels at the beginning of the twentieth century. These systems embodied pluralist assumptions with their notions of collective representation and third-party dispute resolution, and unions were able to be legally constituted as representatives of employee interests in relation to both members and non-members. The legitimacy afforded to unions under the arbitral system was embedded in extensive institutional guarantees, including exclusive coverage of defined categories of employees and guaranteed recognition and representation rights. Despite the prominence of unions under the arbitral system, it has been argued that employee voice was marginalised as a consequence of the centralisation of industrial relations processes at the national and industry levels (Bray et al. 2001). The gradual decentralisation of the workplace relations system since the 1980s, through a series of legislative reforms under successive Labor and Liberal-National Coalition federal governments beginning in the 1980s, and the growth of HRM within organisations have together contributed to a significant decline in union voice and the emergence of alternative forms of representation, particularly joint consultation and direct voice (Pyman et al. 2006; Holland et al. 2009). It can reasonably be argued that the decline in union representation, and consequently union voice, is not simply the result of factors such as the increasingly instrumental orientation of employees, changes in the occupational and industrial structure of the economy or other considerations. Empirical research demonstrates that there is unmet demand for union membership in Australia – that is, there are employees in non-union workplaces who would join a union if given the opportunity to benefit from union voice channels (Pyman et al. 2009). This is explored more fully in the following section, which draws on our findings from two major national studies on the nature of participation and representation and participation in the Australian workplace.

■ The Australian Worker Representation and Participation Survey (AWRPS)

The AWRPS was undertaken in order to explore the changing nature of worker representation, participation and influence in Australia (Teicher et al. 2005). This section of the chapter reports on data from the surveys undertaken in 2004 and 2010 in order to provide an analysis of the nature and structure of employee voice in Australian workplaces in the twenty-first century. The samples were stratified by Australian state/territory to reflect the geographical distribution of the population as reported in the Australian Bureau of Statistics (ABS) Census of Population and Housing. The samples are broadly representative of the Australian population in terms of demographic characteristics. For purposes of comparison between the 2004 and 2010 samples, unweighted estimates are reported.

■ Non-union voice

Examining non-union voice in the workplace, Figure 7.1 shows that a large majority of respondents reported the presence of an 'open door' policy to discuss problems

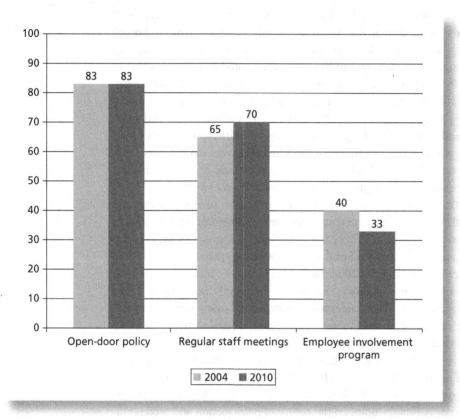

Figure 7.1: Non-union voice arrangements in 2004 and 2010

with their supervisors and/or senior management, as well as having regular staff meetings with senior management in the workplace. The proportion of workplaces with an 'open-door' policy remained the same at 83 per cent in 2004 and 2010, and the proportion of respondents reporting regular staff meetings increased from 65 per cent to 70 per cent over the same period. This indicates that consultation and direct communication remain strong, and in some cases are increasing. However, formal employee involvement programs such as quality circles, which relate to actual decision-making in the workplace, are the least common non-union voice arrangements reported by respondents, and decreased from 40 per cent to 33 per cent over the six years to 2010. This decline is a little surprising, as earlier national surveys (Callus et al. 1991; Morehead et al. 1997) identified the importance and rapid growth in this form of employee voice, which was associated with the introduction of Japanese management techniques into Australia from the 1990s onwards. This decline has to be seen as a concern, as it appears to highlight that real participation and co-decision-making are in decline or, to put it slightly differently, unitarist approaches to management are ascendant. Evidence of a decline could also support Charlwood and Terry's (2007) argument that management use information provision and consultation as a means to make unilateral decisions and reinforce managerial prerogative, influence and control (see also Wilkinson et al. 2004).

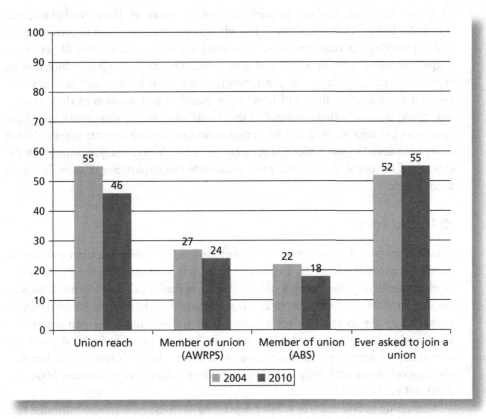

Figure 7.2: Indicators of union voice in 2004 and 2010

■ *Union voice*

Union reach is defined as the presence of a union at the workplace that an employee can join (Haynes et al. 2006). Figure 7.2 shows that the proportion of respondents who report that there is a union at their workplace that people doing their type of work can join has decreased from 55 per cent in 2004 to 46 per cent in 2010. That nearly half of respondents report the absence of union reach should be a matter of concern for Australian unions, in light of a continuous decline in union density and significant investments by the Australian Council of Trade Unions (ACTU) and many affiliated unions in implementing an organising model in contrast to the more passive and less resource intensive servicing model traditionally utilised by Australian unions. (For a more detailed discussion of the models of union action, see Chapter 3.)

Our estimates of union density, though slightly higher than the official ABS figures, reinforce the trend towards decreasing union membership over time in Australia (see Figure 7.2). In 2010, the national ABS estimate for union membership was 18 per cent. In addition to the decline, problems of union supply and reach (availability of a union that a person could join in their workplace) are exacerbated by the incidence of 'free-riding' (receiving the benefits of union membership without joining) in Australia. In 2010, union members represented just over half (52 per cent) of those who had the opportunity to join a union at their workplace; the remainder (48 per cent) were free-riders who enjoyed the benefits of collective action without bearing the costs. In 2004, free-riding was 8 per cent lower (40 per cent), suggesting an increase in free-riding over time. The increase in free-riding may be correlated with declining union reach over the same period. The proportion of workers who reported that they had never been asked to join a union at their current workplace, despite having a union that they could join, slightly increased from 52 per cent to 55 per cent in 2010. Evidence that almost half of the workers surveyed have never been asked to join a union at their current workplace raises questions about the efficacy of the organising model, and accentuates the importance of capitalising on union reach.

■ *Hybrid voice*

In the earlier part of this discussion, we identified the increasing popularity of dual or hybrid forms of voice from the literature. In Australia, we found that the proportion of workers identifying the presence of hybrid voice at their workplace declined from 55 per cent in 2004 to 48 per cent in 2010 (see Figure 7.3). Part of this change may be explained by the increase in the proportion of workers reporting non-union-only voice in their workplace over this period: up from 35 per cent in 2004 to 44 per cent in 2010. Interestingly, and consistent with the problems of union reach identified above, workplaces with only union voice have remained stable between 2004 and 2010 at 4 per cent.

Examining hybrid voice in greater depth, the AWRPS research also indicated that the strongest predictor of managerial responsiveness to employee needs was the combination of direct and non-union representative voice arrangements (Pyman et al. 2006). The effectiveness of hybrid voice channels, rather than a single channel, in Australia is consistent with other empirical studies in Europe, the United Kingdom and New Zealand. In the United Kingdom, for example, Sisson (2000) found that, in cases where a greater number of different participative forms were used, managers were more likely to report benefits. In the United Kingdom, Wilkinson et al. (2004) also found that union and non-union channels coalesced into a systematic alliance so as to complement one another. This notion is further supported by Machin and Wood's (2005) analysis of the British Workplace Employment Relations Study, which found evidence of a complementarity between union and HRM practices. Collectively, the results affirm the value of building and developing complementary, alternative forms of employee voice in the workplace.

The effectiveness of hybrid voice is contrary to the substitution argument, demonstrating that union, non-union representative and direct voice are not mutually exclusive. In specific circumstances, however, union substitution may be seen as a strategic option, or its attraction may arise partly from ideological reasons. This finding in support of the hybrid model resonates with the 'partnership' model that is strongly advocated in Europe, promoting a shared agenda and the compatibility of high-involvement HRM practices with union voice (Boxall & Purcell 2011). Indeed, a

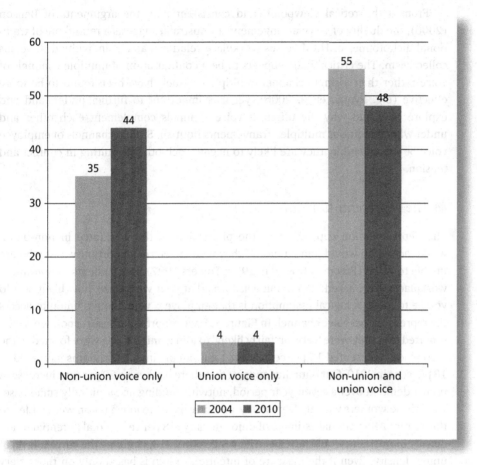

preference for cooperative union–management relations was also identified in the AWRPS among a majority of both union members and non-unionists in the 2004 and 2010 surveys.

In the Australian context, the operation and interaction of multiple voice channels transcends the unitarism–pluralism dichotomy, and underscores the rationale for a plurality of interests and cooperative relations in the employment relationship. For unions and managers, the findings suggest the desirability of an incorporated, mutually reinforcing approach to employee voice, which is predicated on multiple and inclusive channels, collaboration and cooperation. Such arrangements reflect the contemporary workplace, with an increasingly diverse workforce and dynamic and complex environment. Hybrid voice models also resonate with integrative approaches to human resource sustainability and a 'soft' model of human resource management, both of which are underpinned by workforce development and cooperation with unions. As Guest (1995: 136) suggests, unions should be seen as being compatible with principled advocacy of HRM.

From a theoretical viewpoint, and consistent with the arguments of Benson (2000), the duality of voice arrangements in Australia suggests a rethinking of traditional dichotomies of HRM versus workplace relations, and of individualism versus collectivism. The critical issue appears to be a configuration of multiple channels of voice rather than a single channel. Multiple channels have been found to be more effective (e.g. Pyman et al. 2006), yet it is important to further understand and explore how and why the different voice channels complement each other and under what conditions multiple arrangements flourish. Should channels of employee voice be incompatible, they are likely to negate each other, resulting in conflict and tension.

■ *The representation gap*

The 'representation gap' refers to the proportion of the workforce in non-union workplaces who would join a union if they were given the opportunity, but who are unable to do so (Freeman & Rogers 1999; Towers 1997). Respondents in non-union workplaces were asked: 'If a union was formed at your workplace, how likely would you be to join?' A logical assumption is that employees would join a union to access the representative voice channel. In Figure 7.4, we report that those respondents who reported that they were 'very' or 'fairly likely' to join a union if one were formed in the workplace represented 15 per cent of the total sample in 2004, and this increased to 18 per cent in 2010. Our data thus suggest that there has been a 20 per cent increase in unmet demand over a seven-year period, notwithstanding an admittedly small base.

If those workers who are 'very likely' or 'fairly likely' to join a union were added to the current ABS national estimate of union density (18 per cent), total potential union density in Australia would have been 36 per cent in 2010, doubling the current level of union density. Even if the measure of intention to join is based only on those 'very likely' to join a union, union density would have increased by 7 per cent and 6 per cent in 2004 and 2010 respectively. The level of stated unmet demand is actually very similar over time. If those workers who are 'very likely' to join a union were added to the ABS estimate, estimated potential union density in Australia in 2010 would still increase by a quarter to 24 per cent.

Ongoing and increasing unmet demand for union representation and union services should be a significant concern for the union movement, and reinforces the importance of extending union reach. By targeting unmet demand, unions would be able to increase their influence and power in the workplace and obtain greater leverage in influencing the national agenda on workplace relations. In this light, it is notable that right-wing think-tanks like the HR Nicholls Society challenge the extent of union influence on national political agendas on the basis of the small and declining proportion of union members in the Australian workforce. Equally, employers and human resource managers should be mindful of the apparent increase in the demand for third-party involvement in the workplace. At one level, this latent demand may indicate that HRM strategies are not working. On another level, consistent with the Marxist or radical perspective, employees may increasingly perceive management

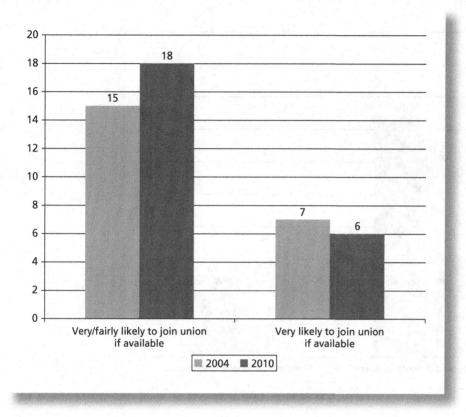

Figure 7.4: Unmet
demand for union
membership in 2004 and
2010

information and consultation strategies as rhetoric, masking enhanced managerial prerogative, influence and control in the workplace.

■ Attitudes to unions

Taking into account the evidence of a representation gap and unmet demand, it is worth exploring the attitudes of employees to unions as the traditional voice of the workforce. As shown in Figure 7.5, the majority of workers in non-union workplaces who believe that a union would make no difference to them personally at the work-place has increased from 67 per cent in 2004 to 74 per cent in 2010. This increase in employees' indifference is arguably consistent with the increase in free-riding, as has already been noted. Significantly, the proportion of employees who are indifferent to unions has increased at the same time that managerial opposition to unions in the workplace has decreased; from 34 per cent in 2004 to 25 per cent in 2010. Overall, then, it seems more likely that the problem is one of union supply and a lack of efficacy in organising in Australia, rather than latent managerial opposition. This finding is a major problem for unions, and has strategic implications for how they organise and represent the workforce. Given unmet demand for unionisation, Australian trade

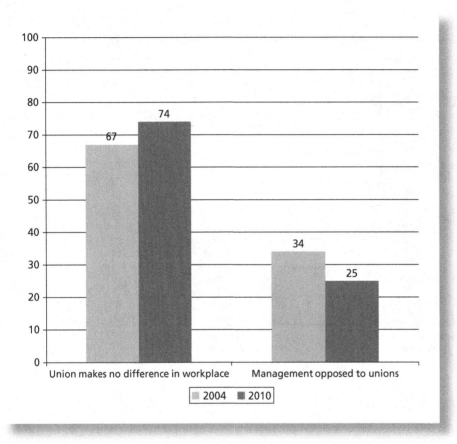

Figure 7.5: Attitudes to
unions in 2004 and 2010

unions must consciously work on their image. Unions must consider how they can demonstrate success and the value of union voice to non-members. After all, there is evidence that there are a core group of 'willing' employees seeking a third party (voice) in their workplace; it is now the case that Australian unions must extend their reach to capitalise on this unmet demand.

■ Satisfaction with influence at work and the industrial relations climate

When exploring issues of satisfaction and influence in the workplace, Figure 7.6 shows that about two-thirds of workers were satisfied with their influence at work in both 2004 and 2010. Nevertheless, this still leaves a significant minority who feel they have less influence and control in the workplace, suggesting the presence of an influence gap. Evidence of an influence gap may further substantiate the notion that management are increasing their prerogative and control in the workplace, at the expense of genuine employee involvement and participation.

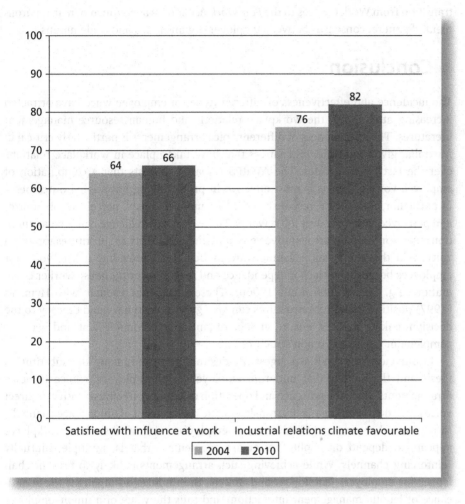

Figure 7.6 also shows that the overwhelming majority of employees had a favourable opinion of the workplace relations climate – that is, they believed that the
relations between management and employees were good. This finding is consistent
with low levels of perceived managerial opposition to unions that were reported
above. In fact, there is a trend towards a more favourable opinion of the workplace
relations climate over time, increasing from 76 per cent in 2004 to 82 per cent in 2010.
This increase may be attributable to, *inter alia*, the changed political and legislative
environment. As we have discussed elsewhere (particularly in Chapters 1, 5 and 8),
the period of the Howard Liberal-National Coalition government was one in which
labour market deregulation was high on the political agenda, and generated much
public debate and division. The election of a Labor government in 2007 resulted in
only a partial retreat from a neo-liberal agenda in workplace relations, but the

Figure 7.6: Influence at
work and industrial
relations climate indicators
in 2004 and 2010

transition from Work Choices to the *Fair Work Act 2009* was conducted in an environment of general consensus between employer organisations and trade unions.

Conclusion

The incidence and effectiveness of different types of employee voice have attracted increasing attention in the workplace relations and human resource management literatures. The effectiveness of different voice arrangements is particularly critical in Australia, given fundamental changes that have taken place in workplace relations over the last three decades. The AWRPS research suggests that a combination of employee voice channels is most effective in predicting organisational outcomes – in particular, managerial responsiveness to employee needs, perceived job control and perceived influence over job rewards. These findings challenge common assumptions that non-union representative voice and direct voice act as substitutes for union voice, and that these voice channels are ineffective in providing a true voice for employees because they lack independence and seek to institutionalise worker cooperation (e.g. Gollan 2005; Kelly 1996b). These arguments resonate with Hyman's (1997) position that direct structures can give greater legitimacy and efficacy to the decision-making process, ensure greater organisational commitment and act as a complement to existing union structures.

In our view, the AWRPS suggest the desirability of rethinking the substitution thesis and the models that underpin employers' and employees' choice of voice arrangements, since the presence and operation of non-union representative or direct voice *per se* do not automatically translate to the replacement of union voice channels. In a practical sense, the effectiveness of employee voice in Australian workplaces appears to depend on a plurality of arrangements – that is, multiple, mutually reinforcing channels. While achieving such arrangements is likely to present challenges for employers, employees and unions, the findings do highlight the significance of labour–management interaction, and thus the value of a union–employer partnership approach predicated on mutual benefits. However, an increasing representation gap and unmet demand for union voice should be of concern for unions and human resource managers, but may in fact provide a stable foundation for the parties to work together for the achievement of mutual gains.

Discussion questions

7.1 What is the meaning and significance of the statement that 'employee voice is only one feature of the broader regulation of the employment relationship'?

7.2 Discuss why employee voice is important for employers and employees in the workplace.

7.3 What are the lessons that the Australian trade union movement should draw from the findings of the Australian Worker Representation and Participation Survey?

7.4 Provide an assessment of the extent to which employers can influence employee voice in the workplace.

7.5 Discuss the extent to which the government should intervene in workplace relations to encourage and shape employee voice in the workplace.

CASE STUDY

The power of the voice

Medicare Australia is a federal government public service agency that plays a key role in the delivery of health services to the Australian community. The agency has key relationships with the medical and pharmaceutical industries and is part of the Department of Human Services. Medicare Australia has approximately 5000 employees nationally and operates a large head office in Canberra, as well as state-based operations. Medicare Australia's operations include more than 250 shopfronts located throughout Australia and three major call centres located in Brisbane, Sydney and Melbourne. The operations team in Medicare Australia accounts for 3500 of the 5000 staff employed.

The terms and conditions of Medicare Australia's employees are governed by their workplace agreement, which traditionally has been negotiated with the Community and Public Sector Union (CPSU). While Medicare Australia estimates that a maximum of 40 per cent of its workforce are union members, it has been prepared to renegotiate solely with the CPSU every two or three years when the workplace agreement expires. The last set of negotiations for the 2007 agreement involved a number of procedural changes being introduced. Not all of these were agreed to by the CPSU; however, Medicare introduced the changes following feedback from staff located throughout Australia. This was the beginning of the 'power of voice' for Medicare Australia.

As the 2007 Medicare Certified Agreement was entering its last 12 months of operation, Medicare Australia embarked on a process to obtain feedback from staff leading into the official negotiation period. This process was commenced as a result of quite specific input from staff, many of whom were not members of the CPSU. These staff felt passionate about their terms and conditions of employment, and wanted either to 'have a say', or for Medicare Australia to also negotiate with a staff representative team, elected by employees. During the initial feedback process, Medicare Australia was keen to incorporate staff representatives in the negotiation process alongside the union. However, the organisation was also aware that the CPSU would oppose this approach. Medicare Australia was looking for ways to broaden its approach to negotiating terms and conditions of employment for staff, and saw this as one possible mechanism that would be truly reflective of their diverse needs and wishes.

The feedback from staff provided Medicare Australia with both an opportunity and a significant challenge. The incorporation of a staff representative team would enable the organisation to negotiate directly – something that some staff wanted to occur. The challenge was union membership. If the 40 per cent membership figure was correct, was it feasible to move away from a union-negotiated agreement?

From the start of the negotiation process, it was made clear to all staff members that the organisation would negotiate the new agreement with both the CPSU and the Staff Representative Team. This decision elicited negative feedback – first from the CPSU, which stated that as it was a union-negotiated agreement, a staff representative team could not be included; and second from the non-union staff members, who claimed that the CPSU did not represent their views or interests, and who as a result wanted a voice at the negotiating table.

Medicare Australia was determined to include the Staff Representative Team as a key player in the negotiation process. The CPSU indicated that it may not be prepared to negotiate with Medicare Australia if the Staff Representative Team was 'in the room at the same time'. The feedback from non-union staff was clear: they wanted a voice at the negotiating table. Medicare Australia officially informed the CPSU that negotiations would commence on the date specified and that the Staff Representative Team would be involved. It further stated that it was prepared to negotiate a non-union agreement if required, although the organisation's preference was to maintain a union agreement.

The CPSU distributed printed material to members and outside Medicare Australia worksites, stating that if the Staff Representative Team was allowed to participate in negotiations, it would enable Medicare Australia to reduce the terms and conditions of employment. During this time, there was a degree of friction amongst union members and non-union employees. While this was a minor distraction to the business operations, it provided a clear signal to Medicare Australia that a number of its employees wanted to negotiate directly with the organisation.

The new agreement was successfully negotiated with both the CPSU and the Staff Representative Team in late 2007. The introduction of the Staff Representative Team provided a benefit to both staff members and the organisation. A number of proposals submitted by the Staff Representative Team were instrumental in an agreement being reached in relation to new terms and conditions of employment. The feedback and satisfaction among staff were significantly higher than in previous years, mainly due to the fact that they truly believed their interests had been represented. The power of staff members' voice was instrumental in the introduction of a different negotiation approach – one that Medicare Australia wants to strengthen for future Certified Agreements.

Written by Brad Nash.

Case study discussion questions

1. What form of employee voice was sought at Medicare and why?
2. From the perspective of the CPSU, was the response of opposing the Staff Representative Team the best one?
3. From the perspective of management, can you envisage a better way of handling the situation that emerged in the agreement negotiations?
4. Inclusion of non-union representation is ultimately limited; how do you envisage that non-union representation could be extended within Medicare to provide ongoing voice for employees?

8

Changing patterns of workplace conflict and dispute resolution

Bernadine Van Gramberg

■ Chapter objectives

This chapter will enable readers to understand the:
- marginalisation of the national industrial tribunal as an attempt to privatise the process of settling workplace disputes
- reinvigoration of the dispute-settlement role of the national industrial tribunal
- decline in the number of strikes and the consequential changes in the patterns of industrial conflict
- evolution and nature of the unfair dismissal jurisdiction and the growth of unfair-dismissal disputes in Australia.

Introduction

Workplace conflict is an inevitable part of the pluralistic nature of organisational life. In Australia, the management of workplace conflict has been at the heart of the political agenda for workplace relations for the major parties. This chapter briefly traces the history of the regulation of workplace conflict since the beginning of the twentieth century and looks at the importance of tribunal conciliation to the settlement of workplace disputes over this time. It then describes the major changes to the system of dispute settlement since the late 1980s, particularly in relation to the differing agendas of the various political parties, employers and unions, which have acted to *decentralise* dispute resolution to the workplace. In doing so, the chapter describes the national tribunal, the Fair Work Commission (formerly Fair Work Australia), examining its relationship with the functioning of dispute-settlement clauses in enterprise agreements required by legislation and the resolution of unfair dismissal disputes, which make up the bulk of the Commission's workload. It then examines the collective and individual manifestations of workplace conflict. The chapter ends with an examination of the decline in strike numbers and concludes that overt conflict is not disappearing in Australia but it is changing to more individualised manifestations.

The development of the Australian workplace relations system

To some extent, the regulation of Australian industrial relations emerged from a strong need to manage workplace conflict rather than to regulate workplace peace. In fact, it evolved from a period of intense strike activity prior to the six colonies forming a federation in 1901. These 'Great Strikes' occurred in the mid- to late 1890s, enveloping the maritime, shearing and mining sectors across several colonies (Svensen 1995). They were triggered by the concerted efforts of employers to avoid collective bargaining and to recognise unions. The union response was quick, concerted and widespread, with hundreds of thousands of employees striking across the colonies. Employer retaliation was just as fierce, and with colonial government support, it commonly involved the deployment of armed escorts for strike breakers (often unemployed striking workers themselves) to worksites.

The ramifications of the Great Strikes were so great in terms of their cost to the developing Australian economy and disruption to society in general that the founders of the Constitution of Australia included clause 51(xxxv), mandating conciliation and arbitration of industrial disputes. Under the *Conciliation and Arbitration Act 1904*, the Commonwealth Court of Conciliation and Arbitration became the first federal body with jurisdiction to conciliate and arbitrate industrial disputes. The effect of this centralised dispute resolution system was that by 1980 wages and conditions were set by either state or federal awards for more than 90 per cent of Australian employees (Ellem & Franks 2008: 51).

During a period of increasing global economic instability and competition, in 1983 the Hawke federal Labor government commissioned a review of the operation of the industrial relations system and required recommendations as to its future direction. In 1985, the *Report of the Committee of Review into the Australian Industrial Law and Systems* (Hancock Report) was released (Hancock 1985). The Hancock Committee had considered a less centralised model of industrial relations for Australia, but concluded that it would be undesirable to move away from a model based on collective representation of employers and employees. The report applauded the centralised system for its ability to pursue Australia's macroeconomic objectives, curb inflation, avoid unemployment and observe the public interest. It maintained that deregulation of the labour market did not take into account the potential power differentials that would exist if employers and employees (through their unions) were left to bargain for wages and conditions in the workplace (Hancock 1985).

The Hancock Report met with a range of criticisms centred around the fact that its rhetoric was not persuasive (Blandy 1985: 453), that it amounted to little more than preferring the 'devil you know [to] the devil you don't' (Fane 1988: 226) and, similarly, that it made a merely 'incremental adjustment' to the industrial relations system, having generally retained the status quo (O'Brien 1994: 449). Nevertheless, it gave rise to the *Industrial Relations Act 1988*, which replaced the *Conciliation and Arbitration Act 1904* and renamed the federal tribunal the Australian Industrial Relations Commission (AIRC). But while retaining an essentially centralised system of industrial relations, for the first time it introduced mandatory workplace-level dispute-resolution procedures for all consent awards and collective agreements (Van Gramberg 2006). In other words, the *Industrial Relations Act 1988* provided an opportunity for employers and unions to negotiate a workplace agreement, and it instigated a process for workplace resolution for disputes arising from these local-level agreements. This provision heralded a future trend in encouraging dispute resolution at the level of the workplace without tribunal intervention for disputes arising under negotiated agreements, a point that will be taken up later in the chapter. This, of course, was the turning point which gave rise to the term 'workplace relations'.

As outlined above, two sets of voices had considerable influence in the subsequent transformation of Australian industrial relations. First, the right-wing HR Nicholls Society was established as a response to the findings of the Hancock review. The Society, which saw itself as honouring a little-known Tasmanian newspaper editor, Henry Richard Nicholls, who had (reportedly) publicly criticised the Conciliation and Arbitration Commission, included among its aims discussing 'the operation of industrial relations in Australia including the system of determining wages and other conditions of employment' and promoting 'reform of the current wage-fixing system' (HR Nicholls Society, 2012). The Society has been vociferous in its attack on the AIRC, the predecessor of the Fair Work Commission, across the years, calling for its removal (e.g. Moore 2004).

Second, in its policy document *Towards an Enterprise Based Industrial Relations System* (BCA 1987), the Business Council of Australia (BCA) emphasised the need to remove third parties (notably unions, but also the AIRC) and focus on the direct employee–employer relationship, a position endorsed by the unitarist ideology of the emerging human resources management (HRM) profession. The BCA outlined a vision for setting wages in each workplace, in which employers would negotiate directly with individual employees or single-enterprise unions (consisting of workers). Then, in its later report, *Enterprise Based Units: A Better Way of Working*, the BCA proposed that the pluralist industrial relations system in Australia was outmoded because of its assumption of conflict in the employment relationship:

> We need to jettison the 'industrial relations' mindset within our enterprises where it still rests on the outmoded assumption of conflict, and move to 'employee relations' in which industrial relations becomes a subsidiary part of relationships at work. (BCA 1989: 5)

The assumed consequence of jettisoning the industrial relations mindset and its central premise of the inevitability of industrial conflict was that employee relations (a more unitarist replacement) would avoid such conflict, because the focus would be more about 'relationships at work'. Further, the BCA promulgated a vision in which, by removing unions from the workplace, industrial conflict would essentially disappear, and managers and supervisors would be then be able to smooth away any local-level conflicts with workers. This argument was influential on the federal Labor Party government. In 1993, the *Industrial Relations Act 1988* was amended by the *Industrial Relations Reform Act 1993*. As described in Chapter 5, the main contribution of the *Industrial Relations Reform Act* was to introduce enterprise bargaining, which commenced the process of decentralising wage-setting to workplaces, where employers, employees and unions would make agreements that would then be certified by the AIRC, provided certain – largely procedural – conditions, were met. The implications for dispute resolution also changed, with an increased expectation that employers and employees would resolve their matters in the workplace rather than relying on the AIRC. To this end, when a workplace dispute was referred to the AIRC, the tribunal was required to check that the parties had made some effort to resolve the matter in-house in the first instance.

In 1996, the Howard Liberal-National Party Coalition government passed the *Workplace Relations Act*, which continued the evolution of workplace relations in Australia by providing for non-union contracts between employers and workers – effectively individual contracts, known as Australian Workplace Agreements (AWAs). For further discussion of this legislation, see Chapter 5. At this time, it was seen as important that the AIRC undertook conciliation rather than arbitration, and that workplaces resolved their own disputes to a greater extent. For the first time, a model (or, more correctly, a default) dispute-resolution process was included in the legislation inserted for use by to enterprise agreements (individual workplace agreements); this provided for private mediation rather than referral to the AIRC (Schedule 9, sub-regulation 30ZI (2)). An indication that the Howard government intended to broaden the involvement of private mediators was evident in its release of three reports that extolled the opportunities for these practitioners in Australian workplaces (Reith 1998, 1999a, 1999b, 2000).The legislative package completed the decentralisation process by removing the AIRC's power to undertake compulsory arbitration. The *Workplace Relations Act 1996* was later amended to include a model dispute-settlement procedure in Division 2 of Part 13 for parties to collective agreements. This model became the default mechanism when a workplace agreement did not specify any procedure for resolving dispute at the workplace (Stewart 2009).

In 2005, following an electoral victory in which the Howard government unexpectedly gained control of the Senate, the *Workplace Relations Act 1996* was overhauled by the government. The *Workplace Relations Amendment (Work Choices) Act 2005*, better known as Work Choices, was enacted. It established the Australian Fair Pay Commission as the vehicle for minimum wage rises (removing this function from the AIRC) and utilised the corporations power (s. 21) in the Australian Constitution to extend the application of individual workplace agreements to constitutional corporations, effectively overriding state legislation dealing with workplace relations for corporations. This dramatically increased the number of workplaces subject to the federal jurisdiction.

Importantly, the Work Choices regime delivered the government's vision for privatising dispute resolution by restricting parties' access to the AIRC and, at the same time, by making it easier for parties to employ a private mediator. The *Work Choices Act* limited the AIRC's ability to offer a range of dispute-resolution techniques (particularly arbitration), but did not impose the same restrictions on these private dispute-resolution providers. The Act also limited the range of disputes that could be heard by the AIRC (s. 694). The clear preference of the government for private mediators rather than the AIRC was expressed in the Explanatory Memorandum to the Work Choices amendments, which promised to:

> establish a system of registered private alternative dispute resolution (ADR) providers that will support genuine choice between the AIRC's dispute settling expertise and other dispute resolution specialists (House of Representatives 2005: 21

In practice, Work Choices made the process of submitting a dispute to the AIRC far more onerous than opting for a private provider. While this might have been a potential bonanza for law firms and private mediators, the Howard government was defeated at the 2007 election before the full implications of the privatisation of workplace dispute resolution could be realised fully.

It was not long before the changes proposed by the incoming Rudd Labor government in 2009 once again reshaped Australian workplace relations and dispute resolution through the enactment of the *Fair Work Act 2009*. The new legislative regime that took effect on 1 January 2010 came with the motto 'Forward with Fairness' as a way of flagging the intended removal of the 'harshest' aspects of Work Choices (Gillard 2008). While emphasis was still placed on resolving disputes in the workplace, the *Fair Work Act* introduced a simpler model for dispute resolution under Schedule 6.1 of the Fair Work Regulations 2009. Although less prescriptive than the *Workplace Relations Act 1996*, it nevertheless outlined the way disputes were to be handled in the workplace. In brief, the Act specifies that parties must first attempt to resolve their dispute at the workplace level before allowing either party to refer the dispute to the Fair Work Commission. Interestingly, the *Fair Work Act* continues to allow any independent third party other than the Fair Work Commission to resolve disputes (including by arbitration), subject to the parties consent (s. 740). The *Fair*

Work Act also made significant changes to unfair dismissal laws by removing most of the previous exclusions, in part delivering the new prime minister's promise to remove the harshest aspects of the previous laws. We turn now to describe the national tribunal, the Fair Work Commission, as a precursor to a discussion of its main workload: the settlement of unfair dismissals.

The national tribunal: the Fair Work Commission

The Fair Work Commission has its headquarters in Melbourne, with subsidiary offices in each of the eight states and territories of Australia. Like its predecessors, the AIRC and Fair Work Australia, its members are appointed from the fields of industrial relations, law and economics (AIRC 2009). the Fair Work Commission is a government-funded and operated national institution with a range of responsibilities relating to workplace relations, including the provision of dispute resolution through mediation, conciliation, expression of opinions or recommendations and undertaking binding arbitration (see *Fair Work Act 2009*, s. 595). However, the Act provides that the Fair Work Commission can only exercise these powers if they are outlined in the dispute-resolution procedure of the workplace or agreed upon by the parties involved. Hearings at the Fair Work Commission may be conducted by a single member sitting alone, or three or more members comprising a Full Bench.

As indicated earlier in this chapter, the focus of tribunal settlement of workplace disputes is the conciliation function. While conciliation is not defined in the *Fair Work Act*, the Fair Work Commission website describes the exercise of its jurisdiction over unfair dismissals as

> an informal, private and generally confidential process where a Fair Work Australia conciliator assists employees and employers to resolve an unfair dismissal application by agreement. The conciliator is independent and does not take sides, but works to bring the parties to an agreed resolution (Fair Work Australia 2012b).

In Australia, this type of settlement is highly successful – for example, in 2008–09, 75 per cent of unfair dismissal applications were settled by conciliation. This high rate of settlement by the tribunal was maintained at above 70 per cent over time (see Figure 8.1).

Within six months of the establishment of Fair Work Australia, the precursor to the Fair Work Commission, the rate of settlement of unfair dismissal claims in conciliation was 81 per cent (Figure 8.1). While more recent figures show that the conciliation settlement rate fell slightly in 2011 to 76 per cent (Fair Work Australia 2011), the rate is nevertheless impressive given that the number of cases coming before the tribunal had more than doubled from 17 658 lodgements in 2008/09 to 37 262 in 2010/11 (Table 8.1).

Workplace dispute resolution

As described above, all enterprise agreements must contain a dispute-settlement procedure. Section 186(6) of the *Fair Work Act* provides that in certifying an agreement, the Fair Work Commission must be satisfied that it includes a dispute-resolution

Table 8.1 AIRC/Fair Work Australia caseload between 2008 and 2011

	AIRC (2008–09)	AIRC/FWA (2009–10)	FWA (2010–11)
Lodgements	17 658	44 720	37 262
Hearings and conferences	11 526	21 770	24 178
Published documents	4 861	11 281	11 684

Source: Fair Work Australia (2011) (involving 10 367 matters).

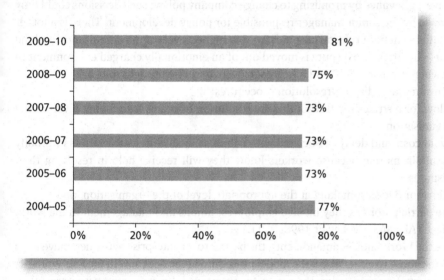

Figure 8.1: Conciliation settlement rate of termination of employment matters 2004/05 to 2009/10
Source: AIRC (2009); Fair Work Australia (2010).

procedure. The procedure may allow either the Fair Work Commission or 'another person who is independent of the employers, employees or employee organisations' to settle disputes (s. 186(6)(a)), but it must allow employees and employers to be represented (s. 186(6)(b)). That employees are able to be represented in dispute-resolution procedures both recognises the inequality of power between employers and employees and enables there to be a witness to the proceedings.

Dispute-resolution procedures generally allow for a series of stages of consultation and negotiation in the workplace. Most procedures commence with the employee who has a grievance and provide that the immediate supervisor whose responsibility it is to attempt to resolve the matter must be consulted. Many grievances are resolved at this early stage; however, if the dispute is not resolved, the dispute-resolution procedure progresses to the next stage, which requires more senior managers in the organisation to become involved and can also provide a role for unions. A well-designed procedure will provide for resolution by a third party where the parties are unable to reach agreement. Typically, this final step will provide for resolution either by an industrial tribunal or an agreed mediator.

The essence of a dispute-resolution procedure is that it is intended to provide a low-cost alternative to industrial action. For this reason, it is imperative that during the drafting stages the parties undertake to refrain from taking industrial action while a dispute is proceeding through the steps of the procedure.

The progressive nature of a dispute-resolution procedure is intended to ensure that decisions are made at the appropriate level of the organisational responsibility. This means, for example, that if a grievance arose over the start and finish time of an employee, it would not be appropriate for this to progress from line to senior management. Managers at this level would be unlikely to be privy to the relevant organisational detail to resolve such an issue, and would most likely need to seek advice from line management. Conversely, it would be impossible for a line manager to attempt to resolve a grievance by promising to change company policy; such decisions could only be made by the senior manager responsible for policy development. There is another potential benefit in referral of some issues to higher levels of the organisation and the union – in effect, the dispute is moved out of an emotionally charged environment to one where 'cooler heads' and a fresh perspective can be brought to bear.

In summary, dispute-resolution procedures:

- allow for a strike-free flow of dispute resolution from lower to higher levels in the organisation
- avoid costs and delays associated with tribunals by dealing with matters internally
- maintain morale because workers know they will receive help in resolving their disputes
- allow for decision-making at the appropriate level of the organisation, and
- are participatory as they involve employees, unions and management in the workplace (Alexander & Lewer 1998: 271).

Since the Work Choices amendments, the parties to an enterprise agreement have been able to choose to either adopt the model procedure in the Act (now in the Fair Work Act Regulations) or to develop their own for insertion into their enterprise agreement. Table 8.2 provides a schematic overview of the model dispute-resolution procedure.

The model term allows workplaces to follow three basic steps when there has been a dispute over a matter arising under the agreement or a dispute over the National Employment Standards (NES) (see Chapter 5 for a discussion of these standards). Failure to settle at the workplace may give rise to either party notifying the Fair Work Commission of the dispute to seek its intervention. Regulation 6.01(5) provides for the Fair Work Commission to intervene in two stages. First, the Fair Work Commission will use mediation, conciliation or express an opinion, or make a recommendation in order to resolve the dispute. If this fails to settle the matter, the Fair Work Commission may arbitrate and make a binding determination on the parties. The model term also compels parties to continue work as normal while the dispute is in the process of resolution, either in the workplace or at the Fair Work Commission (Regulation 6.01(6)).

In line with the shift away from collective disputes and industrial action, applications to the Fair Work Commission have increasingly arisen from individual disputes that are related mostly to dismissals. Application for relief from termination of employment constituted the highest workload of the tribunal even before the *Fair Work Act* was implemented. Taking the last year for which complete data are available 2008/09, there were 7994 claims lodged; of these, 3234 (41 per cent) alleged that

Table 8.2 Model Term for Dealing with Disputes for Enterprise Agreements

1. An employee who is a party to the dispute may appoint a representative.
....
2. The parties to the dispute must try to resolve the dispute at the workplace, by discussions between the employee or employees and relevant supervisors and/or management.
....
3. If discussions at the workplace level do not resolve the dispute, a party to the dispute may refer the matter to the Fair Work Tribunal.
....
4. The Fair Work Tribunal may use mediation, conciliation in the first instance and arbitration if necessary to resolve the matter.
....
5. Work will continue normally while the dispute-resolution process is underway.
....
6. The parties agree to be bound by a decision made by the Fair Work Tribunal.

Table 8.3 Termination of employment lodged in states and territories, 2005/06 to 2008/09

Year (1 July–30 June)	2005/06	2006/07	2007/08	2008/09	2009/10
Vic	3224	2019	2275	2638	N/A
NSW	1296	1511	1712	2428	N/A
Qld	420	737	944	1319	N/A
WA	317	394	422	762	N/A
SA	159	307	416	499	N/A
Tas	83	75	111	151	N/A
ACT	136	75	100	104	N/A
NT	123	55	87	93	N/A
Total	5758	5173	6117	7994	13 054

Source: AIRC (2006, 2007, 2008, 2009).

termination was harsh, unjust or unreasonable (unfair dismissal), 1687 (21 per cent) alleged that termination was unlawful and 3073 (38 per cent) alleged that it was both unfair and unlawful. Under the Work Choices amendments that preceded the *Fair Work Act*, there were restrictions that precluded many potential claims from being lodged. In particular, under the *Fair Work Act* the previous exclusion of unfair dismissal claims from employees from firms with 100 or fewer was removed. Hence, 4.3 million additional employees immediately had access to protection from unfair dismissal, as evidenced in a 30 per cent (5208 cases) increase in claims within the first six months following implementation of the *Fair Work Act* (DEEWR 2010). The state of Victoria recorded the highest number of cases at 2638, followed by New South Wales (2428) and Queensland (1319), with 1609 originating from other states and territories (AIRC 2009). Given the vast workload associated with claims for unfair dismissal (see Table 8.3), it is pertinent now to further examine this jurisdiction.

■ The development of the unfair dismissal jurisdiction

As noted above, disputes over claims for unfair dismissal make up the bulk of work of industrial tribunals in Australia, at both the state and federal levels. Dismissals that are harsh, unjust or unreasonable are considered to be unfair dismissals, and come under the jurisdiction of the industrial tribunals (Stewart 2011). Dismissals that are unlawful are those where employment rights (for instance, the rights under the anti-discrimination laws) have been breached or where employees have been harmed in their employment by reason of membership or non-membership of a union, and these are normally settled by the courts (see Chapter 5). This section overviews the changes in unfair dismissal laws since they became part of the federal tribunal's jurisdiction, and provides an update on the operation of the Fair Work Commission in resolving these claims.

The *Industrial Relations Act 1988* was amended in 1993 by the *Industrial Relations Reform Act*, which allowed the AIRC to conciliate unfair dismissal disputes. The legislation provided relief to employees who were dismissed without a valid reason relating to either their capacity or their conduct based on the operational require-ments of the organisation. It was the employer's duty to demonstrate there was a valid reason for the dismissal, but thereafter the employee had to demonstrate that the dismissal was harsh, unjust or unreasonable (*Industrial Relations Reform Act 1993*, s. 170EDA). Applications alleging unfair termination went to the AIRC for conciliation and could be arbitrated with the consent of the parties. Those cases not settled in conciliation or not arbitrated by consent were referred to the (then) Industrial Relations Court of Australia, which could make orders to reinstate a dismissed employee and could provide compensation either in addition to the reinstatement or instead of it (*Industrial Relations Reform Act 1993*, s. 170EE). The new jurisdiction quickly grew into a major component of the AIRC's workload and was the subject of criticism on both sides of the political divide, with many seeing it as being overly favourable to employees (Stewart 2009).

In 1996, the incoming Howard government retained the AIRC's jurisdiction over unfair dismissals but added the requirement that the tribunal implement a 'fair go all round' policy (*Workplace Relations Act 1996*, s. 170CA(2)). At the time, this was justified as an attempt to encapsulate the perspective of all parties and balance their interests in resolving disputes. In practice, however, the 'fair go all round' principle made it easier for employers to defend unfair dismissal claims (Robbins 2005). In its next term of office, the Howard government's radical *Work Choices Act 2005* went still further, removing the AIRC's power to make orders for compensation and restricting the types of employees who were eligible to lodge unfair dismissal claims by excluding those who worked in firms with fewer than 100 employees, employees dismissed for genuine operational reasons, those who had not completed a six-month qualifying period and seasonal employees. These amendments were justified partly on the grounds that if the potential for unfair dismissal claims was reduced there would be a large positive impact on job creation. But the harshness of the unfair dismissal provisions in the *Work Choices Act* resulted in criticisms that the government had breached ILO Convention 150 on Termination of Employment at the Initiative of the Employer 1982. The defeat of the Howard government in 2007 meant that the full impact of its unfair dismissal provisions could not be evaluated against claims that it would create greater overall employment.

As explained above, the passage of the *Fair Work Act* restored unfair dismissal provisions to many types of employees, emphasising reinstatement as the primary remedy, with compensation to be awarded only where reinstatement was not in the best interests of the employee or the employer's business. There are still some exclusions regarding access to the unfair dismissal provisions. For instance, Part 3(2) of the *Fair Work Act* specifies that employees from small businesses (fewer than 15 employees) can only make an unfair dismissal claim after a 12-month minimum employment period, while employees of larger businesses can bring an unfair dismissal claim after six months' employment. Those employees not covered by an award or agreement cannot bring a claim if their remuneration is more than the prescribed ceiling of $113 800. Other categories of employee who cannot use the provisions are those dismissed due to 'genuine redundancy', those employed on specified-term and specified-task contracts, trainees (where their employment ends on completion of the training agreement) and casual employees who do not meet the requisite minimum employment periods.

Specifically, there are several criteria under Chapter 3 of the *Fair Work Act* that need to be met to establish unfair dismissal. First, the dismissal must be harsh, unjust or unreasonable. Second, the dismissal must not be a case of genuine redundancy; and third, if the worker was employed by a small firm, the dismissal must have been consistent with the Small Business Fair Dismissal Code, which apples to those firms with fewer than 15 employees (s. 385). Next, the tribunal must decide whether there was a valid reason for the termination and must take into account a range of provisions under section 387, such as whether the person was notified of that reason, whether the person was given an opportunity to respond to any reason related to their capacity or conduct, whether the person was refused a support person to assist with discussions relating to dismissal and whether there was a warning if the dismissal related to unsatisfactory performance.

The *Fair Work Act* also contains provisions in section 385 pertaining to the capacity of the employer, such as the degree to which the size of the firm would impact on the ability of the employer to follow procedures in effecting the dismissal, the degree to which the absence of dedicated HRM specialists or expertise in the enterprise would be likely to impact on the procedures followed in effecting the dismissal and any other matters that the Fair Work Commission considers relevant. This provision represents some continuity with the previous 'fair go all round' policy, which also took into consideration the capacity and resources of employers in the process.

The method used by the Fair Work Commission to resolve unfair dismissal disputes is to hold a private conference with a conciliator, either by phone or on site at the workplace, both of which provide a more informal setting for dispute resolution

(*Fair Work Act 2009*, s. 625). These conciliators are not members of the Fair Work Commission, but are employed as public servants under the Act. If the conference fails to settle the matter, the parties may refer their dispute to the Fair Work Commission. A recent evaluation of the work of the conciliators revealed that over 90 per cent of the conciliations were held by telephone and more than 80 per cent of cases settled in this way (Weame et al. 2010).

Once it receives a referral for an unfair dismissal dispute, the Fair Work Commission has the opportunity to consider whether a hearing is the 'most effective and efficient way to resolve the matter' (*Fair Work Act 2009*, s. 399), which means that the matter may not be heard at all. Alternatively, the tribunal may decide the matter on the documents lodged in the absence of a hearing (ss. 396–7). Should a hearing take place, the Fair Work Commission is not bound by the rules of evidence and procedure (s. 591), which is another provision to help ensure the dispute-resolution process is less formal and more expeditious than a curial setting.

◼ Workplace conflict and its manifestations

The discussion so far in this chapter has centred on the fact that workplace conflict has driven changes to Australian workplace relations laws over the last three decades. Conflict and particularly strikes have been linked with pluralism, the ideology behind traditional, collective industrial relations (Fox 1974). As Abbott (2007: 62) notes, 'industrial relations are based on the assumption that there is an ever-present potential for conflict between competing workplace groups, and therefore rules and institutions for its regulation are necessary'. More recently, we have seen that changes to workplace relations have focused on decentralising employment regulation to the level of individual employees and their employers. This 'relationship'-centred focus brings with it the more unitarist assumption that individualism is preferred to collective relationships (particularly those involving unions), and is less likely to result in conflict (Fox 1974). The assumption that the removal of unions will lessen the occurrence of conflict can be tested by considering how patterns of industrial conflict in Australia have changed since decentralisation of the industrial relations system. Before moving to this discussion, it is pertinent to consider how workplace conflict is most commonly manifested.

Workplace conflict can be described as either manifested by collectives of workers or by individuals. Examples of collective conflict include industrial campaigns such as strikes, bans on performing certain duties and stop-work meetings. These collective manifestations are associated with groups of employees and often with union involvement. Of necessity, these activities are also highly organised. They require planning and employee support; in Australia, such activities are regulated under law. We consider the classification of legal and illegal industrial action later in the chapter, but for more detail see Chapter 5. This kind of overt conflict can also happen at an individual level, perhaps when an employee with a grievance lodges a claim with a supervisor or a tribunal because of a perceived injustice which has been done to them. The level of overt collective industrial action including strikes has been falling steadily in Australia and in other developed nations. This might appear to vindicate that those promoting a decentralised workplace relations framework. However, the absence of strikes does not mean an absence of conflict. It may simply mean that this particular manifestation of overt conflict has been suppressed or is not an available option, and that employees become limited in how they express their dissatisfaction or their sense of injustice. Given that the level of individual overt action in the form of claims to tribunals and courts has been rising, this represents a key shift from overt collective industrial action in Australia. We explore this as part of a discussion of declining strike activity in the following section.

■ Is workplace conflict disappearing in Australia?

The Australian Bureau of Statistics (ABS 2011d) documents a range of overt forms of industrial action, including 'unauthorised stop-work meetings; general strikes; sympathetic strikes (e.g. strikes in support of a group of workers already on strike); political or protest strikes; rotating or revolving strikes (i.e. strikes that occur when workers at different locations take turns to stop work); unofficial strikes; and work stoppages initiated by employers (e.g. lockouts)'. Such industrial action is officially recorded if the number of days lost reaches ten in a particular firm. Equally, industrial action is recorded if ten employees from a particular firm stop work for one day. This calculation is in accordance with the international guidelines adopted by the 1993 International Conference of Labour Statisticians. Figure 8.2 shows the dramatic decline of industrial action in Australia between 1969 and 2011.

As indicated earlier, it is tempting to conclude that the decline of strikes in Australian workplaces over the last two decades marks the end of workplace conflict. However, there is abundant evidence suggesting the existence of widespread but less visible conflict in the form of individual and small-group disputes. This phenomenon is not confined to Australia; rather, it seems to be an international trend with Bingham (2003) finding a decline in collective disputes in the United States but a concurrent rise in individual conflicts. Walker and Hamilton (2011: 40) have observed similar trends in the United Kingdom, where individual employees have filed claims and lawsuits with greater frequency than in the past, leading them to conclude that 'individual disputes may now be the most relevant indicator of conflict'. Also in the United Kingdom, Goddard (2011: 283) recently asked: 'If conflict is fundamental to the employment relation, has it simply been diverted into alternative, these less organised and less overt forms since the 1970s?'

In Australia, these less organised forms of conflict include bullying, interpersonal and individual grievances submitted to industrial or equal opportunity tribunals, workers' compensation claims (including stress-related claims), absenteeism and labour turnover. There is ample evidence for the growth of these types of workplace conflict. For instance, the number of complaints to the Australian Human Rights

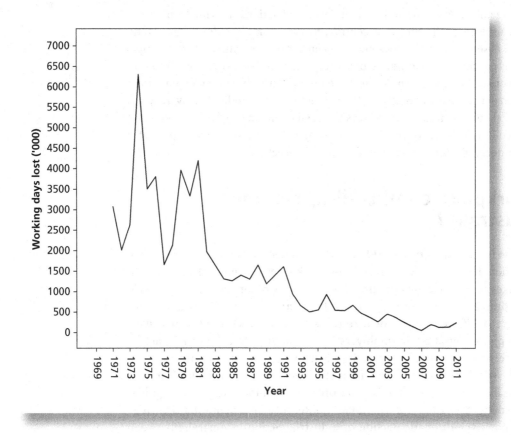

Figure 8.2: Industrial
disputes and days lost in
Australia over time
Source: ABS (2011d).

Commission (AHRC) and its predecessor, the Australian Human Rights and Equal
Opportunity Commission (HREOC) rose by 80 per cent to 2517 between 2006 and
2010, and most of these disputes were from workplaces. Employment-related complaints constituted 88 per cent of all complaints under the *Sex Discrimination Act
1984*, 65 per cent of complaints under the *Age Discrimination Act 2004*, 44 per cent of
complaints under the *Racial Discrimination Act 1975* and 36 per cent of complaints
under the *Disability Discrimination Act 1992* (AHRC 2010: 39). A year later, the AHRC
(2011) again reported that employment-related issues led the complaints under the
discrimination Acts: 88 per cent of all complaints under the *Sex Discrimination Act*, 66
per cent of complaints under the *Age Discrimination Act*, 35 per cent of complaints
under the *Racial Discrimination Act* and 31 per cent of complaints under the *Disability
Discrimination Act*.

A more telling picture of the level of dysfunction in workplaces is shown by the rise
of informal inquiries to the AHRC (particularly in relation to workplace bullying,
unfair dismissal, sexual harassment and discrimination on the basis of race and
disability), which grew to 19 968 in 2010, up 76 per cent over the previous five
years. Informal inquiries are made by employees seeking advice and information,

often at an early stage of their conflict, and may herald future claims. At the same time, the AIRC reported an increase in disputes referred from failed workplace dispute-settling procedures from 851 in 2004/05 to 1243 in 2009 (AIRC 2009). While notifications of unresolved workplace disputes fell back to 810 in 2011, the number of notifications of collective disputes related to enterprise agreements grew from 245 in 2006/07 to 1748 in 2010/11 (Fair Work Australia 2011). We have already seen that unfair dismissal claims make up the greatest part of the workload of the Fair Work Commission, and this figure is growing. More generally, these figures indicate an increasing inability of workplace parties to resolve their conflicts without the assistance of the federal tribunal. Clearly, while strikes have subsided, workplace conflict in Australia has not.

The cost to workplaces and the economy from this type of individual and group conflict is high. The Productivity Commission (2010: 287) reports that the annual costs to the economy could be as much as $36 billion. The costs include the emotional strains on individuals, their families, communities and society, as well as their related costs on businesses. For example, Fox and Stallworth (2008) note that workplace bullying alone results in loss of productivity, a rise in the number of accidents, diminished corporate reputation, high turnover, absenteeism, strained loyalty, distrust, sabotage, resentment, uncivil climate, decreased communication and potential escalations to workplace aggression or violence, as well as the direct costs of legal liability and higher workers' compensation. Much of the damage to workplaces is caused by the adverse behaviours of those who feel aggrieved (Goldman et al. 2008). Disputes impact not only on employers but also on the health of workers (Kieseker & Marchant 1999). Increasingly, it is being recognised that illnesses may be induced or exacerbated by workplace conflict.

We cannot conclude that workplace conflict is disappearing. Given the general assumption that union membership is related to workplace conflict, the presence of unions in workplaces and their relationship to the manifestations of conflict also require some exploration.

■ The role of unions in workplace conflict

Australia has one of the most comprehensive regulation and reporting regimes for trade unions in the world. Employee organisations (and employer associations) must be registered in accordance with the *Fair Work (Registered Organisations) Act 2009* (ROA). Under the *Registered Organisations Act*, trade unions have a range of rights and responsibilities in relation to their members' industrial interests. Unions have the right to enter business premises to investigate suspected breaches of the *Fair Work Act 2009* – that is, awards or enterprise agreements that relate to affected employees. The national union confederation, the ACTU, plays key roles in national wage cases (for those employed on the minimum award system) and test cases in labour law before the courts, and deals with inter-union disputes. The nature of the ACTU and its activities are considered in Chapter 2.

Australian federal law provides limited legal opportunities for unions to strike, as they are restricted to periods of time when a contract is being negotiated, and then only with the permission of the Fair Work Commission. Virtually all industrial action undertaken outside of that regime may be subject to some form of legal sanction arising either at common law (breach of contract or economic torts) or under certain statutes (e.g. secondary boycott provisions in the *Trade Practices Act 1974* and sanctions under state and federal industrial legislation). Strikes in essential services, such as law enforcement, air-traffic control and sanitation are heavily regulated by federal and state laws.

Trade union membership in Australia peaked at about 61 per cent in 1954 and, while it remained steady over a number of years, it has been declining steadily since the mid-1970s (Ellem & Franks 2008: 46; see also Chapter 3 for a fuller discussion). More recently, it fell from 20 per cent in August 2009 to 18 per cent in August 2010, representing a decrease of 47 300 employees in just 12 months. Figure 8.3 shows

Figure 8.3: Proportion of trade union membership in main job by industry
Source: ABS (2012d).

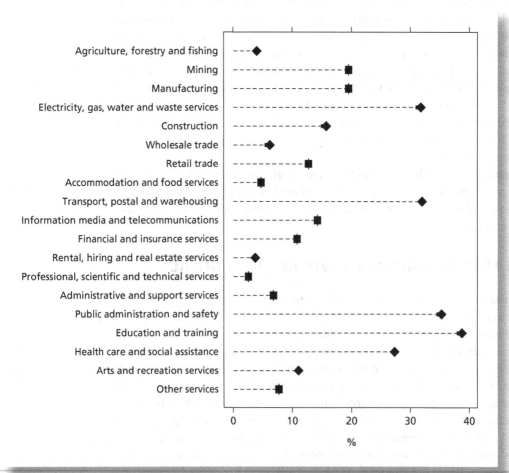

the current levels of union membership by industry in Australia. The ABS (2012) reports that membership is still relatively high in the utilities, transport, public administration, health care and education. It is lowest in agriculture, wholesale trade, the hospitality industry, real estate services, professional services and administrative support services.

There is speculation that the decline of union membership is associated with the decline of industrial action (including strikes) in Australia. This is true to the extent that industrial action requires organisation, planning and consultation, and traditionally unions have provided this to their members. Unions are also registered for the purpose of representing their members in industrial tribunals, so these disputes have an avenue via which they can be resolved. Laws pertaining to strikes envisage that unions are the entities that submit the relevant documentation to the tribunals so the matters can be heard. In the absence of unions in most industries, there are now few mechanisms for strikes or other types of collective action to proceed legally. Therefore, it is not surprising that strikes have decreased in an environment of declining union membership. However, while the decline of unions is likely to have contributed to the decline of collective industrial action, as is evident from the discussion above, it has not led to the demise of workplace conflict. With or without unions, employees still experience injustice and unfairness at work. In the absence of an appropriate union, these employees have lost one avenue for dealing with their disputes, either individually or collectively; instead, a range of other avenues have opened up for them to have their disputes resolved, including claims under discrimination laws, occupational health and safety regulations and workers' compensation rules.

Conclusion

The Australian workplace relations system was born out of a period of intense and often violent strikes, which were harmful to both society and the developing economy. The fact that the Great Strikes spread rapidly across the various Australian colonies led to the insertion into the Australian Constitution of a clause providing for compulsory conciliation and arbitration for disputes that crossed the border of any one state (s. 51(xxxv)). The ensuing *Conciliation and Arbitration Act 1904* established the federal tribunal and provided a registration and regulation process for unions that, over time, has increasingly restricted unions' ability to take industrial action such as strikes. Unions themselves have decreased in both number and membership, driven by a combination of political and unitarist managerial ideologies that have variously portrayed them as unwelcome intruders into the employment relationship and the harbingers of workplace conflict. At the same time, workplace legislation in Australia has gradually decentralised dispute resolution from its traditional focus on the federal tribunal to workplaces. Enterprise agreements must contain a procedure for settling workplace disputes, and while these may provide for the tribunal or another third party to assist in dispute settlement, employers and employees must attempt to settle matters themselves in the first instance. While many disputes are now settled in workplaces, there has been a growing caseload of unfair-dismissal disputes lodged with the Fair Work Commission (formerly Fair Work Australia) and its predecessor, the Australian Industrial Relations Commission. At the same time, strikes have almost disappeared in Australia. With the increasing demise of unions in the Australian workplace, it has become too easy to attribute the decline of strikes to either the removal of union influence or the success of the unitarist model of workplace relations. Rather, the rise of individual disputes in the form of increasing court and tribunal cases for unfair or unlawful dismissal, harassment, bullying, workplace stress and so forth demonstrates that workplace conflict remains a significant part of the employment relationship.

Discussion questions

8.1 It has been said that regulation of Australia's workplace relations system emerged as an attempt to regulate workplace conflict rather than to maintain workplace peace. Do you agree? Explain.

8.2 If workplace conflict is inevitable, what are the roles of governments, employers and unions in its management?

8.3 There has been ongoing debate in Australia over whether the federal industrial tribunal (now the Fair Work Commission) should have the power to arbitrate a workplace dispute. What are the advantages and disadvantages of such a power?

8.4 Resolving unfair dismissal disputes continues to form the bulk of the Fair Work Commission's workload. What do you believe are the key factors contributing to this?

8.5 The decline of strikes in Australia has coincided with the increase of individual disputes such as harassment and bullying. This pattern has emerged from the interplay of a number of interrelated factors. Explain, considering the role of governments, employers and unions in Australia.

Monitoring and surveillance in the employment relationship: the new frontier

Peter Holland and Anne O'Rourke

■ Chapter objectives

This chapter will enable readers to understand the:
- concept of workplace monitoring and surveillance and its growth and development
- ways in which monitoring and surveillance are challenging traditional conceptions of the employment relationship
- important policy and workplace regulation issues associated with monitoring surveillance
- invasive nature of monitoring and surveillance in the workplace
- paradox associated with monitoring and surveillance in the workplace, particularly in relation to the role of human resources managers.

Introduction

The impact of the neo-liberal agenda, the shift in distribution of employment to the service sector, the growth in casual, temporary and contract employment and a decline in union membership have combined to create a context in which employees' ability to resist managerial control has been reduced. In this situation of weakened resistance, the availability of new information technologies for the monitoring and surveillance of employee performance has enhanced the type, depth and intensity of management supervision. However, like any new technology, the impact of information technology is mediated by the social context and power relationships within which it is introduced.

The range and types of management monitoring vary considerably, from the detailed control of the interactions of call centre staff with customers and GPS tracking of employee movements to the checking of employee emails and internet access. The former is similar to the scientific management methods of work measurement adopted in factories in the first half of the twentieth century, whereas the latter relates to what is appropriate activity during working hours. Visual surveillance of employees with digital cameras during working hours and employer monitoring of social networking sites have also added to the managerial repertoire for controlling employees. This latter group of activities needs to be distinguished from the more traditional issues of work process control, since such surveillance techniques raise civil liberties issues with respect to privacy and the person. Similar concerns about civil liberties are raised by employer use of advances in medical testing, which have also made it possible for employees to be tested for drug use and for genetic propensity to particular types of illness.

This chapter examines the nature and the implications of the uptake of new technologies for monitoring and surveillance, and assesses their impact on the employment relationship. It also explores the arguments for monitoring and surveillance, the types of monitoring and surveillance that are now available and the paradoxes and problems of this monitoring in the contemporary workplace. To help frame these issues and the current debate, we also examine the emerging case law to provide an insight into the development and interpretation of monitoring and surveillance in the workplace.

Monitoring, surveillance and the employment relationship

> Everyday employees work under the unblinking gaze of video cameras (both hidden and overt), [urinate] into cups in order to get or keep a job, swipe a card or wear a badge to create a trail of movements, and/or drive a vehicle equipped with a Global Positioning System that closely monitors their out-of-office behaviour. (Lane 2003: ix)

As this statement illustrates, the level, depth and intensity of monitoring and surveillance that can be undertaken in the workplace are immense. Equally, it demonstrates the rapid pace of technological advances. Since this statement was made less than a decade ago, micro-chipping and genetic testing of employees, while not commonplace, have become the latest trends extending the boundaries of monitoring, surveillance and privacy, both inside and outside the workplace. Moreover, this is happening at a time when trade unions – a major purpose of which is countering management power and control – are in decline in most advanced market economies. Adding to these developments, the twenty-first century has seen the emergence of social networking sites, which have the potential to provide further information to employers and to disrupt the boundaries between professional and private life as never before. All these changes are progressing at a rate often far in advance of the adaptive capacity of employment laws, and the institutions and practices of workplace relations.

Furthermore, advances in information technology, combined with diminished costs, have created a significant shift in the availability of monitoring and surveillance systems and strategies. Issues such as drug testing, for example, were once seen as applicable to critical incident professions only (such as pilots), or were associated with large organisations that had the resources to undertake such operations. However, drug testing is now feasible for most organisations. In addition, the movement of work into cyberspace has created a new dimension in terms of monitoring employees' time usage and website visits. Even issues such as genetic testing of employees and tagging through radio frequency identity devices (RFIDs) and global positioning systems (GPS) are now within the reach of most organisations.

The issues and debates traverse a range of theoretical perspectives within workplace relations, including the areas of ethics and privacy, and consequently create new challenges for the employment relationship. In turn, it is necessary for management, employees and their representatives to understand the impact of such changes. Employers in particular need to consider the value of engaging in monitoring and surveillance – not only intangible cost-benefits, but also intangible aspects such as trust within the employment relationship. An undermining of trust and morale can have an injurious effect on the ongoing employment relationship and the profitability of the organisation. This is particularly important in an era when employers readily increase monitoring and surveillance simply because they can (Wallace 2004). The managerial desire to monitor needs to be weighed against issues of trust, respect for employee privacy and autonomy, increasing skill shortages and a 'war for talent', as well as the psychological contract that increasingly is indicating that a workforce which is not content with the work environment will leave. However, employees in casual, temporary or contract employment, with little bargaining power in their employment relationship, may accept such monitoring and surveillance as the price they have to pay for having access to work. Further, in the call centre industry, where some employers have adopted a 'burn and churn' human resources strategy, issues of trust are not paramount (Russell 2009).

The complex issues and the debates that surround the implementation of these processes need to be more fully understood, if for no other reason than the challenge they pose to the 'bedrock' of good workplace relations.

Why monitoring and surveillance?

Employers have several grounds upon which to argue for, and undertake, monitoring and surveillance of the workforce. The first is that, in many cases, employees represent the organisation and so the organisation is liable for their actions. These actions may include defamation, harassment, inappropriate comments or bullying of other employees. Certainly, the initial use of email was often perceived as a private communication channel sent in an 'electronic' envelope, resulting in employees often being more candid or casual in their communications due to their misconception of the lack of permanency of the email on the system.

The second reason for monitoring and surveillance of employees is concern about productivity. The internet, more than any other tool in the workplace, opens employees to the world – indeed, many would find it difficult to work without the support of the internet. However, the opportunities to be distracted by social networks and other non-work-related use of the internet reduce productivity, and 'cyberslacking' (as it has become known) is a growing issue in many organisations.

The third key element of monitoring and surveillance is security and legal concerns. The volume of critical data stored and moved within organisations, and the speed at which information can be transferred electronically, can leave organisations vulnerable to sabotage as disgruntled employees leak sensitive information.

Finally, the issue of legal compliance is an important aspect of this new world of work. Increasingly, organisations are developing e-management retention policies to ensure protection against potential litigation issues, as so much communication now takes place in a cyberspace. While this is a more passive approach to monitoring and surveillance, it does require the organisation to actively monitor e-communications across a range of areas. From this perspective, it can be argued that the employer is acting in a responsible manner by increasing its monitoring and surveillance of the workforce. However, like the employment relationship, there are two sides to this issue, and how employers use and develop their monitoring and surveillance policies and practices can be seen as a reflection of their attitudes to the employment relationship.

Types of electronic monitoring and surveillance

Email

Email has become ubiquitous in the workplace as a quick and simple way of passing on organisational information, both internally and externally. In this global workplace, it allows work to be transmitted over large distances, quickly and cheaply. However, along with the many advantages there are also dangers, based primarily on the misconception that emails are private and easily removed by the 'click of a button' by both the sender and receiver. The problem for users of email is that, despite this widely held assumption that emails are private, most Australian case law starts from the presumption that the employer is entitled to monitor email use within the organisation. The following cases illustrate the approach of the court and tribunal to email use in the workplace.

In *Australian Services Union v Ansett*, an employee was dismissed from employment on the basis that she had distributed a bulletin of the Australian Municipal, Administrative, Clerical and Services Union (ASU) relating to the enterprise bargaining agreement to ASU members using Ansett's internal email system. Ansett argued that the distribution of the bulletin through the internal email system constituted misconduct, breaching the terms of the employment agreement and entitling them to terminate her employment. The Federal Court of Australia found that the union delegate should not have been dismissed because dissemination of union material via the email system did not breach Ansett's email or IT policy. Ansett's email policy stated that use must be 'for the purpose of performing authorised lawful business activities'. Justice Merkel said that, as Ansett had entered into an agreement with the union to have a Joint Work Group to discuss employment issues, it was important to communicate the outcomes of meetings to the employees. While the court found that the use of the email system to distribute the union bulletin was implied within the policy, Justice Merkel added the qualification that this did not constitute a general authorisation for distribution of union material via email. Rather, union communication may be regarded as authorised if it relates to a process established by the employer as an integral part of negotiating and implementing workplace change.

In *Willmott v Bank of Western Australia Ltd*, the employer detected sexually explicit cartoon images on the email system during routine monitoring of its computer system. Upon investigation, Willmott admitted to storing the images on his work computer but denied they were pornographic. He was subsequently dismissed for breach of the employer's email policy. However, on appeal, the Western Australian Industrial Commission found that the employee had breached the company's internet/email policy, but the breach was trivial and did not warrant termination of employment. The Commission described the emails in question as dirty jokes of the kind found in a secondary-school playground or in the possession of undergraduates. In reaching its decision, the Commission also considered the employer's failure to explain to employees what constituted inappropriate or offensive material.

More recently, in *Griffiths v Rose*, the Federal Court upheld the dismissal of a public servant who accessed pornographic material from home using an employer-provided computer which, unknown to him, was loaded with 'desktop logging software'. This conduct was found to have breached the employer policy – in this case, the Australian Public Service Code of Conduct. This was followed by another case, *Batterham and Others v Dairy Farmers Ltd*, where 15 employees were dismissed for receiving and sending inappropriate material, including pornography, through the company email system. Seven employees challenged their dismissals, denying that they had sent inappropriate material, and challenged a distinction that the employer had made between hard- and soft-core pornography. However, the federal tribunal, Fair Work

Australia (now the Fair Work Commission), rejected their denials, commenting that in 2006 the company had dismissed three workers for similar offences. Subsequently, the company had instituted a series of training sessions, developed an email policy and required all employees to sign an agreement stating that they understood and would comply with the policy. The email policy provided that email could only be used for business purposes and could not be used in an inappropriate manner, which included the transmission of pornographic, sexually explicit or otherwise offensive material. The tribunal said that the employer had explained in 'clear and unequivocal' terms how the email system was to be used; however, the employees had 'blissfully ignored the risk they were taking'.

■ Internet

The internet also provides an extensive 'window on the world', and information at the touch of a button; however, it has the potential to be the greatest cause of productivity losses in the modern workplace. From pornography to gambling, through to seeking a new job, the online environment provides the capacity for employees to cyberslack. As well as exposing the organisation to reduced productivity, it can also open the organisation to costly electronic viruses.

The majority of legal cases involving internet use concern downloading pornography and other offensive material. These cases – usually involving termination of employment – frequently overlap with cases involving misuse of the email system, as the latter often involves the transmission and dissemination of material downloaded from the internet. For example, in *Queensland Rail v M Wake*, the Full Bench of the Australian Industrial Relations Commission (AIRC) overturned an earlier decision by a single commissioner reinstating an employee who was summarily dismissed by Queensland Rail for breach of its internet and email policy. The employee had used the system to download and disseminate pornographic material over a number of years. The conduct by the employee included saving images on his computer and creating a shortcut from his desktop to the images. The images had also been transmitted through the employer's internet system. Queensland Rail had instituted a policy titled 'Appropriate Use of Electronic Communications System Specification', which explained the meaning of 'appropriate use'. The policy also stated that a breach would result in termination of employment. The policy was reinforced by a Code of Conduct, and Queensland Rail had undertaken appropriate training and education to ensure that employees understood the requirements of the policy. The Full Bench found that Queensland Rail was entitled to dismiss Wake, due to the comprehensive steps it had taken to implement its policy and to ensure that employees were aware of the policy and understood the implications of a breach.

A more complex example is provided by *Christos v Curtin University of Technology*. Christos, who was employed as a Senior Lecturer at Curtin University, was dismissed from his employment on the ground of serious misconduct in relation to breaches of the university's Information and Communication Technology (ICT) policy. The alleged breaches included:

- allowing a computer belonging to the university to be used inappropriately and in violation of the university's principles, policies and procedures
- permitting a minor (the employee's son) to access offensive and pornographic material from the internet
- allowing a minor to breach the *Copyright Act 1968* by downloading or otherwise copying files, CDs or DVDs to the computer
- allowing offensive and pornographic material to be stored on the computer
- allowing MP3 files to be stored on the computer, and
- creating and allowing a document identifying a large number of pornographic and offensive websites to be stored on the computer.

The employee challenged all these allegations, although he acknowledged that he did allow some MP3 files to be stored on his computer, he claimed to be unaware that this was a breach of the policy. Under the university's ICT policy, any university-owned machine, whether utilised in the workplace or at home, must only be used for work-related purposes, and then only by the person authorised to use the computer. The evidence showed that one of the employee's sons had transferred the pornography to the computer, and it was conceded that Wake gave his son ready access to the computer when he was not using it. In addition, a document named 'meme.text' containing some 500 pornographic web references was also found on the computer, which the employee claimed was research for a book on the relationship between sex and words. This text was stored on a disk which the employee had asked his son to download on the computer. While the Commission stated that there was no evidence to suggest that the son had viewed the contents of the file, they said that allowing the son access to the file was improper and constituted a major breach of the university's policy. The Commission found that the employee had breached the university's policy in allowing the computer to be used for non-work-related activities without written authorisation; that the employee had breached the policy in allowing his son access to the computer; that he had breached the policy in allowing his son to copy music files or music copied from CDs to be stored on the computer; and that allowing the meme. text file to be stored on the computer and giving his son access to the file constituted a major breach of the university's policy. As a result, the Commission found that the termination of employment for misconduct was valid.

Although a significant proportion of the cases concerning termination of employment for misuse of the email or internet system involve downloading pornographic or offensive material, in one case just attempting to access the internet was sufficient to terminate employment. In *Owusu-Ansah v Danoz Direct Pty Ltd*, an employee had attempted to access the internet after being directed not to do so. He tried to access Yahoo but was limited to the first page. He argued that he had not actually 'surfed' the net, as he was blocked from doing so. Fair Work Australia found that his dismissal for misconduct was valid, as it was irrelevant that he could go no further than the first page; the point was that he should not have attempted to access the internet at all.

A number of conclusions can be drawn from these cases. First, email usage must be confined to business purposes. Second, courts and tribunals place significant importance on the existence of workplace policies or codes of conduct in relation to email and internet usage. Such policies and codes set the parameters for employees, and make it easy to establish employee breaches of workplace codes concerning appropriate and responsible use of employer computer systems. Third, the courts do not make a distinction between the workplace of the employer or the employee's private space. For example, in *Griffiths v Rose*, the AIRC took as axiomatic the blurring of public and private space; accessing the employer's information technology system from home transferred Mr Griffiths into the public space governed by the employer. Likewise, in *Kenny v Epic Energy*, an employee was dismissed after he had accessed pornographic sites on six occasions over a period of seven months from his home computer using the company's account. The fact that an employee was utilising the computer at home was not a defence to a breach of the employer's policy.

■ *Social networking*

The phenomenon of social networking through sites such as Facebook, MySpace and professional sites like LinkedIn have become major aspects of e-communication in recent years. From a workplace relations perspective, the consequences of these new tools are being experienced in a wide range of workplace and organisational issues, from productivity to the damage of organisational reputation where employees make inappropriate comments about their employer. Issues of privacy and security have also been raised in connection with social networking sites.

There is a limited amount of evidence that demonstrates employer concerns over internet usage. In the United Kingdom, a survey of 226 senior human resource practitioners found that human resources managers' major concerns with social networking were time-wasting, loss of productivity, security issues and inappropriate activities (Woolnough 2008). These concerns were accentuated by a lack of social media and e-communication policies. The *Social Networking Regulation Pulse Survey* of 10 000 employees, reported by the US-based Institute for Corporate Productivity, found that the leading issue for organisations with social networking was the leaking of confidential information (HRFocus 2009). This is illustrated by a case against a former Hay Recruitment consultant, who transferred confidential information to his LinkedIn site. In this British case, the court ordered the previous employee of Hay to disclosure documents relating to business contacts and addresses he had uploaded on to the professional networking site during his employment with Hay. It is notable in the judgment there was no mention of Hay having a relevant internet use policy. The case highlights growing employer concern about the strength of confidentiality agreements, and also their policies on the use of social networking websites at work (Davies 2011).

Other cases emerging around social networking issues include the example of an employee of the UK retail chain Argos, who was terminated following misconduct involving comments on Facebook. Another case involved the sacking of a Virgin Airlines cabin crew member for posting critical comments about customers and the organisation's safety standards (Garnham 2009), while in a third case the British Transport Police (BTP) gave a written warning to a senior staff member who had posted explicit details of his sex life and photos (in uniform) on his Facebook page. This episode also forced BTP to update its policies regarding social networking (Woolnough 2008).

A key point arising from this discussion is the manner in which organisations deal with these issues, which are communications external to the worksites and not on workplace systems. Employees' off-duty and private social networking activities about their personal and professional life are increasingly becoming areas for conflict. This is also an area of increasing concern from a recruitment perspective as employers increasingly search social networking sites to undertake background checks on potential employees.

This escalating use of online information highlights the increasing blur between professional and private lives. As many commentators have argued, employers need to consider the implications of social data mining (or backgrounding) and utilisation of online information, as it may give rise to legal actions for discrimination. This is particularly the case if these sites include aspects of the candidate's political or sexual orientation, ethnicity and personal interests. This reinforces the perception that privacy concerns with regard to social networking sites are not well understood by either employers or employees. For example, in Australia there have been a number of cases involving employers checking employees' Facebook sites, which have resulted in disciplinary action or termination of employment. One case involved a prison officer who faced disciplinary action after making comments on Facebook about his employer. In a second case, a corporate bank employee was dismissed for using the word 'recession' in a Facebook profile. In a third, a teacher was disciplined over comments she made about being bullied (Moses 2009). These cases illustrate the complex nature of the new technologies and the problematic character of managing social networking spaces that blur the traditional boundary between private and professional life. Case law in this area is still in its infancy. However, with the ever-increasing use of social networking sites, regulation – whether through workplace policy, codes of conduct or the inclusion of clauses pertaining to internet use in employment contracts – is likely to increase, leading to further legal challenges and the development of case law.

■ RFIDs/GPS devices and chipping

Radio Frequency Identification Devices (RFIDs) are a good example of technological functional creep. Functional creep occurs where the introduction of a piece of technology – in this case, for tracking freight – leads to other uses such as employee tracking. The creation of this new technology continues to extend the boundaries of the workplace, further increasing the capacity of the employer to monitor the activities of the employee.

As noted, RFIDs and Global Positioning Systems (GPS) devices initially were developed as a way of tracking freight. However, these can just as easily be used for the tracking of the people who are transporting this freight. These devices can show the length of journey and stops taken during that journey. This enables highly sophisticated tracking of drivers in the field away from supervisors. This has recently been taken to a new level with the micro-chipping of staff on the grounds of security. An example of this development is provided by a US organisation that requires staff working in the high-security areas of the organisation to have a micro-chip implanted. Somewhat paradoxically, while security is cited as the foremost reason for this micro-chipping, security researchers have remarked on the ease with which such micro-chips can be skimmed and cloned by a hacker (Libbenga 2006). Once this is taken into account, this issue of the level of monitoring and surveillance of the individual can be seen as significantly more intrusive and invasive than traditional forms of workplace supervision and surveillance. For example, at the Star City Casino in Sydney, uniforms had RFIDs implanted in them, and when workers challenged this, management gave the reason that there had been a number of thefts of uniforms and that the purpose was not to track the movements of employees. However, bearing in mind the cost of the uniforms, the number stolen and that the uniforms had little commercial value, this use of implanted chips seemed to be a disproportionate response. However, the employees' union (the Liquor, Hospitality and Miscellaneous Union) eventually accepted this increased level of employee monitoring, arguing that the casino was already a highly monitored site (Bibby 2007). This illustrates – albeit somewhat strangely – the acceptance of functional creep regarding monitoring and surveillance by a union and the reality of the union's bargaining position in relation to these issues.

■ *Video surveillance*

Workplace surveillance has been described as a ubiquitous management approach, giving rise to Orwellian notions of workers under constant surveillance by management (Sprague 2007). Video surveillance expands the experience of management omnipresence by subjecting the employee to permanent visibility and display, and thereby undermining the integrity and autonomy of the employee. In contrast to many European countries, where the concept of workplace privacy is well entrenched and workplace surveillance is tightly regulated, Australian law has only recently begun to address the issue of video surveillance in the workplace. As of 2011, only two states and the Australian Capital Territory (ACT) have implemented laws specifically governing workplace surveillance.

New South Wales was the first Australian state to pass workplace-surveillance laws, with the enactment of the *Workplace Video Surveillance Act 1998*. This Act governed the use of covert video surveillance in the workplace, making it an offence for an employer to engage in covert video surveillance, other than for the purpose of establishing whether an employee was engaging in unlawful activity, and where such surveillance had been authorised by a covert surveillance authority. The Act was repealed and replaced by the *Workplace Surveillance Act 2005*, which expanded the 1998 Act by including all forms of surveillance and additional requirements for camera, computer and tracking surveillance. In relation to video or camera surveillance, the 2005 Act governs both covert and overt surveillance and requires that camera surveillance not be undertaken unless the camera or device is clearly visible and signs notifying people that they are under surveillance are present at the entrance. Covert surveillance is prohibited unless authorised by a 'covert surveillance authority', as defined in the legislation. Permission to undertake covert surveillance at the workplace cannot be given to an employer by a magistrate, unless an employer can show that there are 'reasonable grounds' to justify its issue. In determining reasonable grounds, a magistrate must have regard to the seriousness of the unlawful activity with which the application for covert surveillance is concerned. If the application involves covert surveillance of a recreation room, meal room or any other area at a workplace where employees are not directly engaged in work, a magistrate must have regard to the affected employees' heightened expectation of privacy when in such an area. Once an employer is granted permission to institute covert surveillance in the workplace, the operation must be overseen by a surveillance supervisor for the authority. The Act prohibits any surveillance of an employee in any change room, toilet facility, or shower or other bathing facility at a workplace.

The New South Wales approach was followed in Victoria in 2006 with the *Surveillance Devices (Workplace Privacy) Act 2006*, which amended the *Surveillance Devices Act 1999* to enhance its operation in workplaces. These changes to the Act were made as a result of a Victorian Law Reform Commission (VLRC) inquiry that found employee privacy in the workplace was not adequately protected (VLRC 2005). The Act applies to all employers, and prohibits them from knowingly installing, using or maintaining optical surveillance devices or listening devices to observe, listen to, record or monitor the activities or conversations of a worker in a toilet, washroom, change room or lactation room in the workplace.

The most comprehensive legislation concerning video surveillance in the workplace is the Australian Capital Territory's *Workplace Privacy Act 2011*. This law was developed within the framework of the *Human Rights Act 2004*, which includes a right not to have one's privacy interfered with in an unlawful or arbitrary manner. The Act covers data, tracking and optical surveillance, and states that an employer can only conduct surveillance if the employer has provided written notice to employees. The notice must be given at least 14 days before the surveillance, and must state the type of surveillance, how it will be conducted, whether it is intermittent or continuous, and the purpose for which the employer wants to conduct the surveillance. Additional requirements for optical surveillance are that the device must be visible and that a sign is visible at the entrance of the workplace, informing people that they may be under surveillance. Like the New South Wales law, covert surveillance is strictly regulated, requiring an employer to demonstrate to the Magistrates Court that there is reasonable suspicion that an employee is engaging in unlawful activity, what actions the employer took to detect the unlawful activity, a description of the proposed surveillance device and when the covert surveillance may be conducted. In addition, the employer must give the name of any persons designated as a surveillance supervisor. The Magistrates Court must be satisfied that such a person has the experience or expertise to be a surveillance supervisor, and is independent of the employer.

There is a benefit to be gained from uniform legislation at the federal level to ensure consistency and standard community expectations. However, to date the

Australian government has been reluctant to enact privacy legislation specifically related to the workplace. It is an area that will require governmental responses in the future. This is particularly the case given the development of web cameras, hand-held video cameras and mobile phone cameras. Such technology makes covert surveillance effortless and simple, and in addition to raising issues pertaining to the employer–employee relationship, provides the potential for employees to surreptitiously film other employees.

Invasive aspects of workplace monitoring and surveillance

Alcohol and drug testing

The potential dangers that substance abuse poses in the workplace are well documented, causing substantial costs in both human and economic terms. While acknowledging the lack of accurate data concerning drug use in the workplace, the International Labor Organization (ILO) estimates that between 3 and 15 per cent of fatal work accidents in Australia are related to drug and alcohol use. The relationship between alcohol, drug use and accidents at work is an important issue, because occupational health and safety (OHS) legislation in Australia places an obligation upon employers to provide a safe workplace for all employees and visitors to sites that they control. Employers are subject to strict liability under this law, and face significant fines if found to be in breach of the Act. The fact that employer liability extends to employees' actions and/or omissions, regardless of the employee's state of mind, provides a key justification for drug testing in the workplace.

Research undertaken in the United States suggests that drug testing in the workplace in both employment and pre-employment situations has been a major factor in reducing absenteeism and accidents, and is the most common method of removing the issue of substance abuse in the workplace. This evidence provides a compelling case for implementing drug testing to ensure that employees meet their contractual obligations to a satisfactory standard and that employers meet their duty of care requirements under OHS legislation. Implicit in this argument is that those employers who have not implemented drug-testing policies and programs are maintaining unsafe workplaces (Holland & Wickham 2001). However, the cost-effectiveness and overall value of drug testing have been questioned:

> The American Civil Liberties Union cites analysis by a committee of the National Academy of Sciences (NAS) which found that most workers who use illicit drugs never use them at work, and when they use drugs on their own time, they do so in a way that does not affect work performance. (Gip 1999: 16)

Performance within the scope of the contract of employment is an important and related consideration in the drug testing debate. DesJardine and McCall (1990) ask what level of performance are employers entitled to expect? If an employee's productivity is satisfactory, arguably that person is meeting their contractual obligations. It follows that knowledge of drug use on the grounds of productivity is not relevant to an employer. In addition, while duty of care is an important issue, not every job has the potential for unintentional harm to other workers. For this reason, the issues of privacy, control and fairness in the employment relationship need to be considered by employers, employees and their unions when drug testing is implemented in the workplace. From the union perspective, the main consideration is the right to privacy (Scott-Howman 2004).

Using Mill's principle of liberty, Bowie and Duska (1990: 89) contend that employees have the right to do whatever they wish, provided that it does not harm the employer. It follows that if a person chooses to take illicit drugs outside of paid work time, it is of no concern to the employer, provided it does not impinge on work performance (Bowie & Duska 1990; Greenwood, Holland & Choong 2006). In addition, drug testing suffers from accuracy problems, in that tests cannot determine whether the effects of illicit drugs – which may remain in the system for days and even weeks – will substantially impair or affect performance. Webb and Festa (1994) note that the link between drug usage and on-the-job injuries is at best tenuous. Drug testing may also uncover other medical conditions or over-the-counter or prescribed drugs used by employees (such as Insulin or metabolites of morphine), which have the potential to affect the employment status or tenure of workers. This creates concern over an employee's right to 'informational privacy', and gives rise to a legitimate concern that drug testing can be used by employers to go on a 'fishing trip' if appropriate limits are not put in place. Specifically, mandatory drug testing may be open to improper or malicious use to intimidate or target employees who undertake activities that may be unpopular with management, such as union activism (Webb & Festa 1994). Therefore, the use of drug testing within the workplace may create an atmosphere of insecurity, oppression and anxiety in employees, and could actually result in lower performance and higher labour turnover, as well as increase industrial unrest. Indeed, Quinlan, Bohle and Lamm (2010) claim that this has been an important consideration for Australian managers of US-based organisations that have pursued the introduction of drug-testing procedures. In addition, Bahls (1998: 82) notes that the internet is replete with tips on how illicit drug users can evade drug tests and detection.

Within the larger context of the employment relationship, work culture and the social environment have also been identified as critical and complex factors impacting on the drug testing debate. For example, a culture of drug use – both legal and illicit – in isolated locations has been linked to different ways of life, the work environment and the physical location of work (Daly & Philp 1995; Quinlan, Bohle & Lamm 2010). As Allsop and Pidd (2001: 5) highlight:

> In a variety of cultures, formal and informal pressures still encourage weekly after work team building and relaxation based on alcohol consumption. Sanctioned drugs such as caffeine and tobacco have been embraced in ritualised breaks in worktime.

Indeed, a study of alcohol consumption in the Pilbara mining region of Western Australia found that alcohol consumption was 64 per cent above the state level (Daly & Philp 1995). A subsequent study by Midford and colleagues (1997) in mining-related worksites found that alcohol consumption was greater than the national average, while binge drinking was found to be more prevalent and was related to shiftwork and isolation from family.

Aside from the explicit focus on the mining industry, Berry and colleagues (2007) found risky levels of drinking behaviours among 44 per cent of the Australian work-force. While research has focused upon the link between the nature of the work and associated drug use, issues of control, alienation and stress, linked with individuals' perceptions of their powerlessness, have been identified as factors related to drug use in the workplace (Quinlan, Bohle & Lamm 2010). As Midford (2001: 46) argues:

> In the workplace, holding the view that drug use is a problem for the individual worker is functional from the point of view of the employers, because it avoids any exploration of how the workplace may contribute to the problem. However, to gain an understanding of workplace drug problems, one must look at a full range of factors that influence patterns of drug use.

The Australian Council of Trade Unions (ACTU) does not support the introduction of any form of biological testing of workers for alcohol or other drugs in the workplace, except in very limited circumstances and subject to joint union and employer agree-ment. This pluralist stance adopted by the ACTU is based upon the premise that the need for control and prevention measures arises only when drugs and alcohol are misused to the extent that the user cannot properly and safely carry out regular duties. In considering an appropriate response in a particular workplace, there must first be involvement of union representatives, and second an examination of the broad environmental factors pertaining to the individual workplace or industry. Research demonstrates that the key issues in the misuse of alcohol and other drugs are: hazard-ous work; a poor work environment; unrealistic deadlines; a lack of job satisfaction; a lack of worker participation and control; inadequate training and supervision; and work culture and shiftwork (Holland, Pyman & Teicher 2005). Indeed, the fatigue generated by these factors, combined with increased deregulation of the Australian labour market, raises major issues regarding occupational health and safety (ACIRRT 1999). As Nolan (2000: 2) argues:

> Employees and unions have questioned why random drug testing has assumed such priority in an industrial climate where increasing demands have been placed upon workers to work twelve-hour shifts. Evidence suggests that it is fatigue and not impair-ment through drug and alcohol abuse that leads to the majority of accidents.

If management is truly interested in these issues, the ACTU argues that a more holistic approach should be adopted – for example, including fatigue-monitoring and man-agement systems. This broadens the drug-testing debate and raises the critical issue of fitness for duty. The question of fitness for duty often raises a more subtle and complex issue of control in the workplace. Unions tend to see the introduction of measures such as drug testing as management exercising increased control under the guise of managerial prerogative, and as a strategy to marginalise the countervailing power of unions – particularly where there is an absence of consultation. This was certainly highlighted as a key theme in the implementation of drug testing in the case of South Blackwater Coal (Holland & Wickham 2001). This clash over control can potentially become a major source of conflict between management and unions. The need to strike a balance between the employer's legal obligation and employees' rights is a complex and sensitive issue that currently pervades the development and implementation of drug-testing policies.

Traditionally, the concept of fitness for duty meant little more than pre-employment screening of employees to determine their capacity to meet the requirements of the job. More recently, as explained above, fitness for duty has often been manifest in testing regimes designed to detect impaired capacity to perform the duties of a position. Such approaches have often proved controversial, due to the process by which regimes are implemented and deficiencies in the tests themselves (Holland & Wickham 2001). However, the BHP Pilbara case provides a point of reference for to how to approach these issues, despite there having been an industrial dispute around the development of drug-testing procedures. Through an Employee Assistance Program, and appropriate testing safeguards implemented in conjunction with a consultation process with unions, BHP Iron Ore Mines in the Pilbara Region of Western Australia was able to develop a comprehensive drug-testing program deemed fair by the courts.

The need for a more holistic and pragmatic approach has led to advocacy of a non-discriminatory testing regime for a wide range of physical and psychological factors that may impair performance (Nolan & Nomchong 2001). While the search for appropriate tests remains problematic, the philosophical underpinning of this approach is that the causes of impairment are not confined to circumstances within the employee's control, and may be significantly affected by workplace conditions under the employer's control. Adopting this type of approach is likely to reduce the likelihood of industrial conflict over drug and alcohol testing in workplaces.

■ Genetic testing in the workplace

While genetic testing is not at significant levels in Australian workplaces, the implications for employment of such testing (for genetic disorders and family history) are considerable, and take monitoring and surveillance in the workplace to new levels of intrusion with regard to informational privacy. Genetic testing is effectively the acquiring of information about an individual, either directly or from their family medical history, through biological samples that may reveal predisposition or occurrence of diseases or other physical conditions. From a workplace perspective, the focus is on occupational health and safety-related diseases, and can include specific tests for:

- employees at risk of a work-related disease
- employees' susceptibility to workplace chemicals
- employees who have been exposed to harmful chemicals, and
- employees who have been exposed to harmful radiation.

However, concern remains about what such examinations are actually testing for, and who has access to this information. As research continues to indicate, genetic testing cannot clearly determine the susceptibility of an employee to these risks. It would also be expected that if employers adopted safe working practices in relation to the management of dangerous chemicals or radiation, this would prevent employees from being exposed to such dangers.

An indication of the increasing availability and pervasiveness of this type of testing occurred when a major health insurer, NIB Health, offered these tests to its customers and promised that the results would not affect eligibility for continued health cover. It is worth noting in this context that DNA kits are now being sold in drugstores in the United States. Following this increased availability, it could be considered only a matter of time before such tests are as common as drug and alcohol testing in the workplace.

The paradox and problems of monitoring and surveillance in the workplace

As Wallace (2004) notes, while organisations may use monitoring and surveillance for specific purposes, in an era of declining union power, these new tools give more power and scope for organisations to use them simply because they are available, and once in use these techniques allow for functional creep. This statement goes to the very heart of the employment relationship and employers' attitudes to their workforce in regard to the levels of trust and control management allow employees. The paradox of this situation is that the rapid rise in the level of monitoring and surveillance has coincided with the emergence of human resource management (HRM). While initially this might not seem at odds with the unitarist philosophy of HRM, in order to develop successful workplace relations, an HRM approach is based upon the development of a long-term relationship with the workforce built upon trust. As research has found, and as discussed in Chapter 6, trust in the employment relationship is positively associated with a range of desired employee attitudes – for example, job satisfaction and organisational commitment – and desired work behaviours, including organisational citizenship behaviours and turnover. Consequently, trust has been identified as a critical variable affecting the efficiency and performance of organisations. As Kiffin-Peterson and Cordery (2003) note, the management of an organisation can ill afford to ignore the influence of trust on employees' attitudes and the employment relationship. Trust enables cooperation, and is therefore a key element when it comes to judging how employees view their relationship with management; it can also be a source of competitive advantage for organisations. Westin (1992) found in his research that failure by management to implement monitoring and surveillance in a participatory way damaged the trust relationship between management and employees.

In addition, the issue of control within the employment relationship is highlighted in the nature and extent of monitoring and surveillance. Sempill (2001) argues that electronic monitoring can be used as a tool to reinforce employer power by promoting the enforcement of employee obedience. It is this imposition of technology by an employer that can be seen to contribute to the erosion of employees' rights and increased powerlessness in the employment relationship – and, as a consequence, to a decline in organisational trustworthiness. The consequences of this excessive monitoring and surveillance can lead to employee well-being problems associated with stress and alienation, leading to high levels of turnover. Equally, excessive monitoring and surveillance can lead to employee resistance and sabotage (Ball 2010). This has been well documented in the research on call centres, which have emerged as one of the fastest growing sectors in Australia. Described in various negative terms, including as 'dungeons with telephones', 'electronic sweatshops' and 'assembly lines in the head', call centres have attracted a reputation for having high levels of surveillance, with annual turnover rates commonly in excess of 30 per cent, despite the fact the work is essentially standardised and routine. This attitude to the employment relationship falls neatly within a Marxist perspective of workplace relations, which places a power imbalance at the heart of the employment relationship. Indeed, the use of monitoring and surveillance can be a mechanism intended to heighten this imbalance by increasing employer control over the workforce.

In this context, the actions of management towards employees are continually evaluated and assessed by both employees and their representatives. Those actions that violate trust can create an atmosphere of distrust, and consequently employees and their representatives may be less willing to develop a committed relationship with management and a more likely to seek redress through industrial action or turnover. It follows that management decisions to develop policies and practices that focus on monitoring and surveillance have to be considered against the potential effect on the employment relationship, as such policies and practices can influence employees' perceptions of the trustworthiness of an organisation or the organisational climate of trust. Monitoring and surveillance policies and practices are therefore central to the employment relationship and the 'exchange' between employees and management.

Conclusion

It is clear the rapid development of technologies blurring the boundaries of work and work and private space has had a significant impact on the nature and extent of monitoring and surveillance of employees and, as the case law indicates, organisations have been catching up with the consequences of these changes. In addition, the nature and extent of monitoring and surveillance take us back to the fundamental nature of the employment relationship, in terms of trust and mutual respect. Monitoring and surveillance strategies can be seen as a litmus test of the true perspective of management and its relationship with employees. This has a major impact on the nature of the employment relationship. As the case study of Semco (opposite) illustrates, organisations should consider the genuine need for, or requirements of, implementing monitoring and surveillance policies and practices – why they are doing it and at what cost in terms of the intangibles – such as trust and the employment relationship – that they may be sacrificing.

▪ Discussion questions

9.1   Outline and evaluate the cases for and against monitoring and surveillance in the workplace.

9.2   What are the potential implications for employers who 'data mine' prospective employees?

9.3   What are the major issues associated with developing drug-testing procedures in the workplace?

9.4   Discuss this statement: 'Genetic testing opens up a whole new set of issues in the workplace'.

9.5   Monitoring and surveillance technologies offer employers increased capacity to control workers and also to erode their privacy. How adequately have unions, HR professionals and industrial tribunals responded to these challenges?

CASE STUDY

An alternative approach: the post-Fordism road

While this chapter has provided a critical analysis of and sense of inevitability about developments in monitoring and surveillance in the workplace, some companies are developing more positive workplace cultures based on mutual respect, trust and cooperation. Often described as a post-Fordist approach, it is characterised as a workplace culture in which monitoring and surveillance are minimal, where the workforce and management build a trusting relationship where work is discussed and allocated, the pace of work is jointly determined and autonomy is maintained. This is what underpins the work culture at the Brazilian industry giant Semco. Below are excerpts from an interview with Ricardo Semler on the issue of monitoring and surveillance.

Ricardo Semler: set them free

For nearly 25 years, Ricardo Semler, CEO of Brazil-based Semco, has let his employees set their own hours and wages, and even choose their own IT. The result is increased productivity, long-term loyalty and phenomenal growth. So what about monitoring and surveillance?

Semler on network security

One of the things I've noticed is IT people want to make sure that their systems are intact, private, confidential ... but they think nothing whatsoever of invading the e-mail privacy of their own employees. That's very interesting to me, because it's not only a double standard, but a violation of constitutional rights. Companies have taken the blind assumption that because the system is theirs, then anything that people do on it has to be available to them. I think it's a very hypocritical mode, and it deals with fundamental freedom issues that I don't think people have completely thought through.

Semco and employee emails

Staff searched for a software or system that would make it impossible to spy on people's email. They couldn't find one and had to customise one.

Semler's response when asked whether employees worked fewer or longer hours under the new policy

Last week CNN spent four days with a bunch of our guys probing in all directions, and they concluded that our people balance their lives much better, and that there is an unusually high number of people who take their kids to school, etc. But a recent statistic of ours shows that 27 per cent of our people are online on Sunday at 8 p.m. – 27 per cent. So they probably do work hard.

As Semler notes, in the long run this system is really an unforgiving one, because it is up to you to figure out how to best spend your time. Nothing happens if you don't come in to work on a Monday morning. But if you're sitting on a beach on Monday morning at 11 o'clock and you are alone, maybe it's worth it to work that bit harder. How do you really measure the value of that kind of moment?

Source: Wieners (2004).

Case study discussion questions

1. Why does the Semco approach seem so radical?
2. Reflecting on the Semco approach to monitoring and surveillance, do you think it would work in an organisation in which you currently work or have worked? Explain why or why not.

Diversity and disadvantaged workers

Santina Bertone and Devaki Monani

■ Chapter objectives

This chapter will enable readers to understand the:
- nature of labour market disadvantage and its various categories
- intersecting nature and changeability of labour market disadvantage
- connections between disadvantage, industry restructuring and the dismantling of labour market protections
- implications of labour market disadvantage for workplace relations.

Introduction

In the second decade of the twenty-first century, the Australian workforce presents an unusual degree of diversity. Race and culture, gender, disability, age, lifestyles and changing family responsibilities are among the key diversity characteristics of an expanding population and labour force. This diversity has been fuelled by sustained mass immigration, the increasing workforce participation of women, the need to retain older and skilled workers and demands for equitable employment participation by traditionally marginalised groups, such as people with disabilities and Indigenous people. In this chapter, the nature and extent of each of these forms of diversity will be addressed, and the implications of this diversity for workplace relations examined. This analysis will also look at the interaction between diversity and disadvantage, and industry restructuring and economic change.

In this discussion, we conceptualise diversity and disadvantage as multifaceted, such that individuals can be characterised by a range of types of diversity and disadvantage – for example, women can be seen as disadvantaged because of gender, but in some cases also as low-skilled migrants, older workers, persons with a disability or members of a minority religion. Besides the multifaceted character, diversity and disadvantage can be seen as evolving over time so that negative attitudes abate, as in the case of Greek and Italian migrants who are now seen as more mainstream compared with more recent arrivals from Asia.

Disadvantage, industry restructuring and the dismantling of labour market protections

The disadvantages that can arise from diversity among groups such as migrants, women, Indigenous people, older employees and the disabled are magnified both by structural changes to the economy, such as the growth of the services sector and opening up of the trade-exposed sector to international competition, and also by the removal of protections in the labour market. This disadvantage manifests itself as growth in various forms of precarious employment, such as increasing levels of casual and part-time work, and under-employment (these issues are also considered in Chapter 2). These changes to labour market regulation have also resulted in greater wage dispersion within and between industries. The periodic crises of capitalism, such as the Global Financial Crisis (GFC) of 2008, also bear more heavily on disadvantaged employees, who are more exposed to unemployment and loss of income.

The Australian economy has undergone major restructuring since the dismantling of most tariffs and quotas during the Hawke and Keating federal Labor governments and the floating of the exchange rate in the early 1980s. Australian industries are now open to international competition, and must differentiate themselves from their competitors in order to survive in the international marketplace. As detailed in Chapters 1 and 2, the share of jobs in manufacturing – which employed a large proportion of unskilled migrant workers – has continued its steep decline since the 1970s, now accounting for little more than one in 10 jobs. As a result, the majority of employment is now found in the service industries, particularly health and community services, financial services, retail, hospitality and tourism, and education. Mining and agriculture are major generators of export income, but provide relatively few jobs.

These broader structural changes have contributed to a significant redistribution of national incomes and wealth away from the more disadvantaged in Australian society towards the richest. In the context of declining employment opportunities and increasing international competition, the bargaining power of disadvantaged workers is eroded further, potentially leading to a further deterioration in incomes and working conditions, especially in light of continuing falls in trade union membership (discussed further in Chapter 3).

Disadvantaged workers have also been affected adversely by changes in workplace relations laws, both in the period up to 2007 and following the enactment of the *Fair Work Act 2009*. For a more detailed explanation of these developments, see Chapters 3 and 5. As a result, there is now far greater dispersion and variability in terms and conditions of employment than in the days of the centralised arbitration system operating for most of the twentieth century.

Those workers whom we define as disadvantaged are exposed to a number of risks, including long-term unemployment (since disadvantaged workers are usually the first to lose their jobs or find it harder to commence their working lives); a prolongation of short-hours working, leading to reduced income over a longer period of time (short-hours working kept many manufacturing employees in jobs during the GFC); greater work intensification and job insecurity due to instability in the markets and survival strategies by companies; and increased risk of discrimination at the point of recruitment, as employers become more selective at times when unemployment is rising.

Moreover, the focus on competitiveness has caused some employers to increase workloads and reduce staffing ratios, leading to the phenomenon of 'work intensification', or requirements to complete more work in a given time. Work intensification has also affected employees at both the low and high ends of the skill spectrum (Watson et al. 2003). Added to these changes in work organisation has been a substantial rise in the incidence of 'non-standard' contracts, including part-time and casual jobs, and labour hire arrangements. It is estimated that approximately one-quarter of all Australian workers fall into the non-standard employment category (Masterman-Smith & Pocock 2008). For many workers, this can mean not being able to secure long-term employment that generates sufficient income. At the other extreme, many professional and managerial workers are working increasingly long hours (Watson et al. 2003). There is also a gender divide in these new working patterns, as women are more heavily represented in non-standard employment, such as part-time and casual jobs, while men are over-represented among long-hours workers.

Young people and older workers are also more likely to be offered non-standard or precarious employment. Particular dangers are posed by the broader structural changes, and the periodic crises of capitalism such as the GFC, for members of disadvantaged groups, who are often struggling to maintain competitiveness and employability in the labour market.

Intersecting nature and changeability of diversity and disadvantage

Overlaying the cultural and gender diversity of the workforce are major issues associated with age, religion, socio-economic status, disability, family and care responsibilities, sexual orientation and lifestyles. Being female, immigrant or disabled does not occur in isolation; these states intersect and occur together, as suggested above. Nor are they value-free: the way in which society views and constructs these ways of being has important implications for how individuals experience their lives and contribute to the workplace. The concept of 'race' is socially constructed, as there is no genetic basis for differentiating between people (Hollinsworth 2006). Gender, disability and age intersect with culture, race and religion to create new opportunities and often barriers to work and careers. It is not the case that these influences are additive; rather, as Hollinsworth (2006: 54–5) observes:

> Race is experienced through gendered forms and gender is experienced in race-specific ways. Which aspects of our identity are foregrounded depends on the circumstances. Privileging one among various such identities denies this situationally shaped sense of oneself.

Moreover, it has been observed that the 'lived' reality of race can change over an individual's lifetime, as a person becomes acculturated to the host society and accumulates more 'whiteness' – similar to the way in which earlier immigrant groups (such as Italians and Greeks) become more accepted into the community, compared with more recent arrivals (such as Asians and Muslims).

It is also worth noting the fundamental fluidity and changeability of some of the constructs that make up diversity in the workforce and the associated conditions that lead to disadvantage. There has been a tendency to view people as falling into certain fixed categories, particularly for the purposes of equal employment opportunity legislation and managing diversity policies. People are seen to be either male or female, able-bodied or disabled, immigrant or Indigenous. Yet, on closer examination, it is clear that life transitions and choices, crises and discontinuities (both in and outside of paid work) can lead to significant changes in both the objective and subjective experience of disadvantage in the workforce. Examples of this include professionals and managers of both genders finding themselves becoming disabled, sole parents, old, ill or otherwise marginalised by their work and life experiences – or, conversely, immigrants acquiring social and cultural capital in Australia over time and becoming more integrated into the host society.

It is also important to reflect on the meaning of terms such as 'disadvantaged', which appears in the title of this section. In the discussion below, we show that, in many respects, being different from the dominant Anglo-Celtic male group (the norm), which continues to hold most power in Australian workplaces, can be linked to disadvantage – in terms of unemployment, income, status, career and benefits. Consequently, workforce disadvantage can be seen as a relative concept. However, the situation is complex, with some members of disadvantaged groups having access to better paid jobs and careers than others, depending on their skills, immigration category, period of arrival, age, degree of whiteness and ethnicity. Many immigrants work in professional and technical jobs, while some Anglo-Celtic male youths exhibit high rates of unemployment (usually linked to early school leaving and poorer socio-economic status). As previously noted, even educated white Anglo-Celtic Protestant males can face major life-changing transitions such as illness, disability, divorce, single parenthood and ageing, which can move them into a disadvantaged status *vis-à-vis* other members of the workforce.

Migrants

Race and cultural difference in Australia

Before examining the main characteristics of post-war immigration and the employment experience of migrants, and subsequently that of Indigenous people, it is important to place these issues in the context of the debate about whether we have adopted a positive attitude to multiculturalism and tolerance. Australia prides itself on being a 'remarkably tolerant' nation, and multiculturalism is portrayed by politicians as a highly successful policy for managing cultural diversity in the population. White privilege is consistently denied, and racism – where it is recognised – is seen as aberrant and isolated in form. Hage (1998) is critical of the underlying notion of tolerance, seeing it as yet another way in which white Australians affirm their ownership of the nation and their rights to regulate who belongs. But Hodge and O'Carroll (2006: 57) caution that tolerance is not a 'crisp, binary' concept – even a limited amount of tolerance can be valuable and, 'like taxation … it is part of the social contract in a pluralist society'.

Officially, Australia is no longer a 'white' nation. The repeal of the 'White Australia' policy (1901–58) enabled people of any race or background to be admitted as permanent residents and accorded due protection under the law. Certainly, the majority of skilled migrants who have arrived since 2000 have not been 'white', coming predominantly from the Asian region. However, racism is seen to continue in a variety of ways – in community attitudes, in the workplace, in the media and in myriad day-to-day interactions. Hollinsworth (2006) provides a thorough review of the evidence in early twenty-first-century Australia, and concludes that racism still thrives.

Post-war migration

In 2006, Australia had a population of 21 million, a quarter of whom were born overseas and originated in one of more than 200 countries (ABS 2006b). Altogether,

44 per cent of Australians were either born overseas or had at least one overseas-born parent (ABS 2006b). Almost three-quarters of the overseas born were from either Europe or Asia. This cultural diversity was reflected in similar proportions in the Australian workforce, with 13 per cent of the workforce born in non-English speaking (NES) countries and 23 per cent being born overseas (Department of Immigration and Citizenship 2008b). In comparison, the percentage of overseas-born workers in other industrialised countries is considerably lower, ranging from 15 per cent in the United States, 9 per cent in Germany and 5 per cent in the United Kingdom to just 1.3 per cent in Japan (Hayashi & Moffett 2007). Only Canada, with an overseas-born workforce of 19.2 per cent, is comparable to Australia (Hawthorne 2006).

In the post-war era, Australia embarked on a mass immigration program that has consistently added 1–1.5 per cent annually to the population (in gross terms), with the level only falling during economic downturns. Early post-war policy favoured the entry of British settlers; however, when insufficient numbers were attracted from this source, the large-scale entry of Eastern European refugees in the 1940s and later Southern European immigrants in the 1950s and 1960s began, followed in the 1970s and 1980s by people from the Middle East, South-East Asia, North Asia and finally Africa (Bertone 2008). Before the late 1980s, immigration policy focused on numbers and family reunion. After the late 1980s, with the emphasis on developing Australia as a knowledge economy, the emphasis shifted towards skilled migration and away from family reunion. A detailed points-based entry test gave priority to applicants who were young, well educated, literate in English and qualified for high-demand jobs in which local skills were in short supply.

This points test was reinforced in 1997 by the then federal Liberal-National Party Coalition government to apply to both principal applicants and more distant relatives. By 2002, the majority (58 per cent) of permanent migrants entering the country were skilled, a figure that rose to 70 per cent by 2008. A new temporary immigration scheme was also introduced to admit skilled immigrants on an employer-nominated basis for periods of up to four years. A marked rise in the numbers of overseas students also occurred during this time, with most students coming from India and China. Changes to immigration rules allowed these students to apply for permanent residency while still onshore.

By 2006, almost three-quarters of the overseas-born population were born either in Europe (47 per cent, or 2.1 million) or Asia (27 per cent, or 1.2 million) (ABS 2006b). The top 10 countries of birth for the overseas-born population, in numerical order, were: United Kingdom, New Zealand, Italy, Vietnam, China, Greece, Germany, Philippines, India and the Netherlands (Leuner 2007). English continued to be the dominant language, but 17 per cent of the population (3 million people) reported speaking a language other than English (LOTE) at home (ABS 2006b). Three-quarters of these people were first-generation overseas-born immigrants, and just over one-fifth were second-generation immigrant Australians. What are the employment experiences of the immigrant newcomers, and what are the implications in the workplace?

■ *Employment experience of migrants*

The workplace relations literature dealing with immigrant workers dates back to the 1960s. This literature documents the increasing militancy of immigrant workers, particularly in motor vehicle and steel manufacturing (see Lever-Tracy & Quinlan 1988). It also investigates issues such as the experience of immigrant women in manufacturing (Stephens & Bertone 1995); the relationship between immigrants and their trade unions (Bertone & Griffin 1992); and the impact of training reform and workplace relations changes, such as award restructuring and enterprise bargaining, on immigrant workers' employment and conditions (Callus & Knox 1993; Charlesworth 1997). This literature also documents the effects of economic restructuring (including tariff reductions, outsourcing and the shift to service industries) (for example, see Weller 1999; O'Loughlin & Watson 1997) on immigrant jobs, livelihoods and working life. Much of this literature emphasises the multiple disadvantages experienced by immigrant workers, such as low pay, harsh working conditions, vulnerability to restructuring and a higher risk of unemployment.

Reflecting the working-class composition of the early post-war waves of immigration, research tended to focus on immigrants working in blue-collar jobs within manufacturing, transport and logistics, building and construction, and public utilities such as gas, water and postal services. By the late 1980s and into the 1990s, however, researchers were pointing to the increasing intakes of skilled immigrants and the quite different employment challenges this raised (see Birrell & Hawthorne 1997). By the beginning of the twenty-first century, it was clear that immigrant employment in Australia had diversified to a significant extent, with immigrants gaining a strong foothold in professional and para-professional jobs, while they were still over-represented among low-paid blue-collar occupations (Bertone 2008).

The challenges faced by the 'new breed' of immigrants now included poor recognition of overseas-gained qualifications and experience; over-qualification for their jobs; high rates of unemployment in the early settlement years (remaining high for some groups, such as refugees); blocked career paths and under-representation in public sector employment (Bertone, Leahy & Doughney 2004); and discrimination in recruitment on the basis of non-Anglo-Celtic names (Leigh 2009).

■ Female employees and the family

■ *Parental leave*

Recent decades have seen the sustained entry of women into the Australian workforce. Pocock (2003) observed that in 35 years the workforce participation rate of women had grown by 19 per cent, while the male rate had fallen by 12 per cent. Over the same period, the growth in workforce participation was especially pronounced among women of child-bearing age, with 44 per cent of women in paid jobs working part-time. By 2006, women's workforce participation rate had risen to 58 per cent, amounting to 46 per cent of a workforce of 9.1 million. However, the increased participation of women as paid workers has not led to a generalised reduction in their traditional responsibilities in the home, such as caring for children and other family members, doing housework and other unpaid domestic labour. This paradox leads to a range of diversity challenges for the optimal management of women in organisations.

Balancing paid work with family responsibilities remains a challenge for a large number of Australians. Women continue to carry the burden of unpaid caring work, which means that changing workplace culture and practices to be supportive of women's caring responsibilities is a vital goal in terms of ensuring gender equality in the workplace. Examples of changes that are required in this area include improved access and entitlements to parental leave, flexible work practices, provision of afford-able and high-quality child care, attention to working hours, closing the gender pay gap and action to address 'informal' workplace cultures that act to exclude women or diminish the value of their participation.

In relation to maternity leave, as early as 1979 the Australian government legis-lated for an entitlement to 12 months' unpaid maternity leave after 12 months' qualifying service with an employer. It was not until 2011 that the first national Paid Parental Leave scheme started. It provides eligible working parents with 18 weeks of Parental Leave Pay at the National Minimum Wage (which was $606.40 per week as of 1 July 2012). Parental Leave Pay is fully funded by the Australian government under the *Paid Parental Leave Act 2010*. Father and partner pay provides eligible working fathers and partners who share the care of a child born or adopted from 1 January 2013 with up to two weeks' pay at the rate of the National Minimum Wage. Eligibility for paid leave requires the mother to have worked for approximately 13 months (392 days) before the birth of the child.

Before the enactment of the *Paid Parental Leave Act*, paid maternity leave was provided in some industries and some larger private sector workplaces, but overall, only one-third of employed pregnant women in Australia could access any paid maternity leave. The duration of paid maternity leave varied from six weeks to three months. The utilisation of paid paternity options or parental leave by male partners was even lower, at 25 per cent. The introduction of the Paid Parental Leave scheme does not allow employers to use the parental leave payments to in any way substitute for existing employer-provided benefits. Although there is a right to 12 months' unpaid parental leave in Australia, paid parental leave in Australia is of relatively short duration, particularly compared to other nations, making it difficult for some families to combine the arrival of a child with work and income maintenance.

■ Child care and female participation in the workforce

Paid parental leave is one of several options in a range of 'time-based policies' that may be designed to support women and men in the care of their children and other family members. There remains an urgent need to develop a systematic and stable means of funding child care that allows women and men to participate in the labour market. Flexible work arrangements are also required to allow for parents to provide child care and participate in household work, thereby addressing both gender equality and the need for greater workforce participation and national productivity. Iceland and Sweden have pioneered the development of policies that include extensive parental leave *and* child-support schemes, resulting in high participation rates for women as mothers. Notably, these two countries have higher percentages of mothers in paid employment than the average for all women employed across OECD countries (OECD 2007b).

The workforce participation rate of 72.9 per cent for Australian women in the childbearing age group (25–44 years) is the eighth lowest in the OECD, lagging behind Sweden (86.4 per cent), Portugal (84.8 per cent) and Canada (81.8 per cent). Overall, in Australia, the gender gap in labour force participation – which we refer to as the incomplete female revolution in Chapter 2 – is 16 per cent (ABS 2008), compared with Canada at 12 per cent and Sweden at 5 per cent (World Economic Forum 2008). Against this background, Australia would need to increase its participation rate for women aged 25–44 years by 7.1 per cent – approximately 209 000 women – to reach a participation rate equal to that in Canada. Compared with other countries, when Australian women are employed, they are also more likely to be employed part-time, and this is often associated with low wages, as explained in Chapter 2.

In its current form, the Australian labour market does not offer maximum scope for flexible family arrangements, despite these being identified as the 'most effective strategy for retaining staff' – more effective than the offer of financial incentives. As a strategy for providing flexibility, part-time employment is most closely connected with cost-saving measures (for further discussion of this issue within two service sector industries, see Chapter 12). Hence part-time work is more prevalent in lower paid sectors such as personal services, retail and hospitality, where women tend to be concentrated.

To the extent that these jobs are casual, the incumbents do not receive leave loadings or superannuation benefits. Part-time jobs are also more likely to be casual or provide no job security. Australia has a high incidence of casual employment, with women engaged in 70 per cent of part-time and casual work (Preston & Burgess 2003). Part-time jobs are also less likely to offer opportunities for professional development and career advancement. In effect, by working part-time, many Australian women are accepting inferior work.

Severe skill shortages were evident before the onset of the GFC, including in traditionally female-dominated professions such as nursing (which also relies heavily on the importation of skilled immigrants). In the absence of workplace arrangements that give sufficient attention to ensuring flexible work practices for both parents, women are likely to continue to 'choose' part-time work due to a lack of other feasible options or to stay out of the paid workforce altogether. Flexible working initiatives will need to focus on the aspect of caring *per se*, whether for children or for elderly or disabled relatives. In order to have real choices in the labour market, men and women need to be able to access quality part-time work that provides the full range of benefits and career paths.

For immigrant women, the issues may differ: they are more likely to work-full time (Bertone & Leuner 2008). Immigrant women are also more likely to be concentrated in blue-collar jobs within the manufacturing industries, although increasingly they are spread across a range of service industry jobs, including the professions. Despite – or perhaps because of – these differences, the need for flexible working arrangements, paid parental leave and appropriate child care are just as relevant for immigrant women. Moreover, both immigrant women and Australian-born women are under-represented in managerial jobs relative to their workforce share.

■ Gender pay gap

Beyond the issue of work–life balance, which has been a recent focus in the academic and policy literature, is the long-standing issue of the gender pay gap and entrenched gender stereotypes, which limit the range of jobs that women perform and the associated remuneration and career paths. Although the gender pay gap has narrowed considerably since the implementation of equal pay decisions by the industrial tribunals, in 2005 women's full-time ordinary time earnings were 15 per cent below the male average, and this increased to 17 per cent by 2010. That the gender pay gap persists in Australia highlights the operation of a range of factors, including occupational segregation, under-valuation of female-dominated jobs, male-dominated organisational cultures and the gendered division of family labour (Strachan, Burgess & Henderson 2007).

■ Family division of labour

Finally, the issue of working hours is particularly significant in its effects on the division of labour at work and home. A recent Human Rights and Equal Opportunity Commission (HREOC) report found that one-third of men were working longer than 45 hours per week, with fathers of young children being more likely to work longer hours (HREOC 2007). These figures suggest that work cultures strongly encourage long working hours, with negative implications for women who cannot, or are not willing to, work long hours, due to family and other obligations. The effects of long working hours cultures can undermine women's career opportunities and potential for salary advancement.

Unless these issues are addressed at the level of public policy, skill shortages are likely to continue, and increases in national productivity may continue to be sluggish. Women's aspirations and potential for full workforce participation will not be realised, and workplaces will be perceived as less fair as a result. Barriers facing women and immigrants in the labour market – particularly for skilled immigrants – act as a brake on the capacity of the economy to fully utilise its productive capacity. The benefits of fully integrating women from diverse backgrounds (immigrant, Indigenous, disabled, younger and older women, women with children and women without children) into the labour market include the 'capacity to attract a wider range of quality employees, reduced staff turnover, less absenteeism and lateness, enhanced staff performance and motivation, a competitive edge and innovation contributing to improved effectiveness' (ILO 2004, cited in Strachan, Burgess & Henderson 2007).

In summary, there is a considerable literature on the many strategies that organisations can use to achieve better outcomes for women in the workplace; these include paid maternity leave, flexible work practices, strong equal employment opportunity policies, targeted employment programs, monitoring of workforce data and progress against targets and diversity committees.

■ Anti-discrimination legislation

Strengthening of the legislative framework is also required in order to facilitate women's labour force participation. Although federal and state legislation prohibiting gender discrimination in employment is long-standing and operates throughout Australia, there are still important gaps. At the federal level, the principal laws are the *Sex Discrimination Act 1984*, the *Fair Work Act 2009* (which contains some equity provisions) and the *Equal Opportunity for Women in the Workplace Act 1999*. Each state and territory also prohibits gender discrimination, and the *Public Service Act 1999* and *Equal Employment Opportunity (Commonwealth Authorities) Act 1987* contain significant equal employment opportunity provisions for federal public servants. The *Sex Discrimination Act* applies to all private sector employers and relies on an individual complaint process to address direct and indirect discrimination based on sex and related attributes. The *Equal Opportunity for Women in the Workplace Act*, in contrast, applies to large private sector employers (100 employees or more) and is more proactive in requiring employers to take systematic action to achieve equal opportunity for women in the workplace; however, it is limited in its coverage and has weak enforcement powers.

The deficiency of the anti-discrimination laws, such as the *Sex Discrimination Act*, is that they are reliant on individuals making a complaint and successfully making a case for redress. The decision in a given case generally cannot address systematic discrimination across workplaces or industries. In comparison, the *Equal Opportunity for Women in the Workplace Act* recognises that discrimination is both historical and systematic, and needs to be tackled in a comprehensive manner, but is limited to large private sector employers. With no effective penalties for non-compliance, the *Equal Opportunity for Women in the Workplace Act* also lacks a genuine capacity to regulate all employers within its coverage.

■ Indigenous Australians

Indigenous or Aboriginal and Torres Strait Islander people make up 2.4 per cent of the Australian population (ABS 2009a), and in rural areas some still retain their native languages. Their situation, historically and economically, is very different from that of the culturally diverse newcomers. Dispossessed of their lands and subject to harsh paternalistic control by colonial governments and violence from settlers, Indigenous people continue to be treated differently by policy-makers and suffer a range of inferior health, employment and psycho-social outcomes (Hollinsworth 2006).

Closing the gap between Indigenous and non-Indigenous people in Australia in relation to labour market status, education and health, and other measures has been an increasing focus of government policy. For instance, the Council of Australian Governments (COAG) commissioned the Steering Committee for the Review of Government Service Provision to regularly report in relation to Indigenous disadvant-age, measuring performance against a set of key indicators. The Steering Committee has produced five reports to date (in 2003, 2005, 2007, 2009 and 2011); these reflect significant employment and training achievements. However, the reports highlight that more needs to be done to support Indigenous people to gain employment and access to better incomes, particularly in rural and remote areas.

The Rudd Labor government also implemented the Closing the Gap initiative to reduce the disadvantage and increase life outcomes of Indigenous people in terms of early childhood education; reading writing and numeracy; Year 12 attainment rates; employment; life expectancy; and child mortality rates. This initiative requires an annual report on progress in bridging the gap between Indigenous and non-Indigenous Australians (*Closing the Gap: Prime Minister's Report* 2010). Targets have been set in the initiative, such as halving the gap in unemployment rates by 2016.

The 2007 Steering Committee report on Indigenous Disadvantage indicates that the Indigenous unemployment rate fell from 20.5 per cent in 2002 to 12 per cent in 2006, but rose again to 18 per cent by 2010. However, the reported Indigenous unemployment rate would be higher if the implementation of the federally funded Community Development Employment Projects (CDEP) scheme was not factored in. Even with the CDEP and its successor, the Remote Jobs and Communities Program, unemployment among Indigenous people is significantly higher than the average for the population. The Indigenous labour force participation rate is also lower among Indigenous people (56 per cent) than the rate for non-Indigenous people (66 per cent) (ABS 2011e; ABS 2011f). Data from the 2006 Census reveal that 25.6 per cent of Indigenous people worked as labourers, compared with 11.6 per cent of non-Indigenous people. Outside the CDEP, Indigenous people work on average 8.9 hours per week, which is comparatively lower than the mainstream population, with at least 17.5 working hours each week (ABS 2007).

Indigenous Australians are least represented in managerial and professional occupations. The most frequently cited barrier to positive training and employment outcomes for Indigenous peoples is limited literacy and numeracy skills. According to the 2006 Census, approximately 65 per cent of Indigenous people had completed Year 10 or higher, compared with 80 per cent of the non-Indigenous population. Approximately 65 per cent of Indigenous people aged 15 years and over have no post-school qualification, compared with 52 per cent for non-Indigenous people. Aboriginal and Torres Strait Islander adults were 3.2 times more likely to be admitted to hospital for chronic disease than their non-Indigenous peers. In June

2005, Aboriginal and Torres Strait Islander young people aged 17 to 24 years were between 11.5 and 13.9 times more likely to be in prison than non-Indigenous young people. Adults were between 8.8 and 10 times more likely to be imprisoned than non-Indigenous adults (Department of Education and Training, 2006, Queensland Government). Indigenous people are significantly more likely to be employed in the public sector (33.1 per cent) compared with non-Indigenous (16.5 per cent). Indigenous employment in the private sector decreases with remoteness, ranging from 59.3 per cent in non-remote areas to 41.2 per cent in remote areas.

Having reviewed some of the gaps in relation to Indigenous employment and limited options for the majority of Indigenous Australians, one perspective offered is ensuring that Remote Jobs and Communities Program (RJCP) projects be imposed on all employers considering Indigenous employees. However, according to Banks (2009), despite the growth of CDEP beyond expectation, Indigenous workers do not see the potential of personal and financial growth by remaining employed through this avenue. In assessing what needs to be done by government to address Indigenous employment gaps, four areas are crucial: cooperative approaches between Indigenous people and government; community involvement and participation in program design and decision-making (avoiding 'top-down' directions); ongoing government support (considering that government support is inconsistent and is often inadequate in practice); and adequate governance and monitoring of programs (the early intervention and prevention approach).

Disability

According to the ABS survey on Disability, Ageing and Carers in Australia (2003), 1 per cent of people of working age experienced a severe activity limitation, and thereby a lower labour force participation rate. In most cases (88 per cent), the disability was not visible. In comparison, almost 20 per cent of the total Australian population had a disability, but only 53 per cent of these participated in the labour force (ABS 2003).

Employers of people with disabilities overwhelmingly (90 per cent) report that no additional costs were associated with employing these workers and that average attendance and retention rates were favourable (72 and 79 per cent respectively). Despite this, a higher proportion of people with disabilities (8.6 per cent) were unemployed in 2006 compared with the average (5 per cent) (ABS 2006b). The lower socio-economic status and lower levels of employment of people with a disability are key indicators of the economic health and well-being of this group.

According to Kearns (2008), the main issue with regard to low levels of employment among people with disabilities is discrimination at the point of recruitment. Employers often utilise recruitment criteria or 'skill prerequisites' that effectively 'filter out' people with a disability, particularly those with intellectual disabilities. In this area, it is relevant that employability varies across categories of disability. Specifically, educational studies show that hearing- or vision-impaired students in vocational education and training (VET) are more likely to clear exams and have higher employment outcomes than students with intellectual or learning disabilities, including mental illness and acquired brain injuries.

A further barrier for disabled people is the perception that they are 'passive consumers of employment support', and they are often criticised for not being pro-active in seeking work and tending to rely on pensions. However, in the current scenario where a high proportion of jobs are precarious and short-term in nature, disabled individuals are more likely to rely on pensions rather than seeking out such jobs, although some people judged to have a threshold work capacity may be required to work.

In 2010, some 793 000 people in the workforce age group received a Disability Support Pension (DSP). The Australian government provides employment-assistance programs for people with disabilities to work in supported employment settings. Similarly, the Supported Wages Scheme enables people whose productive levels might be lower than average to have their wages aligned to the level of their working capacity. Disability Employment Services are also funded to ensure that placement services are able to secure ongoing and relevant employment for people with dis-abilities. In most circumstances, employers are provided with wage subsidies and grants for modifying workplaces suitable to disabled individuals. Despite these ini-tiatives, in 2001 the Australian Chamber of Commerce reported that only 43 000 people were employed under these Australian government programs and 17 000 of these were employed in supported employment settings (formerly known as sheltered workshops), mostly in business services.

There remain significant challenges in facilitating employment opportunities for people with disabilities – particularly women – again highlighting the multifaceted nature of labour market disadvantage. This group, comprising 20 per cent of all females, continues to be impacted by both gender and disability discrimination. Part of the problem is the limited nature of the *Disability Discrimination Act 1992*, which places an onus on individuals with a disability to lodge complaints with the Australian Human Rights Commission (AHRC); however, reluctance to lodge a com-plaint is likely to lead to systematic under-reporting of discrimination and under-representation of cases at AHRC level.

■ Older workers

In common with other Western countries, Australia has an ageing population profile. In 2006, one in four people was older than 55, compared with one in every 25 people in 1901. It has been forecast that by 2045, a quarter of the population will be over 65 (Kimberley 2009: 8). Life expectancy rates are increasing, with women having the highest life expectancy at 86.1 years (compared with 82.5 years for men). Given these demographic trends, and the increasing demand for skilled labour within a growing economy, the need to retain older workers is increasingly being recognised and promoted. Australian policy-makers are turning their attention to ways to increase the workforce participation of older people in an effort to avert labour shortfalls, maintain tax revenue and improve productivity.

However, the reality is that almost half (45 per cent) of older workers (aged 55 and over) are not in the workforce, having retired or been retrenched, or because they are unable to continue work through ill-health. Moreover, it appears that many organisations do not understand the strategic imperative of retaining older workers as the supply of younger workers shrinks. Research from Australia and New Zealand shows that older people face significant discrimination in gaining or retaining employment (Handy & Davy 2007). Widespread industry restructuring in Australia has led to many older workers being offered early retirement or voluntary redundancy. Women suffer the double jeopardy of sexism and ageism in recruitment and, when they do gain jobs, they are often relegated to less secure, casualised forms of employment, such as 'temping'.

At an organisational level, HRM policies do not seem to have kept pace with the challenges posed by demographic changes. Yet, if the share of over-55-year-olds in the workforce does increase, employers will face the need to manage up to four generational cohorts, with all the complexity arising from this. Clearly, HRM policies and practices will need to develop to meet the needs of older workers and ensure harmonious working relations among the various age groups.

The federal *Age Discrimination Act* prohibits discrimination on the grounds of age (whether against youth or older persons) in employment, education and a range of services. State and territory anti-discrimination laws fill the gaps that exist in the coverage of the federal law. As with other anti-discrimination legislation, remedies at the federal level depend on an individual lodging a complaint in writing and undergoing either conciliation by the AHRC or determination by a federal court. In spite of anti-discrimination laws, employers and recruitment agencies may mask potentially discriminatory practices through recourse to academically legitimated concepts of 'team fit' or 'organisational fit', based on organisational literature. Such concepts often reference a majority culture of younger people in an organisation, for which older workers are considered to be unsuited. For older women, discrimination on the basis of 'looks' or appearance is also an important factor, with younger, more 'attractive' women being preferred for front-of-house or personal assistant roles. All older workers face certain stereotypes in employment, such as perceived lack of relevant skills, resistance to change and new technology, slower pace of work and increased risk of ill-health. However, age discrimination against women takes on more multi-layered psychological dimensions, based on gender-influenced notions of beauty, fashion, domesticity and authority.

In terms of the employment of older workers, there are contradictory forces at play. On one hand, the ageing workforce and a relative shortage of younger entrants are forcing governments to examine ways to encourage older people to extend their paid working lives. On the other hand, employers generally display negative attitudes towards older workers, and many older people themselves face contradictory personal, financial and labour market pressures. Several studies note the need for employers to offer older workers more flexible working arrangements, such as part-time work or short-term contracts, in order to meet their needs and aspirations. On the supply side, the inadequate superannuation coverage of many older workers, increasing life expectancy and greater targeting of the age-pension encourage many older people to remain in or return to the workforce. The question is whether employer policies and older workers' propensities and needs can coalesce to produce mutually desirable outcomes.

Beyond the problem of labour/skill shortages, organisations will find it important to retain organisational and technical knowledge held by older workers, in order to train the next generation of workers and ensure continuity of operations. It is increasingly apparent that organisations will need to explore a range of flexible work options to ensure that older workers are able to combine paid work and retirement, and to increase their motivation to stay on at work. This section has not dealt with issues affecting younger workers (15–24-year-olds), but there is significant evidence that in different ways, with their elevated unemployment rates and vulnerability to low pay and exploitation, they too form a disadvantaged group in the labour market (Biddle & Burgess 1999).

■ Conclusion

Australia has one of the most culturally diverse labour forces in the world and, with its increasing level of cosmopolitanism, exhibits a remarkable tapestry of skills, aptitudes, lifestyles and backgrounds. The challenge for managers and practitioners is to 'harness' the positive aspects of this diversity and ensure that all workers have the opportunity to contribute their skills, talent and labour for the benefit of all. Indeed, diversity management has been one of the major areas embraced by HR managers in Australia.

Our research has shown that the reality of disadvantage has different historical, cultural and empirical dimensions, depending on the nature of the difference foregrounded in any individual case. While disadvantaged groups may share common challenges, they also have their own particular problems and issues, based on history, circumstance and environment. However, as argued in this chapter, it is unhelpful to treat disadvantage as falling into separate and fixed categories. The nature of disadvantage can change over time and with circumstances; it is fluid and multifaceted.

All workers have the potential to fall into the disadvantaged category, but some live with disadvantage all their working lives. As many commentators have pointed out, the dominant stereotype of the typical worker as being white, Anglo-Celtic, Protestant, able-bodied and male, with a full-time support worker at home, leaves the majority of the workforce potentially marginalised and not served well by many workplace cultures and systems, particularly those emphasising long working hours or rapid-change flexibility. In this scenario, it is imperative for managers to adopt tailored and robust diversity strategies to ensure a secure supply of skilled labour at all levels. Making sure that workloads, work environments and working hours suit the needs of disadvantaged workers is an option, but the challenges are considerable. Not to address these challenges risks the under-utilisation of workforce capacity and talent held among individuals who may variously be described as 'disadvantaged' but who are willing and able to work.

Discussion questions

10.1 What is the meaning of the term 'disadvantaged worker', and how and to what extent is it distinct from 'diversity'?

10.2 What is the difference between workforce disadvantage and precarious employment? Illustrate your answer by reference to one or more of the demographic groups discussed in this chapter.

10.3 Explain the rise of casual employment in Australia, placing particular emphasis on its demographic features and relationship to workforce disadvantage.

10.4 Is there any connection between the extent of workforce disadvantage in Australia and economic policy, economic fluctuations and workplace relations laws? Are these factors interrelated? If so, in what ways?

10.5 What is the paradox that exists in relation to the employment of older workers, and why does it persist? Can governments assist in its resolution?

The challenge to workplace health and safety and the changing nature of work and the working environment

Elsa Underhill

■ Chapter objectives

This chapter will enable readers to understand the:
- links between employment insecurity and occupational health and safety (OHS)
- relationship between employment insecurity and poor health outcomes
- connection between the design and management of work and psychological or physical harm
- importance of employee voice in bringing about improved psycho-social well-being at work
- growing challenges to worker involvement in OHS despite its efficacy in reducing occupational illness and injury.

▨ Introduction

Changes in the work environment present significant challenges to workers' health and safety. The pursuit of labour flexibility, intense competitive pressures and the shift towards decollectivism and deregulated labour markets have produced new workplace risks to occupational health and safety (OHS), while eroding the capacity of workers to respond to such risks. Foremost is the challenge posed by the changing nature of employment, specifically the growth of precarious forms of employment, as well as greater job insecurity experienced by permanent employees. The second risk is the surge in psycho-social distress associated with increasingly demanding employment conditions, and third is the decline in occupational health and safety worker representation and consultation, contributing to a void in mechanisms for identifying, monitoring and controlling risks at work. These risks are not inevitable, but reflect choices made by organisations and governments about the priority given to worker health and safety vis-à-vis other economic and political objectives.

▨ Changes in the nature of employment: precariousness and job insecurity

In Chapter 2, we considered the Australian employment model and especially the causes of growing workforce insecurity, and in Chapter 10 we examined the multiple sources of labour force disadvantage. In this section, we return to discuss the issue of 'precariousness' because of its important implications for workplace health and safety.

The nature of employment has changed substantially in recent decades. As firms have pursued greater labour flexibility, an increasing share of the workforce has faced precarious employment, which is characterised by increased job insecurity, more volatile incomes and a reduced capacity to voice workplace concerns. In Australia, the growth in labour flexibility is most readily evidenced through the expansion of casual employment. Around 16 per cent of those in the workforce were employed on a casual basis in 1983; the proportion peaked at 26 per cent in 1998 before stabilising at about 24 per cent in 2010 (ABS 2011a). Initially concentrated in service industries with peaks and troughs in customer demand, such as hospitality and retail, casual employment is now dispersed across a range of industries, including manufacturing, construction, warehousing and health care (ABS 2011g). Most casuals (70 per cent) are employed part-time and, reflecting the expansion of casual employment into industries that formerly were the domain of full-time male workers, an increasing number of casual workers are men, with this category now making up 16 per cent of the male workforce (ABS 2011g).

Temporary agency work (also known as labour hire) is another form of precarious employment that has experienced rapid growth since the late 1980s. Agency workers are hired by an agency and placed with a host employer while continuing to be employed and paid by the agency. Although agency workers make up only 3–4 per cent of the Australian workforce, as in other developed economies, agency workers are disproportionately employed in low-skilled and often hazardous occupations and industries, and their employment creates downward pressures on wages and employment conditions, safety and union membership (Arrowsmith 2006). They are often paid lower wages than those received by their co-workers who are direct employees and are reluctant to join or become active in unions for fear of job loss. They too are hired predominantly on a casual basis (80 per cent of agency workers are estimated to be casuals), paid only for the time placed with a host. While some are placed with one host for an extended period, others 'churn' through multiple host workplaces at very short notice. Indeed, a common problem encountered by agency workers is the 'uncertainty of living by the mobile phone', waiting to be told when and where their next placement will be (Underhill & Quinlan 2011). While temporary agency work originated with white-collar office 'temping', like casual employment more generally, it has since expanded into a diverse range of industries from manufacturing, maintenance work, food processing and ware-housing, through to hospitals and call centres.

A third form of precarious employment is independent contracting, whereby workers supply a service but are not employees. While some independent contractors operate genuine businesses, others are more accurately described as 'dependent contractors' because they are typically reliant on a single employer for work and exercise little discretion in the manner of its performance – they resemble employees but are not entitled to employment-based protections, such as a minimum wage or other employment conditions. Independent contractors make up about 9 per cent of the workforce, a share that has remained relatively stable in recent decades, notwith-standing anecdotal evidence to the contrary. An audit of cleaning-service employers in 2011, for example, found that 22 per cent of employers had misclassified employ-ees as independent contractors) (Fair Work Ombudsman 2011). The extent to which these self-employed workers are dependent rather than independent contractors has not been estimated but is likely to vary by industry and function.

Together, these three types of precarious workers make up just under one-third of the Australian workforce; after allowing for those on fixed-term contracts and other business operators, only 62 per cent of the workforce comprises permanent employ-ees, and 18 per cent of them are part-time (ABS 2011g). Similar developments in the growth of precarious employment have occurred in other advanced economies, although the form differs by local institutional arrangements. Hence, while 13.5 per cent of workers in the European Union were employed on temporary contracts in 2010 (Eurofound 2011), only 9 per cent of German workers were employed in fixed-term jobs (although 20 per cent were employed in low paid 'marginal' employment) (Siefert 2011); one-quarter of British workers were employed part-time and another 6 per cent were in temporary jobs in 2010 (Slater 2011); and around 32 per cent of Spanish workers have been employed in temporary jobs since at least the turn of the century (Malo 2011). This shift in the nature of employment is widespread, and its implications for workers' well-being are increasingly the focus of research and govern-ment inquiries in many countries.

Alongside the growth of less-secure forms of employment has been the expansion of outsourcing, privatisation and repeated rounds of downsizing and restructuring since the 1990s in Australia. Each has contributed to permanent employment becoming less stable, resulting in increasing numbers of workers in precarious employment. One of the most significant developments had been that both Labor and non-Labor governments at the state and federal levels have undertaken privatisation and outsourcing, resulting in a marked shift in employment away from in the formerly stable, unionised public sector to the private sector. By 2010, only 20 per cent of employees worked in the public sector compared with 32 per cent in the mid-1980s (ABS 1985, 2011a). Among private sector employers, a common response to global pressures has been 'offshoring', or other forms of extreme cost-cutting. As we saw in Chapters 1 and 2, employment in manufacturing – another former mainstay of secure employment and unionisation – has fallen steadily over recent decades. In contrast, employment in the service sectors expanded from around 66 per cent of the workforce in 1984 to 78 per cent in 2010 (ABS 1985, 2011a). These shifts in the industry distribution of employment have brought considerable job uncertainty during periods of change, and resulted in a greater proportion of the workforce facing 'softer' health and safety risks (such as psycho-social risks), including concerns about work intensification and declining quality of jobs.

Although these changes began in the 1980s, they were hastened by changes to workplace relations laws implemented by both Labor and Liberal-National Coalition governments, as discussed in previous chapters (see especially Chapter 5). Prohibitions on collective agreements that contain clauses restricting the use of agency and casual workers in effect provided an incentive to utilise insecure forms of employment, while prohibitions on including basic conditions – such as rest breaks and minimum breaks between shifts (raising concerns about issues such as fatigue) – both increased workplace health and safety risks during the years of the Howard Liberal-National Coalition government. Prohibitions on paid union training (including OHS training) and restrictions on the right of entry to union officials also eroded the capacity of unions to respond to OHS issues. Further, the elimination of unfair-dismissal protections for many workers undermined their confidence in raising health and safety concerns. Removing protection from unfair dismissal was regarded as a impeding enforcement of OHS laws by government inspectors because it was more difficult to shield complainants from employers, particularly in small workplaces (Quinlan, Bohle & Lamm 2010). Although many of these collective rights have been reinstated since 2010, union membership remains at historically low levels, leaving gaps in OHS worker representation. Also, despite the reinstatement of many of these rights, there are few signs of employer reliance on precarious forms of employment being reversed. Consequently, as we shall see below, health and safety concerns arising from precarious and insecure employment have continued.

■ Precarious employment and health and safety at work

Evidence that the changing nature of employment was detrimental to worker health and safety began to emerge in the 1990s, and was consolidated in a study by Quinlan,

Mayhew and Bohle (2001). Their review of more than 100 studies of job insecurity and downsizing reported that more than 80 per cent of studies found that OHS had been adversely affected by this development and only part-time employees experienced ambiguous effects. A further review of international research on outsourcing and subcontracting found poorer OHS outcomes in 23 out of 25 studies, while the exceptions (one in subcontracting and the other in home-based work) yielded 'mixed' results (Quinlan & Bohle 2009). Narrower reviews of research into temporary employment (e.g. Virtanen et al. 2005) have also revealed a clear preponderance of studies identifying a negative association between OHS outcomes and precarious forms of work.

Drawing upon the commonalities revealed across studies, Quinlan and Bohle (2004) developed the Economic and Reward Pressure, Disorganisation and Regulatory Failure (PDR) model to explain why precarious employment impacted negatively on workplace health and safety. The model groups explanatory factors into three categories. The first, *economic and reward pressures*, includes elements of economic pressure and power that are both immediate to the job – such as piecework payment systems – and part of the broader labour market – for example, irregular income streams of precarious workers and lack of income support following injury. It encompasses sources of income insecurity that influence safe work practices, such as low job and income security and intense competition for work, which can contribute to a range of hazardous practices, including work intensification, 'cutting corners', accepting hazardous tasks, working when injured and multiple job-holding (Quinlan & Bohle 2004). An OHS inspector, for example, described his experience with subcontractors in the following terms:

> Every site we go on they have subcontractors there and . . . it certainly creates problems because if they don't get the job done they don't get paid so they'll work longer hours, they'll try and take that shortcut unfortunately because they'll get the job done quicker . . . (cited in Quinlan, Johnstone & McNamara 2009: 564)

The second factor, *disorganisation*, encompasses characteristics that tend to emerge in organisations that lack a commitment to a stable workforce. It includes the exacerbation of complex, ambiguous rules and procedures, and changes to work rules and practices, which become lost among the myriad 'visitors' to the workplace. In these circumstances, OHS knowledge and management systems become fractured, while inter-worker communication, task coordination and lines of management control are weakened. Under-qualified, under-trained and inexperienced workers who lack familiarity with the workplace become more commonplace. In this setting, precarious workers are less able to collectively organise or to be 'heard' at the workplace. Importantly, disorganisation should not be seen simply as an outcome of oversight, but rather as a characteristic feature of the relationship between contingent workers and their employers. The use of temporary workers affects employer attitudes to induction, training, participation in workplace committees and other activities, with implications for safety (Quinlan & Bohle 2004: 93).

The third category, *regulatory failure*, refers to the extent to which OHS and employment regulation are weakened through the complexity of precarious employment and inter-organisational contracting arrangements. Gaps in coverage emerge in employment protection and minimum entitlements; compliance is weakened as employee knowledge of entitlements declines or is undermined by their labour market vulnerability; and enforcement processes encounter hurdles, such as identifying those with legal responsibility and the opportunistic liquidation of business entities to avoid prosecution. Another element of regulatory failure is inconsistent or discriminatory aspects of both the form and implementation of regulation practices that bear most heavily on those in precarious employment (including foreign and undocumented workers). Quinlan and colleagues' (2009) study of OHS inspectors' perceptions of the problems associated with changing employment arrangements also highlights how these complexities stretch already limited inspectoral resources, because of the need to continually explain obligations to multiple parties at single worksites and to undertake follow-up visits to the multiple office locations associated with those parties. Table 11.1 summaries the key risk factors associated with the three components of the PDR model.

Underhill and Quinlan's (2011) analysis of the injury experience of temporary agency workers in Australia demonstrates how PDR factors contributed to a higher risk of injury and more severe injuries for agency workers compared with traditional, directly hired workers. The agency workers were predominantly employed as casuals, and many were injured early in a placement; 18 per cent were injured during the first week of their placement and 35 per cent within the first month. By contrast, only 5 per cent of comparable directly hired workers were injured during their first month of employment. The irregular work and income of temporary workers resulted in economic pressures to accept any placement available, to work intensely to ensure another placement would be offered, and not to report injuries for fear of job loss (contributing to relatively minor injuries becoming more severe). Some agency workers were placed to perform tasks for which they were neither qualified nor experienced (including, in one case, a youth who was fatally injured), and such training as was provided by the agency employer or the host was often inadequate. Three-way communication between workers, agencies and hosts in relation to workplace risks

Table 11.1 Risk factors associated with the Economic and Reward Pressure, Disorganisation and Regulatory Failure (PDR) model

Economic and reward pressures	Disorganisation	Regulatory failure
Insecure jobs (fear of losing job)	Short tenure, inexperience	Poor knowledge of legal rights, obligations
Contingent, irregular payment	Poor induction, training and supervision	Limited access to OHS, workers' compensation rights
Long or irregular work hours	Ineffective procedures and communication	Fractured or disputed legal obligations
Multiple job-holding (e.g. may work for several temp agencies)	Ineffective OHSMS/inability to organise	Non-compliance and regulator oversight (stretched resources)

Source: Underhill and Quinlan (2011).

was often fractured and, when workers raised OHS and workplace concerns, employers and hosts 'passed the buck' between one another, with neither resolving the issue. Workers also risked dismissal or being offered a placement too far from home to be practicable, as a consequence of raising concerns or taking time off to recover from minor injuries. Once injured, the majority in this sample were offered no further placements, notwithstanding having recovered from their injuries.

These findings in relation to temporary agency workers are not unique to Australia. Studies undertaken in the United States (e.g. Smith et al. 2010), France (e.g. Francois 1991), Spain (e.g. Benavides et al. 2006) and Finland (e.g. Hintikka 2011) have found that agency workers experience a higher rate of injury than directly hired workers, while studies in Canada (e.g. Lippel et al. 2011) and Sweden (e.g. Aronsson 1999) have identified similar practices contributing to OHS risks for agency and on-call workers.

The risks associated with precarious work also extend to poorer health. A study of poorer health outcomes among precarious workers in Canada (Lewchuck et al. 2003) led to the development of the 'employment strain' model, which identifies seven components of employment strain that are common to precarious employees and contribute to poorer health. These are uncertainties arising from lack of control over access to work (employment uncertainty); earnings unpredictability; household precariousness (providing basic needs); scheduling; work location; task; and workload. Not only were precarious workers more likely to report poorer health, they were also more likely to report being tense at work and exhausted after work. These stress-related symptoms were an outcome of the uncertainty or employment strain continually faced by precarious employees. Clarke et al. (2007), in further tests of the model, distinguished between the importance of employment relationship uncertainty, support and effort. Those in unsustainable precarious employment who preferred but were unable nor expected to find permanent employment experienced high employment and income insecurity, poorer health outcomes and the least access to social support at work, both from their household and in the community. As Clarke et al. observe (2007: 325): 'Their employment situation both creates a need for support but makes it more difficult for workers to access it.' Only the small proportion of workers who were satisfied with precarious employment reported good health and social support, leading them to consider their work arrangements sustainable in the longer term.

Over the past decade, a number of governments have initiated inquiries specific to OHS and changing employment, or have included changing employment in the terms of reference of broader inquiries into OHS (e.g. Dean 2010; NIOSH 2002; Stewart-Compton, Mayman & Sherrif 2009). The response of the Australian government has been among the more innovative to date. The model national OHS laws, which commenced in 2012, broaden the responsibilities of organisations to ensure that they provide a safe and healthy work environment for all workers, not just the organisation's employees. The laws are intended to overcome the complexities and confusion that flow from multi-employer worksites, such as those that arise when contractors and temporary agency employees are engaged by organisations (Johnstone 2011). However, the risks confronting precarious workers originate in part from their acute job insecurity, a problem derived from gaps in employment rather than OHS regulation. These risks also flow from a lack of knowledge about their employment rights, including the right to compensation once injured. Injured casual workers, for example, are three times more likely than permanent workers to not apply for workers' compensation, because they either believe they were not covered or are not aware of entitlements (ABS 2011h). Lastly, the continual exposure to organisational restructuring and downsizing noted earlier has produced work environments in which precarious workers increasingly are joined by permanent employees in being exposed to chronic uncertainty and its associated detrimental health impacts.

■ Organisational change, job insecurity and health

There is now consistent evidence that job insecurity contributes to psychological ill-health, and that the higher the level of insecurity, the more ill-health increases (Ferrie et al. 2008). Importantly, perceived job insecurity – when workers are fearful or continually worried about job loss – shows a stronger direct relationship with poor health than objective insecurity, such as when the nature of the employment contract is insecure (Strazdins et al. 2004). Also, while it might be thought that those with poorer psychological health are more likely to be located in less secure employment, studies that have measured changes in psychological health over the duration of employment from secure to insecure status have confirmed that the direction of causality is from job insecurity to poorer health (Ferrie et al. 2008).

The Whitehall study (also known as the Stress and Health Study) was among the earliest to identify the adverse health consequences of job insecurity. These studies analysed data collected from more than 10 000 British public servants, beginning in 1985 (for further details, see the study website at <http://www.ucl.ac.uk/white-hall>, accessed 20 December 2012). Baseline screening commenced in the mid-1980s, and data-collection continued over a 15-year period, during which there was substantial restructuring and privatisation. Workers who experienced chronic job insecurity reported poorer self-rated health and greater levels of psychiatric morbidity (depression) than those whose jobs remained secure; those whose jobs shifted from secure to insecure also experienced elevated blood pressure. Neither alcohol consumption nor smoking behaviours accounted for these outcomes. Some adverse effects were enduring, with poor psychological health evident for extended periods after job security returned, notwithstanding improvements in self-reported health (Ferrie et al. 2008). Similar outcomes have been found in other industry sectors and countries (e.g. Virtanen et al. 2002). The impacts of job insecurity are not limited to psychological health. Poorer physical health, including fatigue, chronic insomnia, migraines, colds and flu-like symptoms, as well as musculoskeletal disorders, have all been identified (Ferrie et al. 2008).

Employees who remain in downsized organisations – the 'survivors' – have been shown to experience a number of health problems associated with increased job demands, including those flowing from subsequent under-staffing, often accompanied by increased uncertainty about their own future in the organisation. As in the studies reported above, outcomes include anxiety, depression, poorer self-reported health, musculoskeletal problems and heart disease (see Quinlan 2007 for a review of such studies). Increased rates of workplace injury have also been identified in studies of downsizing in the health sector, along with increased violence at work (Ferrie et al. 2008). While many studies of the health effects of downsizing rely on workers' self-reported health status (typically the General Health Questionnaire, an internationally recognised reliable and validated evaluation tool), the small number of studies utilising objective data have found a greater likelihood of the use of anti-depressant prescription drugs, elevated blood-sugar levels (a potential precursor to diabetes), blood pressure and early retirements on medical grounds (see Ferrie et al. 2008 for a review of such studies). A Danish longitudinal study of public sector restructuring found a high level of 'burnout' (physical and psychological fatigue and exhaustion), accompanied by cynicism, detachment from the job and a lack of professional accomplishment among more than 1000 respondents (Anderson et al. 2010). Although consultants had been engaged to assist with communication during restructuring, it was found that a lack of worker involvement in the process contributed to these poor mental health outcomes.

Faced with the uncertainty and pressures associated with employment in organisations undergoing cost-cutting, employees have been found to respond with high levels of presenteeism (attending work while ill), estimated to be more costly to organisations than absenteeism; excessive (and often unpaid) working hours; delaying vacation leave (with an associated risk of burnout); and reluctance to report OHS problems or take part in OHS committees (Quinlan 2007). Organisational change is so pervasive that job insecurity – even for permanent employees – is now considered an ongoing feature of the labour market (Ferrie et al. 2008). The policy implications of such an assessment point to the need for the promotion of reductions in job insecurity across the workforce, not only for precarious workers.

Growing prevalence of psycho-social hazards and the changing workplace environment

Alongside job insecurity are a range of other employment characteristics that together make up the psycho-social work environment. Known as psycho-social risks, these hazards involve 'those aspects of the design and management of work, and its social and organisational contexts, that have the potential for causing psychological or physical harm' (Leka & Cox 2010: 125). While the poorer health outcomes associated with job insecurity and organisational change include psycho-social outcomes (especially to the extent that these outcomes are associated with distress), the most commonly recognised health outcome of psycho-social risks is occupational or job stress.

Workers experiencing occupational stress face considerable difficulty in accessing workers' compensation, including a greater likelihood that the claim will be investigated and rejected, and a reluctance of doctors to support such claims. It is perhaps unsurprising that recent Australian data on workplace injuries show that those with job stress were least likely to receive workers' compensation (78 per cent of those who claimed to have job stress did not receive workers' compensation), yet were most likely to require five or more days of leave in order to recover (compared with all other injury types) (ABS 2011h). This survey also found that 4.9 per cent of the workforce have self-reported work related stress or another mental condition (ABS 2011h). Other surveys suggest that this phenomenon may be more prevalent and have significant costs. LaMontagne and colleagues (2008) estimate that in 2003, 13.2 per cent of male workers and 17.2 per cent of female workers in the state of Victoria were likely to suffer depression attributable to job strain. Between 2006/07 and 2010/11, it was reported that there had been a 54 per cent increase in workers' compensation claims for stress (notwithstanding a relative restrictive definition of the disease), and that such claims accounted for one in five serious claims (requiring one or more weeks off work) (Comcare 2011). The cost of depression across the Australian workforce was estimated to be \$12.6 billion per year in 2007, based upon an estimated 1.54 million workers (14.7 per cent of the workforce) suffering depression. This included \$3.4 billion attributed to lost productive time and \$8.9 billion attributed to job turnover or employee replacement costs (LaMontagne, Sanderson & Cocker 2010). Under the circumstances, it is not surprising that workers' compensation claims for occupational stress are regarded as just the 'tip of the iceberg'.

Surveys in the European Union also report high levels of work-related stress, with between 20 and 30 per cent of workers reporting that their health was at risk because of work-related stress in 2007 (Leka et al. 2011). The cost of work-related stress, depression and anxiety was estimated to be more than £530 million in the United Kingdom, and between €830 million and €1656 million in France, in 2009 (Eurofound 2009). Importantly, from the perspective of worker entitlements to compensation for work-related injuries, the International Labour Organization (ILO) recognised occupational stress as an occupational disease (where a direct link is established between exposure to risk factors and a mental disorder) in 2010 (Leka et al. 2011). Such recognition represents an important step in terms of employers bearing responsibility for minimising exposure to known risks.

Of the explanations for occupational stress, Karasek's (1979) model is the most widely accepted and tested. His job demands/job control model identifies a significant interactive relationship between levels of job demands, job control and mental strain. Put simply, 'job strain increases with the relative excess of demands over decision latitude' (1979: 5). 'Job demands' were defined to include variables such as working fast, working very hard, excessive workloads, and whether the job was hectic or sufficient time was allowed to complete tasks. 'Job control' included factors such as the degree of discretion over task organisation, the repetitive nature of tasks and participation in decision-making. The combination of high demand and low job control produced 'job strain', which in turn is measured by exhaustion and depression indicators. Further, increased exposure to high-strain jobs contributed to unresolved strain and was manifested in poor mental health. It was found that social support can mitigate only some of this risk.

More recent studies have estimated that job strain doubles the risk of depression (LaMontagne et al. 2008). Further, an Australian study of managers and professionals found that the combination of job strain and job insecurity markedly increased the odds of suffering both mental and physical health problems (Strazdins et al. 2004). Belying the accepted view that work is always good for you, Broom and colleagues (2006) analysed a sample of almost 2500 Australians aged 40–44 years, and found that those who reported job strain, job insecurity and low levels of ability to find a new job if their current employment ended were more likely to report that they suffered depression than those who were unemployed.

There are two other models worthy of brief consideration. The first is the *effort/reward imbalance model* (Siegrist 1996), which emphasises the imbalance between efforts expended by employees and the rewards provided by employers, including non-tangible recognition. Additional variables of low social support, including support from co-workers and supervisors, have also been joined with this model when identifying higher-risk practices (Bultmann et al. 2002). This model has been expanded to include the level of job security as a reward, offering a potential explanation for the poor outcomes associated with job insecurity noted above (Silla, Gracia & Peiro 2005). The second model is the *organisational justice model*, which posits that a lack of procedural and relational justice within organisations contributes to occupational stress (Kivimäki et al. 2007). In this study, organisational injustice was found to be associated with poorer health, with the highest level of risk occurring when injustice was combined with a high effort-to-reward imbalance.

Interventions to reduce the risk of job stress take three forms. The first of these are primary organisational level interventions, which focus upon the cause of stress – such as job design, work pace or the operation of a joint-workplace OHS committee. The second are secondary individual-level interventions, which focus upon modifying individual responses to stress to facilitate better responses to stressful situations, such as stress or time management programs. Finally, there are tertiary interventions, which involve treating those exhibiting symptoms of stress. LaMontagne and Keegel (2010) point out that primary interventions offer the maximum benefit to individuals and organisations because of their focus upon causal factors. They also affirm the importance of meaningful participation of those targeted by such interventions:

> Participation is a particularly important principle in job stress intervention because it is integral to the prevention and control of job stress itself. Participation is a concrete enactment of job control, demonstrates organisational fairness and justice, and builds upon mutual support among workers and between workers and supervisors. (LaMontagne & Keegel 2010: 8)

Egan and colleagues' (2007) review of 18 studies examined health outcomes following interventions that increased employee involvement in decision-making. It concluded that most interventions led to improved health. This outcome was reinforced by a review of 19 studies of task restructuring (Bambra et al. 2007), which found that only those interventions that reduced job demands resulted in improved health, and that increased job demands tended to affect health adversely.

However, both the reality of employee involvement and the robustness of research findings on employee health have been questioned, particularly in those cases in which employee participation was direct rather than representative, and where psycho-social risks were conceptualised in individual rather than collective terms. As Walters (2011: 604) points out, 'many of the factors which have contributed to this declining influence [of trade union representation in OHS] are the same ones that contribute to the rise in psycho-social risks and their effects at work'. From the various findings on the link between employee well-being and employee participation, we see the importance of research on employee voice – an issue that is considered further in Chapter 7.

The potential for effective employee involvement in mechanisms to reduce psycho-social risks, however, is also central to proposals emanating from the European Union. A major project piloting an integrated risk-management approach to psycho-social risks was undertaken and a 'European Framework for Psycho-social Risk Management' developed that endorses the participatory approach and promotes 'ownership' by all stakeholders (managers, workers and their representatives) as a key component of psycho-social risk assessment (Leka & Cox 2010). The effectiveness of this approach is yet to be evaluated fully. Nor has such an approach been well supported in Australia, where a revival in the popularity of behaviour-based approaches to health and safety (such as the promotion of employee resilience) has shifted attention back to individualised responses, rather than a focus upon organisational-level sourced problems. As Shaw and Blewett (2000: 465) observe, the:

> resurgence of worker behavior as a sufficient explanation for occupational ill-health and as the most effective target for interventions to improve OHS . . . [is depriving] workers of the power to act on their environment, only on their behaviour.

Worker involvement is also diminishing as a result of a number of other changes occurring in the working environment, considered in the next section.

The demise of worker involvement in workplace health and safety

The scope for and importance of worker involvement in occupational health and safety has been touched upon throughout this discussion – for example, the absence of precarious workers' involvement at the most rudimentary level of raising individual concerns heightens their risk of injury, while interventions that enhance workers' involvement in decision-making have been linked to improved health outcomes. Here we turn to the role of formal involvement in OHS workplace processes, namely worker OHS representatives and worker participation in joint OHS workplace committees, and the scope for precarious workers being represented in OHS matters at work.

Workplace health and safety is often partitioned off by management from other collective concerns at the workplace. It is regarded as an area requiring expertise or, particularly in the case of small businesses, a problem created by reckless workers – otherwise known as 'the careless worker' syndrome – and therefore requiring behavioural change rather than corrections and improvements in production and work processes. Yet research has found consistently that collective worker involvement is essential to the development of a safe and healthy workplace; that effective OHS is not the domain of experts (although their input is necessary); and that a safe workplace is an outcome of deliberate actions by both management and workers.

Since the 1980s, most Australian states have enacted OHS legislation supporting (to varying degrees) worker health and safety representatives and joint OHS committees, and this approach is also embodied in the new, national model for OHS laws (which has so far been enacted at the federal level and in the Australian Capital Territory, Northern Territory, New South Wales and Queensland). Worker health and safety representatives generally are involved in day-to-day activities such as risk assessments, monitoring practices and investigating problems when they arise, as well as making representations to management. Joint OHS committees are composed of management and worker representatives, and are intended to have higher-level policy-orientated functions. Quinlan, Bohle and Lamm (2010: 344) distinguish these functions as monitoring and enforcement by worker representatives and problem-solving by OHS committees. Some states mandate that workers make up at least 50 per cent of the members of an OHS committee to ensure that these bodies are not dominated by management's interests.

Statutory endorsement of formalised worker representation in OHS is well supported by research on the impact of such involvement, particularly when unions are part of the process. In the United States, deaths from hydrogen sulphide were less frequent in unionised than non-unionised workplaces, and fewer illnesses and injuries were recorded in the public sector when workers were involved through an OHS committee. In Canada, a reduction in lost-time injuries was associated with health and safety committees, while worker empowerment was consistently associated with lower injury rates (Johnstone, Quinlan & Walters 2005). In the European Union, active union representation and participatory management have been associated with improved sickness absence rates in Norway, and interaction between works councils and unions (including a willingness by unions to mobilise union power) contributed to increased employer compliance with statutory obligations to involve workers in OHS in the Netherlands (Popma 2008). In the United Kingdom, analysis of the Workplace Industrial Relations Survey data identified both higher injury rates in workplaces where management did not consult over OHS, and lower rates when joint consultative arrangements were in place (Walters & Nichols 2007). Other studies have found a positive relationship between worker representation and improved OHS practices, such as tackling OHS issues and getting things done (Walters & Nichols 2007); paying closer attention to risks embedded in company processes, such as psycho-social workloads; and raising awareness of OHS issues and improving compliance with OHS statutory requirements (Popma 2008). No such studies have been conducted in Australia in recent times, although Biggins and Holland's (1995) findings are consistent with the international studies. A feature of these international studies is that effective worker involvement also involves trade unions, and direct employee participation has not been shown to have an equivalent impact (Walters & Nichols 2007).

A three-step process is thought to explain why unionised workplaces with active worker involvement result in lower injury rates and more effective preventative approaches to OHS (Walters & Frick 2000). First, workers draw on union resources for expertise and training, enabling an informed, independent voice that can be exercised without fear of discrimination. Both the quality and quantity of such training have been shown to be crucial to worker representatives developing and being integrated into workplace health and safety in European studies. Second, the independent voice provided by unions, when coupled with additional work activities such as hazard identification (made possible because of the knowledge and expertise gained from the union), helps shape the OHS management system, including its responsiveness to OHS problems. Third, the nature of the OHS management system will in turn determine the extent to which hazards are identified and either removed or controlled (Walters & Frick 2000). Other explanations for the direct link between reduced injuries and union-supported worker representation emphasise the greater knowledge of the work environment and the associated risks that are held by workers compared with their managers. Also, worker representatives can act as 'watchdogs' on managers to ensure that the health and safety interests of their constituents are not compromised by a management focus on maximising production and profit – which may be prioritised above optimal OHS management' (Loudoun & Walters 2009: 181).

Walters and Nichols (2007) caution that there are preconditions to effective worker representation and consultation. These include legislative support for the role of OHS representatives; demonstrable senior management commitment to both OHS and participative approaches, as well as the capacity to support participative approaches; competent identification, evaluation and control of risks by management and workers; trained and informed autonomous representatives supported by external unions; and consultation and communication between the OHS representatives and those they represent. The discussion below focuses on the first of these preconditions.

In Australia, there is no systematic collection of data on the number or location of workplace OHS representatives or joint OHS committees; however, the limited evidence suggests that OHS representatives are only found in unionised workplaces, and that the numbers have diminished substantially since the mid-1980s (Quinlan, Bohle & Lamm 2010; ABS 2011a). The weakening of trade unions has meant that the institutional infrastructure – including access to independent expertise, training and support in disputes over OHS – has slowly eroded in Australia, thereby undermining participative processes (Johnstone, Quinlan & Walters 2005). Limited overseas evidence suggests that a similar pattern of decline is occurring – for example, in the United Kingdom, the WIRS points to a fall in the number of workplaces undertaking consultation over OHS matters between 1998 and 2004

(Walters 2011). In Sweden, where legislation has supported worker OHS representation for almost a century, the number of workplace representatives has remained
relatively stable, but they have reported greater levels of harassment and lower
levels of resources under the less favourable political and labour market environment that has emerged over the past decade (Frick 2011).

Legislative support for OHS worker representation is thus insufficient when other
institutional and political settings are hostile to unionisation and worker involvement.
A Victorian survey of more than 800 OHS representatives, for example, reported that
32 per cent had been intimidated or bullied by their employer and/or manager for
raising OHS issues (Victorian Trades Hall Council 2004: 11). Similarly, a survey of 41
584 workers (mostly union members) undertaken by the ACTU reported that 27 per
cent of respondents agreed with the statement that 'employees who speak out about
issue as safety are frowned upon'. A parallel public survey of 1000 workers found that
26 per cent agreed with the same statement (ACTU 2011). A smaller, national survey
of 762 managers (54 per cent) and non-managers (46 per cent) conducted by Safe
Work Australia drew more positive results: 90 per cent of respondents agreed that
they were 'not afraid to challenge unsafe situations or unsafe work practices' and a
similar proportion (89 per cent) agreed that 'employees are encouraged to raise
health and safety concerns in your workplace' (Job & Smith 2011).

To overcome the perception of disadvantage that flows from voicing OHS concerns,
the Victorian *Occupational Health and Safety Act 2004* was amended in 2009 to
strengthen the protection against organisations that discriminated against workers
who raised OHS issues. A large stevedoring company was the first to be prosecuted
under this provision; it was fined A$180 000 in 2011 for having suspended and threat-
ened to dismiss a worker (who was also an OHS representative) who had refused to use
a new method for unloading steel from vessels, because the OHS committee had not
been consulted before its introduction (a legal requirement), and he and other workers
were not familiar with the new process (OHS Alert 2011). The *Fair Work Act 2009* also
protects workers who are adversely affected for raising OHS issues, as we noted in
Chapter 5. This protection was demonstrated by a recent Federal Court decision grant-
ing an injunction preventing a large manufacturer from giving a final warning on
dismissal to a health and safety representative following disagreement over unsafe
practices (*Automotive, Food, Metals Engineering, Printing and Kindred Industries Union
v Visy Packaging Pty Ltd (No. 2)*. These two examples illustrate the need for demonstrable enforcement of the employment rights of OHS representatives to support their
OHS activities. Without such support, workers will continue to be reluctant to voice
concerns or become OHS representatives.

We now move to consider the second major barrier to worker involvement in
improving OHS: the capacity for employees to be represented on these issues in view
of the changing nature of employment and the low incidence of OHS representatives
across Australian workplaces. The growth in precarious employment, along with
greater job insecurity experienced by permanent employees, has produced an environment in which an increasing proportion of the workforce are either excluded from
OHS participatory processes or are prevented from participating due to fear of job

loss. For example, Keegel and colleagues (2010) found that casual employees were least likely to participate directly in OHS issues – for example, through conversations with management – as well as through representative mechanisms. Union members were also found to be two-and-a-half times more likely to be involved in direct forms of participation than non-union members, suggesting that even direct participation may be contingent upon unionisation. Underhill's (2008) survey of temporary agency workers in Victoria found that a substantial minority – around one in four – reported being either dismissed for raising OHS concerns, or did not voice their concern for fear of dismissal; a similar proportion found their concerns were ignored when raised. Host employees – often resentful about the presence of agency workers, whom they perceived as a threat to their own employment – were also reluctant to incorporate them into OHS committees or represent them in relation to host OHS issues. Consultation over OHS within temporary agency firms has also been found to be problematic, with downward communication rather than consultation being most common (ACREW 2007). Other practical impediments to the involvement of precarious workers in workplace OHS issues also exist. Part-time workers (including part-time casuals) are less likely to be engaged in workplace issues, less likely to have received appropriate training and, in the case of workplaces where worker involvement was discouraged, less likely to risk their employment or discrimination by becoming involved in representative processes (Johnstone, Quinlan & Walters 2005).

The growth in outsourcing and the resulting presence of multiple employers in a single workplace complicate the issue of establishing employee representation in OHS, as well as which employer should respond to the concerns raised. As Johnstone, Quinlan and Walters (2005: 95) observe, worker OHS representation and joint OHS committees

> presume an identifiable and relatively stable group of employees located together or in very regular contact, and working for a single employer . . . new work patterns break this nexus or on OHS weaken it to the point where it would be extremely difficult for these mechanisms to be used effectively.

The model national OHS laws are intended to overcome these complexities; however, they presuppose the presence of workplace OHS representatives. As we have demonstrated, this has been undermined by declining unionisation. While worker involvement in OHS has consistently been shown to improve workplace health and safety, the assumption that workers can exercise their voice regarding OHS issues without fear of discrimination and without union support is not well founded.

▪ Conclusion

The focus of this chapter has been on occupational health and safety outcomes in a changing work environment; however, it is clear that underpinning many of these issues are changes in the workplace relations environment and legislation. Over recent decades, the political economy of many developed countries has shifted markedly to neo-liberal policies, which have promoted deregulation of the labour market and discouraged unionism – either directly through regulatory constraints on collective bargaining, or indirectly through encouraging employers to adopt more anti-union approaches. These changes have weakened workers' capacity and ability to respond to OHS issues, and have limited their access to legislated benefits and protections once they are injured. Precarious workers are more likely to be injured; workers with job insecurity are more likely to experience poorer health outcomes; and the changes in the nature of organisations and jobs have been accompanied by increased levels of job stress. The capacity of workers to respond to these issues through workplace consultative processes has diminished.

The regulatory settings for OHS in Australia have been relatively stable since the mid-1980s. The increased risks that have emerged have resulted mostly from the deregulation of the labour market and the subsequent increased power of employers to determine employment conditions without sufficient regard to OHS considerations. These changes in employment regulation arguably have undermined the intent of OHS regulation – such as employee involvement – while also creating new risks such as psycho-social hazards. In addition, these changes have created an environment where the risk and the associated costs of workplace injuries, which were intended to be borne by employers through workers' compensation systems, increasingly are borne by injured workers and the public health system. As we explained in Chapter 1, this is one of the consequences of the advance of neo-liberal ideas. In this way, the social inequalities in health experienced elsewhere are likely to become more pervasive in Australia, notwithstanding a universal health system to support workers once they are injured.

There are nevertheless indications that other developed economies have started to address some of these concerns. The European Parliament passed a non-legislative resolution on mental health in 2009, which included a call to employers to 'promote a healthy working climate, paying attention to work-related stress, the underlying causes of mental disorder in the workplace, and tackling those causes' (Leka et al. 2011: 1051). It also called on the European Commission to 'require businesses and public bodies to publish annually a report on their policy and work for the mental health of their employees on the same basis as they report on physical health and safety at work' (Leka et al. 2011: 1051). In Belgium, for example, employers are now required to regularly screen their organisation and collect data on antecedents of stress and well-being. But these developments are taking place in a socio-political environment with a tradition of social dialogue.

In Australia, where re-regulation of the labour market has been strongly resisted, even under a Labor government, the prospect of such an approach being adopted seems remote. Safe work practices and a healthy environment benefit employers, workers and society, yet OHS often remains a contested issue – or, in the case of both precarious workers and those subject to job stress, is simply overlooked. There is a need to reconsider the economic and social benefit of 'workplace flexibility' when the health effects are so pervasive.

▪ Discussion questions

11.1 What are the three forms of precarious employment? How does their increasing prevalence potentially impact on workplace health and safety?

11.2 Discuss the implications of the rise of neo-liberal policies for the development of workplace health and safety.

11.3 Explain and evaluate the Economic and Reward Pressures, Disorganisation and Regulatory Failure (PDR) model as it applies in Australia.

11.4 'The consequences of the increasing precariousness of employment for workers' physical and mental health are not confined to the direct consequences of their employment insecurity.' Evaluate this statement.

11.5 How is employee voice linked to improving workplace health and safety, and worker health and well-being?

11.6 'Declining union density and the rise of precarious employment together threaten the cornerstone of the Australian approach to regulating workplace health and safety.' Discuss.

Part III

Workplace Relations in Action

From reactive flexibility to strategic flexibility in retail and hospitality

George Lafferty

■ Chapter objectives

This chapter will enable readers to understand the:

- nature and causes of labour market flexibility in two industries that are high users of precariously employed workers
- attraction of many employers in retail and hospitality towards a minimalist approach to workplace flexibility, despite policy settings that facilitate employee-oriented flexibility
- international literature demonstrating that the strategic implementation of flexible working practices can be beneficial to both employers and employees
- potential for implementing flexible working arrangements in a way that reduces the adverse impacts of events such as the Global Financial Crisis (GFC).

▪ Introduction

As illustrated elsewhere in this book (see especially Chapters 2, 10 and 11), there has been a widespread shift in recent decades from full-time, 'standard' employment towards part-time, 'non-standard' employment, both in Australia and internationally. This trend has brought with it a proliferation of less secure, peripheral labour market participation. Focusing on retail and hospitality, two closely related industries that are characterised by high levels of 'non-standard' or precarious employment, this chapter examines how the strategic implementation of flexible working arrangements can enable people to achieve more secure and less peripheral labour market participation. The policy impetus for this discussion is provided primarily by the provisions of the *Fair Work Act 2009* in relation to flexible working arrangements, set within the context of Australia's experience during the Global Financial Crisis (GFC). The chapter indicates ways in which the use of flexible working arrangements can be implemented to expand equitable labour market participation and to reduce the impact of macro-economic fluctuations.

Under the *Fair Work Act 2009* (s. 65, 'Requests for Flexible Working Arrangements'), workers with caring responsibilities for children under school age or aged up to 18 with a disability now have a legislated right to request more flexible hours of work. The *Fair Work Act's* flexible work provision, which is included in the National Employment Standards (NES) create an opportunity for the strategic implementation of flexible working arrangements (see Chapter 8 for a discussion of the evolving role of the human resources [HR] function). The chapter explores how the potential benefits from this provision might be maximised to expand the available labour force available to employers, while enabling employees to achieve working arrangements that provide greater job security and career progression.

In this chapter, we focus on the *strategic* implementation of flexible working arrangements in the retail and hospitality industries – that is, implementation processes that integrate the interests of employers and employees towards the achievement of common organisational goals. How can flexible working arrangements be extended on a long-term basis through organisational policies, enterprise agreements and workplace practices, rather than being used as ad hoc responses to short-term operational considerations or individual employee conditions? To what extent can organisations move beyond basic compliance with legislative requirements towards consultative decision-making processes that lead to the strategic implementation of flexible working arrangements? How can flexible working arrangements be implemented to attain such goals as employee retention and the more effective matching of positions to available employees (both actual and potential)?

The chapter also examines the initial impact of the flexible working arrangements provisions in the *Fair Work Act* through an analysis of recent enterprise bargaining agreements in the retail and hospitality industries. To what extent have bargaining processes led to the introduction of flexible working arrangements clauses that seek to combine the needs and aspirations of both employers and employees? A consistent concern in this discussion is how flexible working arrangements – particularly different forms of part-time work – can contribute to broader social and economic goals, including the achievement of greater labour market resilience during cyclical downturns.

National policy and international developments

This discussion is framed by three additional national policy developments within the macroeconomic context of global economic fluctuations. First, the findings of the national Intergenerational Report (Commonwealth of Australia 2010: vii–xvi) illustrated the adverse consequences of an ageing population and the pressing need to expand the available labour force. Second, the 2011 federal Budget stressed the national priority of increasing labour market participation among five groups: young people; single parents; long-term unemployed people; people with disabilities; and older workers (Commonwealth of Australia 2010–11). Third, the federal government report, *A Stronger, Fairer Australia* (Department of Prime Minister and Cabinet 2009) highlighted how large numbers of people continue to suffer the effects of social exclusion, including unemployment, low incomes, job insecurity and poor housing – a situation exacerbated by the economic downturn (ABS 2010c; O'Loughlin, Humpel & Kendig 2010). These goals of expanding the labour force, greater flexibility for employees, increasing labour market participation and strengthening social inclusion provide the chapter's policy framework, within which we integrate the strategic implementation of flexible working arrangements in retail and hospitality.

The international background is provided by global responses to economic downturn, most notably the Group of 20 (G20) Nations London Jobs Summit of April 2009. The Summit established three priorities, which closely parallel the national issues outlined above: the expansion of productive employment; assistance for the most vulnerable members of society; and a greater supply of both jobs and skills (G20 2009: 1). It concluded that more flexible, 'non-standard' working arrangements could contribute significantly to achieving these goals. In Australia during the GFC, flexible working arrangements – including part-time work – aided labour market resilience, partially compensating for a decline in full-time employment. Yet, although there is anecdotal evidence that many employers responded to the downturn by reducing hours of work, flexible working arrangements were not adopted in a strategic manner (see van Wanrooy et al. 2009: 34–35). Given current uncertainties in the international economy, the chapter investigates how the strategic implementation of flexible working arrangements, particularly in part-time employment, might increase labour market opportunities and generate more sustainable employment in the retail and hospitality industries.

Despite the potential benefits afforded by flexible working arrangements, limited progress has been made towards their widespread strategic implementation, in Australia or internationally (Danziger & Walters Boots 2008; Golden 2008; Homung,

Rousseau & Glaser 2008). Consequently, several countries – including Australia – have introduced legislation to encourage flexible working arrangements. Some European countries, including France, Belgium, Germany and the Netherlands, even provide a comprehensive right to flexible working arrangements for all employees (Hegewich 2009: 2). However, Australia's 'right to request' provision most closely resembles the more limited legislation in both the United Kingdom and New Zealand that provides employees with caring responsibilities the 'right to request' flexible working arrangements. In the United Kingdom, the benefits following legislation introduced in 2003 have included: higher productivity; improved retention of skills and knowledge; reduced costs of recruitment and training; lower labour turnover and absenteeism; improved work–life balance, health and well-being; and increased labour force participation (Department for Business Innovation and Skills 2010: 10–14; DTI 2006). In New Zealand, employees with caring responsibilities were given a legislated right to request more flexible hours of work in 2007, and there is already evidence of similar gains from this provision (New Zealand Department of Labour 2009).

In Australia, there is a considerable unmet demand for greater flexibility in working hours from employees (Productivity Commission 2011). The range of flexible working arrangements – which vary in their suitability for different industries, occupations and positions – includes:

- *Annualised working hours*. This allows workers with caring and other responsibilities or commitments to work for less than a full year – for example, 40 weeks – while spreading their remuneration over 52 weeks. This allows workers to take blocks of time off work, such as during school holidays, while continuing to be paid in every pay cycle.
- *Reversible part-time positions*. Often used as a staff-retention strategy, this arrangement allows employees to move from full-time to part-time work, with a guarantee that they can return to full-time employment within a certain period of time.
- *Flexi-time or variable hours*. These can range from quite substantial changes (such as a compressed working week, in which the same number of working hours is performed over fewer days) or minor forms of flexibility that may have a high value for employees, such as the ability to vary start and finish times. 'Flexi-time bandwidth' provisions allow employees to work within a 'bandwidth' of, for example, three hours before or after 'normal' start and finish times, thus providing employers with a reliable labour supply and employees with a considerable degree of personal flexibility.
- *Homeworking*. This form of working, which can reduce demand on scarce facilities such as office space, provides an opportunity for employees to focus on larger projects that require long-term concentration; it also reduces the time, expense and environmental costs associated with commuting. There are potential pitfalls, such as occupational health and safety considerations and the possibility of overwork.
- *Telework*. As the use of computer and communication technologies to work away from a central office, telework shares the main possibilities and problems of homeworking. However, with the onset of online retailing and hotel booking, the potential for its expansion in these two industries may have increased.

• *Job sharing.* A voluntary arrangement where a specific full-time job is shared by two or more employees, with pay and entitlements provided on a pro rata basis. Strictly speaking, all the duties of the particular role and accountability for performing that role are shared. Job sharing could be suitable for many retail and hospitality employees, including people with childcare or other caring responsibilities, older workers seeking a bridge to retirement and younger workers who may be combining paid work with study. For example, job sharing might enable older workers to continue their labour market participation at reduced hours, while sharing their knowledge with their job-share partners, such as younger people entering the labour force (see also Chapters 10 and 11 for further discussion of this issue).

In retail and hospitality in particular, flexible working arrangements – such as flexible, part-time work – can provide entry points for many employees, while ensuring the highest number of suitable applicants for available positions – for example, by providing working hours that are matched to child-care requirements. It is also a way for (potential) employees to manage family commitments. Yet current labour market policies are geared strongly towards placing unemployed people (particularly the long-term unemployed) in full-time employment (Fowkes 2011), when more flexible, part-time work may be more suitable in many situations. Not only do a considerable number of people not want to work full-time, but moving from unemployment to full-time employment may not offer the best avenue towards long-term labour market participation: the most vulnerable workers (including the long-term unemployed) are the ones most likely to fall back into unemployment. Therefore, a more strategic use of part-time flexible working arrangements (as discussed in Chapter 10), linked to broader labour market interventions, could play a stronger role in increasing labour market participation, particularly among priority groups identified in current labour market policies: young people, single parents, long-term unemployed people, people with disabilities and older workers.

Downturn, recovery and flexibility

Retail and hospitality employment is often associated with significant disadvantage and insecurity, as we saw in Chapters 2 and 11. Both industries have similar patterns of high rates of participation by women with children, young people and older workers. They are also notable for high levels of part-time and casual work, under-employment and labour turnover, as well as low proportions of workers with post-school qualifications. During the most recent economic downturn following the GFC, the most vulnerable sections of Australian society were affected severely, as jobs were distributed unevenly between industries and occupations, across different age groups and between men and women. For example, labour market participation by younger people (aged 15–24) declined considerably, with potentially longer-term damaging effects for labour market participation (Robinson, Long & Lamb 2011: 8–12). However, part-time work made a valuable contribution to maintaining overall levels of labour market participation (ABS 2012c).

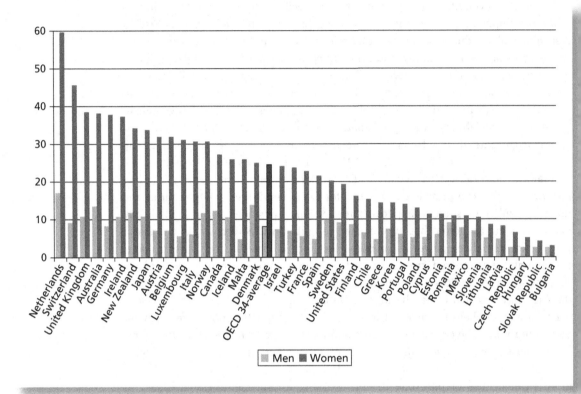

Figure 12.1: International Incidence of Part-Time Employment, 2009
Part-time employment as a proportion of total employment
Source: OECD Family database (n.d.).

In Australia, part-time workers are classified as those who are identified by the Australian Bureau of Statistics (ABS) as those workers (including unpaid family workers) who 'usually worked less than 35 hours a week (in all jobs)'. Therefore, someone working in multiple part-time positions that amount to 35 or more hours weekly is classified as a full-time worker. There are also significant international variations in the criteria used to classify a worker as 'part-time'. These include the number of hours worked, whether unpaid family workers are included in employment statistics and whether or not statistics are based on self-assessment by workers. Therefore, some caution is required when drawing international comparisons on the incidence of part-time work. Nonetheless, by any measure Australia has one of the highest rates of part-time employment in the OECD (see Figure 12.1).

As we saw in Chapter 2, part-time employment accounts for approximately 29 per cent of total employment and comprises around 45 per cent of women's employment and 15 per cent of men's employment. The incidence of part-time work is highest among women in the main child-rearing age range, older male workers and younger workers.

Since November 1991, when there were 1 359 700 part-time employees in Australia, there has been a generally continuous increase in part-time employment, with only a few periods of downturn. Following a brief, minor contraction in overall part-time employment, by November 2011 total part-time employment was 2 943 100 (ABS 2012a). Within the context of overall growth, over the 20 years to 2012, part-time employment among men has grown at a faster rate than it has among women. This fact suggests that the growth in part-time employment may not be based entirely on employee preferences and may not indicate a widespread move to family-friendly work practices.

Nationally, retail and hospitality are the industries with the two highest rates of part-time employment, and within the broad category of 'part-time' they include very high proportions of casual workers – although casual positions have declined as a proportion of overall part-time employment since the 1990s (ABS 2011a). These industries exhibit high levels of flexibility in terms of variation in days of the week worked each week, number of hours worked from week to week, prevalence of weekend work and levels of casual employment (ABS 2010a). In these industries, the major forms of flexibility appear to be temporal and numerical, and both are largely 'employer-driven' rather than 'employee-focused' forms of flexibility.

Most business activity in retail and hospitality is both price-sensitive and labour-intensive, with wages consuming considerably higher-than-average proportions of overall expenses. Wages in both industries have long been firmly anchored at the lower end of the earnings spectrum, as can be seen Table 12.1.

Table 12.1 Earnings ($), August 2010: retail, hospitality (accommodation and food services), all industries

Industry	Male full-time	Female full-time	Total full-time	Male part-time	Female part-time	Total part-time	Total male	Total female	Total
Retail	1075	852	979	311	334	327	803	522	642
Hospitality	964	785	886	287	287	287	604	431	507
All industries	1364	1086	1263	453	473	468	1218	805	1024

Source: ABS (2010a).

Despite the relatively low wages in retail and hospitality, employers in both industries consistently have resisted significant wage increases. Most recently, they have opposed any rise in the minimum wage arising from Fair Work Australia's 2011–12 *Minimum Wage Review* (Australian Hotels Association 2012; National Retail Association 2012). Yet there is little evidence that profits have been suffering as a consequence of higher wages. In the year to December 2011, total profits in retail grew by 11.2 per cent, and in accommodation and food services total profits grew by 14.5 per cent, while total wages growth in both industries was 3.1 per cent (ABS 2012b). As noted in Chapter 2, a similar but more extreme pattern has been exhibited in the United States over a long period of time.

Despite the extensive decentralisation and deregulation of the past two decades, employers in both retail and hospitality continue to pursue further flexibility in employee wages – for example, demanding more commission-based remuneration, conditions and working hours, particularly the freedom to engage more part-time and casual workers (see Australian Hotels Association 2012; National Retail Association 2012; Productivity Commission 2011). The rapid rise of internet-based commerce has acted as a stimulus for these demands. Such innovations as online bookings and self-check-ins have had some impact on hospitality, but the internet has had the greatest impact on retail. Online shopping accounted for 6 per cent of all retail spending in 2010, with projected growth rates of between 10 and 15 per cent annually (Productivity Commission 2011: 87). This trend has generated increased employer pressure for greater operational flexibility in 'bricks-and-mortar' retail establishments, in order to compete with online retailers – particularly overseas.

The main unions in retail, the Shop, Distributive and Allied Employees Association and in Hospitality, United Voice (formerly the Liquor, Hospitality and Miscellaneous Union), have long been at the forefront of resisting demands for employer-driven flexibility, which have tended to sideline more employee-focused flexibility. This task has been made considerably more daunting by low rates of union membership in the two industries, especially hospitality. In August 2010, only 29 200 (4.8 per cent) of a total of 667 800 employees in the hospitality industry were union members in their main jobs (ABS 2010c).

Union membership in the retail sector was substantially higher at 169 700 (15.4 per cent) out of a total of 1 103 000 employees, although still below the national average of 18.3 per cent. The vast majority (161 500) of unionised retail workers are in store-based employment, such as at Woolworths and Coles. Union membership tends to be much higher in larger organisations, and a major factor that differentiates the two industries is that large employers are far more prevalent in retail than in hospitality. While retail accounts for only 6.5 per cent of all Australian organisations, it employs 21.3 per cent of all employees, indicating the importance of major retail chains and department stores. Smaller employers are substantially more important in hospitality: accommodation and food services account for 5.5 per cent of all employing organisations but only 4.2 per cent of all employees. Therefore, while retail and hospitality are closely related industries with several overlapping areas – for example, fast food – there are also notable differences. Overall, the considerable majority of employees in retail and particularly in hospitality remain in non-unionised, usually smaller workplaces, dependent mainly on industrial award provisions (minimum wages and conditions of employment stipulated by the Fair Work Commission – formerly Fair Work Australia – or by state industrial commissions). Hospitality is the industry with by far the highest proportion of award-only employees: in May 2010, the figure was 45.2 per cent (291 600 employees). Retail has the fourth-highest proportion of award-only employees: 22.3 per cent (204 900) (ABS 2010b). The significance of award-only employment is that it implies that wages are not set by collective bargaining, and that they are likely to be lower and closer to the national minimum wage.

These are two industries that have high levels of part-time and casual employment, low pay and low levels of unionisation, in which employees have borne the brunt of employer demands for greater operational flexibility and managerial prerogative. Nonetheless, they offer considerable potential for more strategic implementation of flexible working arrangements, given that they already exhibit high proportions of part-time work – albeit often to accommodate employers' rather than employees' requirements. In the next section, we assess the impact of economic downturn on retail and hospitality employment, and look at how flexible working arrangements might contribute to future labour market resilience and participation in the two industries.

Responding to downturn

Employees in both retail and hospitality are particularly vulnerable to macro-economic and market fluctuations, having experienced considerable job losses during the economic downturn. Between February 2001 and February 2012, both retail and hospitality experienced an average annual increase in full-time employment of approximately 1 per cent, below the national average for the period of just under 2 per cent, while over the same period the two industries were consistently well above the national averages in part-time employment growth (ABS 2012f). During the GFC from the latter part of 2007, this trend largely continued with growth in both retail and hospitality employment being largely confined to part-time positions, which partly compensated for losses of full-time jobs (see Table 12.3).

As can be seen from Table 12.2, overleaf, total employment in both industries was maintained reasonably well during 2007–08. It was only in the August quarter of 2009 that total retail employment fell below 1.2 million for the first time since May 2007. However, full-time retail employment reached its peak of 705 300 in the November 2007 quarter. The growing importance of part-time employment in sustaining overall employment is evident: whereas in the November 2007 quarter part-time employment accounted for 44.1 per cent of total retail employment, by May 2009 that proportion had increased to 48.8 per cent. Despite signs of recovery since late 2009, the retail industry has failed to reach the overall employment levels attained in November 2007. In hospitality, the story is somewhat different and the contribution of part-time employment is even more significant. Full-time employment in the industry has remained quite stable since February 2007, with part-time work providing the main source of employment growth. By February 2012, part-time employment accounted for just almost 60 per cent of total hospitality employment.

Signs of recovery are evident in the recruitment trends in both industries. From July 2010 to June 2011, 73 per cent of retail employers and 76 per cent of hospitality employers recruited new employees (DEEWR 2011). Matching positions and working arrangements with potential job seekers and the respective expectations of employers and employees represents a particular challenge, however. In retail and hospitality between July 2010 and June 2011, the average number of applicants for sales worker vacancies was 6.4, but the average number of suitable applicants was only 2.1. In retail, 5.8 per cent of advertised vacancies in the 12 months to July 2011 remained unfilled, while in hospitality 5.5 per cent of advertised vacancies remained vacant.

Table 12.2 Employment in retail and hospitality, February 2007 to February 2012

Quarter	Full-time retail	Part-time retail	Total retail	Full-time hosp.	Part-time hosp.	Total hosp.
Feb 2007	659.1	540.4	1199.5	331.5	377.2	708.7
May 2007	641.7	545.1	1186.8	319.6	391.4	710.9
Aug 2007	655.5	556.3	1211.8	322.8	395.9	718.7
Nov 2007	705.3	558.0	1263.3	314.6	376.4	691.0
Feb 2008	699.2	542.3	1241.6	329.4	378.0	707.5
May 2008	660.3	580.0	1240.4	323.9	395.3	719.2
Aug 2008	637.6	579.4	1217.0	326.7	398.3	725.0
Nov 2008	637.1	583.9	1221.1	317.7	394.4	712.1
Feb 2009	641.8	593.8	1235.6	310.4	403.3	713.6
May 2009	629.2	599.7	1229.0	320.2	412.9	733.1
Aug 2009	603.4	566.2	1169.6	308.0	444.5	752.5
Nov 2009	642.0	572.1	1214.2	316.2	435.3	751.5
Feb 2010	607.9	591.9	1199.8	319.0	421.3	740.3
May 2010	617.8	582.2	1200.0	339.0	435.1	774.1
Aug 2010	613.7	590.2	1203.9	307.5	430.0	737.6
Nov 2010	639.0	611.0	1250.1	344.8	427.7	772.5
Feb 2011	641.8	607.6	1249.4	353.3	444.1	797.5
May 2011	624.1	610.0	1234.1	335.8	460.8	796.5
Aug 2011	642.2	577.8	1220.0	332.2	448.0	780.2
Nov 2011	647.9	574.0	1222.0	327.2	439.8	767.0
Feb 2012	646.0	568.3	1214.3	324.9	413.2	738.1

Note: All figures in '000s.
Source: ABS (2012f) and previous years.

The continuing importance of traditional, informal methods of recruitment and job-seeking is noteworthy. During the 12 months to June 2011, 43 per cent of employers used informal methods (including 30 per cent using 'word of mouth' and/or approaching a job seeker, 10 per cent using direct approaches by a job seeker, and 6 per cent placing a sign in a window or using a billboard). In contrast, only 22 per cent used the internet, 14 per cent used a recruitment agency and a meagre 5 per cent used Job Services Australia (the government-funded national job-finding network), while 39 per cent continued to use newspaper advertisements. The use of informal methods indicates a continuing role for face-to-face, local recruiting methods. A strategic approach to recruiting would seek to integrate these methods effectively according to the job concerned and the relevant labour market – for example, local, national or international. Flexible working arrangements of various types can provide one strategy through which the needs and expectations of employers and employees can be matched more effectively within prevailing labour market conditions.

The appropriateness of different flexible working arrangements is highly context-dependent on industry, occupation, workplace and individual circumstances. Yet organisational policies and enterprise agreements can provide frameworks within which flexible working arrangements can be implemented in a coherent, equitable fashion. The next section assesses whether there is evidence of a shift towards more strategic implementation of flexible working arrangements within enterprise bargaining processes in the retail and hospitality sectors.

Bargaining for flexibility

The inclusion of a flexible working arrangements provision in the *Fair Work Act* (s. 65) and the NES, as a basic employment entitlement, was intended to provide a platform for 'genuine discussion between employers and employees about flexible work arrangements for working parents' (Gillard 2010). NES 2 provides:

1. **Requests for flexible working arrangements** – allows parents or carers of a child under school age or of a child under 18 with a disability, to request a change in working arrangements to assist with the child's care.

Retail and hospitality agreements concluded between 1 January 2010 and 28 November 2011 were examined in order to evaluate the extent to which the NES had prompted a shift to negotiated flexibility provisions. Are there initial signs of a more strategic, collaborative bargaining approach to the implementation of flexible working arrangements? Are the parties developing clauses in agreements that go beyond the statutory Individual Flexibility Agreement and flexible working arrangements minima? (See Chapter 5 for further discussion of these types of arrangements.) The findings of this study are summarised in Tables 12.3 and 12.4 (overleaf). The *Fair Work Act* requires every modern award and enterprise agreement to include a 'flexibility' term. A model flexibility term is provided in the Fair Work Regulations 2009. The term 'Standard IFA' is used here to refer to agreement clauses that are identical to, or do not substantively differ from, the wording of this model term. Where an enterprise agreement does not include its own flexibility term, it is taken to include the model term. The NES stipulate minimum entitlements for employees. These include the right to request flexible working arrangements. The term 'Standard Flexible Working Arrangements' is used here to refer to flexible working arrangements clauses that are identical to, or do not substantively differ from, the wording of this provision in the NES.

A continuum emerged in both industries, from those agreements with no mention of flexible working arrangements to those that have produced quite detailed strategies for their implementation. Although the latter include only a small minority of agreements at present, they provide examples that could be

Table 12.3 Retail industry flexibility provisions	
Standard IFA	57
Standard Flexible Working Arrangements clause	25
Silent on IFA	4
Silent on Flexible Working Arrangements	34
Modified IFA clause	1
Modified Flexible Working Arrangements clause	3
Total agreements	62

Table 12.4 Hospitality industry flexible provisions	
Standard IFA clause	60
Standard Flexible Working Arrangements clause	32
Silent on IFA	4
Silent on Flexible Working Arrangements	37
Modified IFA clause	8
Modified Flexible Working Arrangements clause	2
Total agreements	72

followed more widely. For example, the following indicates the strategic implementation of flexible working arrangements to reduce reliance on casual and short-term employment, while also ensuring that part-time employees will have access to career paths:

> Flexible part-time employees will be employed to minimize the need to engage casual employees and temporary employees. Flexible part-time employees will be given the opportunity to progress within the classification structure in the same way as other employees. (Blue, Sydney Enterprise Agreement 2010, clauses 7.2.2, 7.2.3)

On the other hand, numerous examples remained of the blunt assertion of employer-driven flexibility. For example:

> For the purpose of increasing productivity and efficiency and improving customer service, employees shall: (a) perform all work within the grade in which they are employed and those of lower grades; (b) perform all work which is incidental or peripheral to their main task(s) or function(s); (c) not impose or enforce demarcation barriers between food and beverage tasks they are required to perform; (d) perform work at any work location as required by the STC during the period of the engagement. (Sydney Turf Club Food & Beverage Enterprise Agreement, clause 10.1)

In some cases, the standard clauses were modified significantly – as in the following case, which excludes parents of children with a disability up to the age of 18:

> In accordance with the National Employment Standards, a team member who is a parent of a child under school age (or has the responsibility for the care of a child under school age), may request … (Lovisa Enterprise Agreement 2010, clause 4.9)

In many cases, especially in the hospitality sector, agreements were silent on flexible working arrangements, while a small number were silent on IFAs; in those cases, the statutory minima contained in the NES still apply. However, the absence of specific provision for flexible working may be of some practical concern, since it may indicate that the issue was not considered in constructing these agreements and that employees may be unaware of the statutory requirements. Flexible working arrangements and such provisions as conversion from casual to part-time employment have been part of bargaining processes in retail and hospitality since the 1980s; however, typically they formed part of a process of concession bargaining. Assessment of the specific contribution of the NES flexible employment provision and whether the *Fair Work Act* overall has contributed to any change in the culture of bargaining (especially in light of the Act's good-faith bargaining requirement in s. 228) would require extensive discussion with the respective parties and further analysis of enterprise agreements and bargaining.

There is considerable international evidence that broad support for flexible working arrangements is achievable (Plantenga & Remery 2009). Crucially, employers (including small and medium-sized employers) who have exhibited initial opposition to flexible work legislation have subsequently reported few problems, as the practical benefits have become increasingly evident (Hegewisch 2009: 44–55). Recent research by Fair Work Australia (now the Fair Work Commission) supported these conclusions. The *Fair Work Act* (s. 653) requires the general manager of the Fair Work Commission to conduct research into Individual Flexibility Agreements and requests for flexible working arrangements, including the circumstances in which requests are made, the outcomes and the circumstances in which requests may have been refused. In its report, the panel reviewing the Act recommended that the right to request flexible working arrangements should be extended to include a 'wider range of caring and other circumstances' and that the employer should 'hold a meeting to discuss the request, unless the employer has agreed to the request' (McCallum, Moore & Edwards 2012: 99).

Conclusion

The retail and hospitality industries are already characterised by considerable diversity in the jobs they provide and the composition of their labour forces. Strategies for implementing flexible working arrangements need to be matched more effectively to the specific situations of various (actual and potential) employees – for example, workers with children aged under 5, workers over 55 or workers with disabilities. Flexible working arrangements can contribute to the achievement of more equitable labour market participation that accommodates family and other commitments, reducing divisions between the 'included' majority in reasonably secure employment and an 'excluded' minority of welfare dependants and the insecurely employed. Thus the integration of flexible working arrangements within broader policy and socio-economic goals can extend their significance beyond their usual domain of achieving work–life balance. As several commentators (for example, Skinner & Pocock 2011) have noted, the 'right to request' provision of the *Fair Work Act* is restricted to employees with specific caring responsibilities; provides only a formal requirement for employers to consider individual requests for flexible options; and provides no right of redress where employers refuse such requests. To a substantial extent, the provision is very little, very late.

There is a demonstrable need to match types of flexible working arrangement to life-cycle stages of workers, and varying commitments and aspirations. Many people do not want full-time employment – and their reasons are often related to life-cycle considerations, such as child-rearing, study commitments, responsibility for providing care to aged relatives and planning for retirement (see also Chapter 10 for discussion of these issues). Not only can provisions for flexible working arrangements contribute to staff recruitment and retention, they can also provide mechanisms whereby organisations can improve working conditions for employees and build a generally more productive working environment, as was considered in Chapter 6. The location of flexible working arrangements within both enterprise agreements and organisational policies can facilitate their integration with organisational strategy, linking them to consultative decision-making processes. 'Strategic' approaches in this respect require the *meaningful* participation of all relevant parties, whereby planning processes integrate competing interests, in order to take us beyond a simple dichotomy between 'employer-driven' and 'employee-focused' forms of flexibility.

▪ Discussion questions

12.1 Why have some Australian employers opted for a minimalist approach to the implementation of flexible working practices instead of a more strategic approach?

12.2 Which types of work and flexible working arrangements do you believe would make employment in (a) a large supermarket (with more than 250 employees); and (b) a small hotel (with around 20 employees) most attractive to:

　(i)　a 21-year-old man studying full-time at TAFE

　(ii)　a single mother with two children aged 3 and 7

　(iii)　a 49-year-old former mine worker who has been unemployed for two years

　(iv)　a wheelchair-bound female university graduate aged 28

　(v)　a 58-year-old woman who is currently in full-time clerical work, but looking to reduce her working days and travel time?

Restructuring Victorian public hospitals and the implications for work and work organisation

3

Richard Gough and Pat Brewer

■ Chapter objectives

This chapter will enable readers to understand the:

- manner in which market-driven cost-cutting policies have played out in public hospitals, through a case study of one Australian state (Victoria)
- process of work intensification in nursing and the its intersection with a range of management tools and measures developed for hospitals
- temporary nature of the successes of the nursing union in campaigning for improved staffing and better health care under a Labor government
- ways in which measures of performance can be manipulated to suggest improved performance of public hospitals
- consequences of work intensification in terms of the experience of employees and the implications for their health and well-being.

Introduction

This chapter examines the impact of an Australian state government (Victoria) applying an aggressive, neo-liberal reform agenda on the delivery of public sector hospital care and on nursing staff in particular. These changes were set in the context of a response to increasing labour costs and also disproportionately higher non-labour costs due to new pharmaceuticals, new diagnostic equipment and technology (White & Bray 2005: Congressional Budget Office 2008). However, the response of the Kennett Liberal-National Coalition government in Victoria to these cost pressures was to introduce more radical neo-liberal influenced changes to public hospitals than those implemented by the New South Wales state Labor Government (White & Bray 2005). These changes also coincided with the introduction of enterprise bargaining nationally during the 1990s, which allowed for enterprise-level collective bargaining over wages and conditions, with the aim of improving productivity (see also Chapters 1 and 5). However, centralised control over staffing budgets by state health departments left relatively little actual control of these issues in the hands of local hospital management (White & Bray 2005).

In Australia, nursing work in acute-care hospitals is provided by qualified nurses, and the use of nursing assistants (staff assisting patients with eating, dressing and making basic observations) is very limited. This is in contrast to other Anglo-American countries, such as the United States and United Kingdom, where extensive use is made of nursing assistants, most of whom have few or no formal qualifications. The Australian model of health care has been sustained by the different state branches of the nurses' union, the Australian Nursing Federation (ANF), membership of which has increased nationally from around 100 000 in 1994 to more than 200 000 in 2011 (ANF 2011). In Chapter 1, we explained that the precepts of neo-liberalism include a preoccupation with reducing government expenditures and reducing the size of the public debt.

In the health sector, expenditure reduction is hard to achieve; however, governments have tried to curb the rate of growth of the health budget. In the case of Victoria, in line with the neo-liberal precepts of cutting budgets and shrinking the public sector (see Chapter 1), these efforts have taken several forms, beginning with cutting the numbers of clinical, managerial, administrative, cleaning, catering and general staff (the outcomes for nursing staff are discussed below). The second form was restructuring and reorganising the management of hospitals. For instance, in Victoria in the 1990s, under the Kennett Liberal-National Coalition government, the autonomous status of hospitals with their management boards was replaced by metropolitan health networks, which included hospitals and also the delivery of other health services. These networks had small, accountable boards, which had a business focus and consisted of professionals appointed by the Health Minister. Third, the outsourcing of services such as radiology, pathology, dental technicians, lawn-mowing, security, engineering and maintenance, and food services was attempted, but in some cases these services remained in-house – either due to successful internal tenders or the inability of outsource delivery to achieve demonstrable efficiencies in areas like pathology (Stanton, Young & Willis 2003). In general, however, the attempt to outsource non-clinical services did lead to cuts in job numbers and to job intensification, with greater job flexibility and changed work practices.

The fourth measure designed to curb expenditure growth occurred in the latter years of the Kennett Liberal-National Coalition government; this was the privatisation of some public hospitals. Plans were put in place for a major hospital in north-eastern Melbourne, the Austin and Repatriation Hospital, to be redeveloped and operated by a private company and for a new private hospital to be developed in Gippsland in regional Victoria, replacing the existing public hospital. Charges were introduced in some emergency departments, as well as fees being introduced for some categories of patient who received medical services but were not admitted.

The final, and possibly most important, change was the introduction of throughput measures of performance – the so called Casemix funding of hospitals. Casemix is based on average times taken to treat patients with particular types of illness – for example, the removal of an inflamed appendix compared with the replacement of a heart valve. These procedures are classified into Diagnostic Related Groups (DRGs). The average time of patient stay required for treatment and recovery prior to discharge was benchmarked against the performance of individual hospitals. Hospitals were then funded on the basis of the average length of stay and not the actual length of stay of particular patients. Public hospitals also introduced a range of Key Performance Indicators (KPIs), such as number of discharges per shift and the length of patients' waiting time in an emergency department before admission to a ward.

In the next section, we discuss the implementation of the neo-liberal-inspired health-care reforms in Victorian hospitals. In the third section, the increasing intensification of nursing work resulting from these reforms is analysed using statistics on changes to Victorian hospitals' performance from 1996 to 2009. These data clearly indicate a significantly increased number of patients being treated due to higher patient turnover (flows) and decreased numbers of beds during the 1990s. The changes in health policy with the election of a Labor Party state government in 1999 (first led by Premier Bracks from 1999–2007 and then by Premier Brumby from 2007–10), leading to increases in the number of nurses, is examined next. Necessarily, this part of the discussion also examines the successful industrial campaign conducted by the ANF Victorian Branch to achieve better nurse-to-patient ratios. Despite the improved ratios, increased patient flows and insufficient beds continued to put pressure on nurses to increase the number of patients discharges, which is a time-consuming activity. This outcome is examined through an analysis of the results of interviews with 75 nurses (in 2008–09 in three public hospitals) about their levels of job stress and the associated causes.

Implementing a market-driven model in Victorian public hospitals

The 1992 election of the Kennett Liberal-National Coalition government in Victoria led to major changes in the management and funding of public acute-care hospitals.

These changes reduced the staffing levels and numbers of beds at the same time as the demand for in-patient health services was increasing. By the mid-1990s, the number of nurses in the public hospital system was reduced by 2000 (Gordon, Buchanan & Bretherton 2008). Between 1995/96 and 2001/02, patient admissions increased by 26 per cent and nurse staffing numbers fell by a further 5 per cent. These changes were complemented by the adoption of the Casemix classification and costing of illnesses (White & Bray 2005). The DRGs allowed for comparison of length of stay per treatment between acute-care hospitals, and enabled the government to put pressure on hospital managements to reduce bed days and increase patient flows in order to reduce treatment costs. As a result, it was necessary to either change work systems or intensify the work of other staff, such as nurses (Willis 2005).

These Casemix-related cuts in spending were achieved partly by the arbitrary way in which base payments for each service, as distinct from the relativities between services (for example, the difference in cost between a heart valve operation and appendix removal), were set, since no realistic assessment of the actual cost of a service was made to set the base amount (Antioch & Walsh 2002; Duckett 1998). As a result, about $190 million was cut from hospital funding with the introduction of Casemix in 1993 (Gordon et al. 2008). Another shortcoming of the DRGs is that they did not effectively account for the nursing input for a particular illness, which can be quite variable according to the level of acuity or severity of the patient's condition (Gordon, Buchanan & Bretherton 2008).

A further major change was the decentralisation of the management of hospitals, with middle management made responsible for recruitment and rostering. In an environment of decreased nursing numbers, in order to keep shifts staffed, nurse managers made increased use of agency nurses, who were paid at least double the rate paid to ongoing staff (Gordon, Buchanan & Bretherton 2008). Increased use of agency staff also placed pressure on more senior staff in wards because of the need to monitor agency nurses, who were not familiar with the protocols and procedures of the ward in which they were working. Full-time nursing staff also tended to go part-time so that they could work as agency staff.

Another broad policy direction taken by the Victorian government in order to contain costs was to reduce the number of acute care overnight hospital beds, particularly in the period from 1995 to 2002 (Sammut 2008). This change was justified by the large increase in 'same-day' or out-patient surgery, made possible by technological improvements such as 'keyhole' surgery, which is much less invasive than older methods (Grey, Yeo & Duckett 2004). This was seen as offsetting the need for patients to be admitted for several days and, certainly for those aged 65–74, there has been a decline nationally in multi-day admissions by 4.2 per cent over the period 1993–2002 (Mackay & Milliard 2005). However, for patients aged over 75 years, admissions increased by 21.6 per cent from 1993–2002, and the proportion of admissions for this age group was greater than the increase in their proportion of the population at large (5.8 per cent compared with 1.8 per cent).

Impact of the changes

The results of the changes initiated by the Kennett government to cut public hospital costs and improve efficiency can be seen in a range of indicators of hospital perform-ance, which point to higher workloads and increased work pressures for nurses. These indicators, which relate to the increased flow of patients through public hospitals, include the average length of patient stay, the annual throughput of patients per bed (caseflow rate) and the bed occupancy rate. Increased patient flows resulted in higher turnover of patients in wards in a situation where, as explained above, nurse numbers decreased and the number of patients treated increased significantly. Greater turn-over of patients also meant that nurses had to spend more of their time completing time-consuming admission and discharge procedures at the cost of providing direct patient care.

The first indicator, reduction in average length of stay, meant that nurses had to deal continuously with very ill patients, without the relief of having recovering patients who needed less attention. As indicated above, the average length of stay of patients in acute-care hospitals was affected by the Casemix system of benchmark-ing of DRGs, which placed pressures on hospitals to match the lengths of stay for particular illnesses to those of the best-performing hospital.

The issue of definitions needs consideration before we can correctly interpret the data on the average length of hospital stay. In the Australian figures, computations of the average length of stay have been affected by the method of measurement, which combines multi-day and same-day patients. However, the average length of stay can also be measured by excluding same-day patients. Including same-day admissions in the measure with multi-day admissions biases the average length of stay downwards. In order to obtain a more accurate understanding of changes in length of stay, we also use the OECD (2007) measure of average length of patient stay, which is defined in terms of average multi-day patient stay.

The average length of stay for multi-day patients in acute care hospitals in Victoria between 1995/96 and 2002/03 oscillated around 6.6 days, but from 2004/05 to 2008/09 the average decreased by 6 per cent according to the Australian Institute of Health and Welfare (AIHW) (AIHW 1997–2010). However, the combined same-day and multi-day figures showed a different trend, with a decline in average length of stay of 12 per cent between 1995/96 and 2001/02 and a further decline of 11 per cent between 2002/03 and 2008/09. This discrepancy between the two measures of patient stay was driven by the large increase in same-day patient admis-sions of 20 per cent between 1995/96 and 2001/02, a change from 44.4 per cent to 53.1 per cent of patient admissions. As a result of the government policy of closing public hospital beds, which was advocated on the grounds of technological advances in surgical techniques, there was an increase in same-day patients in Victoria, with the number of beds per 1000 population declining by 12 per cent between 1996/97 and 2001/02 (from 2.7 to 2.4 beds per 1000 people). Subsequently, this ratio stabilised at about 2.4 per 1000 population until 2008/09.

The second indicator, the caseflow rate (annual throughput of patients per bed, measured by dividing admissions by number of beds) increased by 47 per cent between 1995/96 and 2001/02, from 64 to 94 patients. From 2002/03 to 2008/09, the rate of change slackened, with a rise in throughput of patients of only 11 per cent from 97 to 108. Such increases in caseflow point to increased pressures on nurses due to the need to attend to more admissions and discharges during a shift.

The third indicator of patient flows, bed occupancy rates, rose by 24 per cent between 1995/96 and 2001/02, from 78 per cent to 97 per cent, and then stabilised until 2008/09. However, figures for multi-day bed occupancy indicate a very similar pattern of increase to the combined same-day and multi-day bed occupancy rates. The level of bed occupancy is a critical factor in the level of stress suffered by nursing staff. This is demonstrated in research undertaken over a four-year period on 6699 nurses in Finland, which revealed that exposure to bed occupancy rates over 85 per cent for more than six months was associated with increasing rates of commencement of anti-depressants (Virtanen et al. 2008). Nurses exposed to 95 per cent occupancy rates were twice as likely to commence use of anti-depressants, compared to those experiencing 85 per cent bed occupancy rates (2008). In the larger of the three hospitals studied, occupancy rates were 107 per cent in 2007 (Anonymous Health Network 2008). More generally, the link between psychosocial factors, stress and depression was demonstrated comprehensively across a range of industries.

The intensification of nursing work, combined with the number of nurses in the public hospitals under the Kennett government, led many nurses to either leave the industry altogether or to shift to nursing work in private sector hospitals or to other non-hospital nursing jobs. This exacerbated the growing shortage of nurses and also the ageing of the nursing workforce, which had an average age above 40 years (Auditor-General Victoria 2002). There was also a shift of nurses from full-time to part-time work from 37.4 per cent in 1988 to 42.8 per cent in 1998.

The above analysis clearly shows how the implementation of the neo-liberal agenda in acute care hospitals, through cutbacks and increases in work intensity in the 1990s, created a situation of crisis due to nurse shortages. This situation had to be remedied by Victoria's incoming Bracks Labor government in 1999.

■ The Bracks–Brumby Labor governments

The period of the Kennett Liberal-National Coalition government (1992–99) was the 'high water mark' of the implementation of neo-liberal reforms in Victoria. It is clear that cost-cutting and increased in patient flows had exacerbated a nursing shortage in Victoria by 2000. Nurses were leaving the profession due to work intensification (ACCIRT 2002) and direct reduction in the number of jobs in public hospitals.

With the election of the Bracks Labor government, there was a retreat from some aspects of the neo-liberal policy in public health. Privatisation of hospitals was abandoned and the state budget provided funds for building new hospitals. The work situation of nurses also improved. Nurse staffing numbers rose by 33 per cent from 2001/02 to 2008/09, whereas patient admissions rose by only 20 per cent over the period 2002/03 to 2008/09. In the four years to 2004, some 5200 extra acute-care, aged-care and psychiatric nurses were recruited (Pike 2004).

Despite more nurses returning to acute-care hospitals and the hiring of overseas nurses and new graduates, during the period 2002–04, nurse shortages – particularly in some specialist areas – continued to be a problem (Gordon, Buchanan & Bretherton 2008). The number of admitted overnight patients in Victorian public hospitals increased by 10 per cent in the period 2002/03–2008/09, and the number of same-day patients increased by 19 per cent over the same period, according to AIHW data. To stem the rising costs of contract staff, the Labor government required public hospitals to move from reliance on agency staff to 'bank staff' – that is, casual staff directly employed by a particular hospital and not through nursing agencies – thus reducing costs and incentives for full-time staff to join agencies.

While these changes were occurring, in the period following the election of the Labor government, the Victorian branch of the ANF was running an industrial campaign in support of claims for a new enterprise bargaining agreement. The campaign, 'Nursing the System back to Health', focused on the need of the public health system to have sufficient labour and skills to maintain quality standards of patient care (Gordon, Buchanan & Bretherton 2008). Central to the nurses' campaign was a call for the introduction of fair nurse-to-patient ratios to reduce work pressures. Their industrial campaign culminated in the tactic of closing one in five beds in all public hospitals, in turn forcing hospitals to cancel elective surgery. The campaign continued for over six months, and the ANF's refusal to compromise on the nurse-to-patient ratios led to the case being referred to the Australian Industrial Relations Commission (AIRC) for private arbitration (Gordon, Buchanan & Bretherton 2008). That private arbitration was used in this case was a consequence of the Howard federal Liberal-National Coalition government having enacted the *Workplace Relations Act 1996* (see Chapter 5). In the private arbitration, the ANF argued that no reliable and consistent system existed for measuring nursing work-loads. The employer industrial association, the Victorian Health Industry Association (VHIA), argued for a patient dependency system (severity level of patient illness). The ANF responded that such systems depended on top-down recognition of patient dependency and that experience elsewhere suggested that nurses' assessment of patient acuity (severity of illness) was often discounted or ignored by senior managers. It also argued that overseas research had demonstrated that lowering nurse-to-patient ratios also significantly reduced adverse outcomes and mortality for patients (Aiken et al. 2002).

In August 2000, Commissioner Blair ruled in favour of nurse-to-patient ratios. In acute-care wards, the ratio established was five nurses to 20 patients on day shift. This ratio allowed nurses to vary the number of patients for whom they cared on a shift, depending upon the acuity of illness of their patients – for example, a nurse with two very ill patients might give her other two patients to two other nurses, who then might each have five patients on a shift. This change partly drove the increase in nurse staffing that followed in subsequent years. As a result of the decision, 1300 effective full-time nursing positions were created (Hospital Circular 4 2001). It also made workloads for nurses more manageable and was positively received by nurses, as discussed below.

While the Bracks Labor government had been elected on a campaign of restoring public hospitals and increasing nurse staffing, and hence supported Commissioner Blair's decision, this commitment was not sustained. While initially accepting of the AIRC decision on nurse-to-patient ratios, in subsequent enterprise bargaining rounds, the government argued for their abolition. In the 2004 bargaining round, under direction from the government, the VHIA argued for abandoning the ratios, whereas the ANF argued for their extension to other areas of nursing and demanded more staff. In the next bargaining round, in 2007, the VHIA and the Brumby Labor government again attempted to remove nurse-to-patient ratios in order to contain wage costs. Finally, the ANF succeeded in extending the ratios, and 500 nurses were added in public hospitals as the result of a campaign that again successfully mobilised public support (Gordon, Buchanan & Bretherton 2008). The building of community alliances in this was one of the strategies considered in Chapter 3.

However, during the period of the Bracks–Brumby Labor government, continued cost increases resulting from the introduction of new technology and the needs of an ageing population led to pressures on the health budget. The policy of decreasing the number of acute hospital beds (discussed above), combined with efforts to continuously increase patient flows and achieve higher bed occupancy rates, remained the focus of hospital managements responding to Health Department policies (Auditor-General Victoria 2008). However, higher levels of bed occupancy in wards led to a conflict between the logic of efficient bed utilisation (achieving close to 100 per cent bed occupancy) and the need to have sufficient beds available in wards so that emergency patients did not have to remain in emergency departments for long periods. By 2009, the government came to insist on the need for hospitals to meet a KPI that 80 per cent of patients had to be admitted to the wards from the emergency department within eight hours. This demonstrates the constant tension between the public's increasing expectations of government services and the preoccupation of governments in Australia and overseas with reducing expenditure and achieving budget surpluses; a similar situation was observed in the examination of the Australian Public Service in Chapter 15.

Although the Labor government under both Premiers Bracks and Brumby increased nurse staffing, key indicators of work intensification such as patient flows (average length of stay, bed occupancy rates and caseflow rates) continued to increase. The number of beds per 1000 people also remained relatively static, while the numbers of multi-day and same-day patients increased considerably. The increasing number of same-day patients indicated a higher level of acuity in multi-day patients, thus increasing workloads for Victorian nurses.

The performance measures-driven approach to hospital management, advocated by government agencies such as the Auditor-General (Auditor-General Victoria 2008) in his report on managing patient flows and the VHIA, failed to comprehend the increased staffing and other patient-related costs of running hospitals at near 100 per cent bed occupancy rates and with increasing patient throughput. Importantly, the higher levels of bed occupancy led to increased workloads with no downtime, in a manner analogous to that experienced by employees working in a lean production regime in automobile assembly plants (Rinehart, Huxley & Robertson 1999).

Meeting these performance measures led to contradictions, because moving patients out of emergency departments required vacant beds in wards. In turn, this led to increased pressures on nurses and other clinical staff to push patients through the system. The failure to increase the number of beds because of greater numbers of same-day surgery patients also ignored the impact of an ageing and sicker population. Hence, although the ANF managed to improve the work situation for nurses, it was not able to counteract managerial strategies aimed at meeting government-imposed performance targets.

Nurses' views of work pressure

The impact of work intensification on workers' health and well-being was discussed above, and also in Chapter 11; we now explore these impacts from the perspective of the nursing workforce. Our interviews with Victorian nurses, conducted in 2008/09 in a large teaching hospital and two suburban hospitals, revealed the benefits of the nurse-to-patient ratios for both staff and patients; these included more manageable patient workloads and the potential for cooperation between staff to help one another with high-dependency patients. Such flexibility helped to ameliorate the impact of increased patient acuity by making cooperation between nurses over high-acuity patients possible, whereas a strict adherence to a ratio of one nurse to four patients could leave another nurse in a very stressful situation. This cooperation between nursing staff often arose from a feeling that members of a ward were part of an informal team, and this feeling only broke down under extreme pressure. However, there were examples where informal teams did not form, and a rigid interpretation of the ratios as being one nurse to four patients did occur. Despite these positive responses, nurses surveyed in the three hospitals reported increased work speed and effort between 2003 and 2008, as can be seen in Figure 13.1.

The survey findings on work speed were explained by the nurses who we interviewed; they also identified the causes of increased work pressures as arising from the issues mentioned above, including the increase in patient flows and patient acuity. These views are explored more below.

Patient flows

The above responses regarding nurse-to-patient ratios by nurses in the three Victorian acute-care hospitals indicate that the reduced ratios of patients to nurses, combined with teamwork, have had a positive impact on workloads and patient care. However, the responses also highlight aspects of the nurses' work environment, such as

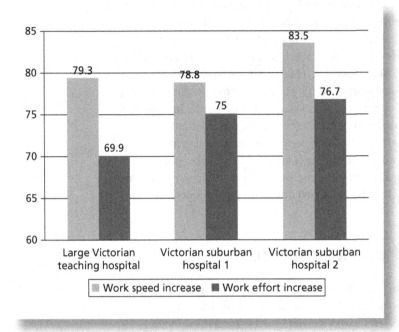

Figure 13.1: Change in work speed and effort, 2003–08

increasing patient acuity and complications, faster patient flows and insufficient beds, which counteracted the positive influence of the ratios in ameliorating work intensity.

The increase in patient flows – namely, shorter length of stay, increased case flows and higher bed occupancy rates – can be identified as a major source of work intensification. As we have demonstrated, increased numbers of patient discharges generated increased workloads due to the documentation required for patient discharges and in liaising with other health-care providers, including pharmacies, social workers, outside rehabilitation services, home nursing services and out-patient services. Also, there was work intensification arising from ensuring that patients and their relatives understood the medications that were prescribed and that they received the necessary care and treatment advice required for recovery.

The nurses stated that the accelerated rate of admissions and discharges and associated increased workflow pressures were driven by the interaction between meeting local targets or KPIs and the Casemix average length of stay criteria for discharges. A Nurse Unit Manager (NUM) in one of the suburban surgical wards captured the interaction well:

> The pressure now is on how we perform … whether we get our patients out based on the length of stay or we have key performance indicators that demand that we get at least one patient out of the ward by 10 o'clock so that we don't have a bottleneck down in emergency.

Another unit manager in charge of a surgical ward in the teaching hospital developed this account of work pressure:

In actual fact I reckon it is really hard slog. I reckon it is hard slog everywhere. In the ward areas, because of the patient flow and bed push to get people out of there, to get people out of ICU just so others can come in, and we are a trauma hospital now getting much sicker people that don't stay for long, so you haven't got the luxury of somebody recovering, you know, for ten days post surgery.

An NUM in charge of an intensive care unit in the teaching hospital explained the difficulty of balancing the management demands to meet the KPIs and the pressure on her staff:

it's still about the KPI and the money and making sure the numbers are right. So that's where I have to push back – and there was a case a couple of weeks ago where we were absolutely crazy, people were working their bums off and extra shifts and whatever, and I just said, 'Tomorrow, we're not doing any elective surgery, we need a break'.

The resultant number of discharges in a ward was identified as a barometer of work pressures. An NUM in charge of a medical ward in the teaching hospital commented: 'We fluctuate between two and six [discharges] a day. Six would be a bad day.' An NUM in charge of a surgical ward in a suburban hospital said:

I just think the pace, the actual pace, the physical pace that we have to do it at, you know, it's nothing for us to have 10 or 12 admissions and discharges in one day, and that's an awful lot of turnaround.

Another nurse who was in charge of a surgical ward in the teaching hospital described the pressure to both admit and discharge patients:

And, you know, the acuity is high, the complexity is high, the number of patients we need to get in per day and get out per day is really high, and there's an enormity … And there is enormous pressure to get those people [patients from ICU and theatre] in and to create capacity for them, and also to safely discharge out.

A suburban hospital NUM commented on the extra burden of paperwork associated with the discharge of elderly patients:

That's another thing that really bogs them down, is paperwork. I mean, as far as – it's safety measures as well. It's knowing that they're safe, and the concern about elderly people and where they're actually being placed and where they're going, and knowing that they're leaving here safely is a big concern.

An NUM in a surgical ward of the teaching hospital commented on the impact of the increased volume of discharge paperwork:

Most of the time your patient is gone and you are still doing paperwork two to three hours later to bring it up to speed, because you do not have time to do it then, because you have three other things going on.

▪ Insufficient beds

Insufficient beds and very high levels of bed occupancy in hospitals are issues that have a significant impact on access to in-patient beds in wards by emergency patients and patients coming from operating theatres and intensive care units, as well as greatly increasing the pressures on nursing staff. A report by the Auditor-General

(Auditor-General Victoria 2008) identified the need to improve patient flows to relieve what has been termed 'bed block' between emergency departments and wards. There has been some official recognition that there is incompatibility between an efficiency agenda requiring very high levels of bed occupancy and patient access to wards from emergency departments (2008: 15). However, there is no recognition in this report of the pressures placed on nursing staff by increased patient flows, high bed occupancy levels and inadequate bed numbers.

The inadequate number of beds in acute-care hospitals has resulted from state government policies premised on the assumption that the shift to same-day care and shorter patient stays reduces the need for beds. As indicated above, this bed shortage has also been exacerbated by the increasing demand from patients over 75 years (Auditor-General Victoria 2008; Sammut 2008). The Brumby Labor government and the subsequent Baillieu Liberal-National Coalition government set a KPI for hospitals to keep emergency patients waiting no longer than eight hours. This has added to the pressures on nursing staff to discharge patients to make beds available.

An NUM in the teaching hospital identified that the throughput pressure highlighted the need for more beds, commenting that:

> You know, you can argue you can open 30 beds and you'll still be in the same position that you are today. Because you'll fill them, there's no doubt you'll always be in 100 per cent full. But certainly to help with some of that, opening extra beds would be beneficial.

A NUM in charge of the intensive care ward in the large teaching hospital commented about the demand for beds:

> If you go there today, it is crazy. It's 24 beds today; they're all full, and we've got six other patients needing beds in here. So I've actually got two nurses out in the wards looking after sick patients on the wards until we can get the beds in here and get them in here and stuff.

Conclusion

In 1992, a Liberal-National government came to power in Victoria and implemented a program of neo-liberal reforms based reducing the role of the state and using the market as the way to efficiently deliver health and a range of other public services, including power generation and distribution, prisons and major highways. Our analysis of patient flows, staffing levels, patient numbers and bed numbers demonstrates that the major reduction in government funding and work intensification for nurses occurred under the Kennett Liberal-National government. The succeeding Labor government, while retreating from privatisation and outsourcing, left in place systems of managerial accountability and output based funding (Casemix) and reduced bed numbers, which continued to put pressure on the public hospital system. This provides a demonstration that neo-liberal ideology and policies are not the preserve of one political party; rather, the types of political compromises entered into will differ according to the circumstances.

To counteract this pressure on the system, the Australian Nurses Federation successfully campaigned to achieve and retain nurse-to-patient ratios, which resulted in higher levels of staffing. The Bracks Labor government, faced with the growing costs of health care, including capital funding for hospitals, and with a neo-liberal aversion to public sector borrowing for infrastructure, continued to press for increased patient flows and did not increase in bed numbers on a per capita basis. It first tried unsuccessfully to regain control of costs by using collective bargaining to eliminate nurse-to-patient ratios. However, the Labor government was more nuanced in its application of neo-liberal policies than its Liberal-National precursor, as it sought to respond to political and industrial pressures applied by a union with well-developed community alliances.

Discussion questions

13.1   How have Victorian governments attempted to cut costs in public health? Was this process simply sensible financial management?

13.2   What were the measures of work intensification in Victorian public hospitals? Was there any evidence of this having adverse health consequences for the nursing workforce?

13.3   What were the changes in public hospitals following the election of a state Labor government? Did this constitute the end of neo-liberal policies in Victorian public health?

13.4   Is there any evidence that the adverse consequences of work intensification can be alleviated by forms of employee participation, particularly teamwork? Do these findings resonate with the literature discussed in Chapter 11?

13.5   How effective was the union in improving health outcomes for patients and the working environment of its members?

Global supply chains and workforce flexibility in automotive components

Malcolm MacIntosh

■ Chapter objectives

This chapter will enable readers to understand:

- how global supply chains influence local production arrangements in the automotive components sector
- the importance of a broad systemic understanding of the factors influencing production and work arrangements
- interactions between production practice, work organisation and human resources management (HRM) practices
- how external economic and regulatory factors influence the organisation of work and production
- the ways in which employee voice operates in relation to production strategies and the pressures that shape work and work organisation.

Introduction

In this chapter, we examine the role of workplace relations practices and policies at Futuris, Australia's largest domestic automotive components company. We will show the ways in which competitive pressures, government policy and industrial negotiations have shaped and changed the experience of work and workplace relationships in the company. The components industry is one in which the globalisation of markets has shaped production scale and strategy; it is an industry in which labour negotiations and the content of enterprise agreements provide the framework for productive efficiency and the experience of work, and also an industry in which communications and employee involvement have to serve sometimes conflicting management and employee needs. Many of the issues raised in this case study have salience in other locations, because the industry is inherently global in its orientation through its part of global value chains in the automotive sector.

To provide a context, we begin with an overview of the automotive sector, as that industry frames and defines the manner in which automotive components companies operate. Next we provide the relevant findings of a research project undertaken by the author into changing work practices in the automotive components sector. The research included an examination of enterprise agreements in several companies, including Futuris, Autoliv and TI International. Only one of these companies, Futuris (the focus of this chapter), is Australian-owned. The research draws on focus group discussions with employees and interviews with managers in each of the companies included in the research.

The automotive industry

The automotive industry has been described as a pre-eminent example of global production (Dicken 1999: 316). The major motor vehicle producers (MVPs) are organised globally, with the assembly of products occurring across the globe. The ownership of the industry has until recently been concentrated in Europe, North America and Japan, but there has been some recent growth in Asian-based companies outside Japan – notably Korea, India and China. More importantly, there has been a significant change in the location of manufacturing plants towards countries where demand is increasing, with new centres for production in China, India and Thailand. The annual production of motor vehicles in China now exceeds that in the United States. In Korea, a substantial motor industry has developed over a period of two decades, underpinned by major investment by government and North American car companies, while the Indian industry is expanding with acquisition and growth based on its large domestic market. A submission to the recent Australian Government Automotive Review (Bracks Review) noted that the centre of mass for the production of passenger vehicles (light vehicles) has shifted towards Asia (Federation of Automotive Products Manufacturers 2008: 12). These shifts have clear implications for the Australian industry.

The Australian motor vehicle industry is currently focused on the subsidiaries of three global manufacturers: GMH, Toyota and Ford. The industry faces a particular problem with a relatively small domestic market. This has led local manufacturers to pursue export markets, with varying levels of success. As MVPs operate within a global corporate structure, their access to overseas markets is itself governed by corporate priorities rather than unrestricted choice. For further insights into the nature of globalised production, see Chapter 1.

For the Australian automotive sector, government policy has provided an important framework shaping the way the MVPs, and consequently components companies, have managed their operations. Until the 1980s, the industry grew behind a 'wall' of tariff protection and other government support mechanisms (such as guaranteed fleet purchases), which fostered low levels of efficiency and innovation (Wright 2006; see also Chapter 2). In the late 1980s, a new approach to domestic manufacturing was developed, known colloquially as the Button Plan after the federal minister then responsible for its development. This plan instituted a planned reduction in tariff protections, thereby more directly exposing local manufactures to global competition (Lansbury & Saulwick 2006). Compensating support for retraining and redundancy payments for displaced workers allowed a relatively orderly transition to the new competitive environment, which also resulted in a rationalisation of the number of MVPs sustaining a local presence.

Wright (2006: 56) summarises the development of industry policy in the sector, concluding that 'the Australian state has played a key role in making the industry more efficient and reorienting the activities of producers to survive the pressures of import competition'. Nevertheless, the logic of the policy position adopted in the 1980s, together with changes in the global markets for vehicles and changing currency rates, has led to significant challenges for the industry (Australian Government 2008b). As the Federation of Automotive Parts Manufacturers (FAPM) explained in its submission to the Automotive Industry Review, the underlying reality of the Australian automotive sector is one of a small market place for manufacturers (FAPM 2008). According to the Bracks Review, the proportion of Australian manufactured vehicles sold has declined from 30 per cent of all vehicle sales in 2002 to 19 per cent in 2007 (Australian Government 2008a: 1). Allied with this decline in the sales of locally manufactured vehicles, the proportion of components sourced from Australian manufacturers has declined with successive model changes (Australian Government 2008b: 12).

The components sector

Automobiles are assembled from a great many components. As the industry has developed in complexity and scale, the task of developing constituent components has increasingly been delegated to a growing body of specialist components companies (Lewchuk & Robertson, 1997). These companies tend to be organised hierarchically. Some companies specialise in the design and manufacture of major sub-systems of final vehicles, such as transmission or braking systems, while others manufacture less complex products such as door handles. As a consequence, companies manufacturing components make up a significant sub-sector of the automobile industry and, like the MVPs, they are often organised globally.

In Australia, components manufacturers have ranged from small family companies to subsidiaries of multinational companies (MNCs). The development of global supply chains for automotive components has led to qualitative and quantitative changes in the Australian industry. In 1990, there were approximately 127 members of the peak industry body, the FAPM, but this had declined to 55 companies by 2012. However, the composition of the sector has also changed. In the early period, the majority of components companies were Australian-owned and many were part of diversified companies. More recently, from the mid-1990s, the industry has become more concentrated, with subsidiaries of overseas components companies dominating the supply of complex components (Cooney & Sewell 2008: 135).

One effect of this greater integration into global supply chains for components has been the relative ease with which the MNCs can transfer production outside Australia. An example is the Australian subsidiary of the global supplier of safety systems, Autoliv, which moved its Australian production facility to China in order to be closer to a major and emerging market. An interesting contrast to this is provided by the American-owned supplier of fuel lines, TI International, which fabricates products in Australia for Australian MVPs using basic materials imported from its own Chinese plant. This decision is largely dictated by the physical size of the finished product, which would be costly to import from China because of the space required. A further variation on the theme of global supply is to be found at Futuris, which has maintained its Australian plants but has expanded its activities offshore through a deliberate policy of developing joint ventures and subsidiary operations in other countries closer to larger product markets (Sprague 2012: 15). In each case, the changes reflect the increasing globalisation of components manufacturing.

■ The workplace relations framework

Since the early 1980s, Australian governments have changed the legislative and institutional framework of the workplace relations system. These efforts began with the Hawke federal Labor government's Prices and Incomes Accord with the Australian Council of Trade Unions (ACTU) in 1983, and developed under the subsequent Keating Labor government with legislative changes aimed at decentralising industrial relations; these developments were considered in Chapters 5 and 8. However, the most dramatic changes in the system took place under the Howard Liberal-National government, beginning with its 1996 legislative changes embodied in the *Workplace Relations Act* and later amendments. As we have explained above, the enactment of the *Fair Work Act 2009* brought further major changes to the workplace relations framework. How these changes impacted on workplace relations in the components sector is of particular interest.

First, there has been a move from reliance on awards towards workplace and enterprise agreements across the industry. This decentralisation reflects changes in the role of the national tribunal, the Fair Work Commission (formerly Fair Work Australia). Second, there have been important changes in the way industrial agreements are negotiated in the vehicle and components sectors. By 1996, the characteristic practice was that industrial agreements were negotiated through company-level bargaining within an industry framework. Unions used the industry framework to spread the best bargaining outcomes across the sector, a practice known as 'pattern bargaining'. Together, these changes encouraged a stronger focus on enterprise and workplace bargaining; combined with legal limitations on union industrial action, this facilitated greater authority from employers in bargaining outcomes.

The logic of production

The other important feature of the global industry is the use of a more or less common language to describe the principles of production and supply across the sector, in particular the notion of 'lean production' (Womack, Jones & Roos 1990). While the idea was not defined in any direct manner in Womack, Jones and Roos's book, it was based on the authors' understanding of the management and supply chain practices that appeared to have contributed to the success of Toyota as an international vehicle manufacturer. The novelty of the lean production model lies in part in its systemic approach to the process of manufacturing, which includes production processes, but also extends to management of the supply chain for components, thereby extending the scope of management beyond the boundaries of the MVP.

Supply-chain relationships

In the lean production philosophy, the supply of components is aligned across the supply chain to match market demand. In this system, the supply of components 'just in time' (JIT) is a key principle designed to minimise waste and excess stocks of components and products. The underlying principle of eliminating waste also implies greater attention to quality.

Long-term contractual relationships were proposed as ideal for the achievement of the mutual gains expected across the key supply criteria of price, quality and timely delivery. In the system described by Womack, Jones and Roos (1990), this supplier–buyer relationship is pictured as a win–win situation in which there is a degree of mutual dependence. The essential building blocks of the new relationship are stated to be trust, shared risk and opportunity, along with cooperative behaviour in inter-organisational relationships. The outcomes are expected to be quality, and delivery in time and at prices that reflect the productivity and reduced waste of lean production processes.

A more analytical view of the supply-chain relationship is provided by Gereffi (2002), who describes the relationship in the automotive sector as a 'production-led' supply chain, one in which the relationships are generally hierarchical and it is the priorities of the final producer that determine those participating in the process. Increasingly, MVPs rely on suppliers to provide either discrete components or increasingly complex sub-products for inclusion in the final product. The supply chains linking a components manufacturer and MVP are designed to deliver these products to the final assembly line in a reliable and planned manner. The situation that emerged in the final decades of the twentieth century was described in a submission to the Australian government's review of the automotive industry:

> the chains are led to the final product and the assembly plant, and are tightly controlled by MVPs. Everything is carefully forecast, planned and tracked. Development matches to the orders of the product plan, sourcing to the rhythm of the assembly plan. (FAPM 2008)

For components manufacturers, the underlying logic of this relationship is presented as a range of requirements for product quality, price and delivery, which are embodied in the formal contracting arrangements. Invariably, these requirements are complemented by detailed and quite prescriptive auditing systems, which are designed to integrate supplier production behaviour with the requirements of the MVP. These requirements have a direct impact on the organisation of work and working relationships, as they specify aspects of work performance. In other words, workplace relations in the context of a global supply chain must be heavily shaped by the requirements of the major vehicle producers, because otherwise alternative sources (offshore) of components will have to be found.

In Australian companies, the supply relationship is governed closely by contractual arrangements that have implications for work practices and management in the supply companies. These contracts include clauses specifying how the supplier will be expected to demonstrate competence in manufacture, assembly and even design. Contracts normally include clauses that specify how the quality of the product will be measured, the cost of the product and expectations as to how and when the product will be delivered. Each of these requirements creates a need for the managers of supplier companies to create management processes to respond to the customer requirements. As reported by managers in supply companies, the hierarchical relationship is one in which the buyers – the MVPs – exercise the 'upper hand'. These decisions influence the scope of work undertaken by production workers and the standards expected of them. Quality is invariably specified in quite precise terms – for example, as the number of errors acceptable per million parts. To ensure that these standards are reached, suppliers are expected to adopt proprietary auditing processes provided by the MVP, generally referred to as quality systems. Supplier company managers acknowledge that error-free production is a key requirement that tends to drive training, job allocation and the organisation of work responsibilities.

In the Australian situation, cost has generally been interpreted as a reduction of costs across the period of the contract, but in a tortuous use of language, this is presented by the MVPs as sharing in the efficiency gains of long-term contracts.

These demands create some pressure towards a cost-oriented approach to production with manning levels, wages and work methods all conditioned by the cost constraints experienced by the company. Finally, the delivery regime is normally geared to the needs of final production. As daily production requirements vary, suppliers must operate in a flexible manner with an ability to vary the pace and volume of production to balance the cost of reworked components or storage while meeting customer requirements. Taken together, these requirements and the way they are specified in supply contracts create a work environment in which workers are made aware of the overall production priorities and are expected to exercise a relatively high degree of responsibility for the quality of their operations – sometimes referred to as 'quality at source'.

At Futuris, it was evident that each of the MVPs had a slightly different approach to the contractual relationship, a situation identified in a study by Gereffi, Humphrey and Sturgeon (2005). Managers and – interestingly – many workers were able to describe the character of those relationships very clearly. One MVP was described by a middle-level supervisor in one of research companies as 'bureaucratic' and intimidating. Moreover, it was suggested that the relationship was driven largely by cost. A second of the MVPs was described as very directive in its relationships. The third MVP was seen somewhat differently, and was described in terms similar to those applicable to the 'lean production' model – that is, cooperative and problem oriented. In two other companies examined in the research, managers described the relationship with Toyota as positive in that Toyota acted in a supportive manner in attempting to improve quality and productivity and to develop work systems that would contribute to those outcomes. The auditing system associated with the Toyota Quality System, and the inclusion of team leaders and supervisors from the supplier companies in Toyota training programs, reinforced this perception. These observations indicate that corporate strategies and styles can influence the working environment of management and employees in supplier companies.

Production processes

At the production management level, the 'lean production' system is built around the notion that production priorities and processes should be determined in accordance with product demands. This is referred to as a 'pull' system, rather than on the basis of machine or productive capacity, referred to as a 'push' system (Vidal 2007; Cook & Grase 2001). For this system to work, all aspects of the production system – including labour – need to be flexibly deployed, so as to allow variation in the volume and nature of production taking place. An immediate consequence of this is that employees should be capable of moving between jobs and of adjusting their work to suit different product types. This implies that the workforce is either flexible in size and disposition, or that workers themselves can move across tasks and processes. The first option involves numerical flexibility of changes in overall staff numbers or hours worked. The latter is normally referred to as functional flexibility, and implies a degree of shared skills and abilities across the workforce. There are important implications for employee security, skills and workloads in these choices. However, the lean model is generally assumed to refer to functional flexibility, where responsibility for quality assurance and minor maintenance is placed on production teams, and team members are trained to enable task-sharing. This encourages a more relational approach to the work relationship (as opposed to a task-based one) between managers and employees as quality assurance and team responsibility require higher levels of trust and engagement with management requirements than might be induced in a less stable work arrangement. Where employers resort to numerical flexibility, workplace relationships take on a much more transactional character.

In the present context, of particular interest are the implications of the lean production idea for the organisation of work. There are a range of challenges to the view that lean production is a new paradigm of work that values human skills and abilities more than traditional mass production systems. The criticisms include empirical evidence that the new system may accentuate stress and unsafe work practices, and that it is simply a refinement of traditional mass production or Taylorist approaches to work organisation (see Chapter 11; Berggren 1992; Babson 1995; Parker & Slaughter 1993; Lewchuk & Robertson 1997). After reviewing such critiques, Vidal (2007) concluded that the degree to which different manufacturing plants in his study had achieved the core idea of worker involvement in decisions about quality and process improvement implicit in the 'lean production' model could be explained by an understanding of the local context in each plant. He identified three factors that could explain the limited application of lean production principles: the strategic orientation of management; organised worker power; and workforce disposition – that is, workers' propensity to resist and shape new work practices (2007: 204). Vidal used this framework to classify the workplace changes pursued in each of his cases. An important outcome of his research is confirmation of the different ways in which lean production initiatives may vary according to the way managers approach change, how worker interests are organised and their ability to resist or accommodate the changes.

The focus of the research reported in this chapter is more on management strategies and processes, and the way that they accommodate or challenge formal workplace relations arrangements, as well as worker motivations and interests. Here, we concentrate most directly on how the strategic position facing managers influences human resources management (HRM), production practices and work organisation, and how each in turn shapes workplace relations. The study incorporates consideration of the changes outside the workplace, whereas Vidal focuses on the dynamics of change within. Accordingly, we move next to examine the strategic position of the company, including its organisational relationships (particularly through supply chains); its production technology and organisation; the context of HR management; and worker responses and experience.

The Futuris case

Strategic orientation

Futuris is an operating subsidiary of a larger conglomerate corporation that operates across several industry sectors. The company's development suggests a strong commitment to establishing a sustainable position in the automotive components sector. The company's involvement in this sector began with the manufacture of air-conditioning units for local MVPs in the 1980s, but later expanded to steering columns and parts for seats. The local market had relatively low production volumes, making it difficult for manufacturers to pursue high levels of capital investment, which in part explains this early diversification. Production was a mix of basic fabrication and assembly of parts, some bought from other suppliers. At that time, the company's operations were characterised by a distinctive approach to management, reflecting contemporary ideas about building employee involvement and satisfaction (employee voice).

In the 1990s, the company underwent structural change, resulting in more distinctive product specialisation with plants serving the requirements of MVPs. The company expanded through the takeover of smaller local production facilities, which consolidated its position as a manufacturer of seating and door trims. The company pursued a position in global supply chains based on its relationships with MVPs in Australia, together with its ability to manage to their supply requirements. As a result, the company grew in a period of 20 years from an organisation with plants in two states to one larger local plant with interests in offshore plants in China, Mexico and Brazil. This growth has been funded from within the corporate group, and control remains in the headquarters, located in Melbourne.

Production organisation and strategy

Futuris has built its position as a supplier to MVPs through attention to the basic requirements of error-free products delivered on time and at an agreed price. The availability of a relatively experienced workforce in each of its manufacturing locations facilitated training for the specific requirements of Futuris processes, while the management culture promoted the value of building trust between managers and operational staff. At the time of this study, the plant incorporated a range of semi-automated sub-processes designed to reduce human error and improve efficiency. Accompanying the changes in technology has been a systematic approach to codifying operating procedures, while computer based production coordination has reduced demands on supervisors. In one focus group, it was suggested that these changes fell short of the MVP's expectations. As explained above, production systems in supply chain relationships are shaped by the contractual arrangements in place. At Futuris, the importance of the contract was attested to by focus group participants. In one area, the company departed quite distinctively from the norms of a JIT system by reinstituting buffer stocks for finished goods; this arrangement allowed for up to two days of finished goods on site. The change, which is a departure from the JIT principle inherent in lean production, enabled Futuris managers to smooth the flow of work and reduce the disruption of abrupt changes in demand. Some operators suggested that 'error chasing' in products was also disruptive, and that the buffers allowed the whole production system to operate more continuously. However, it was also observed that problem-solving on the shop floor was encouraged by a 'no-blame' approach by managers. One operator contrasted his experience at Futuris with a more negative experience at a nearby German components manufacturer.

■ Context and strategy for human resources management

At the plant level, HR is led by a small team of practitioners. The senior manager participates in plant-level strategic decisions through her membership of the Plant Management Committee and, consistent with the approach outlined in Chapter 6, all members of the HRM group see their role as supporting the strategic directions being pursued by the company. The overall framework of their approach could be described as focused on building employee competence and engagement. At the operational level, the group concentrates on selection, training, communication, and health and safety. Selection processes are relatively sophisticated, with personality and behavioural testing used to assess the potential for new employees to 'fit' with the work environment. The objective of these techniques is also to assess supervisory potential, as the company has actively sought to identify people with the ability to provide leadership from within as it has expanded.

Training for employees has been central to the development of production capability. While most operators talked of on-the-job training, training was undertaken quite systematically and based on measurable competency outcomes. The overall objectives of training included cross-skilling within teams. The classification structure outlined in the enterprise bargaining agreement included a clear link between cross-skilling and remuneration. Supervisors and team leaders were encouraged to undertake formal training in supervision and management through TAFE, with company support. The company's training policies attracted strong support from staff.

Occupational health and safety were given a high priority in the belief that this was not only a means of preventing accidents and injuries, but would also build employee respect and commitment. The company also embarked on an ambitious ergonomic project to redesign jobs and standardise operating procedures, to align them more closely with the physical capacity of operators. The project was aimed at reducing injury occasioned by ergonomic job demands that exceeded the physical ability of operators, but was again part of a larger program of building trust in management. Focus group discussions confirmed that staff at all levels responded positively to the company's approach to health and safety. In this sense, Futuris exemplifies the way in which job design to maximise autonomy can improve worker well-being, and promote better health and safety (see Chapter 11 for further discussion).

The company attached importance to communications with employees. Focus group respondents saw communications positively and, while there was some criticism of the style of communication, it was reportedly improving. There was a relatively wide view among operators that many of the issues raised by management colloquially referred to as 'State of the Nation' addresses were not of any real interest to employees; on the other hand, supervisors generally viewed these sessions as valuable. One operator observed wryly that 'they give us what they want … but keep some stuff to themselves. The stuff they don't tell us is what we want to know.'

Another comment from a group of long-serving operatives was that communication (as well as the use of cross-functional teams) had declined from that experienced a decade earlier. This suggests that the process of integrating employees from other companies whose operations had been taken over by Futuris had created strains on the more relaxed interaction experienced in the 1990s. It is also possible that the 'State of the Nation' addresses reached their primary target of keeping supervisory staff aligned with the company's direction but did not address the interests and concerns of operatives. The greater cynicism of operators to communication practices was an indication that the task of building a shared vision was likely to be prolonged.

Consultation over work practices was less evident. Operators suggested that consultation over workplace changes, changes to equipment, layout and operating procedures were often undertaken in ignorance of employees' views. Operators explained this approach in several ways. One saw it as laziness, and suggested that managers only reacted when their main customer demanded action on an issue. Another operator suggested that engineers and managers had different priorities to people on the shop floor, and were not really interested in making jobs easier to undertake. A related comment was that errors in engineering solutions were unlikely to emerge until production operators experienced difficulties in implementing the changed job requirements, making it easier for engineers and managers to meet immediate pressures without reference to their longer-term effects. Supervisors and team leaders tended to be more analytic about the deficiencies in consultation, suggesting in one case that the pressures on managers were different and were not understood by operators. This may have been an allusion to the stress placed on managers to meet the expectations of MVP customers.

Performance management processes were defined in the enterprise bargaining agreement, with a central role given to a consultative committee for implementing standards and processes. However, focus-group participants did not appear to be aware of the formal consultative process. Not surprisingly, supervisors and team leaders saw the idea of measuring work outcomes in a positive light.

Focus groups did not reveal any deep-seated opposition to the performance management system, and the following comment by one operator suggests that the system may have been seen as a reasonable one: 'You take pride in your work, I suppose, because you are more accountable here … I think because there is a bit more accountability here [than at Holden] that people do put in the extra effort.' This comment and the overall reaction of operators to questions about performance management need to be seen against a background in which performance failures were not subject to 'blame', but resolved in a cooperative and constructive manner.

■ *The workplace experience*

Production systems had a number of outcomes for supervisors and production operators in the plant. All focus-group participants expressed the view that work had become more difficult, and that operators were busier than previously. Some operators explained the situation with some resentment, blaming the increased workloads on earlier redundancies. In contrast, the team leaders found the work demands constant but satisfying in that they felt busy and engagement with supervisory tasks was positive for that group. The difficulties felt by operators appeared to be centred on the pace of work, as well as changes in job requirements resulting from layout changes and the range of products on which operators worked. The negative comments about the more complex roles were invariably balanced with a comment that Futuris was a better place to work than other components companies.

Shared responsibilities for quality and functional flexibility within production teams are a central tenet of the 'lean production' model. At Futuris, teams were composed of groups of workers organised around a range of production tasks. There was usually some tangible sub-component or outcome associated with each group, and there was an explicit focus on the development of shared and complementary task-related skills. The measurement of performance and output provided a focus for the activity of these groups of workers. As explained above, the selection and training of team leaders is quite systematic and thorough. Focus group participants attested to the cooperative spirit within their teams. One operator suggested it was driven by necessity as well as an element of goodwill: 'People and task sizes vary, so people need to help one another.' In terms of the skills that people brought to the job, the level of cross-skilling varied between teams and was as low as 20 per cent of the team in several cases. In that situation, the ability to assist one another was limited by the skill levels available.

A related issue was the use of cross-functional teams in which managers and employees from a range of organisational units would work together as project teams to review or redesign work arrangements. While such project teams had been used in the past, they appeared to have fallen into disuse under the pressure for managers to make quick responses to the MVP on production issues. Supervisors and employees were equally critical of the demise of these cross-functional project teams. Supervisors were critical of the loss of efficiencies that resulted, while employees and team leaders expressed concern over the introduction of changes in work arrangements without effective consultation or engagement with those most affected by them.

In summary, the production team working arrangements were generally consistent with the proposals embodied in the lean production literature (Womack, Jones & Roos 1990), although the failure to maintain cross-functional project teams for process improvement and redesign of work arrangements suggests that the imperatives of customer needs could dictate a more top-down approach to process and production improvements.

■ *Workplace relations*

The company's approach to production management is reflected in the content and orientation of its enterprise agreements and, more directly, in the HRM policies adopted. The content and tone of the enterprise bargaining agreements negotiated between 2001 and 2007 were distinctly oriented towards management priorities. An over-arching clause in these agreements focused on the importance of responding to competitive pressures and identified areas for improvement. While they expressed a common concern for industry policy, the agreements effectively endorsed the competitive logic advanced by employers. They incorporated opportunities for numerical flexibility in the form of the ability of managers to change the spread of working hours, shift breaks and overtime. Functional flexibility was encouraged by linking job-related skills development to financial rewards. Overall, the orientation in the company is towards a production-centred approach to HRM and work organisation, with lean production serving the purpose of a narrative for explaining the way work is organised.

As indicated above, unions were in a much more defensive position in the industry following the legislative changes of the Howard Liberal-National Coalition government (see Chapter 3). They appeared to have reduced leverage in the plant, as indicated by the ability of managers to undertake a survey of employee attitudes to numerical flexibility without union agreement or involvement. Doubtless this situation was exacerbated by the continuing instability in the global motor vehicle industry and, in Australia, by the actual or threatened withdrawal or scaling down of the operations of the local vehicle manufacturers. It is instructive that, in each focus group, workers were asked whether they 'trusted' management and their unions respectively. The answers were consistently negative for both management and unions, suggesting that there was an instrumental approach to the work situation, in which work demands and pressures were tolerated for the relative security of the work situation. This might be explained by the common appreciation that the employment situation in the industry was fragile – ironically, a message reinforced by the lean production narrative.

■ Conclusion

By setting the case of a local vehicle components manufacturer in the context of the global vehicle manufacturing sector, we can see the intricate connections between workplace experience and the many factors shaping the strategies of companies in the industry and the employment relationship within those companies. The corporate structure of their customers, the MVPs, emerges as a significant element in determining the size, range of activities and the management practices adopted by the component manufacturers. Supply-chain relationships are important in determining a focus for day-to-day management practice and for longer-term financial stability. In this context, Futuris has sought greater production efficiencies, not only through technology but through changes in work practices and arrangements.

Collective negotiations continue to provide a framework for working conditions, but they reflect management priorities, and HRM practices increasingly focus on individual relationships. Interviews with the HRM staff further elaborated this point. The pursuit of the many technical aspects of lean production arrangements faced little opposition from a workforce instrumental in its outlook and unions weakened by internal difficulties and reduced influence at industry level.

These observations help explain the rather cynical view expressed by employees regarding the degree of trust they had in management and unions respectively. While all kinds of incidents could be adduced to explain some of the negativity, the fact that it was almost a universal sentiment suggests a degree of resignation or an instrumental view of the workplace. Nonetheless, Futuris was widely held up as a superior work experience compared with those many workers had experienced elsewhere in the industry.

■ Discussion questions

14.1   'The automotive industry is a powerful demonstration of the way in which global forces impact on the Australian economy and workplace relations, but the choices made by governments reflect neo-liberal prescriptions.' Discuss.

14.2   Identify the changes that have occurred in workplace relations in the automotive components sector over time. Analyse the forces driving these changes.

14.3   How well does the model of 'lean production' implemented in the automotive components industry fit with the notion of employee participation in decisions on issues such as the organisation of work?

14.4   In the case study in this chapter, what type of employee voice has emerged? What are the key features that indicate this?

The Australian Public Service: the challenges ahead

Bernadine Van Gramberg,
Julian Teicher and Brad Nash

■ Chapter objectives

This chapter will enable readers to understand the:
- ways in which the Australian Public Service (APS) has changed both procedurally and structurally in an era in which market principles are pervasive
- impact of adopting a private enterprise approach to management, both at the level of service delivery and in managing its workforce
- challenges of workforce planning in light of demographic changes in the sector
- effect of decentralisation policies on the ability to operate as one APS
- internal and external environmental factors that most impact on effective public service delivery – especially the impact of changes of government on workplace relations arrangements and management.

Introduction

The Australian Public Service (APS) comprises a suite of agencies and departments charged with providing a diverse range of services to a growing and changing Australian population. From schoolteachers, nurses, armed-forces personnel and other direct service providers, to those who work in the administration of policy and program development, the operations of the APS span the public, private and not-for-profit sectors as each has become involved in the delivery of government services. The delivery of these services does not exist in a vacuum. Governments in Australia and most developed nations are influenced in their decision-making by the prevailing views and ideologies – not the least of which is neo-liberalism. As we explained in Chapter 1, these ideologies are driven by beliefs regarding how best to use public taxes and income to deliver government services. This chapter examines the APS by providing an overview of the service and an account of the challenges it faces in providing government programs, payments and services, while seeking to implement private sector management practices. It also highlights the issues that are facing the APS with regard to attracting and retaining a suitably skilled workforce in an environment of increased pressure to cut costs and reduce its size.

An overview of the APS

The APS can be classified as delivering three sets of services: first, the services that form an important part of the nation's social welfare system (for example, public housing, community services); second, the services provided to people with specific needs (for example, aged care and disability services); and third, the services that are used by all citizens at some stage of their lives (for example, education and training, health services, police services and emergency services). The delivery of these services occurs through a number of mechanisms:

- direct delivery through a government provider role
- funding external providers through grants or the purchase of services (a 'purchaser' role)
- subsidising users (through vouchers or cash payments) to purchase services from external providers
- imposing community service obligations on public and private providers
- providing incentives to users or providers, such as reducing tax obligations in particular circumstances (known as tax expenditures) (APSC 2011).

When compared with other nations, the expenditure of the APS to deliver its complex set of programs and services is low. A recent report by Whelan (2011: 15) notes that Australia's contribution of 35 per cent of GDP to fund the APS falls well behind nations such as France (53 per cent), Germany (44 per cent), the United Kingdom (47 per cent), Canada (40 per cent), New Zealand (42 per cent) and the United States (39 per cent). Whelan argues that recent political pressure on Australian governments to return surplus budgets has meant that the dominant mechanism to deliver efficiencies has been cost-cutting. Indeed, this was also the finding of a recent report into the reform of Australian government administration by the Advisory Group on Reform of Australian Government Administration (Moran 2010). Before examining this and other government reports on the strategic direction of the public service, it is important to consider the challenges the APS faces as a service-deliverer.

APS demographics

Each year, the Australian Public Service Commission (APSC) conducts an APS-wide survey, *The State of the Service Report*. The 2010–11 report highlights that there were more than 166 000 APS employees working within 97 agencies at June 2011, an increase of just over 1 per cent compared with the 164 400 employees at June 2010. A further 130 000 to 140 000 employees in Australian government administration work in government agencies other than APS agencies. The agencies with the largest growth in 2010/11 were the Department of Defence, which grew by 4.9 per cent, the Department of Immigration and Citizenship, up by 12.7 per cent, and the Australian Taxation Office (ATO), which grew by 3.6 per cent. Figure 15.1 highlights these changes in APS employment between 1992 and 2011.

Figure 15.1: APS
employees, 1992–2011
Source: APSC (2011).

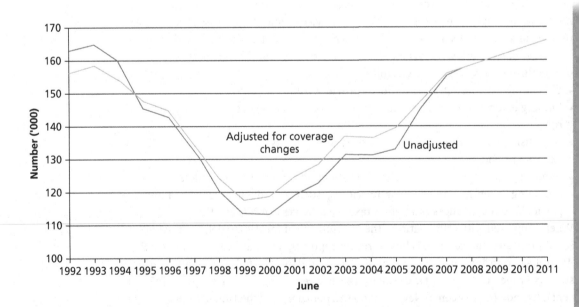

Most APS staff (92.4 per cent) can be classified as having ongoing employment rather than fixed-term, fixed-task or intermittently employment. The proportion of non-ongoing employees in the APS has fallen over the past 15 years, suggesting a greater stability of employment in the sector. However, the pattern of ongoing employment varies between agencies, with larger agencies employing a greater proportion of ongoing staff. Small agencies are noted for hiring non-ongoing employees to cover peaks and troughs in work demand. In June 2011, at least 21 smaller agencies had about one-quarter of their staff employed as non-ongoing. Further, non-ongoing employees tend to be younger than the APS average (21 per cent are aged 25 or younger) and comprise slightly more women (59.7 per cent) than men. More generally, however, the APS is a feminised workforce with women accounting for 57.6 per cent of all APS employment (APSC 2011: 85–90).

The *State of the Service Report* (APSC 2011) highlights that the median age for ongoing employees in the APS was 42 years compared with 39 years in 1997. The APS therefore has an ageing workforce with the bulk of its employees around 45 years of age. This reflects a combination of low levels of recruitment, natural attrition and downsizing in the sector over time. The ageing profile represents a strategically important issue for the APS: under the government superannuation scheme, employees aged over 45 years now will be eligible for retirement in the next 10 years, and they account for 43.7 per cent of the ongoing workforce.

The greatest contributing sector to employment in 2010 was new employees aged over 60 years, while at the same time the employment of those aged under 25 years fell to 3.9 per cent. In this respect, the APS is atypical of Australian employers (see Chapter 10 for further discussion of this issue). The lack of replenishment of the APS workforce, in particular with Generation Y employees, is a major challenge for all departments and agencies. Further, the APS has not been able to satisfy the career progression aspirations of Generation Y employees, often resulting in them deciding to leave and pursue other career options. Without strategies to retain this key component of a future workforce, the APS could suffer from a significant skills and capability shortage in the years to come, which we consider later in the chapter.

The APS as a service deliverer in a changing environment

The APS plays a pivotal role in assisting the Australian government in determining policies, developing legislation and ultimately in delivering services; these are functions that impact on all Australians. In a workplace relations context, the fact that the APS employs approximately 166 000 people, through its various departments and agencies, each with their own enterprise agreements and HR policies, means that developments in this sector are likely to influence other large employers, both directly or indirectly. At the same time, it is emphasised that the two greatest influences over change in the APS come from changes in government and developments in the private sector.

First, changes are often driven by the government of the day, elected with particular mandates and policy directions. A key point of difference for the APS compared with private sector organisations is that a change in government usually results in changes in ministers and their portfolios, and this requires the APS to rework its existing policies and programs, and even its organisation structures. Often, even a change of prime minister significantly alters APS strategy. Over the past three decades, however, the one continuing theme through each change of government has been the political determination to make savings and deliver efficiencies in service delivery. At the same time, the APS is required to continue to provide a strong, high-quality service to a customer base that is becoming increasingly demanding in its expectations of government service delivery.

In this era of tighter budgets and increased expectations, an interesting dynamic for the APS is the reference to 'customers' in its policies, compared with more traditional terms such as 'citizens' or 'the public'. Recently, the APS has changed the way in which it refers to the Australian public a number of times, often switching between 'citizen' and 'customer'. The choice of terminology is important in the present context because, while the language of customers is usually associated with markets for goods and services, it is also a feature of public-management developments in Anglo-American countries.

Together with the shift to the rhetoric of customers, one of the key changes in the APS has been the adoption of private sector management practices and techniques on the assumption that private sector organisations have stronger processes in place for managing staff (Rainey 1999). Arguably, one outcome of the private sector orientation is that APS managers have enjoyed an expanded role with more power, particularly as a result of the increased focus on accountability and decentralisation of human resource policies and procedures to the team level. Indeed, the Moran Report (Advisory Group on Reform of Australian Government Administration 2010) notes that policy development is now even more devolved than previously. There is an expectation that public managers will determine policy direction with stakeholders: 'In the public service, policy collaboration, both between agencies, and with external groups, such as academia, business and the broader community, is essential' (2012:20).

One of the consequences of introducing private sector practices into the APS has been restructuring and rationalisation, largely driven by government's increased focus on 'efficiency dividends'. These so called dividends are actually a flat percentage of operating budget that is removed from the base funding of each department or agency for the upcoming financial year to represent a saving. The Moran Report (2010: 29) notes that dividends are used by agencies as the main efficiency mechanism, and in the year 2008–09 they yielded savings of around $662 million. The aim of efficiency dividends is to encourage the APS to explore all options to improve its effectiveness and efficiency, through technology, work practices or a combination of both. However, these are based on the premise that there are continual compounding efficiencies to be found and realised. The approach drives management at all levels to implement only those strategies that focus on achieving the cost-cutting outcomes they seek. These practices are considered later in this chapter.

■ The imperative for workforce planning and capacity building in the APS

The term 'workforce planning' has been at the centre of recent debates in formulating an APS strategy that ensures continued service delivery in the face of the impending retirements of a sizeable portion of its employees. According to the Australian National Audit Office (ANAO 2002: 11), workforce planning is a 'key strategic activity cascading from an organisation's corporate planning process', enabling it to 'best use its human capital to achieve its outputs and outcomes'. In 2003, the federal government's Management Advisory Committee, in its *Organisational Renewal* report (Management Advisory Committee 2005), recommended that agencies undertake workforce planning, and to this end the ANAO developed a practice guide that was circulated to departments and agencies in 2001. Despite this quasi-directive, the ANAO (2008) has found that workforce planning in APS agencies has been inadequate.

Workforce planning in the APS is needed in order to address a range of challenges beyond an ageing workforce. These include:
• continuing reports of chronic skills shortages
• a fiercely competitive labour market (expected to intensify in key skill areas)
• a tightening fiscal environment
• increasingly demanding expectations of the APS to improve service delivery to the public, and
• policy responses and regulatory frameworks as community needs change and evolve. (APSC 2011: 115)

The *State of the Service Report* for 2011 highlights that only 26 per cent of agencies had a documented workforce plan in place, and 36 per cent had no plan. The lack of workforce planning is underpinned by a lack of planning capability. Some researchers have indicated that many agencies do not have the necessary skills to forecast their workforce requirements for the future – in other words, they are not able to undertake workforce planning very well. In order to manage risks to service delivery, each year the APSC surveys its agencies to determine the nature and extent of these workforce risks over the next five years. Table 15.1 (overleaf) highlights the most commonly cited workforce risks, such as being unable to address capability gaps; problems in retaining and recruiting skilled employees; the lack of career paths; and a loss of corporate knowledge. The inability to address these risks places a significant strain on employment relationships across the APS and, despite numerous reports from the ANAO and Commonwealth Ombudsman, across the APS there remains either reluctance or an inability to adequately address this issue.

A focus on capability-building featured in the recommendations of the Moran Report (Advisory Group on Reform of Australian Government Administration 2010: 44), in order to overcome problems in workforce planning. The concept of capability comes from the resource-based view of an organisation that considers employees one element in the bundle of practices and assets belonging to an organisation and

Table 15.1 Workforce risks facing APS agencies in the next five years 2010–15

Workforce risk	% of agencies
Inability to address capability gaps due to a changing operating environment	53
Inability to retain appropriately skilled employees	52
Inability to recruit appropriately skilled employees	48
Limited career advancement or mobility opportunities for employees	38
Loss of corporate knowledge or talent due to retirement	38
Skill shortages which impact on agency capability	36
Under-developed management or leadership capability among middle managers	36

Source: APSC (2011).

contributing to its sustained competitive advantage. The Moran Report (2010: 24) describes workforce capability as 'the skills, knowledge and abilities that employees of a high performing public service must possess'. The government has documented some evidence on the nature of the skills that are in short supply. For instance, the Moran Report (2010: 24) notes that in 2008–09, 34 per cent of agencies reported information and communication technologies (ICT) as a critical area, while 29 per cent reported a shortage of policy and research skills. Other reported skills shortages were found in project management. The report suggests that these figures have remained relatively constant over the past five years. According to some, one problem faced by the APS is that, unlike the private sector, changing government priorities can profoundly change the set of skills and knowledge required of the APS (Walsh, Bryson & Lonti 2002). Nevertheless, these findings sit uncomfortably with a view that employees should be seen as valuable assets of the APS.

The key question facing the APS is: Why did the evolution of good workforce planning practices which was initially promoted through the set of guidelines issued in 2001 not achieve its desired outcomes? We have so far canvassed the lack of adequately skilled resources and capabilities available within agencies to undertake this task. We now turn to another contributing factor: the devolution of human resource functions to individual agencies. Some researchers have suggested that the lack of central coordination in relation HR operations makes it difficult, if not impossible, to develop a whole-of-APS approach to issues such as workforce planning (e.g. Colley 2001).

▪ Devolution and wage-setting in the APS

During the mid-1980s, under the Hawke Labor government, the APS began modelling its operations on those of private sector organisations, with particular attention to cost-cutting, flattening organisational structures, devolving decision-making and especially those decisions related to recruitment, classification and payment of staff. The transfer of power from the previous Public Service Board to department secretaries was one of many changes designed to ensure that the APS operated by the principles of 'efficiency and effectiveness' (Teicher & Barton 2002). As described in Chapter 1, these changes occurred as organisational responses to the international and national influences of neo-liberal thinking – though in the public sector these ideas were often referred to as New Public Management (NPM) (Hughes 2003). While the term NPM is now sometimes described as an inadequate descriptor of a coherent set of practices, it nevertheless serves as a useful paradigm to capture the sorts of changes that have been implemented by governments across the world in the 1990s as they have grappled with the economic rationalist aims of creating smaller government, extending private ownership and promoting a sense of agency self-management.

The increased emphasis on the management and control of staff at the department level has facilitated the increased individualisation of the employment relationship (Van Gramberg & Teicher 2000). This occurred through the adoption of private sector practices such as individual performance reviews and the dismantling of the concept of a career service as hiring became more flexible in terms of introducing part-time, fixed-term and fixed-task employees.

The election of the Howard Liberal-National Coalition government in 1996, followed by the introduction of the *Workplace Relations Act 1996* and then the Work Choices amendments of 2005, marked the movement of the employment relationship to one directly between employees and employers through decentralised collective bargaining; the introduction of individual agreements (Australian Workplace Agreements or AWAs); and minimising the role and impact of unions such as the powerful Community and Public Sector Union (CPSU). The period of the Howard government also led to further de-layering of the APS with the control of workplace relations shifting to department secretaries. These developments can best be understood when read in conjunction with the discussion of the changes to employment law in Chapter 5.

The decentralisation of workplace relations in Australia has had a profound impact on the manner in which the APS determined the employment terms and conditions of its staff. Remembering that the APS had historically been a centralised civil service with pay and conditions largely set centrally, including by the Public Service Board and with a single award, the introduction of a decentralised approach where each agency is considered a quasi-enterprise has meant that terms and conditions of employment have differed over time, depending on the agency and its bargaining power.

APS agencies were enabled to negotiate enterprise agreements directly with their staff, but with oversight from the Department of Finance, whose role was to assess the affordability of the proposed agreement. These agreements almost invariably involved unions and other employee representative groups, and the bargaining framework was administered by the Department of Employment and Workplace Relations (DEWR) and its successors. The Howard government agenda for reforming APS workplace relations was clear: it wanted to 'create an environment which promotes a culture of continual improvement, foster innovation in pursuing public policy goals and to make individual and team performance count', and enterprise agreements were seen as the main vehicle to deliver these benefits (O'Brien & O'Donnell

2000). But the Howard Liberal-National Coalition government also had a clear ideological mandate to individualise workplace relations, and the APS as a key employer was used as the major platform to roll out individual agreements and to reduce the influence of the public service unions (O'Brien & O'Donnell 2007). Public sector agency heads were charged with the responsibility for 'negotiating' AWAs with their Senior Executive Service and making them available to all other staff; non-union agreements were also implemented. By 2007, almost 12 per cent of APS staff had their employment regulated by AWAs (Forsyth et al. 2008).

The election of the Labor Party in 2007 created another shift in the APS workplace relations landscape. Two key goals of the new government's framework were to remove AWAs and return, where appropriate, to a revised collective bargaining model. The *Fair Work Act 2009* was introduced and the Australian Government Employment Bargaining Framework was rewritten and implemented to reflect these goals. The Bargaining Framework operates within the legislative framework of the *Fair Work Act*, the *Public Service Act 1999* and other Commonwealth laws. The 2009 revisions also incorporated the duty to bargain in good faith and further revisions in 2011 shifted responsibility for supervising the APS workplace relations framework from the Department of Education, Employment and Workplace Relations to the APSC. While the Bargaining Framework provides agencies with broad guidelines for collective bargaining – including the ability to have Senior Executive Service (SES) staff included in the collective agreement – they face a financial cap of 3 per cent in staff pay increases, which is likely to prove problematic in subsequent rounds of bargaining.

The Bargaining Framework has provided the APS with three distinct options for managing terms and conditions of employment. The first is the return to collective bargaining arrangements with employees, a possibility that has driven a revival of the importance and role of the CPSU. The second and third options concern the ways in which the terms and conditions of SES staff and other key staff may be managed. This is a new development because, under the Howard government, the SES was given no option other than employment under an AWA. One way of managing SES terms and conditions is that agency heads can issue a determination, which is a legislative instrument made under section 24(1) of the *Public Service Act 1999*. These determinations are generic across the SES cohort, ensuring consistency across agencies while still allowing agencies to set salary bands for other senior staff. The other way of managing terms and conditions of senior staff is through a common law arrangement that allows agencies to negotiate individual terms and conditions with a particular employee. At this stage, this type of salary-setting is not common in the APS.

One APS, one service?

Over the past two decades, the APS has moved from an essentially centralised bureaucracy to a decentralised set of agencies, each with control over its employment relationships with their employees. Despite this, the APSC often refers to the public service as being 'One APS', which suggests a homogenous operating model with an over-arching infrastructure (Management Advisory Committee 2005). In practice, this is not how the APS operates, and it has been suggested that the issues facing the sector now come as a direct result of the years of the devolution and decentralisation associated with NPM (Colley 2001; ANAO 2002). The decentralised nature of the APS suggests that, rather than being one service, it is more a series of independent quasi-enterprises, all working for the Australian government yet implementing business models and practices that in some cases are not complementary when comparing agencies.

The level of decentralisation has negatively impacted on the ability of managers to set and deliver APS-wide or 'whole-of-government' strategies. Indeed, it is paradoxical that at a time of increasing fragmentation of the public service, Australian governments have regularly resorted to approaches to complex policy problems by requiring agencies and departments to collaborate and offer a seamless service. However, the disparity among agencies in terms of staffing levels and their ability to recruit is reflected in their varying abilities to focus on the key strategic planks set by government. For instance, the Moran Report (Advisory Group on Reform of Australian Government Administration 2010) notes that while over 70 per cent of agencies have a service charter to improve the quality of their services, there is no APS-wide charter that sets common goals among agencies. In other words, there is no whole-of-government strategy on service delivery. The report also notes that as a result of decentralisation, there has been an increase in the number of forms and procedures because each agency creates its own documents. This has led to the observation that 'the Department of Innovation, Industry, Science and Research has identified at least 9600 online forms for business to use in dealing with the three levels of government [federal, state and local]' (Advisory Group on Reform of Australian Government Administration 2010: 19).

Another set of operational discrepancies between agencies arises from their differing abilities to plan or to hire qualified staff. For instance, following the enactment of the *Fair Work Act 2009* and the termination of the AWAs, collective bargaining has occurred across the APS. The new approach has resulted in an increased span of ordinary working hours and other changes to conditions of employment – and, in some cases, significant increases in pay. But these benefits have particularly been linked to larger agencies. The traditional revenue-generation and social policy-delivery agencies such as the ATO and Centrelink have been able to use their size and ability to gain significant injections of funding, which has resulted in a growth in salaries and conditions to a point where these are clearly two of the highest paying agencies in the APS. For other, smaller agencies, the gap between the higher- and lower-paying enterprise agreements has widened. Further, the higher-paying agencies have been able to attract key staff from other agencies with the lure of increased employment conditions and future promotional opportunities. This approach further diminishes the skills base of smaller agencies while doing nothing to enhance the skill base across the APS.

While, on one hand, decentralisation has had the effect of making a single or 'whole-of-APS' approach more difficult to achieve, on the other hand – ironically – public service unions have seen decentralisation as a mechanism for achieving more homogenous terms and conditions of employment. One key example is provided by enterprise bargaining. In the previous round of enterprise negotiations, the union succeeded in creating a large number of enterprise agreements with a common expiry date on or around 30 June 2011. While little management consideration was given to the common end-date of these agreements at the time (largely due to agencies being able to conclude their own agreements), the impact was profound. As the APS headed into 2011, the government faced tougher economic conditions, and it was decided that the APS would offer minimal pay increases in the soon to be renegotiated enterprise agreements. The CPSU mobilised its members and led a successful campaign across the APS, resulting in a number of the management-proposed enterprise agreements being rejected by employees. Agencies particularly impacted on by this campaign were the ATO, Australian Customs and Border Protection and the newly formed Department of Human Services (bringing together Centrelink, Medicare, the Child Support Agency and the Commonwealth Rehabilitation Service Australia). Each agency was then required to reconsider its offer to staff, which created the opportunity for the CPSU to negotiate across-agency terms and conditions. The outcome was a larger than expected pay increase and a set of other conditions that were similar across a number of agencies. While this did not result in a complete standardisation of employment conditions across the APS, it highlighted that the union's strategy to drive consistent outcomes across the APS was working. With these agreements now certified with three-year expiry dates, the CPSU can look forward to the next round of enterprise bargaining in 2014.

■ Work intensification and stress in the APS

The introduction of private sector management practices was primarily based on the premise that the public service was suffering from waste and inefficiency, and that private sector practices would remedy this (Orchard 1998). We have emphasised that the APS response to this malaise focused heavily on cost-cutting. In turn, some researchers have noted that 'doing more with less' led to increased workloads for many APS employees. A typical response to the requirement to increase efficiency was 'leaner', flatter structures, and efforts to directly achieve operational efficiencies but with a static workforce. This observation is supported by findings that APS agencies are achieving higher levels of output and an increase in the pace of work, but this has been accompanied by an overall reduction in the levels of job satisfaction among staff (Brunetto, Farr-Wharten & Shacklock 2011). Moreover, the weight of evidence presented in Chapter 11 suggests that work intensification is likely to have costs in terms of workers' health and well-being.

Under continuing pressure from reduced budget allocations, cost-cutting remains a major source of low staff satisfaction as APS agencies reduce workforce size and still maintain or improve service delivery. This has driven attempts to implement flexibility in workload distribution by moving staff to other positions in order to complete work that is outstanding. While it can be argued that APS staff members 'own' their classification level, they do not own their function, and they can be allocated to any role provided the pay is at their level. Two key practices underpin the problems associated with this type of flexible labour utilisation. First, in order to fill skill gaps, the APS has recruited staff because they possess particular skill sets and qualifications. However due to shortages of suitably qualified staff in areas that are accorded greater priority, these employees may be redeployed, and over time their specialist skills cease to be utilised. Professional staff with extensive qualifications can be reduced to performing administrative processing of claims and payments, which at times has led to them to lodge disputes through the CPSU. Second, the practice of moving staff to other jobs can result in employees working in areas in which they are not skilled, and where there is often a lack of training to equip them to gain the skills required. Ultimately, there is an increased level of attrition, stress or higher levels of unplanned leave. In other cases, industrial disputation occurs, with unions contesting the progressive deskilling of staff. This can be linked to complaints about the lack of career planning, which is a major concern raised by staff – particularly when they are moved. These concerns are highlighted in the *State of the Service Report*:

> negative comments generally related to issues such as a mismatch between the position description and the job, deteriorating work conditions, poor leadership, lack of communication, lack of learning and development opportunities, and a lack of opportunity for career advancement. (APSC 2011: 196)

This managerial practice has several repercussions, which result in lower staff morale. For instance, recent research has pointed to a number of public employee concerns in relation to working conditions, particularly around the lack of consultation over workforce changes, lack of career opportunities, lack of learning and development and the need for longer hours with no monetary compensation (Brown et al. 2009). All these factors may lead to a significant decrease in job satisfaction, lower employee morale and loss of discretionary effort. As discussed earlier, the ANAO has been critical of the lack of effective workforce planning across the APS; when this is coupled with government pressure to increase efficiency dividends, the result is a somewhat volatile workplace relations environment.

The changes that have taken place across the APS over the past three decades have challenged the traditional public service model. While there is no doubt that the APS continues to be responsive to the needs of the government of the day, and that it delivers strong services and programs, internally it grapples with the challenges canvassed in this chapter. These have included challenges in dealing with an ageing workforce; a focus on cost-cutting that appears to have driven ad hoc approaches to hiring and deployment of staff and lack of workforce planning; and decentralisation and devolution, which have resulted in multiple agencies – each with its own approach to workplace relations and work processes – contributing to a lack of consistent outcomes across the sector, vulnerability to union strategy and difficulty implementing a

'One APS' vision. The next section turns to the development of the Service Delivery Reform program as a way forward for the APS to deal with many of these issues.

The services super agency

During 2010/11, the Minister for Human Resources and Social Inclusion, Tanya Plibersek, announced a four-year 'roadmap' for a major reform of the APS and its key service-delivery agencies: the Service Delivery Reform (Department of Human Services 2011). This was designed to integrate social policy service-delivery agencies under a single new federal Department of Human Services. As indicated above, this move integrates four key social service providers: Centrelink, Medicare Australia, the Child Support Agency and the Commonwealth Rehabilitation Service Australia (CRS) into a co-located provider of multiple services. This change came formally into effect on 1 July 2011.

The move can be likened to an extension of the initiative that led to the creation of Centrelink, as the key objective of the service-delivery reform was to make it easier and quicker for the public to access government services in a 'one-stop shop'. It also has other benefits in reducing duplication, delays and inconvenience incurred by customers in a multiple-agency environment. In addition, the reform incorporates provision of services and information through technological improvements delivered online, over the phone and through face-to-face appointments. This means that many of these services are offered through co-located facilities with a single website and common phone number (Department of Human Services 2011: 7). The reform represents an important step back towards a recentralisation of services from the highly devolved, multi-agency environment in which the APS has operated for the past 15 years.

The development of the Department of Human Services is now well into its implementation phase, and there are expectations of significant efficiency and service-delivery benefits to be realised via greater integration of staff (and subsequent staffing decreases), shared services (such as HR, payroll and property services) and infrastructure (for instance, co-located offices). As noted above, this consolidation is also likely to significantly reduce the duplication of work previously done by the four constituent agencies.

In the previous multiple-agency environment, terms and conditions of employment varied considerably across the APS. With the move to a single entity providing these four sets of human services, one of the first challenges facing the new department was how it would negotiate and implement a new enterprise agreement, to bring together approximately 40 000 staff who had worked under four separate enterprise agreements, each containing some clauses that were unique to their particular agency. Terms such as hours of work, minimum hours per week, pay structures, HR policies and similar work performed by staff at different classification levels are typically different across the four APS agencies. Without a new enterprise agreement in place, the department would have been limited in its ability to move staff between programs and services as part of the integration process.

The department's approach to developing a new enterprise agreement was novel in attempting to create an agreement within planned budget parameters, rather than taking the best terms from the four existing agreements. But not everything went to plan. The agreement was put to a staff vote early in the 2011/12 financial year, and was rejected by the vast majority of employees. In part, this was due to the CPSU's successful campaign, which highlighted that some important demands had not been met, including retaining the APS 3–4 broadband and protections for staff rostering, improving overtime provisions, providing pay increases that addressed cost of living increases, and retaining remote office locations such as the key centres in Darwin and Cairns (CPSU 2011). After considerable renegotiation and redrafting, leading to revised pay increases and other benefits, the enterprise agreement went to a second vote in late 2011. This time the agreement was passed by staff, and the department now has the new human resource framework it needs to proceed with its workforce-management plan.

An emerging workplace relations challenge for the new department comes from the fact that the success of the venture is heavily dependent on the technology that will assist in distributing work across numerous locations around Australia. This technology is a 'double-edged sword' because, while there is general acceptance that it will provide flexibility and timeliness in delivering services and information, there are staff concerns regarding the department's workforce-management plan. Staff concerns relate to the potential impact on their jobs and careers, particularly in relation to new training requirements, job redesign, job removals, redundancies and job creation. The CPSU (2012) has described the new Work Management System as a computerised tool that will match employees' skills using 'tags' to specialist tasks anywhere in Australia, and that can be performed online or by phone. This tool will ensure that staff hired with specialist skills will be allocated to tasks requiring those skills. While this addresses the current problem of qualified staff being allocated duties outside their expertise, there is also a concern that staff will be restricted to particular tasks within their existing expertise, leading to a lack of diversity in their work and reduced opportunities for advancement (CPSU 2012).

Conclusion

The centralist approach upon which the Australian Public Service was built and has functioned was designed specifically to deliver government policy and programs in a standardised and consistent way across the country. This approach had its drawbacks in terms of being complex, slow-moving and formulaic in response to policy challenges and problems. With the advent of neo-liberal policies – often described as New Public Management – across the 1980s, the APS devolved into a set of some 97 agencies by June 2011. Each of these agencies had a relatively independent management, including the ability to negotiate its own enterprise agreements with staff and to determine its own work processes. In the abstract, this set of developments can be seen as enhancing efficiency and enabling more targeted and flexible service provision.

In this chapter, we have also described the challenges faced by the APS as it continues to deliver programs and services, and manage workplace relations, as a decentralised set of agencies. Many of these challenges have been fuelled by the continuing focus on cutting costs and doing more with less. Rather than focus on describing and analysing the changed set of workplace relations arrangements in the APS, we have paid particular attention to two key, related issues: shortages of appropriately skilled staff, and workforce planning. We saw how years of restrictions on recruitment, and periodic downsizing and hiring practices concentrating on short-term or fixed-task positions, have created an ageing workforce. We have seen also how work intensification arising from cost-cutting has led to reduced job satisfaction at all levels, and a loss of talent and exacerbation of the demographically derived actual and potential skill shortages. Such developments lead us to question whether short-term efficiencies have been won at the expense of longer-term efficiency and effectiveness.

As we have explained above, historically the APS was much more cohesive, and it could reasonably be described as a service. In the sphere of workplace relations, the development of agency-based setting of pay and conditions has undermined the concept of a unified service, and has at best inhibited mobility and at worst led to a flow of talent from low-paying to high-paying departments and agencies. The present government's way forward on some of these issues has been through its Service Delivery Reform program, which has seen the integration of four key social service providers into one Department of Human Services. This will impact on the current workforce in terms of how their jobs are designed and on their future careers. Nevertheless, the integration has already created the opportunity for a single enterprise agreement, bringing together the terms and condition of work for the four previous agencies into a coherent and standard package for staff. This has the support of the CPSU, and may make workplace bargaining in the future less of a burden than it has been in the past.

Despite this interesting development, there remains a fundamental concern that there has been a long-standing unanimity by major political parties on the need to generate Budget surpluses and, in turn, the need to increase public service efficiency. As the end of the term of office of the current Labor government draws closer, it seems that future changes to the APS may again focus on cost-cutting at the expense of workforce planning and development.

Discussion questions

15.1   How has the neo-liberal agenda played out in the APS? In what ways did it differ between Liberal-National Coalition and Labor governments?

15.2   Why did the evolution of workforce planning not achieve its desired outcomes?

15.3   What were the workplace relations consequences of the decentralisation of the APS.

15.4   How could workplace relations be managed better in the APS, recognising that governments are likely to continue policies of fiscal restraint?

16

Conclusion: the current state of Australian workplace relations

*Julian Teicher, Peter Holland and
Richard Gough*

▦ Introduction

In this book, we have applied the label 'workplace relations' to our study in order to enable us to focus on those features of the regulation of work and employment that are distinctive, and reflect Australia's history, economy and society. At the same time, we have attempted to place the study in its international context and to emphasise those things in the Australian experience that are shared by other nations. This attempt to draw out what is shared as well as that which is distinctive is at the heart of our emphasis on the impact of globalisation and neo-liberalism (Chapter 1) and the Australian employment model (Chapter 2), which draws out what is distinctive and shared with other developed nations.

The major features of the Australian system of bargaining – the labour market and the interrelated welfare system and economic context – have been considered, both in the thematic chapters and the analytical case study chapters. These features form what can be called the interacting elements of the Australian employment model. They conform to aspects of the liberal or Anglo-American model of capitalism, but also are the result of the unique historical development of the Australian workplace relations, economic and welfare system. Structural changes to the economy and the labour market – such as the shift from manufacturing to knowledge and services, and the growth of female employment – are common to the social democratic and conservative model of capitalism, as well as the liberal one (see Chapter 2 for further discussion of these models). However, the ways in which these changes are played out in these three models show significant differences due to the trajectories of political history, including the interactions between the state, employers and unions. The evolution of these trajectories continues in each of the three models, and is influenced by underlying economic and technological forces.

Clear patterns of economic and technological change, and the integration of economies, are apparent in the post-war era. Until the 1970s, increases in capital productivity and the related rate of profit on fixed capital (total amount of capital invested to give a particular level of profit) led to increased investment (accumulation) and employment. These changes were accompanied by increases in labour productivity. The resultant situation of full employment enabled unions – composed largely of industrial workers – to achieve significant gains in real wages and other benefits, which cumulatively led to upward shifts in the share of wages in national income. In the 1970s, a fall in capital productivity and the rate of profit led to a crisis of investment and growing unemployment among the advanced market economies. This crisis and the accompanying inflation led some business elites, economists and lobby groups to identify union power and the resulting growth in real wages as the cause of 'stagflation' and other economic problems. This was also the period of the emergence of the market-driven, neo-liberal political agenda of privatisation, contracting out, deregulation of markets (particularly finance and labour) and the shrinking of the welfare state.

A key part of the neo-liberal agenda was the increasing of interest rates in the late 1970s, without regard to the consequences for investment or employment, ostensibly to reduce inflation – which was seen by some as a greater evil than unemployment – but also to ensure greater returns on financial investment. Increased interest rates increased the borrowing costs of the state and pushed governments towards budget deficits. When capital productivity and the rate of profit bottomed out in the 1980s and then started to increase, it could have been expected that investment and employment would rise. However, increased dividends to shareholders and higher interest rates meant that the increased profitability benefited financial capital more than it did productive capital and employment. The US case is somewhat different in that as, a reserve currency, it was able to import capital despite having negative national savings.

The relative stagnation of real wages in Australia and the fall in the wage share of national income since the mid-1980s, combined with growing inequality of earnings, is an indication of the impact of the neo-liberal agenda, which bears down on employees and promotes financial capital at the expense of productive investment. The weakened position of unions due to declines in coverage and membership, and increasingly restrictive laws – particularly in the liberal model – exacerbated the situation.

The Australian model of workplace relations

We have given particular attention to the Australian employment model because it places the study of workplace relations integrally within state policy and within the social and economic contexts. In these contexts, we have identified several of the key aspects of this framework for more detailed attention.

Unions and bargaining

While there has been a sustained assault on unions over recent decades, due to the intertwining of government policy at state and federal levels that has aimed to margin-alise union influence in both the workplace and the wider society, unions remain significant participants in Australian society. In part, the continued influence of unions reflects the fact that there is a continuing demand for union voice (see Chapter 7); it is also due to the fact that the election of Labor governments has tended to moderate some elements of the neo-liberal agenda. It is noteworthy that, while union membership density has suffered a sustained and large decline, unions remain one of the largest – if not *the* largest – organised social grouping in the country. Given that union membership has fallen from 43 per cent of the workforce in 1992 to 18 per cent in 2011 (ABS 2011a), the key role of unions in protecting employment conditions and wages, and preventing the growth in low-pay, higher levels of inequality and sub-standard employment conditions, is being undermined by decreases in union membership and coverage – particularly in emerging areas of employment and in services more generally.

The shift away from industry or national bargaining has been pronounced in the neo-liberal model countries like the United Kingdom and United States. In Australia, legislation implemented at the national level by the Howard Liberal-National

Coalition government and its Labor successor (see Chapter 5) has prohibited 'pattern' or industry bargaining (except in special cases), and this weakens the bargaining role of employer associations as well as unions. The bargaining position of unions has been improved somewhat under the *Fair Work Act 2009*, in that the bargaining in good-faith provisions makes it unlawful for employers to refuse to bargain with unions. However, the process provides little assurance of the nature and extent of the gains that can be won, as this ultimately may fall to the exercise of bargaining power. Also, the onerous procedures to be complied with for unions to engage in industrial action have been carried over from the Work Choices legislation. Not only do these place a considerable procedural burden on unions seeking to undertake action, but the range of circumstances in which industrial action may be undertaken is restricted, certainly in historical terms, and the penalties for engaging in unlawful action provide a considerable disincentive against strikes and other forms of action.

Chapter 3 canvasses the reasons for union decline, emphasising the growth of the more poorly organised service sector, the role of governments at the state and federal levels with neo-liberal philosophies in legislating to focus the employment relationship at the individual level, and increasing constraints on the role of third parties like unions. The decline of the trade union membership from 61 per cent in 1961 to 18 per cent currently is dramatic. An important aspect of this decline is the very low levels of membership among employees under 30 years of age; another is the fact that unions still remain largely the preserve of men – 35 per cent compared with 18 per cent among women. However, the Australian Worker Representation and Participation Survey research (see Chapter 7) demonstrates that there is considerable unmet demand for union services, much of it among younger workers; there is also evidence of unions having failed to access many in the pool of potential members.

The industry case studies provide a more nuanced view of what is happening to unions. In the health sector (see Chapter 13), we see that the nursing union (the Australian Nursing Federation) has grown from about 100 000 members to more than 200 000 in the period 1994–2012. The Australian Nursing Federation (ANF) is particularly strong in public hospitals and, as an occupational union, provides access to career advice, training and insurance against negligence claims at work for its members. It has been engaged in an ongoing struggle to get better workloads for nurses and has gained improved nurse-to-patient ratios for its members in Victoria. Most ANF members are female, and this goes against the trend for women to have casual jobs with low levels of both unionisation and pay, as occurs in other service sectors like retail and hospitality.

However, even where unions still have strong coverage, as in the automotive parts industry (see Chapter 14), the impact of globalisation is very significant. The linking of these companies to international supply chains and the competition from cheaper offshore suppliers has significant impacts on work organisation, which are beyond union control. In some cases this leads the companies to close their Australian operations. Unfortunately – and unrealistically – much of the public discourse on workplace relations is premised on the idea that if only there could be still more increases in labour market flexibility (lower labour cost), Australian businesses would become competitive. The illusory nature of that proposition is borne out by the discussion of international regulation in Chapter 4.

The decline in unionisation is significant in two ways that are linked: the idea of union renewal, and participation in issues beyond the workplace. In examining strategies for union renewal, Chapter 3 points to the shortcomings of the centralised arbitral model and also raise questions about the efficacy of the organising model adopted from the United States by the Australian Council of Trade Unions in the late 1990s. Attempts by unions to adopt a model of involving the community in campaigns certainly offer a wider base on which to achieve union aims – for example, the James Hardie Company asbestos campaign and the 'Your Rights at Work' campaign run during the lead-up to the 2007 federal election. However, despite the success of these recent examples cited by the authors, so far these are isolated cases rather than an evidence of a successful strategy by the trade union movement.

In considering the future of unions, the recent revival and expansion of international union mobilisation are important. The strategies of international union organisations obviously allow for coordinated campaigns to resist the efforts of multinational companies to degrade wages and working conditions in particular countries. The attempts by these international organisations, such as Global Union Federations (GUFs), to promote better work and to encourage a new social movement–based approach to unionism have yet to show that they can effectively combat the forces of neo-liberalism. In this regard, the discussion in Chapters 3 and 4 is particularly instructive, and leads us to conclude that the potential of effective mobilisations against international finance remains just that: potential. The real challenge here is to create sufficient organisational structures for effective mobilisation on the one hand, and then the capacity to engage with governments and international organisations to influence policy outcomes in a global setting on the other. For example, in the context of the Euro Crisis of 2012, union voices appear to have been peripheral to the deliberations of the EU nations, while economic protests by the unemployed have continued in many parts of Europe. This is somewhat surprising, given the strong emphasis within the European Trade Union Institute on social justice and workers' rights.

■ Employee voice

Given the fall in union membership and coverage, the ways in which employees can have an effective voice in organisations is important. The research on what employees want (see Chapter 7) indicates that at least 36 per cent would prefer to have a union presence – the representation gap. This does not, however, preclude the possibility of communication between management and employees. Such hybrid communication may be positively received by employees, who may also want the assurance of having a union to support them. The high level of about 50 per cent of employees who have not asked to join a union is also an indication, for various reasons, that the unions have not been able to successfully embrace the organising model. The existence of employees at unionised workplaces who are willing to freeload on their colleagues, when they have moral or other reasons for not being union members, also adds to the problems facing unions. Such attitudes have become more prevalent in a society where individualism is promoted by business and political elites.

Another source of support for employees in organisations without a union voice is the human resources (HR) department. In the literature discussed in Chapter 6, the role of HR staff as supporting staff is considered – although we note that there is continuing ambivalence and uncertainty as to the exact role that HR managers should play in Australian organisations. Indeed, there are roles – such as counselling and mediation of disputes between employees – where HR potentially can play a valuable role as professionals exercising a degree of independence of management. However, HR staff are also servants of the corporation, whose primary responsibility is to align employees to the values of the organisation and whose career depends on this focus in the employment relationship. Such alignment is also premised on the view that there is a unity of purpose between employers and employees, and disputes arise largely from third-party intervention.

Current employer HR strategies have also involved much greater monitoring and surveillance of employees. As we saw in Chapter 9, while monitoring of employee performance goes at least as far back as the origins of scientific management, information technologies allow for detailed control over employees' performance, and readily available and cheap laboratory tests allow for testing of employees for a wide range of drugs. The growth of call centres, which often have few or no union members, and where employees' online performance can be continuously monitored, together with the use of GPS systems that make employees' locations always available, are prime examples of utilising information technology. The use of cameras for surveillance has become less popular, as the surreptitious use of such technology for monitoring monitor employees is generally precluded by privacy laws. Depending upon the industry and strength of unions, such practices have been contested, but they clearly show the extent to which employers will go to control their employees to increase productivity if there is no resistance. At the same time, it is evident that the law around monitoring and surveillance in the workplace is not finally settled, and that HR has a role to play in ensuring that employer regulation of the use of internet technologies during working time (however widely defined) neither offends community standards nor impinges on the high-performance culture that many employers expect.

■ Dispute settlement

The issue of settling disputes about pay and conditions in organisations has rested largely with the Fair Work Commission's predecessors. The traditional barometer of disputes has been the number of strikes, but over the past 20 years strikes have declined to very low levels. The decline in unions in workplaces has led to a vacuum in terms of organising strike action and progressing disputes to industrial tribunals. As explained in Chapter 8, the role of settling disputes outside the organisation has been replaced to some extent by the individualisation of conflict, and in some cases by resorting to determinations by industrial and anti-discrimination tribunals. These developments have occurred in the context of the creation of bodies such as the Australian Human Rights and Equal, Opportunity Commission (HREOC) and its successor, the Australian Human Rights Commission (AHRC) to hear complaints from employees. Such bodies have seen a major increase in the number of cases brought before them in recent years, as have unfair-dismissal claims before industrial tribunals.

The reintroduction of unfair dismissal rights for employees in enterprises of fewer than 100 employees in the *Fair Work Act* has also led to a greater number of such cases being heard by the Fair Work Commission. There is also a requirement in the *Fair Work Act* that parties will have a disputes procedure, and may refer their disputes to the Fair Work Commission if they are not resolved locally.

■ *Workplace health and safety*

The weakened role of unions and their capacity to represent employees – particularly in the service sector – has been accompanied by what is described in Chapter 11 as the demise in worker involvement in workplace health and safety. Research in this area has demonstrated repeatedly that the involvement of unionised workers is critical to effective health and safety in workplaces. Appropriately trained employee representatives in a unionised workplace are much less likely to be pressured by management when it comes to raising and resolving issues about unsafe work practices. They are also more likely to be able to identify risks than managers, and to frame a culture of workplace health and safety that prevents injuries. An unfortunate consequence of union decline is that in more and more workplaces there is a lack of union voice – or indeed any voice capable of effectively advocating for workplace health and safety.

The major shifts in the structure of industry and the labour market, including the growth in service work and female employment, accompanied by the increase in precarious work and union decline, have provided a basis for a growth in profit share in Australia. As indicated above, the high interest rates and dividend growth that accompanied the adoption of neo-liberal policies have led sections of business to urge further labour market deregulation and undermining of employees' wages and conditions.

■ *Precarious employment*

A key aspect of these neo-liberal strategies is the promotion of various forms of precarious employment. Employers have used the rubric of the need for a 'flexible' workforce as part of this campaign. Precarious employment is a major break from the male wage-earner model of standard employment that developed in Australia in the context of the arbitral model that we referred to in Chapter 1 as the Federation Settlement, and that remained largely intact until the 1980s.

Precarious employment takes several forms. First, by 2010 about two million employees (over 24 per cent) were casual, and 75 per cent of these were part-time.

These employees cannot access sick leave or holiday pay, can be dismissed without notice and are not guaranteed fixed hours of work. Some aspects of the National Employment Standards (NES) under the *Fair Work Act* – such as maximum weekly hours, two days' unpaid carer's leave and two days' unpaid compassionate leave – apply to casuals. A second form of precarious employment is faced by temporary agency employees – about 3–4 per cent of workers. Such work is often low-skilled and hazardous. A third form of precarious employment is dependent contracting; such workers make up about 9 per cent of the workforce. They are contractors in name only, and do not receive the wages and conditions to which they otherwise would be entitled.

Chapter 2 draws our attention to the striking growth in part-time work in Australia. In 1973, 12 per cent of all workers were part-time, but this reached 17 per cent by 1983 and is currently about 25 per cent. About 45 per cent of women and 16 per cent of men are part-time workers. About 70 per cent of casual employees work part-time, and hence are exposed to precarious employment. Although married women and students may often prefer part-time work, about 9 per cent of part-time workers would prefer to work full-time.

■ *Wage dispersion and inequality*

Accompanying the growth in precarious employment has been a growth in wage dispersion, due to the low wages earned by part-time and casual employees and the exceptional growth in the top 10 per cent of employees – particularly the top 1 per cent. Further, the main change has been the ratio of the top decile of wage earners to the bottom decile, which has shifted from 2.91 in 1995 to 3.34 in 2008. The growth in the percentage of low-paid employees (less than two-thirds of the median full-time income) in Australia has been constrained by the minimum wage set by the Fair Work Commission and its predecessors. The minimum wage was as high as 62 per cent of the median wage in 1996/97, but had slipped to 54 per cent by 2010.

In 2009, the proportion of low-paid employees was 14.4 per cent, which is considerably lower than the level of low-paid employees in the United States and United Kingdom, in itself a reflection of the way in which the implementation of a neo-liberal agenda has continually been moderated by political compromises – in this case, legislated minimum standards. Despite this, it is important to note that the low-paid are a large group in Australia, and up to one-third of these people remain trapped at this level for long periods of time (see Chapter 2).

■ *Female employment*

Esping-Andersen's (2009) concept of the incomplete female revolution (see Chapter 2) is less developed in Australia compared with Scandinavian social demo-cratic countries. Female employment in Australia has grown from 45.7 per cent in 1994/95 to 57.2% in 2005/06. Significantly, the proportion of women in work who have children increased from 43 per cent in 1981 to 6 per cent in 2009. However, the dominant form of couple family remains the one-and-a-half job family in Australia, and the family where two full-time partners are working is about 25 per cent, compared with 66 per cent in Denmark.

One result of couple families with both members working full-time is that this adds to general social inequality. There are two reasons for this: first, the tendency of well-educated and employable women to marry partners with similar levels of education and employability, and for women with poor skills and employment prospects to marry partners with similar characteristics; and second, the likelihood that partners with poor skills and employability will work fewer hours than those with high skills and employability.

An important support for the ability of mothers to work full-time is the cost of child care, which in 2004 represented 22 per cent of the average full-time wage in Australia, compared with 5 per cent in Sweden. Also, until 2011 Australia did not have a national paid parental leave scheme, although about one-third of women had access to some form of paid parental leave from their employer. The new scheme, fully supported by the Australian government, provides eligible working parents with 18 weeks of Parental Leave Pay at the National Minimum Wage.

The high proportion of women employed as casuals in industries like retail and hospitality, which have low levels of unionisation and have experienced lower than average wage rises over the past 20 years, puts such women in a disadvantaged position in the labour market. In one area of social services, the recognition of gender discrimination on wages by Fair Work Australia led to significant wage rises in 2011.

Conclusion

The various features of the Australian workplace employment model outlined above show that Australia is aligned on many dimensions with the neo-liberal (Anglo-American) model of capitalism. Although Australia diverges in some ways from the United States and United Kingdom, due to a different history of regulation of its labour market with greater protections for employees' wages and conditions, there has been a shift to a much higher level of precarious employment and a significantly higher level of earnings inequality. This has been accompanied by a collapse over the past two decades of union coverage and an attempt by many employers to replace collective values by a unitary commitment to the values of the organisation. These changes have occurred in the context of the shift of employment to the service sector and the growth in female employment.

At a political level, labour market regulation has been contested in a series of see-sawing changes, with the federal Labor Party undoing some of the neo-liberal changes embodied in Work Choices, through its *Fair Work Act*. However, both sides of politics have largely accepted the broader implementation of market-based policies of neo-liberalism. The reason for this is the dominance of neo-liberal discourse since the 1980s in public debate, and the rising significance of financial capital, which helped to bring on the Global Financial Crisis.

Glossary

Adverse action. Actions taken by employers against employees, prospective employees and independent contractors that are prohibited because they interfere with a 'workplace right' or with lawful industrial activities – for example, dismissal of a female employee on the grounds of pregnancy or a worker because of union membership.

Alternative dispute resolution (ADR). Refers to the alternative processes to judicial determination, in which an impartial person assists those in a dispute to resolve the issues between them. In the workplace context, it refers primarily to mediation, conciliation and arbitration.

Bargaining in good faith. This term does not have a universal definition, but varies with the legislation applying in a particular jurisdiction. In the case of the *Fair Work Act 2009*, it refers to bargaining with an intention to reach an outcome, holding meetings with the other party within a reasonable timeframe and not withholding relevant information. However, it is not comprehensively defined and the interpretation is being developed through successive tribunal decisions.

Better off overall test (BOOT). The yardstick for determining this is whether the employee is better off overall having regard to the relevant modern award. The standard has been raised from the previous 'no-disadvantage' test so that employees must be better off than under the applicable award.

Capability-building. The concept of capability comes from the resource-based view of an organisation, which considers employees as one element in the bundle of practices and assets belonging to an organisation and contributing to its sustained competitive advantage. The Moran Report (Advisory Group on Reform of Australian Government Administration 2010: 24) describes workforce capability as 'the skills, knowledge and abilities that employees of a high performing public service must possess'.

Casemix funding. Based on the average times taken to treat patients with particular types of illness, from admission to discharge; calculated over a group of hospitals.

Community unionism. A coalition of union(s) and non-union groups, with both focused on advancing a specific common goal that is not narrowly industrial but shared – for example, ending cruelty to animals associated with live sheep exports.

Defamilarisation. The process of outsourcing the role of the family through welfare provision, such as making child care available to working parents.

Dependent contractors. Typically, they are reliant on a single employer for work and they exercise little discretion in the manner of its performance. In this way, these workers resemble employees, but dependent contractors are not entitled to employment-based protections such as a minimum wage and overtime payments.

Disadvantaged workers. This group is identified as being exposed to a number of risks, including long-term unemployment, a prolongation of short-hours working, greater work intensification and job insecurity due to instability in the markets and survival strategies by companies, and increased risk of discrimination at the point of recruitment. This term is closely related to precarious employment, because disadvantaged groups such as women, migrants and workers with disabilities are more likely to be employed in precarious jobs.

Dispute-resolution procedure. A dispute resolution procedure is required by the *Fair Work Act* in all Enterprise Bargaining Agreements (EBAs). Such a procedure sets out the steps to be taken to resolve non-compliance with an EBA by a party to the agreement or a dispute about the interpretation of an agreement. The steps in a procedure should escalate from the formal to the informal, and the number of steps and their requirements will vary with the needs of the parties.

Economic and reward pressures, disorganisation and regulatory failure (PDR) model. This model is used to explain why precarious employment impacts negatively on workplace health and safety. The model groups explanatory factors into three categories.

Efficiency dividend. A flat percentage of operating budget that is removed from the base funding of a government agency in the expectation, with the aim of improving efficiency and effectiveness in that unit.

Effort/reward imbalance model. Emphasises the imbalance between efforts expended by employees and the rewards offered in return by employers, including non-tangible recognition. Additional variables of low social support, including support from co-workers and supervisors, and the level of job security, have also been associated with this mode.

Employee resilience. The notion that a series of individualised interventions – typically forms of training – can enable employees to respond positively to, or at least deal with, otherwise difficult situations with equanimity. Such an approach is often presented as an alternative to organisation-level interventions to change the working environment. In the occupational health and safety (OHS) context, this approach shifts the focus from the organisational context to the individual worker.

Employment strain model. This model identifies seven components of employment strain that are common to precarious employees and contribute to poorer health.

Fitness for duty. Historically, this meant little more than pre-employment screening of employees to determine their capacity to meet the requirements of the job. More recently, in the occupational health and safety context, it has been redefined in terms of testing regimes designed to detect impaired capacity to perform the duties of a position.

Functional flexibility. This refers to employees being multi-skilled and, as a result, able to take on a wider range of responsibilities in their jobs. Such multi-skilling can be either horizontal – taking on a range of tasks at a similar level – or vertical – assuming higher-level tasks.

Global value chains. Global value chains refer to suppliers producing parts that are finally assembled into a product by the organisation that designed the product. For example, the Apple iPhone is made of parts produced in a range of countries other than the United States. Each supplier adds value to the product in accordance with the significance of the part it produces.

Greenfields agreement. Broadly means an agreement between an employer and a union or unions in relation to a workplace or enterprise that has yet to commence operations. The term is also defined in the *Fair Work Act 2009*.

Grievance. In the Australian context, this term is defined more broadly than it is in the US system of collective bargaining, which provides a specific meaning. Typically, a grievance will arise from an interpersonal dispute over issues in the workplace. The subject-matter may include personal treatment by colleagues and supervisors, the operation of rules and procedures or the application of payment systems. A grievance may also be collective, and may relate to the operation of an enterprise agreement.

Host employees (employers). Where a temporary or agency worker is placed with an organisation to perform work, the receiving organisation is referred to as the host employer and the employees of that organisation as host employees.

Incomplete female revolution. Refers to the changing roles of women in the family and their level of participation in education and employment. Completeness would exist where families have both partners in full-time employment, with female earnings on average providing approximately 50 per cent of household income, and where there is equal sharing of child-care and housekeeping duties between partners, with social support available.

Individual flexibility arrangement (IFA). Made pursuant to the terms of an award or enterprise agreement. The matters that can be varied by agreement are limited to five:

overtime rates, penalty rates, allowances, leave loading and arrangements for when work is to be performed. It is mandatory that the employee must be better off overall under the individual arrangement than he or she would be under the award.

Job demands/job control. Of the explanations for occupational stress, Karasek's (1979) model is the most widely accepted and tested. His model identifies a significant interactive relationship between levels of job demands, job control and mental strain.

Just in time (JIT). Delivery of components to the production line is a key element of lean production, because it implies a shift to zero buffer stocks. It also implies that component manufacturers can be relied on to provide consistent quality at a given price.

Lean production. A systemic approach to the process of manufacturing originally developed by the Toyota Motor Corporation. It involves eliminating waste in production processes and improving product quality with supervisor and employee involvement. It also extends to obtaining similar results in the supply chain for components.

Mediation. Most simply defined as assisted negotiation. In these cases, the third party – the mediator – is expected to remain neutral and, in essence, to ensure that each party is able to put their views fully and in a way that will enable the other party to understand those views and expectations.

Modern awards. These provide a safety net of employment conditions and wages for employees in particular industries, and they operate in conjunction with the National Employment Standards (NES). These modern awards came about through a process, undertaken by the Fair Work Commission, of consolidation and modernisation of the large number of existing awards, which were created by the national industrial tribunal in its various guises.

National Employment Standards (NES). These standards cover the ten employment conditions: maximum weekly hours of work; requests for flexible working; parental leave and related entitlements; annual leave; personal/carer's leave; compassionate leave; community service leave; long service leave; public holidays; and notice of termination and redundancy. For further details, see http://www.fairwork.gov.au/employment/national-employment-standards/pages/what-are-the-10-nes-entitlements.aspx (accessed 20 December 2012).

Neo-liberalism. A set of ideas advocating market-based processes to decide what gets produced and who acquires it. Neo-liberalism requires that the state vacate all non-core functions and focus on facilitating market-oriented functioning of the economy.

New Public Management (NPM). A term used from the 1980s to describe the adoption of private sector management practices and techniques by governments, but sometimes criticised for lacking specificity.

No-disadvantage test. Introduced in the *Industrial Relations Reform Act 1993* to ensure that the process of negotiating individual and collective agreements was not used to undercut employees' overall pay and conditions. This test was administered by the national tribunal as part of the process of deciding whether to approve agreements. In essence, the test required that the majority of the covered employees would not be worse off, having regard to the relevant award that applied or would have applied to them.

Numerical flexibility. Numerical flexibility refers to the ability of an employer to reduce or expand the number of full-time employees it has as the need arises.

Occupational health and safety (OHS) management system. In essence, a formalised management system to improve occupational health and safety, which consists of a complex set of interrelated program elements. One of the major differentiators of OHS management systems is the underlying management structures and strategies.

Offshoring. The process whereby employers move part or all of their operations to another country, whether by outsourcing or by operating a related company overseas. Typically, offshoring is undertaken to lower costs of labour in the domestic market.

Organisational justice model. Posits that a lack of procedural and interactional justice within organisations contributes to occupational stress.

Organising unionism. An approach adopted by unions to increase membership through the development of workplace delegates, who focus on issues specific to that workplace in order to advance the workers' interests. Such an approach encourages employees to join the union because of its relevance to their needs.

Partnership unionism. An approach where management and unions work together, focusing on common aims. This approach is often adopted as part of the efforts of a company that is struggling to survive financially.

Pattern bargaining. Broadly involves unions making similar or identical claims on a group of employers. In the context of the *Fair Work Act 2009* (s. 412), it is defined as a course of conduct where a bargaining representative for two or more proposed enterprise agreements engages in a 'course of conduct [that] involves seeking common terms to be included in two or more of the agreements relating to two or more employers'.

Precarious employment. This form of employment is characterised by increased job insecurity, more variability in incomes and a reduced capacity to voice workplace concerns. In Australia, the growth in labour flexibility and precarious employment is best demonstrated through the rise of casual employment and the associated risks – for example, unpredictable work hours, lack of access to opportunities for training and lower incidence of unionisation.

Presenteeism. Faced with the uncertainty and pressures associated with employment in organisations undergoing cost-cutting, employees may feel the need to attend work when they are unwell or injured.

Psycho-social work environment. Alongside job insecurity exist a range of other employment characteristics, which together make up the psycho-social work environment. Known as psycho-social risks, these hazards involve aspects of the design and management of work, and its social and organisational contexts – for example, psychological support, organisational culture, person–job fit, workload and protection of physical safety.

Reciprocal alliances. These involve unions joining with community organisations to achieve outcomes that are beneficial to both the unions and community groups. For example, unions wishing to protect members' jobs could join with a community group wishing to retain a government service that is scheduled to be cut.

Registration. Registration gives unions and employer associations the right to represent their members before the Fair Work Commission. Registration is regulated by the *Fair Work (Registered Organisations) Act 2009*. The Act aims to improve workplace relations by encouraging the existence of union and employer associations, which effectively represent the interests of their members and also are accountable to them.

Representation gap. This refers to the proportion of the workforce in non-union workplaces, who would join a union if they were given the opportunity, but who are unable to do so.

Reverse causation theory. Argues that union membership has a negative impact on the workplace due to a variety of issues, including that employees with lower job satisfaction are more likely to join a union to improve their terms and conditions. A second and related point is that unionised workers are more likely to be dissatisfied, because unions raise awareness of management inadequacies, resulting in more negative evaluations of the workplace, which can adversely affect job satisfaction.

Secondary boycott. This refers to pressure applied to an organisation that is not involved in an industrial dispute to influence the outcome of a dispute in a related organisation – for example, taking industrial action against an organisation in order to stop it supplying parts to another organisation where a dispute already exists. This increases the pressure on the organisation affected by such a boycott of supplies to give in to union demands.

Servicing unionism. An archetypal model of union operation in which the union is focused on the delivery of industrial services to its members through methods other than direct rank and file pressure on employers. In contrast to the organising model, the focus is external to the workplace in the Australian context, and tends to particularly linked to industrial tribunals.

Social and cultural capital. Mostly used in sociology, this refers to the idea that individuals derive value from social networks and from education.

Social movement unionism. This is a form of unionism that concerns itself with more than organising workers around workplace issues such as pay and conditions. It engages in wider political struggles for human rights, social justice and democracy, and it is not always clear whether the political objectives are of greater salience than the industrial issues. Social movement unionism grew out of political struggles in developing countries.

Soft law mechanisms. Also referred to as quasi-legal instruments, these include codes of conduct and similar non-government organisation standards that are not legally binding on nation-states or on international economic actors.

Telework. The use of computer and communication technologies to enable employees to perform their work away from a central employment location.

Temporary agency work. This is also known as labour hire. Such workers are hired by an agency and placed with a host employer while continuing to be employed and paid by the agency. Although agency workers make up only a small proportion of the Australian workforce, as in other developed economies they are disproportionately employed in low-skilled and often hazardous occupations and industries, and are often paid wages that are lower than those received by their co-workers, who are direct employees.

Trade union. A collective organisation of employees in the workplace, which traditionally focuses on improving wages and conditions at specific workplaces. In Australia, much union activity has occurred through the role of unions in representing and advocating members' interests in industrial tribunals.

Trade union density. This is a measure of the number of trade union members expressed as a percentage of the total working population.

Unfair dismissal. This occurs when a dismissal is harsh, unjust or unreasonable, and where the dismissal is not a genuine redundancy (an employer no longer requires the work of the employee to be done and has consulted with the worker before redundancy).

Union reach. This is defined as the presence of a union that an employee can join in the workplace.

Union substitution thesis. The proposition that HR managers can provide voice channels that provide an effective substitute for union membership.

Unlawful dismissal. Expresses the notion that dismissal may be unlawful in specified circumstances. Characteristics that may give rise to an unlawful dismissal include race, colour, age, gender, sexual preference, physical or mental disability, marital status, trade union membership, union activity, political beliefs, being pregnant, or having family or carer responsibilities.

Work intensification. The requirement to complete more work in a given time.

Workplace (industrial) relations climate. The state and quality of workplace relations between employers, employees and unions in an organisation.

References

Books, reports and articles

Abbott, B 2007, 'Small firms and trades unions in services in the 1990s', *Industrial Relations Journal*, vol. 24, no. 4, pp. 308–17.

Abbott, K 2007, 'Employment relations: integrating industrial relations and human resource management', *Problems and Perspectives in Management*, vol. 5, no. 1, pp. 61–71.

ACIL Tasman and Colmar Brunton Social Research 2008, *Accommodation, cafés and restaurants industry profile*, Canberra: Fair Pay Commission.

Ackers, P & Payne, J 1998, 'British trade unions and social partnership: rhetoric, reality and strategy', *International Journal of Human Resource Management*, vol. 9, no. 3, pp. 529–50.

Adelaide Now (2009), 'Holden workers to receive training', *Adelaide Advertiser*, 3 April, viewed 7 November 2011, <http://www.adelaidenow.com.au/news/holden-workers-to-receive-training/story-e6freo8c-1225698166610>.

Advisory Group on Reform of Australian Government Administration [Moran Report] 2010, *Ahead of the game: blueprint for the reform of Australian government administration*, Australian Government, Canberra.

Aiken, L, Clarke, S, Sloane, D, Sochalski, J & Silber, J 2002, 'Hospital nurse staffing and patient mortality, nurse burnout and job dissatisfaction', *Journal of the American Medical Association*, no. 16, pp. 187–93.

Alexander, R & Lewer, J 1998, *Understanding Australian industrial relations*, Harcourt Brace, Sydney.

Allsop, S & Pidd, K 2001, 'The nature of drug related harm in the workplace', in S Allsop, M Phillips & C Calogero (eds), *Drugs and work: responding to alcohol and other drug problems in Australian workplaces*, IP Communications, Melbourne, pp. 5–19.

Anderson, I, Borritz, M, Bang Christensen, K & Diderichsen, F 2010, 'Changing job-related burnout after intervention – a quasi-experimental study in six human service organizations', *Journal of Occupational and Environmental Medicine*, vol. 52, no. 3, pp. 318–23.

Anonymous Health Network 2008, *Annual Report 2007–2008*, Anonymous Health Network, Melbourne.

Antioch, K & Walsh, M 2000, 'Funding issues for Victorian hospitals: the risk-adjusted vision beyond Casemix Funding', *Australian Health Review*, vol. 23, no. 3, pp. 145–53.

Anxo, D, Bosch, G & Rubery, J 2010, 'Shaping the life course', in D Anxo, G Bosch & J Rubery (eds), *The welfare state and life transitions*, Edward Elgar, Cheltenham, pp. 1–77.

Appelbaum, E et al. 2010, 'Introduction and overview', in J Gautié & J Schmitt (eds), *Low wage work in the wealthy world*, Russell Sage Foundation, New York.

Aronsson, G 1999, 'Contingent workers and health and safety', *Work, Employment and Society*, vol. 13, no. 3, pp. 439–59.

Arrowsmith, J 2006, *Temporary agency work in an enlarged European Union*, Office for Official Publications of the European Communities, Luxembourg.

Arthurs, H 2002, 'Private ordering and workers' rights in the global economy: corporate codes of conduct as a regime of labour market regulation', in J Conaghan, RM Fischl & K Klare (eds), *Labour law in an era of globalization: transformative practices and possibilities*, Oxford University Press, Oxford.

Atkinson, AB 2008, *The changing distribution of earnings in OECD countries*, Oxford University Press, New York.

Auditor-General Victoria 2002, *Nurse workforce planning*, Victorian Government Printer, Melbourne.

——2008, *Managing acute patient flows*, Victorian Government Printer, Melbourne.

Austen, S, Jefferson, T, Preston, A & Seymour, R 2009, *Gender pay differentials in low-paid employment*, Women in Social and Economic Research (WiSER), report commissioned by the Australian Fair Pay Commission, Research Report no. 3/09, Curtin University of Technology, Perth.

Australian Bureau of Statistics (ABS) various years, *Survey of Employee Earnings and Hours*, cat. no. 6306.0, ABS, Canberra.

——1985, *Labour statistics Australia, 1984*, cat. no. 6101.0, ABS, Canberra.

——2003, *Disability, ageing and carers, Australia: summary of findings*, cat. no. 4430.0, ABS, Canberra.

——2006a, *How Australians use their time*, cat. no. 4153.0, ABS, Canberra.

——2006b, *A picture of the nation: the statistician's report on the 2006 Census*, cat. no. 2070.0, ABS, Canberra.

——2007, *Labour force characteristics of Aboriginal and Torres Strait Islander Australians: estimates from the Labour Force Survey*, cat. no. 6287.0, ABS, Canberra.

——2008, *Labour force Australia*, cat. no. 6202.0, ABS, Canberra.

——2009a, *Australian social trends*, cat. no. 4102.0, ABS, Canberra.

——2009b, *Australian system of national accounts, 2007–08*, cat. no. 5204.0, ABS, Canberra.

——2010a, *Employee earnings, benefits and trade union membership, Australia*, cat. no. 6310.0, ABS, Canberra.

——2010b, *Employee earnings and hours, Australia*, cat. no. 6306.0, ABS, Canberra.

——2010c, *Labor force Australia*, cat. no. 6202.0, ABS, Canberra.

——2011a, *Employee earnings, benefits and trade union membership*, cat. no. 6310.0, ABS, Canberra.

——2011b, *Employee earnings and hours, Australia*, cat. no. 6306.0, ABS, Canberra.

——2011c, *Families in Australia 2011: Sticking together in good and tough times*, report for National Families Week 2011, ABS, Canberra.

——2011d, *Industrial disputes, Australia, 2011*, cat. no. 6321.0.55.001, ABS, Canberra, viewed 1 June 2012, <http://www.abs.gov.au/AUSSTATS/abs@.nsf/Lookup/6321.0.55.001 Explanatory%20Notes1Dec%202011?OpenDocument>.

——2011e *Labour force Australia*, cat. no. 6202.0, ABS, Canberra.

——2011f, *Labour force characteristics of Aboriginal and Torres Strait Islander Australians*, estimates from the Labor Force Survey, cat. no. 6287, ABS, Canberra.

——2011g, *Forms of employment, Australia*, cat. no. 6359.0, ABS, Canberra.

——2011h, *Work-related injuries, Australia 2009–10*, cat. no. 6324.0, ABS, Canberra.

——2012a, *Australian national accounts*, cat. no. 5206, ABS, Canberra.

——2012b, *Business indicators, Australia, December 2011*, cat. no. 5676.0, ABS, Canberra.

——2012c, *Employee earnings, benefits and trade union membership*, cat. no. 6310.0, ABS, Canberra.

——2012d, *Industrial Disputes, Australia*, cat. no. 6321.0.55.001, ABS, Canberra, viewed 1 June 2012, <http://www.abs.gov.au/ausstats/abs@.nsf/Latestproducts/6310.0Main%20 Features2August%202011?opendocument&tabname=Summary&prodno=6310.0&issue =August%202011&num=&view=>.

——2012e, *Labour force, Australia*, cat. no. 6202.0, ABS, Canberra.

——2012f, *Labor Force, Australia, Detailed, Quarterly*, cat. no. 6291.0.55.003, ABS, Canberra.

——2012g, *Yearbook, Australia 2012*, cat. no. 1301.0, ABS, Canberra, viewed 1 June 2012, <http://www.abs.gov.au/ausstats/abs@.nsf/Lookup/1301.0Main+Features1722012>.

Australian Centre for Industrial Relations Research and Training (ACIRRT) 1999, *Australia at work: just managing*, Prentice-Hall, Sydney.

——2002, 'Stop telling us to cope', in *NSW nurses explain why they are leaving the profession*, University of Sydney, Sydney.

Australian Centre for Research in Employment and Work (ACREW) 2007, *Labour hire research report: best practice models for managing joint responsibilities in the labour hire sector*, ACREW, Monash University, Melbourne.

Australian Council of Social Services (ACOSS) 2011, *Submission to the Independent Inquiry into Insecure Work in Australia*, Sydney.

Australian Council of Trade Unions (ACTU) 2008, Submission to the Review of Export Policies and Programmes, 19 May.

——2009, *Resolution global financial crisis*, ACTU Congress, viewed 1 June 2012, <http://www. actu.asn.au/Images/Dynamic/attachments/6556/CongressResolution2009_GFC.pdf>.

——2011, *Voices from working Australia: findings from the ACTU Working Australia Census 2011*, ACTU, Melbourne.

——2012, *ACTU submission to Fair Work Review Panel*, viewed 19 December 2012, <http:// www.deewr.gov.au/WorkplaceRelations/Policies/FairWorkActReview/Documents/ AustralianCouncilofTradeUnions.pdf>.

Australian Government 2008a, *Review of Australia's automotive industry: discussion paper*, Department of Innovation, Industry, Science and Research, Canberra.

——2008b, Review of Australia's automotive industry: final report [*Bracks review*], Department of Innovation, Industry, Science and Research, Canberra.

Australian Hotels Association (AHA) 2012, *Submission in relation to annual wage review 2011–12*, Australian Hotels Association, Canberra.

Australian Human Resources Institute (AHRI) 2007, 'Extreme makeover: does HR need to improve its image?', *HR Pulse Report*, November.

Australian Human Rights Commission (AHRC) 2009, *Current gender equality laws and institutional arrangements in Australia*, AHRC Resource Paper No. 3, October, AHRC, Canberra.

——2010, *Australian Human Rights Commission annual report 2009–2010*, AHRC, Canberra, viewed 20 September 2012, <http://www.hreoc.gov.au/pdf/about/publications/annual_ reports/2009_2010/AHRC2009_2010_complete.pdf>.

——2011, *Australian Human Rights Commission annual report 2010–2011*, AHRC, Canberra, viewed 20 September 2012, <http://www.hreoc.gov.au/pdf/about/publications/annual_ reports/2010_2011/AHRC_AnnualReport10–11_Final.pdf>.

Australian Industrial Relations Commission (AIRC) 1991, *National Wage Case*, October, Print K0300, AIRC, Canberra.

——2006, *Annual report of the President of the Australian Industrial Relations Commission 2005–2006*, AGPS, Canberra.

——2007, *Annual report of the President of the Australian Industrial Relations Commission 2006–2007*, AGPS, Canberra.

——2008, *Annual report of the President of the Australian Industrial Relations Commission 2007–2008*, AGPS, Canberra.

——2009, *Annual report of the President of the Australian Industrial Relations Commission 2008–2009*, AGPS, Canberra.

Australian Industry Group (AIG) 2009, *Fair Work Act, bargaining provisions and the first 100 days*, AIG, Sydney.

Australian Institute of Health and Welfare (AIHW) 1997, *Australian Hospital Statistics 1995–96*, Health Services Series, cat. no. HSE 3, AIHW, Canberra.

——1998, *Australian hospital statistics 1996–97*, Health Services Series, cat. no. HSE 5, AIHW, Canberra.

——1999, *Australian hospital statistics 1997–98*, Health Services Series, cat. no. HSE 6, AIHW, Canberra.

——2000, *Australian hospital statistics 1998–99*, Health Services Series, cat. no. HSE 11, AIHW, Canberra.

——2001, *Australian hospital statistics 1999–2000*, Health Services Series, cat. no. HSE 14, AIHW, Canberra.

——2002, *Australian hospital statistics 2000–01*, Health Services Series, cat. no. HSE 20, AIHW, Canberra.

——2003, *Australian hospital statistics 2001–02*, Health Services Series, cat. no. HSE 25, AIHW, Canberra.

——2004, *Australian hospital statistics 2002–03*, Health Services Series, cat. no. HSE 32, AIHW, Canberra.

——2005, *Australian hospital statistics 2003–04*, Health Services Series, cat. no. HSE 37, AIHW, Canberra.

——2006, *Australian hospital statistics 2004–05*, Health Services Series, cat. no. HSE 41, AIHW, Canberra.

——2007, *Australian hospital statistics 2005–06*, Health Services Series, cat. no. HSE 50, AIHW, Canberra.

——2008, *Australian hospital statistics 2006–07*, Health Services Series, cat. no. HSE 55, AIHW, Canberra.

——2009, *Australian hospital Statistics 2007–08*, Health Services Series, cat. no. HSE 71, AIHW, Canberra.

——2010, *Australian hospital statistics 2008–09*, Health services series, cat. no. HSE 84, Canberra.

Australian Labor Party (ALP) 2007, *ALP national platform and constitution 2007*, viewed 20 June 2012, <http://www.alp.org.au/platform/index.php>.

——2009, *Draft National Platform 2009*, viewed 20 June 2012, <http://www.alp.org.au/platform/index.php>.

——2011, 46th National Conference National Platform, viewed 20 June 2012, <http://www.alp.org.au/australian-labor/our-platform>.

Australian Manufacturing Workers' Union (AMWU) 2010, 'Holden workers hopeful as second shift set to re-commence', 28 June, viewed 9 November 2011, <http://www.amwu.org.au/read-article/news-detail/524/Holden-workers-hopeful-as-second-shift-set-to-re-commence>.

Australian National Audit Office (ANAO) 2002, *Workforce planning in the Department of Immigration and Multicultural and Indigenous Affairs*, Audit Report no. 56, 2001–02, ANAO, Canberra.

——2008, Management of recruitment in the Australian Public Service *2008*, Audit Report no. 31, 2007–08, ANAO, Canberra.

Australian Nursing Federation (ANF) 2011, 'ANF membership hits 200,000', *Media Release*, 15 April, ANF, Canberra.

Australian Public Service Commission (APSC) 2011, *The state of the service report 2010–2011*, APSC, Canberra.

Babson, S (ed.) 1995, *Lean work: empowerment and exploitation in the global auto industry*, Wayne State University Press, Detroit, MI.

Bahls, JE 1998, 'Drugs in the workplace', *HR Magazine*, February, pp. 81–7.

Bailey, J, Price, R, Esders, L & McDonald, P 2010, 'Daggy shirts, daggy slogans? Marketing unions to young people', *Journal of Industrial Relations*, vol. 52, no. 1, pp. 43–60.

Ball, K 2010, 'Workplace surveillance: an overview', *Labor History*, vol. 51, no. 1, pp. 87–106.

Bambra, C, Egan, M, Thomas, S, Pettigrew, M & Whitehead, M 2007, 'The psychosocial and health effects of workplace reorganisation. 2. A systematic review of task restructuring interventions', *Journal of Epidemiology and Community Health*, vol. 61, no. 12, pp. 1028–37.

Banks, G 2009, 'Are we overcoming Indigenous disadvantage?', paper presented at the third lecture in Reconciliation Australia's 'Closing the Gap Conversations' Series, National Library, Canberra.

Bardoel, EA, De Cieri, H & Santos, C 2008, 'A review of work–life research in Australia and New Zealand', *Asia Pacific Journal of Human Resources*, no. 46, pp. 316–33.

Barney, J 1991, 'Firm resources and sustained competitive advantage', *Journal of Management*, vol. 17, no. 1, pp. 99–120.

Barney, J, Ketchen Jr, D & Wright, M 2011, 'The future of resource-based theory: revitalization or decline?' *Journal of Management*, vol. 37, no. 5, pp. 1299–1315.

Barney, JB & Wright, PM 1998, 'On becoming a strategic partner: the role of human resources in gaining competitive advantage', *Human Resource Management*, vol. 37, no. 1, pp. 31–46.

Bartley, T 2005, *Corporate accountability and privatization of labour standards: struggles over codes of conduct in the apparel industry*, viewed 20 August 2012, <http://www.indiana.edu/~tbsoc/privatization2.6.pdf>.

Bartolomei de la Cruz, HG, von Potobsky, G & Swepston, L 1996, *The International Labour Organization, the International Standards System and basic human rights*, Westview Press, Boulder, CO.

Barton, R & Fairbrother, P 2007, 'We're here to make money. We're here to do business: privatisation and questions for trade unions', *Competition & Change*, vol. 11, no. 3, pp. 241–59.

Baumol, W 1967, 'Macroeconomics of unbalanced growth: the anatomy of urban crisis', *American Economic Review*, vol. 57, no. 3, pp. 415–26.

Beer, M, Spector, B, Lawrence, PR, Mills, DQ & Walton, RE 1984, *Managing Human Assets*, The Free Press, New York.

Belanger, J & Edwards, P 2007, 'The conditions promoting compromise in the workplace', *British Journal of Industrial Relations*, vol. 45, no. 4, pp. 713–34.

Bell, S 1997, *Ungoverning the economy: the political economy of Australian economic policy*, Oxford University Press, Melbourne.

Benavides, FG, Benach, J, Muntaner, C, Delclos, GL, Catot, N & Amable, M 2006, 'Associations between temporary employment and occupational injury: what are the mechanisms?' *Occupational and Environmental Medicine*, vol. 63, no. 6, pp. 416–21.

Benson, J 2000, 'Employee voice in union and non-union Australian workplaces', *British Journal of Industrial Relations*, vol. 38, no. 3, pp. 453–59.

Berggren, C 1992, *Alternatives to lean production: work organization in the Swedish auto industry*, ILR Press, Ithaca, NY.

Berry, J, Pidd, K, Roche, A & Harrison, J 2007, 'Prevalence and patterns of alcohol use in the Australian workforce: findings from the National Drug Strategy Household Survey', *Addiction*, vol. 102, no. 9, pp. 1399–1410.

Bertone, S 2008, *From factory fodder to multicultural mediators: a new typology of immigrant work experiences in Australia*, VDM Verlag, Saarbrucken, Germany.

Bertone, S & Griffin, G 1992, *Immigrant workers and trade unions*, Bureau of Immigration Research and AGPS, Canberra.

Bertone, S, Leahy, M & Doughney, J 2004, *Equal opportunity in the Victorian Public Service: working towards equity in cultural diversity*, prepared for the Office of Public Employment, Victoria, Victorian Government Printer, Melbourne, November.

Bertone, S & Leuner, B 2008, *Immigrant women in the service industries: towards a new strategic plan for MCWH 2008 and beyond*, report prepared for Multicultural Centre for Women's Health, Melbourne, January.

Besser, TL 1996, *Team Toyota: transplanting the Toyota culture to the Camry plant in Kentucky*, State University of New York Press, New York.

Bhagwati, J 2004, *In defence of globalisation*, Oxford University Press, New York.

Bibby, A 2007, 'RFID and surveillance in the workplace', *World of Work*, April, 59, p. 16.

Biddle, D & Burgess, J 1999, 'Youth unemployment in Australia and the search for supply side solutions', *Journal of Economic and Social Policy*, vol. 4, no. 1, pp. 83–104.

Bieler, A, Lindberg, I & Pillay, D 2008, *Labor and the challenges of globalization: what prospects for transnational solidarity?* Pluto Press, London.

Biggins, D & Holland, T 1995, 'The training effectiveness of health and safety representatives', in I Eddington (ed.), *Towards health and safety at work: technical papers of the Asia Pacific Conference on Occupational Health and Safety*, Conference Organisers, Brisbane.

Bingham, LB 2003, *Mediation at work: transforming workplace conflict at the United States Postal Service*, IBM Center for the Business of Government, Arlington, VA.

Birrell, B & Hawthorne, L 1997, *Immigrants and the professions in Australia*, Centre for Population and Urban Research, Monash University, Melbourne.

Blackett, A 2000–01, 'Global governance, legal pluralism and the decentered state: a labor law critique of codes of conduct', *Indiana Journal of Global Legal Studies*, no. 8, pp. 401–47.

Blandy, R 1985, 'The Hancock Report: "the last hurrah of the past"', *Journal of Industrial Relations*, vol. 27, no. 4, pp. 452–61.

Block, RN, Roberts, K, Ozeki, C & Roomkin, MJ 2001, 'Models of international labor standards', *Industrial Relations*, vol. 40, no. 2, p. 258.

Blyton, P & Turnbull, P 2004, *The dynamics of employee relations*, 3rd edn, Palgrave Macmillan, Basingstoke.

Bodman, PM 1998, 'Trade union amalgamation and the decline in Australian trade union membership', *Australian Bulletin of Labour*, vol. 24, no. 1, pp. 18–45.

Borland, J 1999, 'Earnings inequality in Australia: changes, causes and consequences', *Economic Record*, vol. 75, no. 229, pp. 177–202.

Bosch, G 2004, 'Towards a new standard employment relationship in Western Europe', *British Journal of Industrial Relations*, vol. 42, no. 4, pp. 617–36.

Bosch, G & Lehndorff, S (eds) 2005, *Working in the service sector: a tale from different worlds*, Routledge, London.

Bosch, G, Mayhew, K & Gautie, J 2010, 'Industrial relations, legal regulation and wage setting', in J Gautie & J Schmitt (eds), *Low wage work in a wealthy world*, Russell Sage Foundation, New York.

Boselie, P, Brewster, C & Paauwe, J 2009, 'In search of balance – managing the dualities of HRM: an overview of the issues', *Personnel Review*, vol. 38, no. 5, pp. 461–71.

Bowie, NE & Duska, RF 1990, *Business ethics*, 2nd edn, Prentice Hall, Englewood Cliffs, NJ.

Boxall, P & Purcell, J 2011, *Strategy and human resource management*, 3rd edn, Palgrave Macmillan, Basingstoke.

Boxall, P, Purcell, J & Wright, P 2007, *The Oxford handbook of human resource management*, Oxford: Oxford University Press.

Bratton, J & Gold, J 1999, *Human resource management: theory and practice*, 2nd edn, Macmillan, Basingstoke.

Bray, M, Waring, P, Macdonald, D & Le Queux, S 2001, 'The "representation gap" in Australia', *Labour & Industry*, vol. 12, no. 2, pp. 1–31.

Brewster, C, Wood, G, Croucher, R & Brookes, M 2007, 'Are works councils and joint consultative committees a threat to trade unions? A comparative analysis', *Economic and Industrial Democracy*, vol. 28, no. 1, pp. 49–77.

Bronfenbrenner, K 2007, *Global unions – challenging transnational capital through cross-border campaigns*, ILR Press, Ithaca, NY.

Broom, DH, D'Souza, RM, Strazdins, L, Butterworth, P, Parslow, R & Rodgers, B 2006, 'The lesser evil: bad jobs or unemployment? A survey of mid-aged Australians', *Social Science & Medicine*, no. 63, pp. 575–86.

Brown, M, Metz, I, Cregan, C & Kulik, C 2009, 'Irreconcilable differences? Strategic human resource management and employee well-being', *Asia Pacific Journal of Human Resources*, vol. 47, no. 3, pp. 270–94.

Brunetto, Y, Farr-Wharton, R & Shacklock, K 2011, 'Using the Harvard HRM model to conceptualise the impact of changes to supervision upon HRM outcomes for different types of Australian public sector employees', *The International Journal of Human Resource Management*, vol. 22, no. 3, pp. 553–73.

Bryan, D 2000, 'National competitiveness and the subordination of labour: an Australian policy study', *Labour and Industry*, vol. 11, no. 2, pp. 1–16.

Bryan, D & Rafferty, M 1999, *The global economy in Australia*, Allen & Unwin, Sydney.

Bryson, A 2004, 'Managerial responsiveness to union and non-union worker voice in Britain', *Industrial Relations*, vol. 43, no. 1, pp. 213–41.

Bryson, A, Cappellari, L & Lucifora, C 2004, 'Does union membership really reduce job satisfaction?' *British Journal of Industrial Relations*, vol. 42, no. 3, pp. 439–59.

Bryson, A, Gomez, R, Kretschmer, T & Willman, P 2007, 'The diffusion of workplace voice and high commitment human resource management practices in Britain 1984–1998', *Industrial and Corporate Change*, vol. 16, no. 3, pp. 394–426.

Bultmann, U, Kant, I, Van den Brandt, PA & Kasl, SV 2002, 'Psychosocial work characteristics as risk factors for the onset of fatigue and psychological distress: prospective results from the Maastricht Cohort Study', *Psychological Medicine*, vol. 32, no. 2, pp. 333–45.

Business Council of Australia (BCA) 1987, 'Towards an enterprise based industrial relations system', *Business Council Bulletin*, no. 32, BCA, Melbourne.

——1989, *Enterprise based bargaining units: a better way of working*, BCA, Melbourne.

Buyens, D & De Vos, A 2001, 'Perceptions of the value of the HR function', *Human Resource Management Journal*, no. 11, pp. 70–89.

Callus, R & Knox, M 1993, *The industrial relations of immigrant employment*, AGPS, Canberra.

Callus, R, Moorehead, A, Cully, M & Buchanan, J 1991, *Industrial relations at work: the Australian workplace industrial relations survey*, Department of Industrial Relations, AGPS, Canberra.

Campbell, I 2007, 'Long working hours in Australia: working-time regulation and employer pressures', *Economic and Labour Relations Review*, vol. 17, no. 2, pp. 37–68.

Campbell, I & Brosnan, P 2005, 'Relative advantages: casual employment and casualisation in Australia and New Zealand', *New Zealand Journal of Employment Relations*, vol. 30, no. 3, pp. 33–46.

Campbell, I, Whitehouse, G & Baxter, J 2009, 'Australia: casual employment, part-time employment and the resilience of the male-breadwinner model', in L Vosko, M MacDonald & I Campbell (eds), *Gender and the contours of precarious employment*, Routledge, London.

Castles, I 1985, *The working class and welfare: reflections on the political development of the welfare state in Australia and New Zealand, 1890–1980*, George Allen & Unwin, Sydney.

Catrice, J & Lehndorff, S 2005, 'Work organization and the importance of labour markets in the European retail trade', in G Bosch & S Lehndorff (eds), *Working in the service sector: a tale from different worlds*, Routledge, London.

Charlesworth, S 1997, 'Enterprise bargaining and women workers: the seven perils of flexibility', *Labour & Industry*, vol. 8, no. 2, pp. 101–15.

Charlwood, A & Terry, M 2007, '21st-century models of employee representation: structures, processes and outcomes', *Industrial Relations Journal*, vol. 38, no. 4, pp. 320–37.

Chartered Institute of Personnel and Development (CIPD) 2003, *Where we are, where we're heading*, HR survey report, CIPD, London.

Chretien, K, Greysen, R & Chretien, J 2009, 'Online posting of unprofessional content by medical students', *Journal of the American Medical Association*, vol. 302, no. 12, pp. 1309–15.

Christopherson, S & Lillie, N 2005, 'Neither global nor standard: corporate strategies in the new era of labor standards', *Environment and Planning A*, vol. 37, no. 11, pp. 1919–38.

Clark, D 1997, *Economic brief*, AFR Books, Melbourne.

Clarke, M, Lewchuck, W, de Wolff, A & King, A 2007, '"This just isn't sustainable": precarious employment, stress and workers' health', *International Journal of Law and Psychiatry*, no. 30, pp. 311–26.

Cleveland, SH 2004, 'Why international labor standards?', in RJ Flanagan & WB Gould IV (eds), *International Labour Standards*, Stanford University Press, Stanford, CA.

Cling, JP, Razafindrakoto, M & Roubaud, F 2010, *The informal economy in Vietnam: study for the ILO*, viewed 20 September 2012, <http://www.tamdaoconf.com/tamdao/wp-content/uploads/downloads/2010/08/DIAL-ILO-Study-Informal-Vietnam-20101.pdf>.

Closing the Gap: Prime Minister's Report 2010, Australian Government, Canberra.

Cockfield, S, Rainnie, A, Buttigieg, D & Jerrard, M 2009, 'Community unionism and union renewal: building linkages between unions and community in Victoria, Australia', *Labor Studies Journal*, vol. 34, no. 4, pp. 461–84.

Coffey, D & Thornley, C 2008, *Lean production: the original myth reconsidered*, in V Pulignano, P Stewart, A Dunford & M Richardson (eds), *Flexibility at work: developments in the international automotive industry*, Palgrave Macmillan, Basingstoke, pp. 83–103.

Colley, L 2001, 'The changing face of public sector employment', *Australian Journal of Public Administration*, vol. 60, no. 1, pp. 9–20.

Collingsworth, T 2002, 'The human rights challenge: developing enforcement mechanisms', *Harvard Human Rights Journal*, no. 15, pp. 183–203.

——2005, 'Using the Alien Tort Claims Act to introduce the rule of law to the global economy', viewed 20 July 2012, <http://www.iradvocates.org/collingsworth220605.pdf>.

Collins, R 1987, 'The strategic contributions of the human resource function', *Human Resource Management Australia*, November, pp. 5–19.

Comcare 2011, 'Mental stress claims on the increase', *Media Release, Australian Government Comcare*, 21 July, AGPS Canberra.

Committee on Freedom of Association ILO 2010, 'Case No 2698: Complaint against the Government of Australia presented by the Communications, Electrical, Electronic, Energy, Information, Postal, Plumbing and Allied Services Union of Australia (CEPU)', in *Reports of the Committee on Freedom of Association, 357th Report of the Committee on Freedom of Association*, June, ILO, Geneva, p. 50.

Commonwealth of Australia 2010, *Australia to 2050: future challenges* [Intergenerational Report], Commonwealth of Australia, Canberra.

——2010–11, *Building Australia's future workforce: trained up and ready for work*, Commonwealth of Australia, Canberra.

Commonwealth Public Service Union (CPSU) 2011, 'Staff overwhelmingly reject Human Services offer', 12 September, viewed 20 August 2012, <http://www.cpsu.org.au/campaigns/news/25363.html>.

——2012, 'Establishing better jobs in DHS', 8 June, viewed 20 August 2012, <http://www.cpsu.org.au/printversion/28647.html>.

Congressional Budget Office 2008, *Technological change and the growth of health care spending*, US Congress, Washington, DC.

Cook, CR & Grase, JC 2001, *Military airframe acquisition costs: the effects of lean manufacturing*, Rand Corporation, Santa Monica, CA.

Cooney, R & Sewell, G 2008, 'From lean production to mass customisation: recent developments in the Australian automotive industry', in V Pulignano, P Stewart, A Dunford & M Richardson (eds), *Flexibility at work: critical developments in the international automobile industry*, Palgrave Macmillan, Basingstoke, pp. 127–50.

Cooper, R & Ellem, B 2008, 'The neoliberal state, trade unions and collective bargaining in Australia', *British Journal of Industrial Relations*, vol. 46, no. 3, pp. 532–54.

Craig, L & Mullan, K 2011, 'How mothers and fathers share childcare: a cross-national time-use comparison', *American Sociological Review*, vol. 76, no. 6, pp. 834–61.

Cranston, M 2000, 'The terminal decline of Australian trade union membership', *IPA Review*, December, pp. 26–7.

Creighton, B & Stewart, A 2010, *Labour law*, 5th edn, Federation Press, Sydney.

Crosby, M 2000, 'Union renewal in Australia – a view from the inside', in G Griffin (ed.), *Trade unions 2000: retrospect and prospect*, Monograph No. 14, National Key Centre in Industrial Relations, Monash University, Melbourne, pp. 127–53.

Crouch, C 2011, *The strange non-death of neoliberalism*, Polity Press, Cambridge.

Cutcher, L 2004, 'The customer as ally: the role of the customer in the Finance Sector Union's campaigning', *Journal of Industrial Relations*, vol. 46, no. 3, pp. 32–6.

Daly, A & Philp, A 1995, *Alcohol consumption in Western Australia, July 1991 to June 1992*, Health Department of Western Australia, Perth.

Danford, A, Durbin, S, Richardson, M, Tailby, S & Stewart, P 2009, 'Everybody's talking at me: the dynamics of information disclosure and consultation in high-skill workplaces in the UK', *Human Resource Management Journal*, vol. 19, no. 4, pp. 337–54.

Daniels, K 2006, *Employee relations in an organisational context*, Chartered Institute of Personnel and Development, London.

Danziger, A & Walters Boots, S 2008, 'Memo on the impact of the United Kingdom's *Flexible Working Act*', Urban Institute, Washington, DC.

Davies, A (ed.) 2011, *Workplace law handbook 2011: employment law and human resources handbook*, Workplace Law Group, Cambridge.

De Vaus, D 2004, *Diversity and change in Australian families: a statistical profile*, Australian Institute of Family Studies, Melbourne.

Dean, T 2010, *Expert Advisory Panel on Occupational Health and Safety: report and recommendations to the Minister of Labour*, Minister of Labour, Toronto.

Delery, JE, Gupta, N, Shaw, JD, Jenkins, G & Ganster, ML 2000, 'Unionization, compensation and voice effects on quits and retention', *Industrial Relations*, vol. 39, no. 4, pp. 625–45.

Department for Business Innovation and Skills 2010, *Impact assessment: extending the right to request flexible working to parents of children under 17*, Department of Business Innovation and Skills, London.

Department of Education, Employment and Workplace Relations (DEEWR), 2009, *Australian Government Employment Bargaining Framework: supporting guidance, September 2009*, Australian Government, Canberra.

——2010, *Wages growth, industrial actions and unfair dismissal: recent trends*, Australian Government, Canberra.

——2011, *Survey of employers' recruitment experiences, combined results for all regions 12 months to June 2011*, Australian Government, Canberra.

Department of Education and Training (Qld) 2006, *Queensland's labor market progress: a 2006 Census of Population and Housing profile*, Government Printer, Brisbane.

Department of Human Services 2011, *Service delivery reform: transforming government service delivery*, Australian Government, Canberra.

Department of Immigration and Citizenship 2008a, 'Fact sheet 15 – population projections', 28 October, National Communications Branch, Canberra.

——2008b, 'Fact sheet 4 – more than 60 years of post-war migration', 17 November, National Communications Branch, Canberra.

Department of Labour 2009, *The effect of the Employment Relations Act on collective bargaining*, Department of Labour, Wellington, NZ.

Department of Prime Minister and Cabinet (DPMC) 2009, *A stronger, fairer Australia*, Commonwealth of Australia, Canberra.

Department of Trade and Industry (DTI) (UK) 2006, *Draft flexible working regulations: summary of responses and government responses to the 2006 consultation*, DTI, London.

DesJardine, JR & McCall, JJ 1990, *Contemporary issues in business ethics*, Wadsworth, Belmont, CA.

Dicken, P 1998, *Global shift: transforming the world economy*, Paul Chapman, London.

Dodge, WS 1996, 'The historical origins of the Alien Tort Claims Statute: a response to the "originalists"', *Hastings International and Comparative Law Review*, no. 19, p. 221.

Doogan, K 2009, *New capitalism: the transformation of work*, Polity Press, Cambridge.

Dowling, PJ & Boxall, PF 1994, 'Shifting the emphasis from natural resources to human resources: the challenge of the new competitive context in Australia and New Zealand', *Zeitschrift für Personalforschung*, no. 8, pp. 302–16.

Drache, D 2000, *The short but significant life of the International Trade Organization: lessons for our time*, Centre for the Study of Globalisation and Regionalisation, University of Warwick, viewed 18 August 2012, <http://wrap.warwick.ac.uk/2063/1/WRAP_Drache_wp6200.pdf>.

Duckett, S 1998, 'Casemix funding for acute hospital inpatient services in Australia', *Medical Journal of Australia*, no. 169, pp. 17–21.

Duffield, C, Roche, M, O'Brien-Pallas, L, Diers, O, Aisbitt, C & Hall, J 2007, *Glueing it together: nurses, their work environment and patient safety – final report*, UTS, Sydney, July.

Duménil, G & Lévy, D 2011, *The crisis of neo-liberalism*, Harvard University Press, Cambridge, MA.

Dundon, T, Wilkinson, A, Marchington, M & Ackers, P 2004, 'The meaning and purpose of employee voice', *International Journal of Human Resource Management*, vol. 15, no. 6, pp. 1149–70.

Egan, M, Bambra, C, Thomas, S, Petticrew, M, Whitehead, M & Thomson, H 2007, 'The psychosocial and health effects of workplace reorganisation. 1. A systematic review of organisational-level interventions that aim to increase employee control', *Journal of Epidemiology and Community Health*, vol. 61, no. 11, pp. 945–54.

Elfring, T 1988, *Service employment in advanced economies: a comparative analysis of its implications for economic growth*, Rijksuniversiteit Groningen, Groningen.

——1989, 'New evidence on the expansion of service employment in advanced economies', *Review of Income and Wealth*, vol. 35, no. 4, pp. 409–40.

Ellem, B & Franks, P 2008, 'Trade union structure and politics in Australia and New Zealand', *Labour History*, vol. 95, no. 1, pp. 43–67.

Elliot, KA 2000, *The ILO and enforcement of core labour standards*, International Economics Policy Briefs, Institute for International Economics, Washington, DC.

'Employer group calls for individual contracts' 2011, *The World Today*, ABC Radio National, 5 September, viewed 20 August 2012, <http://www.abc.net.au/worldtoday/content/2011/s3309844.htm>.

Epstein, G 2005, *Financialization and the world economy*, Edward Elgar, Cheltenham.

Eslake, S 2011, 'Productivity: the lost decade', in H Gerard & J Kearns (eds), *The Australian economy in the 2000s: proceedings of a conference held in Sydney on 15–16 August 2011*, Reserve Bank of Australia, Sydney.

Esping-Andersen, G 1990, *The three worlds of welfare capitalism*, Polity Press, Cambridge.

——1999, *Social foundations of industrial economies*, Oxford University Press, Oxford.

——2009, *The incomplete female revolution*, Polity Press, Cambridge.

Eurofound 2009, *OSH in figures: stress at work – facts and figures*, European Risk Observatory Report, Office for Official Publications of the European Communities, Luxembourg.

——2011, Changes over time – first findings from the fifth European working conditions survey, viewed 20 July 2012, <http://www.eurofound.europa.eu>.

Fair Work Australia 2010, *Annual report*, Commonwealth of Australia, Canberra, viewed 20 July 2012, <http://www.fwc.gov.au/documents/annual_reports/ar2010/FWA_annual_report_2009–10.pdf>.

——2011, *Annual report*, Commonwealth of Australia, Canberra, viewed 20 July 2012, <http://www.fwa.gov.au/documents/annual_reports/ar2011/FWA_annual_report_2010-11.pdf>.

——2012a, Determination re Social, Community, Home Care and Disability Services Industry Award 2010 – MA000100 PR519357 – AM2011/53, January.

——2012b, 'What is Conciliation?', viewed 20 August 2012, <http://www.fwa.gov.au/index.cfm?pagename=dismissalsprocess#conciliation>.

Fair Work Ombudsman 2011, *Sham contracting and the misclassification of workers in the cleaning services, hair and beauty and call centre industries*, Fair Work Ombudsman, Melbourne.

——2012, *Fair Work Ombudsman Mediation Charter*, viewed 25 August 2012, <http://www.fairwork.gov.au/complaints/mediation/pages/default.aspx>.

Fairbrother, P & Hammer, N 2005, 'Global unions: past efforts and future prospects', *Relations Industrielles/Industrial Relations*, vol. 60, no. 3, pp. 405–28.

Fairbrother, P, Paddon, M & Teicher, J 2002, 'Corporatisation and privatisation in Australia', in P Fairbrother, M Paddon & J Teicher (eds), *Privatisation, globalisation and labour: studies from Australia*, Federation Press, Sydney, pp. 1–24.

Fane, G 1988, 'Reforming Australian industrial relations law: a review of the Hancock Report', *Australian Journal of Management*, vol. 13, no. 2, pp. 223–52.

Farndale, E, Paauwe, J, Morris, SS, Stahl, GK, Stiles, P, Trevor, J & Wright, PM 2010, 'Context-bound configurations of corporate HR functions in multinational corporations', *Human Resource Management*, vol. 49, no. 1, pp. 45–66.

Federation of Automotive Products Manufacturers (FAPM) 2008, *Submission to the Automotive Review*, Federation of Automotive Product Manufacturers, Canberra.

Fenwick, C & Howe, J 2009, 'Union security after *Work Choices*', in A Forsyth & A Stewart (eds), *Fair work: the new workplace laws and the Work Choices legacy*, Federation Press, Sydney, pp. 164–85.

Ferrie, JE, Westerlund, H, Virtanen, M, Vahtera, J & Kivimaki, M 2008, 'Flexible labor markets and employee health', *Scandinavian Journal of Work, Environment & Health*, Supplement 6, pp. 98–110.

Fetter, J 2006, 'Work Choices and Australian Workplace Agreements', *Australian Journal of Labour Law*, vol. 19, no. 2, pp. 210–14.

Fetter, J & Mitchell, R 2004, 'The legal complexity of workplace regulation and its impact upon functional flexibility in Australian workplaces', *Australian Journal of Labour Law*, vol 17, no. 3, pp. 276–305.

Fiorito, J 2001, 'Human resource management practices and worker desires for union representation', *Journal of Labor Research*, vol. 22, no. 2, pp. 335–54.

Fisher, C & Dowling, PJ 1999, 'Support for a HR approach in Australia: the perspective of senior HR managers', *Asia Pacific Journal of Human Resources*, vol. 37, no. 1, pp. 1–19.

Fisher, C, Dowling, P & Garnham, J 1999, 'The impact of changes to the human resources function in Australia', *International Journal of Human Resource Management*, vol. 10, no. 3, pp. 501–14.

Forsyth, A 2010, 'The impact of "good faith" obligations on collective bargaining practices and outcomes in Australia, Canada and the USA', Monash University Department of Business

Law & Taxation Research Paper No. 1645714, viewed 20 August 2012, <http://ssrn.com/abstract=1645714>; <http://dx.doi.org/10.2139/ssrn.1645714>.

Forsyth, A, Creighton, B, Gostencnik, V & Sharard, T 2008, *Transition to forward with fairness: Labor's reform agenda*, Thomson, Sydney.

Forsyth, A & Stewart, A (eds) 2009, *Fair work: the new workplace laws and Work Choices*, Federation Press, Sydney.

Fowkes, L 2011, *Rethinking Australia's employment services*, Whitlam Institute, University of Western Sydney, Sydney.

Fox, A 1974, *Beyond contract: work, power and trust relations*, Faber and Faber, London.

Fox, C, Howard, W & Pittard, M 1995, *Industrial relations in Australia: development, law and operations*, Longman, Melbourne.

Fox, S & Stallworth, LE 2008, 'Bullying and mobbing in the workplace and the potential role of mediation and arbitration pursuant to the proposed National Employment Dispute Resolution Act', in SF Befort & P Halter (eds), *Arbitration 2007: workplace justice for a changing environment – proceedings of the sixtieth annual meeting National Academy of Arbitrators*, BNA, Arlington, VA, pp. 161–225.

Francis, H & Keegan, A 2006, 'The changing face of HRM: in search of balance', *Human Resource Management Journal*, vol. 16, no. 3, pp. 231–49.

Francois, M 1991, 'Le travail temporaire en mileu industriel: incidences sur les conditions de travail at la sante des travailleurs', *Le travail humane*, no. 54, pp. 21–41.

Freeman, R 2007, *America works: critical thoughts on the US labor market*, Russell Sage Foundation, New York.

Freeman, R & Medoff, J 1984, *What do unions do?* Basic Books, New York.

Freeman, RB & Rogers, J 1999, *What workers want*, ILR Press, Ithaca, NY.

Frick, K 2011, 'The position of safety representatives in a weakened Swedish OHS system', paper presented to International Symposium on Regulating OHS for Precarious Workers, Deakin University, Melbourne.

Friedman, TL 2005, *The World is Flat: A Brief History of the Twenty-First Century*, Farrar, Strauss and Giroux, New York.

Gaffney, F 2002, 'Reconstituting the collective? Non-union employee representative structures in the United Kingdom and Australia', in PJ Gollan, R Markey & I Ross (eds), *Works councils in Australia: future prospects and possibilities*, Federation Press, Sydney, pp. 149–79.

Gajewska, K 2008, 'The emergence of a European labour protest movement?', *European Journal of Industrial Relations*, vol. 14, no. 1, pp. 104–21.

Gall, G 2009, 'Union organising with "old" and "new" industrial relations actors', in G Gall (ed.), *The future of union organising: building for tomorrow*, Palgrave Macmillan, Basingstoke, pp. 175–86.

Garcia-Serrano, C 2009, 'Job satisfaction, union membership and collective bargaining', *European Journal of Industrial Relations*, vol. 15, no. 1, pp. 91–111.

Garnham, J 2009, 'Why only twits would ignore the potential (and pitfalls) of Twitter', *People Management*, April, p. 23.

Garver, P, Buketov, K, Chong, H & Sosa Martinez, B 2007, 'Global labor organizing in theory and practice', *Labor Studies Journal*, vol. 32, no. 3, pp. 237–56.

Gereffi, G 2002, 'The international competitiveness of Asian economies in the apparel commodity chain', ERD Working Paper Series 5, Asian Development Bank, Manila.

Gereffi, G, Humphrey, J & Sturgeon, T 2005, 'The governance of global supply chains', *Review of International Political Economy*, vol. 12, no. 1, pp. 78–104.

German Socio Economic Panel Survey 2011, DIW, Berlin.

Gibb, E 2005, *International Framework Agreements: Increasing the Effectiveness of Core Labour Standards*, Global Labour Institute, Geneva, viewed 20 August 2012, <http://www.global labour.info/en/2006/12/international_framework_agreem.html>.

Gillard, J 2008, 'Proclamation of *Transition to Forward with Fairness Act*', Ministers' Media Centre, Education, Employment and Workplace Relations Portfolio, 27 March, viewed 12 June 2012, <http://ministers.deewr.gov.au/gillard/proclamation-transition-forward-fairness-act>.

——2010, 'Media Release: Fair Work Week', 4 January.

Gip, MA 1999, 'Drug testing assailed', *Security Management*, vol. 43, no. 12, p. 16.

Goddard, J 2011, 'What has happened to strikes?' *British Journal of Industrial Relations*, vol. 49, no. 2, pp. 282–305.

Golden, I 2008, 'Disparities in flexible work schedules and work-at-home', *Journal of Family and Economic Issues*, vol. 29, no. 1, pp. 86–109.

Goldman, BM, Cropanzano, R, Stein, JH, Shapiro, DL, Thatcher, S & Ko, J 2008, 'The role of ideology in mediated disputes at work: a justice perspective', *International Journal of Conflict Management*, vol. 19, no. 3, pp. 210–33.

Gollan, P 2005, 'Silent voices: representation at the Eurotunnel Call Centre', *Personnel Review*, vol. 34, no. 4, pp. 423–50.

Gollan, P, Markey, R & Ross, I (eds) 2002, *Works councils in Australia: future prospects and possibilities*, Federation Press, Sydney.

Gollan, PJ & Patmore, G 2006, 'Transporting the European social partnership model to Australia', *Journal of Industrial Relations*, vol. 48, no. 2, pp. 217–56.

Gordon, S, Buchanan, J & Bretherton, T 2008, *Safety in numbers: nurse–patient ratios and the future of health care*, Cornell University Press, Ithaca, NY.

Goss, J 2008, *Projection of health care by disease, 2003 to 2033*, Australian Institute of Health and Welfare, Canberra.

Graham, I 2002, 'Global labour agreements: a framework for rights', *The World of Work*, December, p. 2.

Graham, L 1993, 'Inside a Japanese transplant: a critical perspective', *Work and Occupations*, vol. 20, no. 2, pp. 147–73.

Greenwood, MR, Holland, P & Choong K 2006, 'Re-evaluating drug testing: questions of moral and symbolic control', in J Deckop, B Giacalone & CL Jurkiewicz (eds), *Human resource management ethics*, Information Age, Greenwich, CT, pp. 161–80.

Grey, LC, Yeo, MA & Duckett, SJ 2004, 'Trends in the use of hospital beds in Australia: 1993–2002', *Medical Journal of Australia*, no. 181, pp. 478–81.

Griffin, G, Nyland, C & O'Rourke, A 2003, 'Trade unions and the trade–labour rights link: a north–south union divide?' *The International Journal of Comparative Labour Law and Industrial Relations*, vol. 19, no. 4, pp. 469–94.

——2004a, 'Trade promotion authority and core labour standards: implications for Australia', *Australian Journal of Labour Law*, no. 17, pp. 1–81.

——2004b, 'Trade unions, the Australian Labor Party and the trade–labour rights debate', *Australian Journal of Political Science*, vol. 39, no. 1, pp. 89–107.

Griffin, G & Svensen, S 1996, 'The decline of Australian union density – a review', in G Griffin (ed.), *Contemporary research on unions: theory, membership, organisation, and non-standard employment*, NKCIR Monograph no. 8, vol. 2, Monash University, Melbourne, pp. 2226–73.

Group of 20 (G20) 2009, *Global Plan for Recovery and Reform*, Group of 20, London.

Guest, D 1987, 'Human resource management and industrial relations', *Journal of Management Studies*, vol. 24, no. 5, pp. 503–21.

——1995, 'Human resource management, trade unions and industrial relations', in J Storey (ed.), *Human resource management: a critical text*, Routledge, London, pp. 110–41.

——2002, 'Human resource management, corporate performance and employee wellbeing: building the worker into HRM', *The Journal of Industrial Relations*, vol. 44, no. 3, pp. 335–58.

Guest, D & Conway, N 1999, 'Peering into the black hole: the downside of the New Employment Relations in the UK', *British Journal of Industrial Relations*, vol. 37, no. 3, pp. 367–89.

Hagan, KA 2003, *The International Labour Organization: can it deliver the social dimension of globalization?*, Presentation, Meeting Report, Friedrich Ebert Stiftung, Geneva, viewed 20 September 2012, <http://www.fes-globalization.org/geneva/documents/21Nov03_ILOHagenStudie.pdf>.

Hage, G 1998, *White nation: fantasies of white supremacy in a multicultural society*, Pluto Press, Sydney.

Haipter, T & Banyuls, J 2007, *Labour on the defensive? The global reorganisation of the value chain and industrial relations in the European motor industry*, 28th International Working Party on Labour Market Segmentation, Aix en Provence, 5–7 July.

Hall, P & Soskice, D 2001, *Varieties of capitalism: the institutional foundations of competitive advantage*, Oxford University Press, Oxford.

Hammer, TH & Avgar, A 2007, 'The impact of unions on job satisfaction, organizational commitment, and turnover', in JT Bennett & BE Kaufman (eds), *What do unions do?* Transaction, New Brunswick, NJ, pp. 346–72.

Hammond, KH 2005, 'Why we hate HR', *Fast Company*, no. 97, pp. 40–7.

Hampson, I 1996, *Between control and consensus: Australia's enigmatic corporatism*, Working Paper Series No. 105, School of Industrial Relations and Organisational Behaviour, University of New South Wales, Sydney.

Hancock, K 1985, *Committee of review into Australian industrial relations law and systems report*, AGPS, Canberra.

Handy, J & Davy, D 2007, 'Gendered ageism: older women's experience of employment practices', *Asia Pacific Journal of Human Resources*, vol. 45, no. 10, pp. 85–99.

Hardy, T & Howe, J 2009, 'Partners in enforcement? The new balance between government and trade union enforcement of employment standards in Australia', *Australian Journal of Labour Law*, vol. 22, no. 3, pp. 306–36.

Hartnell, CA, Ou, AY & Kinicki, A 2011, 'Organizational culture and organizational effectiveness: a meta-analytic investigation of the competing values framework's theoretical suppositions', *Journal of Applied Psychology*, no. 96, pp. 937–63.

Harvey, D 2005, *A brief history of neo-liberalism*, Oxford University Press, Oxford.

Havana Charter 1948, viewed 20 October 2012, <http://www.worldtradelaw.net/misc/havana.pdf>.

Haworth, N, Hughes, S & Wilkinson, R 2005, 'The international labour standards regime: a case study in global regulation', *Environment and Planning A*, no. 37, pp. 1939–53.

Hawthorne, L 2006, *Labor market outcomes for migrant professionals: Canada and Australia compared*, prepared for Citizenship and Immigration Canada, Human Resources and Social Development Canada, and Statistics Canada, Toronto.

Hayashi, Y & Moffett, S 2007, 'Cautiously, an aging Japan warms to foreign workers', *The Wall Street Journal Online*, 25 May.

Hayes, W & Jerrard, M 2007, 'Traditional and instrumental union and community links: a case study of an ETU campaign', in D Buttigieg, S Cockfield, R Cooney, M Jerrard & A Rainnie (eds), *Trade unions in the community: values, issues, shared interests and alliances*, Heidelberg Press, Melbourne, pp. 215–27.

Haynes, P & Allen, M 2001, 'Partnership as union strategy: a preliminary evaluation', *Employee Relations*, vol. 23, no. 2, pp. 164–87.

Haynes, P, Boxall, P & Macky, K 2005, 'Non-union voice and the effectiveness of joint consultation in New Zealand', *Economic and Industrial Democracy*, vol. 26, no. 2, pp. 229–56.

——2006, 'Union reach, the "representation gap" and the prospects for unionism in New Zealand', *Journal of Industrial Relations*, vol. 48, no. 2, pp. 193–216.

Hearn McKinnon, B 2007, *Behind Work Choices: how one company changed Australia's industrial relations*, Heidelberg Press, Melbourne.

Hegewich, A 2009, *Flexible working policies: a comparative review*, Equality and Human Rights Commission Research Report 16, Institute for Women's Policy Research, Manchester.

Hendry, C & Pettigrew, A 1990, 'Human resource management: an agenda for the 1990s', *International Journal of Human Resource Management*, vol. 1, no. 1, pp. 17–43.

Hepple, B 1997, 'New approaches to international labour law', *Industrial Law Journal*, vol. 26, no. 4, pp. 362–5.

——1998–99, 'A race to the top? International investment guidelines and corporate codes of conduct', *Comparative Labor Law & Policy Journal*, no. 20, p. 353.

Hickey, R, Kuruvilla, S & Lakhani, T 2010, 'No panacea for success: member activism, organising, and union renewal', *British Journal of Industrial Relations*, vol. 48, no. 1, pp. 53–83.

Higgins, HB 1915, 'A new province for law and order: industrial peace through minimum wage and arbitration', *Harvard Law Review*, vol. 29, no. 1, pp. 13–39.

Hintikka, N 2011, 'Accidents at work during temporary agency work in Finland: comparisons between certain major industries and other industries', *Safety Science*, no. 49, pp. 473–83.

Hodge, B & O'Carroll, J 2006, *Borderwork in multicultural Australia*, Allen & Unwin, Sydney.

Hoffmann, J & Hoffmann, R 1997, *Globalization: risks and opportunities for labor policy in Europe*, DWP 97.04.01 (E), ETUI, Brussels.

Holden n.d., 'About Holden', viewed 7 November 2011, <http://www.holden.com.au/corporate/about-holden>.

Holden, L, Scuffhamm, PA, Hilton, MF, Vecchio, NN & Whiteford, HA 2010, 'Work performance decrements are associated with Australian working conditions, particularly the demand to work longer hours', *Journal of Occupational and Environmental Medicine*, no. 52, pp. 281–90.

Holland, P & Pyman, A (2011) 'Trade unions and corporate campaigning in a global economy: The case of James Hardie', *Economic and Industrial Democracy*, vol. 32, no. 2, pp. 307–328.

Holland, P, Pyman, A, Cooper, B & Teicher, J 2009, 'The development of alternate voice mechanisms in Australia: the case of joint consultation', *Economic and Industrial Democracy*, vol. 30, no. 1, pp. 67–92.

——2011, 'Employee voice and job satisfaction in Australia: the centrality of direct voice', *Human Resource Management*, vol. 50, no. 1, pp. 95–111.

Holland, PJ, Pyman, A & Teicher, J 2005, 'Negotiating the contested terrain of drug testing in the Australian workplace', *Journal of Industrial Relations*, vol. 47, no. 3, pp. 326–38.

Holland, PJ & Wickham, M 2001, 'Drug testing in the workplace: the case of the South Blackwater Mine', *The Management Case Study Journal*, vol. 1, no. 2, pp. 1–17.

Hollinsworth, D 2006, *Race and racism in Australia*, Thomson, Melbourne.

Homung, S, Rousseau, DM & Glaser, J 2008, 'Creating flexible work arrangements through idiosyncratic deals', *Journal of Applied Psychology*, vol. 93, no. 3, pp. 655–64.

House of Representatives 2005, Workplace Relations (Work Choices) Bill 2005 Explanatory Memorandum, Parliament of the Commonwealth of Australia, viewed 20 June 2012, <http://www.workplace.gov.au/NR/rdonlyres/D5BBE0D6-A1C9-4342-B97A-9FE1DFB8 B7BA/0/wrawcbill2005em.pdf>.

HR Nicholls Society 2012, 'Welcome to the HR Nicholls Society', viewed 12 June 2012, <http://www.hrnicholls.com.au/index.php>.

HRFocus 2009, 'Twitter is the latest electronic tool with workplace pros and cons', August, pp. 8–9.

Hubbard, L 2007, 'Hard questions facing Australian Labor', in D Buttigieg, S Cockfield, R Cooney, M Jerrard, & A Rainnie (eds), *Trade unions in the community: values, issues, shared interests and alliances*, Heidelberg Press, Melbourne, pp. 11–22.

Hughes, O 2003, *Public management and administration: an introduction*, 3rd edn, Palgrave Macmillan, Basingstoke.

Human Rights and Equal Opportunity Commission (HREOC) 2007, *It's about time: women, men, work and family – final paper*, HREOC, Sydney.

Huzzard, T & Nilsson, T 2004, 'Dancing queen? Partnership, co-determination and strategic unionism in Sweden', in T Huzzard, D Gregory & R Scott (eds), *Strategic unionism and partnership: boxing or dancing?*, Palgrave Macmillan, Basingstoke, pp. 86–106.

Hyman, R 1997, 'The future of employee representation', *British Journal of Industrial Relations*, vol. 35, no. 3, pp. 309–36.

——2004, 'Whose (social) partnership?', in M Stuart & M Martinez Lucio (eds), *Partnership and modernisation in employment relations*, Routledge, London, pp. 251–65.

——2007, 'How can trade unions act strategically?' *Transfer – European Review of Labor and Research*, vol. 13, no. 2, pp. 193–210.

Immervoll, H & Barber, D 2005, *Can parents afford to work? Childcare costs, tax-benefit policies and work incentives*, OECD, Paris.

International Centre for the Settlement of Investment Disputes (ICSID) 2011, ICSID Database of Bilateral Investment Treaties, viewed 20 November 2012, <http://icsid.worldbank.org/ICSID/FrontServlet>.

International Confederation of Free Trade Unions, Asian and Pacific Regional Organisation (ICFTU-APRO) 1997, 'Trade union strategies in a globalising economy', in *International trade, investment and competitiveness*, ICFTU-APRO, Singapore.

International Federation of Building and Woodworkers (IFBWW) 2004, *IFBWW experiences with global company agreements*, IFBWW, Geneva, viewed 20 November 2012, <http://www.ifbww.org/files/global-agreements.pdf>.

International Labour Organization 1919a, Constitution, viewed 20 October 2012, <http://www.ilo.org/public/english/about/iloconst.htm>.

——1919b, 'The Constitution', Part XIII of the Treaty of Versailles, Versailles, viewed 20 October 2012, <http://www.ilo.org/public/english/overview/iloconst.htm>.

——2010, *Report of the CEACR, International Labour Conference*, Report III(1A), 99th Session, ILO, Geneva.

——2011a, 'About the ILO', viewed 20 October 2012, <http://www.ilo.org/global/about-the-ilo/mission-and-objectives/lang--en/index.htm>

——2011b, 'Governing Body', viewed 20 October 2012, <http://www.ilo.org/global/about-the-ilo/how-the-ilo-works/governing-body/lang--en/index.htm>.

——2011c, 'The International Labour Conference', viewed 20 October 2012, <http://www.ilo.org/global/about-the-ilo/how-the-ilo-works/international-labour-conference/lang--en/index.htm>.

International Trade Union Confederation (ITUC) 2009, *Introduction to the Global Financial Crisis unions watch*, viewed 18 November 2012, <http://www.ituc-csi.org/financialcrisis>.

Iverson, RD & Currivan, DB 2003, 'Union participation, job satisfaction and employee turnover: an event-history analysis of the exit-voice hypothesis', *Industrial Relations*, vol. 42, no. 1, pp. 101–5.

Jenkins, R 2001, *Corporate codes of conduct: self-regulation in a global economy*, Technology, Business and Society, Programme Paper Number 2, United Nations Research Institute for Social Development, viewed 19 October 2012, <http://www.unrisd.org/unrisd/website/document.nsf/0/e3b3e78bab9a886f80256b5e00344278/$FILE/jenkins.pdf>.

Jerrard, MA 2007, 'Building alliances to protect jobs: the AMIEU's response to live animal export', in D Buttigieg, S Cockfield, R Cooney, M Jerrard, & A Rainnie (eds), *Trade unions in the community – values, issues, shared interests and alliance*, Heidelberg Press, Melbourne, pp. 185–200.

Jerrard, M, Cockfield, S & Buttigieg, D 2009, 'The "servicing-organising-community continuum": where are Australian unions today?' in G Gall (ed.), *The future of union organising: building for tomorrow*, Palgrave Macmillan, Basingstoke, pp. 97–113.

Jerrard, MA, Cooney, R, Buttigieg, D, Cockfield, S & Rainnie, A 2007, 'Unions in the community: towards community unionism?' in D Buttigieg, S Cockfield, R Cooney, M Jerrard & A Rainnie (eds), *Trade unions in the community: values, issues, shared interests and alliances*, Heidelberg Press, Melbourne, pp. 1–8.

Jerrard, M & Heap, L 2010, 'Trade unions and social justice', in G Strachan, E French & J Burgess (eds), *Managing diversity in Australia: theory and practice*, McGraw-Hill, Sydney, pp. 121–36.

Job, J & Smith, D 2011, *Motivations, attitudes, perceptions and skills: what they said about work health and safety in 2010*, Safe Work Australia, Canberra.

Johnstone, R 2011, 'Dismantling worker categories: the primary duty of care and worker consultation, participation and representation in the Model Work Health and Safety Bill 2009', *Policy and Practice in Health and Safety*.

Johnstone, R, Quinlan, M & Walters, D 2005, 'Statutory occupational health and safety workplace arrangements for the modern labour market', *Journal of Industrial Relations*, vol. 47, no. 1, pp. 93–116.

Kalina, T & Weinkopf, C 2008, 'The increase of low-wage work in Germany: an erosion of internal labour markets?', paper presented to the 28th International Working Party on Labour Market Segmentation, Aix en Provence, 5–7 July.

Kamoche, KN 2001, *Understanding human resource management*, Open University Press, Buckingham, PA.

Karasek, RA 1979, 'Job demands, job decision latitude, and mental strain: implications for job design', *Administrative Science Quarterly*, vol. 25, no. 2, pp. 285–308.

Kearns, D 2008, 'Dumbed down: experiences of disabled people in vocational training and employment in Australia', Submission to the National Mental Health Strategy, Gold Coast, Queensland.

Keegel, TM, Erbas, B, Dharmage, S & LaMontagne, A 2010, *Are precariously employed workers less likely to participate in occupational health and safety?* McCaughey Centre, School of Population Health, University of Melbourne, Melbourne.

Kelly, J 1996a, 'Union militancy and social partnership', in P Ackers, C Smith & P Smith (eds), *The new workplace and trade unionism*, Routledge, London, pp. 41–76.

——1996b, 'Works councils: union advance or marginalisation?', in A McColgan (ed.), *The future of labour law*, Mansell, London, pp. 44–62.

Kelly, P 1992, *The end of certainty: the story of the 1980s*, Allen & Unwin, Sydney.

Kieseker, R & Marchant, T 1999, 'Workplace bullying in Australia: a review of current conceptualisations and existing research', *Australian Journal of Management and Organisational Behaviour*, vol. 2, no. 5, pp. 61–75.

Kiffin-Peterson, S & Cordery, J 2003, 'Trust, individualism and job characteristics as a predictor of employee preference for teamwork', *International Journal of Human Resource Management*, no. 14, pp. 93–116.

Kim, D & Kim, H 2004, 'A comparison of the effectiveness of unions and non-union works councils in Korea: can non-union employee representation substitute for trade unionism?', *International Journal of Human Resource Management*, vol. 15, no. 6, pp. 1069–93.

Kimberley, H 2009, 'Measuring social inclusion in retirement and ageing: the Brotherhood's latest Social Barometer', *Brotherhood Comment*, August, pp. 8–9.

Kirk, R 2009, 'Ambassador Kirk announces new initiatives for trade enforcement', United States Trade Representative, Mon Valley Works – Edgar Thomson Plant, Pittsburgh, PA, 16 July, viewed 20 June 2012, <http://www.ustr.gov/about-us/press-office/speeches/transcripts/2009/ambassador-kirk-announces-new-initiatives-trade-enfo>.

Kivimäki, M, Vahtera, J, Elovainio, M, Virtanen, M & Siegrist, J 2007, 'Effort–reward imbalance, procedural injustice and relational injustice as psychosocial predictors of health: complementary or redundant models?' *Occupational and Environmental Medicine*, vol. 64, no. 10, pp. 659–65.

Kochan, TA 2004, 'Restoring trust in the human resource management profession', *Asia Pacific Journal of Human Resources*, vol. 42, no. 4, pp. 132–46.

——2007, 'Social legitimacy of the HRM profession: a US perspective', in P Boxall & J Purcell (eds), *The Oxford handbook of human resource management*, Oxford University Press, Oxford, pp. 599–619.

König, CJ, Debus, ME, Häusle, S, Lendenmann, N & Kleinman, M 2010, 'Examining occupational self-efficacy, work locus of control and communication as moderators of the job insecurity–job performance relationship', *Economic and Industrial Democracy*, no. 31, pp. 231–47.

Kotz, D 2008, 'Neo-liberalism and financialization', paper presented to conference in honour of Jane D'Arista at the Political Economy Research Institute, 2–3 May, University of Massachusetts, Amherst, MA.

Krafcik, J 1988, 'Triumph of the lean production system', *Sloan Management Review*, vol. 30, no. 1, pp. 41–51.

Kroon, B, van de Voorde, K & van Veldhoven, M 2009, 'Cross-level effects of high performance work practices on burnout', *Personnel Review*, vol. 38, no. 5, pp. 509–25.

Kulik, C & Bainbridge, HTJ 2006, 'HR and the line: the distribution of HR activities in Australian organisations', *The Asia Pacific Journal of Human Resources*, vol. 44, no. 2, pp. 240–56.

Kuruvilla, S & Verma, A 2006, 'International labor standards, soft regulation and national government roles', *Journal of Industrial Relations*, vol. 48, no. 1, pp. 141–58.

LaMontagne, AD & Keegel, TG 2010, 'What organisational/employer level interventions are effective in preventing and treating occupational stress', Institute for Safety, Compensation and Recovery Research, Monash University & McCaughey Centre, VicHealth Centre for the Promotion of Mental Health and Community Wellbeing, University of Melbourne, Melbourne.

LaMontagne, AD, Keegel, T, Vallence, D, Ostry, A & Wolfe, R 2008, 'Job strain: Attributable depression in a sample of working Australia: Assessing the contribution to health inequalities', *BMC Public Health*, no. 8, p. 181.

LaMontagne, AD, Sanderson, K & Cocker, F 2010, *Estimating the economic benefits of eliminating job strain as a risk factor for depression*, Victorian Health Promotion Foundation (VicHealth), Melbourne.

Lane, FS 2003, *The naked employee*, Amacom, New York.

Lansbury, R 2004, 'Work, people and globalisation: toward a new social contract for Australia', *Journal of Industrial Relations*, vol. 46, no. 1, pp. 102–15.

Lansbury, R & Saulwick, J 2006, 'The automotive industry', in P Waring & M Bray (eds), *Evolving employment relations: industry studies from Australia*, McGraw Hill, Sydney, pp. 119–36.

Legge, K 2005, *Human resource management: rhetorics and reality*, Palgrave Macmillan, Basingstoke.

Leigh, A 2009, *Minorities find it harder to get jobs*, media release, Australian National University, Canberra, 17 June.

Leka, S & Cox, T 2010, 'Psychosocial risk management at the workplace level', in S Leka & J Houdmont (eds), *Occupational health psychology*, Wiley-Blackwell, Hovokien, pp. 124–56.

Leka, S, Jain, A, Widerszal-Bazyl, M, Żolnierczyk-Zreda, D & Zwetsloot, G 2011, 'Developing a standard for psychosocial risk management: PAS 1010', *Safety Science*, vol. 49, no. 4, pp. 1047–57.

Leuner, B 2007, *Migration, multiculturalism and language maintenance in Australia: Polish migration to Melbourne in the 1980s*, Peter Lang, Bern.

Lever-Tracy, C & Quinlan, M 1988, *A divided working class?*, Routledge & Kegan Paul, London.

Lewchuk, W, de Wolff, A, King, A & Polanyi, M 2003, 'From job strain to employment strain: health effects of precarious employment', *Just Labour*, no. 3, pp. 23–35.

Lewchuk, W & Robertson, D 1997, 'Working conditions under lean production: a worker-based benchmarking study', *Asia Pacific Business Review*, vol. 2, no. 4, pp. 60–81.

Lewin, D & Mitchell, DJB 1992, 'Systems of employee voice: theoretical and empirical perspectives', *California Management Review*, Spring, pp. 95–111.

Libbenga, J 2006, 'Video surveillance outfit chips workers', *The Register*, February, n.p.

Lippel, K, MacEachen, E, Saunders, R, Werhum, N, Kozny, A, Mansfield, L, Carrasco, C & Pugliese, D 2011, 'Legal protections governing occupational health and safety and workers' compensation of temporary employment agency workers in Canada: reflections on regulatory effectiveness', *Policy and Practice in Health and Safety*, no. 2, pp. 69–90.

Loudoun, R & Walters, D 2009, 'Trade union strategies to support representation on health and safety in Australia and the UK: integration or isolation?' in D Walters & T Nicholls (eds), *Workplace health and safety: international perspectives on worker representation*, Macmillan, Basingstoke, pp. 177–200.

Macfarlane, I 2000, 'Address to Australian business in Europe', London, 26 May, viewed 6 September 2012, <http://www.rba.gov.au/Speeches/2000/sp_gov_260500.html>.

Machin, S & Wood, S 2005, 'Human resource management as a substitute for trade unions in British workplaces', *Industrial and Labor Relations Review*, vol. 58, no. 2, pp. 201–18.

Mackay, M & Milliard, M 2005, 'Trends in the use of hospital beds by older people in Australia: 1993–2002', *Medical Journal of Australia*, vol. 182, no. 5, pp. 252–3.

Malo, M 2011, 'The impact of labour market reform at the margin on different generations: temporary contracts in Spain', in *International Conference Flex Work Research Centre 2011*, Flex Work Research Centre, University of Amsterdam, Leuven.

Management Advisory Committee 2003, *Organisational Renewal*, Commonwealth Government, Canberra.

——2005, *Senior Executive Service of the Australian Public Service – one APS – one SES*, Commonwealth Government, Canberra.

Manning, P 1998, *Spinning for Labour: trade unions and the new media environment*, Ashgate, Aldershot.

Marchington, M 2007, 'Employee voice systems', in P Boxall, J Purcell & P Wright (eds), *The Oxford handbook of human resource management*, Oxford University Press, Oxford, pp. 231–50.

Martin, G & Woldring, K 2001, 'Ready for the mantle? Australian human resource managers as stewards of ethics', *International Journal of Human Resource Management*, vol. 12, no. 2, pp. 243–55.

Masterman-Smith, H & Pocock, B 2008, *Living low paid: the dark side of prosperous Australia*, Allen & Unwin, Sydney.

McCallum, R, Moore, M & Edwards, J 2012, *Towards more productive and equitable workplaces: an evaluation of the Fair Work legislation*, Department of Education, Employment and Workplace Relations, Canberra.

McGinley, GP 1992, 'Of pirates and privateers: the historical background of the *Alien Tort Claims Act* with some suggestions for its future use', *Anglo-American Law Review*, no. 21, p. 138.

Mehaut, P, Berg, P, Grimshaw, D & Jaerling, K, with Van der Meer, M & Eskildsen, J 2010, 'Cleaning and nursing in hospitals: institutional variety and the reshaping of low-wage jobs', in E Appelbaum et al. (eds), *Low wage work in a wealthy world*, Russell Sage Foundation, New York.

Midford, R 2001, 'The nature and extent of drug related harm in the workplace', in S Allsop, M Phillips & C Calogero (eds), *Drug and work: responding to alcohol and other drug problems in Australian workplaces*, IP Communications, Melbourne, pp. 42–56.

Midford, R, Marsden, A, Phillips, M & Lake, J 1997, 'Workforce alcohol consumption: patterns at two Pilbara mining related work sites', *Journal of Occupational Health and Safety Australia and New Zealand*, no. 13, pp. 267–74.

Moody, K 1997, *Workers in a lean world: unions in the international economy*, Verso, New York.

Moore, D 2004, 'Overmighty judges 100 years of Holy Grail is enough', paper presented to the HR Nicholls Society's XXVth Conference, 6–8 August, Melbourne, viewed 20 August 2012, <http://www.hrnicholls.com.au/archives/vol25/moore2004.pdf>.

Morehead, A, Steele, M, Alexander, M, Stephen, K & Duffin, L 1997, *Changes at work: the 1995 Australian workplace industrial relations survey*, Longman, Melbourne.

Moses, A 2009, 'Facebook discipline may be illegal: expert', *Sydney Morning Herald*, 3 April, p. 12.

Murray, J 2004, 'Corporate responsibility discussion paper', *Global Social Policy*, no. 4, p. 171.

National Retail Association 2012, *Annual Wage Review 2011/2012: submission to Fair Work Australia*, National Retail Association, Brisbane.

Naughton, R 2011, 'The low paid bargaining scheme: an interesting idea, but can it work?', *Australian Journal of Labour Law*, vol. 24, no. 3, pp. 214–37.

News.com 2009, 'Holden halves production at SA plant', viewed 7 November 2011, <http://www.news.com.au/holden-halves-production-at-sa-plant/story-0-697292994>.

Nightingale, S, Ossolinski, C & Zurawski, A 2010, 'Activity in global foreign exchange markets', *Reserve Bank of Australia Bulletin*, December, pp. 45–51, viewed 20 August 2012, <http://www.rba.gov.au/publications/bulletin/2010/dec/pdf/bu-1210-6.pdf>.

NIOSH 2002, *The changing organization of work and the safety and health of working people: knowledge gaps and research directions*, Department of Health and Human Services, Cincinnati.

Nolan, J 2000, 'Unions stuffed or stoned', *Workers Online*, 7 September, pp. 1–5.

Nolan, J & Nomchong, K 2001, *Fitness for duty – recent legal developments*, ACIRRT Working Paper No. 69, ACIRRT, Canberra.

Nyland, C & O'Rourke, A 2005, 'The Australia–United States Free Trade Agreement and the ratcheting-up of labour standards: a precedent set and an opportunity missed', *Journal of Industrial Relations*, vol. 47, no. 4, pp. 457–70.

O'Brien, J 1994, 'McKinsey, Hilmer and the BCA: the "New Management" model of labour market reform', *Journal of Industrial Relations*, vol. 34, no. 2, pp. 468–91.

O'Brien, J & O'Donnell, M 2000, 'A changing public sector: developments at the Commonwealth level', *Australian Journal of Public Administration*, vol. 59, no. 4, pp. 59–66.

——2007, 'From workplace bargaining to workplace relations: industrial relations under the Coalition government', in M Pittard & P Weeks (eds), *Public sector employment law in the twenty first century*, ANU e-Press, Canberra, pp. 127–54.

O'Loughlin, K, Humpel, N & Kendig, H 2010, 'Impact of the Global Financial Crisis on employed Australian baby boomers', *Australasian Journal on Ageing*, vol. 29, no. 2, pp. 88–91.

O'Loughlin, T & Watson, I 1997, *'Loyalty is a one way street: NESB immigrants and long-term unemployment'*, ACIRRT, University of Sydney, Sydney.

O'Rourke, A & Nyland, C 2006, 'The recent history of the *Alien Tort Claims Act*', *Australian Year Book of International Law*, Centre for International & Public Law, ANU College of Law, Australian National University, Canberra, p. 25.

OECD 2000, 'Employment in the service economy: a reassessment', in OECD, *Employment outlook 2000*, OECD, Paris.

——2005, *Employment outlook*, OECD, Paris.

——2006, *Employment outlook boosting jobs and incomes 2006*, OECD, Paris.

——2007a, *Employment outlook*, OECD, Paris.

——2007b, *Maternal employment rates, part 2: labor market position of families*, viewed 20 September 2009, <http://www.oecd.org/document/4/0,3343, en_2649_34819)_3783 6996_1_1_1_1.0.0.html>.

——2008a, *Growing unequal: income distribution and poverty in OECD countries*, OECD, Paris

——2008b, *Employment outlook*, OECD, Paris

——2010, *Employment outlook*, OECD, Paris.

——2011, *Employment outlook*, OECD, Paris.

——n.d., OECD Family Database, viewed 20 November 2012, <http://www.oecd.org/els/social/family/database http://www.oecd.org/social/familiesandchildren/38752777.pdf>.

OHS Alert 2011, 'Patrick fined $180K in Victoria's first OHS discrimination conviction', CCH Australia, 24 January.

Orchard, L 1998, 'Managerialism, economic rationalisation and public sector reform in Australia: connections, divergences, alternatives', *Australian Journal of Public Administration*, vol. 57, no. 1, pp. 19–32.

Owens, R 2006, 'Working precariously: the safety net after Work Choices', *Australian Journal of Labour Law*, vol. 19, issue 2, pp. 161–82.

Owens, R, Riley, J & Murray, J 2011, *The law of work*, 2nd edn, Oxford University Press, Melbourne.

Oxenbridge, S & Brown, W 2002, 'The two faces of partnership? An assessment of partnership and co-operative employer/trade union relationships', *Employee Relations*, vol. 24, no. 3, pp. 262–76.

Paauwe, J 2009, 'HRM and performance: achievements, methodological issues and prospects', *Journal of Management Studies*, no. 46, pp. 127–40.

Pagnattaro, MA 2004, 'Enforcing international labor standards: the potential of the *Alien Tort Claims Act*', *Vanderbilt Journal of Transnational Law*, no. 37, p. 203.

Parham, D 2012, 'Australia's productivity growth slump: signs of crisis, adjustment or both?' Visiting Research Paper, Productivity Commission, viewed 20 October 2012, <http://www.pc.gov.au/research/visiting-researcher/productivity-slump>.

Parker, M & Slaughter, J 1993, 'Should the labour movement buy TQM?' *Journal of Organisational Change Management*, vol. 6, no. 4, pp. 43–56.

Pech, J, Nelms, L, Yuen, K & Bolton, T 2009, *Retail trade industry profile*, Australian Fair Pay Commission Secretariat, Canberra.

Peetz, D 1998, *Unions in a contrary world: the future of the Australian trade union movement*, Cambridge University Press, Melbourne.

——2005, 'Decollectivist strategies in Oceania', *Relations Industrielles/Industrial Relations*, vol. 57, no. 2, pp. 252–81.

——2006, *Brave new workplace: how individual contracts are changing our jobs*, Allen & Unwin, Sydney.

——2007, *Assessing the impact of Work Choices one year on*, Department of Innovation, Industry and Regional Development, Melbourne.

Peetz, D & Preston, A 2007, *AWAs, Collective agreements and earnings: beneath the aggregate data*, Industrial Relations Victoria, Department of Innovation, Industry and Regional Development, Melbourne.

Philips, K & Eamets, R 2007, *Impact of globalisation on industrial relations in the EU and other major economies*, European Institute for the Improvement of Living and Working Conditions, Dublin.

Pike, B 2004, '5200 more nurses now in Victoria's hospitals', media release, Minister of Health, 6 October.

Pittard, M 2005, 'Recent legislation and legislative commentary: agreements straying beyond employment matters. The impact of the Agreement Validation Matters legislation', *Australian Journal of Labour Law*, vol. 18, no. 1, pp. 62–8.

——2006a, 'Back to the future: unjust termination of employment under the Work Choices legislation', *Australian Journal of Labour Law*, vol. 19, no. 2, pp. 225–41.

——2006b, 'Fairness in dismissal: a devalued right', in J Teicher, R Lambert and A O'Rourke (eds), *WorkChoices: the new industrial relations agenda*, Pearson Education, Sydney.

——2011, 'Reflections on the Commission's legacy in minimum standards', *Journal of Industrial Relations*, vol. 53, no. 5, pp. 698–517.

Pittard, M & Naughton, R 2010, *Australian labour law: text, cases and commentary*, 5th edn, LexisNexis Butterworths, Sydney.

Plantenga, J & Remery, C 2009, *Flexible working time arrangements and gender equality: a comparative review of 30 European countries*, European Commission Directorate-General for Employment, Social Affairs and Equal Opportunities, Rome.

Pocock, B 2003, *The work/life collision*, Federation Press, Sydney.

——2009, *Low paid workers, changing patterns of work and life, and participation in vocational education and training: a discussion starter*, Centre for Work and Life, University of South Australia, Adelaide.

Pocock, B, Buchanan, J & Campbell, I 2004, 'Meeting the challenge of casual work in Australia: evidence, past treatment and future policy', *Australian Bulletin of Labour*, vol. 30, no. 1, pp. 16–32.

Popma, J 2008, 'Does worker participation improve health and safety?' in *Safety Reps in Europe: a vital asset for prevention strategies*, proceedings of a joint conference of the European Trade Union Confederation and the Health and Safety Department of the ETUI-REHS, Brussels.

Porter, ME 1980, *Competitive strategy: techniques for analysing industries and competitors*, The Free Press, New York.

——1985, *Competitive advantage: creating and sustaining superior performance*, The Free Press, New York.

Preston, A & Burgess, J 2003, 'Women's work in Australia: trends, issues and prospects', *Australian Journal of Labour Economics*, vol. 6, no. 4, pp. 497–518.

Productivity Commission 2003, *Trends in Australian manufacturing*, Commission Research Paper, viewed 20 August 2012, <http://www.pc.gov.au/__data/assets/pdf_file/0005/8447/tiam.pdf>.

——2010, *Performance benchmarking of Australian business regulation: occupational health and safety, research report*, Productivity Commission, Canberra.

——2011, *Economic structure and performance of the Australian retail industry*, Report no. 56, Productivity Commission, Canberra.

Pusey, M 1991, *Economic rationalism in Canberra*, Cambridge University Press, Melbourne.

Pyman, A, Cooper, B, Teicher, J & Holland, P 2006, 'A comparison of the effectiveness of employee voice arrangements in Australia', *Industrial Relations Journal*, vol. 37, no. 5, pp. 543–59.

Pyman, A, Holland, P, Teicher, J & Cooper, BK 2010, 'Industrial relations climate, employee voice and managerial attitudes to unions: an Australian study', *British Journal of Industrial Relations*, vol. 48, no. 2, pp. 460–80.

Pyman, A, Teicher, J, Cooper, B & Holland, P 2009, 'Unmet demand for union membership in Australia', *Journal of Industrial Relations*, vol. 51, no. 1, pp. 5–24.

Quiggin, J 1996, *Great expectations: microeconomic reform and Australia*, Allen & Unwin, Sydney.

Quinlan, M 2007, 'Organisational restructuring/downsizing, OHS regulation and worker health and wellbeing', *International Journal of Law and Psychiatry*, vol. 30, nos 4–5, pp. 385–99.

Quinlan, M & Bohle, P 2004, 'Contingent work and occupational safety', in J Barling & MR Frone (eds), *The psychology of workplace safety*, American Psychological Association, Washington, DC, pp. 81–106.

——2009, 'Overstretched and unreciprocated commitment: reviewing research on the occupational health and safety effects of downsizing and job insecurity', *International Journal of Health Services*, vol. 39, no. 1, pp. 1–44.

Quinlan, M, Bohle, P & Lamm, F 2010, *Managing occupational health and safety: a multidiscipli-nary approach*, 3rd edn, Palgrave Macmillan, Melbourne.

Quinlan, M, Johnstone, R & McNamara, M 2009, 'Australian health and safety inspectors' perceptions and actions in relation to changed work arrangements', *Journal of Industrial Relations*, vol. 51, no. 4, pp. 557–73.

Quinlan, M, Mayhew, C & Bohle, P 2001, 'The global expansion of precarious employment, work disorganization, and consequences for occupational health: a review of recent research', *International Journal of Health Services*, vol. 31, no. 2, pp. 335–414.

Rainey, H 1999, 'Using corporations of public and private organisations to assess innovative attitudes among members of organisations', *Public Productivity & Management Review*, vol. 23, no. 2, pp. 130–49.

Reichel, A, Brandl, J & Mayrhofer, W 2010, 'The strongest link: legitimacy of top management diversity, sex stereotypes and the rise of women in human resource management', *Management Revue*, vol. 21, no. 3, pp. 332–52.

'Reith defends individual choice in IR' 2011, *Lateline*, ABC TV, 21 September, viewed 20 February 2012, <http://www.abc.net.au/lateline/content/2011/s3323022.htm>.

Reith, P 1998, *Approaches to dispute resolution: a role for mediation*, Ministerial Discussion Paper, August.

——1999a, 'The *Workplace Relations Act 1996* – progress to date, and the need for further reform', address to the Australian Institute of Management, 22 February.

——1999b, 'The continuing reform of workplace relations: implementation of the More Jobs Better Pay', *Implementation Discussion Paper*, 6 May, AGPS, Canberra.

——2000, '*Dispute resolution in workplace relations: a possible role for mediation*', address to LEADR, ADR international conference, Sydney.

Renaud, S 2002, 'Rethinking the union membership/job satisfaction relationship', *International Journal of Manpower*, vol. 23, no. 2, pp. 137–50.

Reserve Bank of Australia 2005, 'The Australian foreign exchange and derivatives markets', *RBA Bulletin*, June, viewed 20 February 2012, <http://www.rba.gov.au/Publications AndResearch/Bulletin/2005/index.html>.

Rhoades, L & Eisenberger, R 2002, 'Perceived organizational support: a review of the literature', *Journal of Applied Psychology*, no. 87, pp. 698–714.

Rinehart, J, Huxley, C & Robertson, D 1999, *Just another car factory? Lean production and its discontents*, Cornell University Press, Ithaca, NY.

Robbins, W 2005, 'The case for unfair dismissal reform: a review of the evidence', *Australian Bulletin of Labour*, vol. 31, no. 3, pp. 237–54.

Robinson, L, Long, M & Lamb, S 2011, *How young people are faring: the national report on the learning and work situations of young Australians*, Foundation for Young Australians, Melbourne.

Roos, PA & Manley, JE 1996, 'Staffing personnel: feminization and change in human resource management', *Sociological Focus*, vol. 39, no. 3, pp. 245–61.

Rosen, EI 2005, 'The Wal-Mart effect: the World Trade Organization and the race to the bottom', *Chapman Law Review*, vol. 8, pp. 261–82.

Rudd, K & Gillard, J 2007a, *Forward with Fairness: Labor's plan for fairer and more productive Australian workplaces*, Australian Labor Party, Canberra.

——2007b, *Forward with Fairness: policy implementation plan*, Australian Labor Party, Canberra.

Russell, B 2008, 'Unions in the information economy: info-service work and organizing in Australian call centres', *Journal of Industrial Relations*, vol. 50, no. 2, pp. 285–303.

——2009, *Smiling down the line: info service work in the global economy*, University of Toronto, Toronto.

Sammut, J 2008, *Why public hospitals are overcrowded: ten points for policy makers*, Centre for Independent Studies, Sydney.

Sarkozy, N 2009, President's speech, delivered at the 12th sitting of the ILO Summit on the Global Jobs Crisis, ILO, Geneva, 15 June, viewed 20 August 2012, <http://www.ilo.org/wcmsp5/groups/public/---ed_norm/---relconf/documents/meetingdocument/wcms_108204.pdf>.

Saundrey, R & Wibberley, G 2012, *Managing individual conflict in the private sector: a case study*, ACAS Research Paper 05/12, ACAS, London.

Schuler, R 1992, 'Strategic human resources management: linking the people with the strategic needs of the business', *Organizational Dynamics*, vol. 21, no. 1, p. 18.

Scott-Howman, A 2004, 'Developments in employment law', paper presented to LexisNexis Professional Development In-House Counsel Legal Summit, Sydney.

Sempill, J 2001, 'Under the lens: electronic workplace surveillance', *Australian Journal of Labour Law*, no. 14, pp. 111–44.

Sengenberger, W 2005, *Globalization and social progress: the role and impact of international labour standards*, Friedrich-Ebert-Stiftung, Washington, DC.

Shaw, A & Blewett, V 2000, 'What works? The strategies which help to integrate OHS management within business development and the role of the outsider', in K Frick, PL Jensen, M Quinlan & T Wilthagen (eds), *Systematic occupational health and safety management: perspectives on an international development*, Pergamon, Amsterdam.

Sheehan, C & De Cieri, H 2012, 'Charting the strategic trajectory of the Australian HR professional', *Asia Pacific Journal of Human Resources*, no. 50, pp. 151–68.

Sheehan, C, Holland, P & De Cieri, H 2006, 'Current developments in HRM in Australian organisations', *Asia Pacific Journal of Human Resources*, vol. 44, no. 2, pp. 2–22.

Siefert, H 2011, 'Non-regular employment in Germany', in *2011 JILPT International Seminar on Non-Regular Employment* (proceedings), Japan Institute for Labour Policy and Training, Tokyo.

Siegrist, J 1996, 'Adverse health effects of high-effort/low-reward conditions', *Journal of Occupational Health Psychology*, vol. 1, no. 1, pp. 27–41.

Silla, I, Gracia, JF & Peiro, JM 2005, 'Job insecurity and health-related outcomes among different types of temporary workers', *Economic and Industrial Democracy*, vol. 26, no. 1, pp. 89–117.

Simmons, JA 2003, 'Balancing performance, accountability and equity in stakeholder relationships: towards more socially responsible HR practice', *Corporate Social Responsibility and Environmental Management*, vol. 10, no. 3, pp. 129–40.

Sisson, K 2000, *Direct participation and the modernisation of work organisation*, European Foundation for the Improvement of Living and Working Conditions, Dublin.

Skinner, N & Pocock, B 2011 'Flexibility and work–life interference in Australia', *Journal of Industrial Relations*, vol. 53, no. 1, pp. 65–82.

Slater, G 2011, 'Non-regular employment in the United Kingdom', in *2011 JILPT International Seminar on Non-regular Employment* (proceedings), Japan Institute for Labour Policy and Training, Tokyo.

Sloan, K & Gavin, J 2010, 'Human resource management: meeting the ethical obligations of the function', *Business and Society Review*, vol. 115, no. 1, pp. 57–74.

Smith, CK, Silverstein, BA, Bonauto, DK, Adams, D & Fan, ZJ 2010, 'Temporary workers in Washington State', *American Journal of Industrial Medicine*, no. 53, pp. 135–45.

Sprague, J-A 2012, 'Parts maker gears up for expansion', *Australian Financial Review*, 15 January, p. 15.

Sprague, R 2007, 'From Taylorism to the Omnipticon: expanding employee surveillance beyond the workplace', *John Marshall Journal of Computer and Informational Law*, no. 25 (Winter), pp. 1–32.

Standing, G 2011, *The precariat: the new dangerous class*, Bloomsbury Academic, London.

Stanton, P, Young, S & Willis, E 2003, 'Financial restraint, budget cuts and outsourcing: impact of the new public sector management in Victoria', *Contemporary Nurse*, vol. 14, no. 2, pp. 115–22.

Steering Committee for the Review of Government Service Provision 2003, 'Key indicators', in *Overcoming Indigenous disadvantage*, Steering Committee, Canberra.

——2005, 'Key indicators', in *Overcoming Indigenous disadvantage*, Steering Committee, Canberra.

——2007, 'Key indicators', in *Overcoming Indigenous disadvantage*, Steering Committee, Canberra.

Stephens, J & Bertone, S 1995, *Manufacturing uncertainty: non-English-speaking background women and training*, AGPS, Canberra.

Stewart, A 2009, *Employment law*, Federation Press, Sydney.

——2011, *Stewart's guide to employment law*, Federation Press, Sydney.

Stewart-Compton, R, Mayman, S & Sherrif, B 2009, *National review into model occupational health and safety laws, second report*, Australian Government, Canberra.

Stiglitz, J 2002, *Globalization and its discontents*, WW Norton, New York.

Stone, J 2006, *The origins and influence of the HR Nicholls Society*, Proceedings of 'Lets Start All Over Again', HR Nicholls Society, Sydney, March, viewed 20 January 2013, <http://www. hrnicholls.com.au/archives/vol27/vol27-3.php>.

Strachan, G, Burgess, J & Henderson, L 2007, 'Equal employment opportunity legislation and policies: the Australian experience', *Equal Opportunities International*, vol. 26, no. 6, pp. 525–40.

Strazdins, L, D'Souza, RM, Lim, LLY, Broom, DH & Rodgers, B 2004, 'Job strain, job insecurity, and health: rethinking the relationship', *Journal of Occupational Health Psychology*, vol. 9, no. 4, pp. 296–305.

Svensen, S 1995, *Industrial war: the great strikes 1890–1894*, Ram Press, Wollongong.

Targeted Campaigns Unit, Fair Work Ombudsman 2011, *Analyses: time frames and recoveries*, September, viewed 20 August 2012, <http://www.fairwork.gov.au/Documents/Complaint-time-and-recoveries-analysis-September-2011.pdf>.

Tattersall, A 2004, 'Community unionism: a strategy for union power under neoliberalism', in proceedings of AIRAANZ Conference, *New Economies: New Industrial Relations*, 3–6 February, Noosa, pp. 255–63.

Teicher, J & Barton, R 2002, *The vanishing public sector: employee relations management – Australia in a global context*, Pearson Education, Sydney, pp. 177–82.

Teicher, J, Holland, P & Gough, R (eds) 2006, *Employee relations management: Australia in a global context*, 2nd edn, Pearson Education, Sydney.

Teicher, J, Holland, P, Pyman A & Cooper, B 2005, 'Australian workers: finding their voice?', in P Boxall, R Freeman & P Haynes (eds), *Voice and voicelessness in the Anglo-American world: continuity and transformation in employee representation*, Cornell University Press, Ithaca, NY, pp. 125–44.

Teicher, J, Lambert, R & O'Rourke, A 2009, *WorkChoices: the new industrial relations agenda*, 2nd edn, Pearson Education, Sydney.

Tonelson, A 2000, *The race to the bottom: why a worldwide worker surplus and uncontrolled free trade are sinking American living standards*, Westview Press, Boulder, CO.

Towers, B 1997, *The representation gap: change and reform in the British and American workplace*, Oxford University Press, Oxford.

Traxler, F 1995, 'Farewell to labor market associations? Organized versus disorganized decentralization as a map for industrial relations', in C Crouch & F Traxler (eds), *Organized industrial relations in Europe: what future?* Avebury, Brookfield, VT.

Triplett, JE & Bosworth, B 2006, 'Baumol's disease has been cured: IT and multifactor productivity in US service industries', in D Jansen (ed.), *The new economy and beyond: past, present, and future*, Edward Elgar, Cheltenham, pp. 34–71.

Tsogas, G 1999, 'Labour standards in international trade agreements: an assessment of the arguments', *The International Journal of Human Resource Management*, vol. 10, no. 2, pp. 352–75.

Tufts, S 1998, 'Community unionism in Canada and Labor's (re)organization of space', *Antipode*, vol. 30, no. 3, pp. 227–50.

Turner, L 2005, 'From transformation to revitalisation: a new research agenda for a contested global economy', *Work and Occupations*, vol. 32, no. 4, pp. 383–99.

Ulrich, D 2009, *HR transformation*, McGraw-Hill, New York.

Ulrich, D & Brockbank, W 2005, *The HR value proposition*, Harvard Business School Press, Boston.

Underhill, E 2008, '*Double jeopardy: occupational injury and rehabilitation of temporary agency workers*', PhD thesis, University of New South Wales, Sydney.

Underhill, E & Quinlan, M 2011, 'How precarious employment affects health and safety at work: the case of temporary agency workers', *Relations Industrielles*, vol. 66, no. 3, pp. 397–421.

United States Trade Representative (USTR) 2009, *Trade policy: a level playing field for American workers*, 24 July, <http://www.ustr.gov/about-us/press-office/fact-sheets/2009/july/trade-policy-level-playing-field-american-workers>.

Unocal 2005, 'Final settlement reached in *Doe v Unocal*', media release, viewed 20 February 2012, <http://www.earthrights.org/legal/final-settlement-reached-doe-v-unocal>.

Vallas, SP 2003, 'Why teamwork fails: obstacles to workplace change in four manufacturing plants', *American Sociological Review*, vol. 68, no. 2, pp. 223–50.

van Barneweld, K 2006, 'Australian Workplace Agreements under WorkChoices', *The Economics and Labour Relations Review*, vol. 16, no. 2, pp. 165–91.

Van Buren III, HJ, Greenwood, M & Sheehan, C 2011, 'Strategic human resource management and the decline of employee focus', *Human Resource Management Review*, no. 21, pp. 209–19.

Van Dyne, L, Ang, S & Botero, IC 2003, 'Conceptualizing employee silence and employee voice as multidimensional constructs', *Journal of Management Studies*, vol. 40, no. 6, pp. 1359–92.

Van Gramberg, B 2006, *Managing workplace conflict: ADR in Australian workplaces*, Federation Press, Sydney.

Van Gramberg, B & Teicher, J 2000, *Creating the managerial state: industrial relations and human resource management in the Australian and Canadian public sector*, National Key Centre in Industrial Relations, Monash University, Melbourne.

van Wanrooy, B, Wright, S, Buchanan, J, Baldwin, S & Wilson, S 2009, *Australia at work: in a changing world*, Workplace Research Centre, Sydney.

Van Wezel Stone, K 1996, 'Labour in the global economy: four approaches to transnational labour regulation', in WW Bratton, J McCahery, S Picciotto & C Scott (eds), *International regulatory competition and coordination*, Clarendon Press, Oxford.

Verma, A 2005, 'What do unions do to the workplace? Union effects on management and HRM policies', *Journal of Labor Research*, vol. 16, no. 3, pp. 415–49.

Victorian Law Reform Commission 2005, *Workplace privacy*, Final Report, VLRFC, Melbourne.

Victorian Trades Hall Council 2004, *The view from the front line: a report on the experiences of OHS Reps*, Victorian Trades Hall Council, Melbourne.

Vidal, M 2007, 'Manufacturing empowerment? "Employee involvement" in the labour process after Fordism', *Socio-Economic Review*, no. 5, pp. 197–232.

Virtanen, M, Kivimäki, M, Joensuu, M, Virtanen, P, Elovainio, M & Vahtera, J 2005, 'Temporary employment and health: a review', *International Journal of Epidemiology*, no. 34, pp. 610–22.

Virtanen, M, Pentti, J, Vahtera, J, Ferrie, JE, Stansfeld, SA, Helenius, H, Elovainio, M, Honkonen, T, Terho, K, Oksanen, T & Kivimäki, M 2008, 'Overcrowding in hospital wards as a predictor of antidepressant treatment among hospital staff', *American Journal of Psychiatry*, vol. 165. pp. 1482–6.

Virtanen, P, Vahtera, J, Kivimäki, M, Pentti, J & Ferrie, J 2002, 'Employment security and health', *Journal of Epidemiology and Community Health*, vol. 56, no. 8, pp. 569–85.

Walker, B & RT Hamilton 2011, 'Employee–employer grievances: a review', *International Journal of Management Reviews*, vol. 13, no. 1, pp. 40–50.

Wallace, P 2004, *The internet in the workplace*, Cambridge University Press, Cambridge.

Walsh, P, Bryson, J & Lonti, Z 2002, 'Jack be nimble, Jill be quick: HR capability and organisational agility on the New Zealand Public and Private Sectors', *Asia Pacific Journal of Human Resources*, vol. 40, no. 2, pp. 177–92.

Walters, D 2011, 'Worker representation and psychosocial risks: a problematic relationship?' *Safety Science*, vol. 49, no. 4, pp. 599–606.

Walters, D & Frick, K 2000, 'Worker participation and the management of occupational health and safety: reinforcing or conflicting strategies', in K Frick, PL Jensen, M Quinlan & T Wilthagen (eds), *Systematic occupational health and safety management*, Pergamon, Amsterdam.

Walters, D & Nichols, T 2007, *Worker representation and workplace health and safety*, Palgrave Macmillan, New York.

Waterman, P 2005, 'Labor and new social movements in a globalising world system: the future of the past', *Labor History*, vol. 46, no. 2, pp. 195–207.

Watson, I 2010, *Mobility among the low paid workforce, Australia 2001 to 2008*, ACTU, Canberra.

Watson, I, Buchanan, J, Campbell, I & Briggs, C 2003, *Fragmented futures: new challenges in working life*, Federation Press, Sydney.

Weame, N, Stafford, N, Southwell, A & Battams, J 2010, *Fair Work Australia unfair dismissal conciliation research survey results*, TNS Social Research, Geelong, viewed 20 January 2012, <http://www.fwa.gov.au/documents/dismissals/report.pdf>.

Webb, G & Festa, J 1994, 'Alcohol and other drug problems in the workplace: is drug testing the appropriate solution?', *Journal of Occupational Health and Safety – Australia and New Zealand*, vol. 10, no. 2, pp. 95–106.

Weller, S 1999, 'Clothing outwork: union strategy, labor regulation and labor market restructuring', *Journal of Industrial Relations*, vol. 41, no. 2, pp. 203–27.

Westin, A 1992, 'Analysis of electronic monitoring: employee perceptions of fairness and the climate of employee trust or distrust', *Applied Ergonomics*, no. 23, pp. 35–42.

Wieners, B 2004, 'Ricardo Semler: set them free', *CIO Insight*, 1 April, accessed 16 January 2013, <http://www.cioinsight.com/c/a/Expert-Voices/Ricardo-Semler-Set-Them-Free>.

Whelan, J 2011, *The state of the Australian public service: an alternative report*, Occasional Paper 12, Centre for Policy Development, accessed 6 June 2012, <http://cpd.org.au/wp-content/uploads/2011/08/CPD_OP12_2011_State_of_APS_Whelan.pdf>.

White, N & Bray, M 2005, 'The labour relations of public healthcare reform in New South Wales', in K Wetzel (ed.), *Industrial relations and health reform: a comparative study of five jurisdictions*, Palgrave Macmillan, Melbourne.

Wilkinson, A, Dundon, T, Marchington, M & Ackers, P 2004, 'Changing patterns of employee voice: case studies from the UK and Republic of Ireland', *Journal of Industrial Relations*, vol. 46, no. 3, pp. 298–322.

Willis, E 2005, 'The variable impact of new public sector management and budget cuts on the work intensification of nurses and doctors in one public hospital in South Australia 1994–2000', *Australian Bulletin of Labour*, vol. 31, no. 3, pp. 255–69.

Willman, P, Bryson, A & Gomez, R 2006, 'The sound of silence: which employers choose no employee voice and why?', *Socio-Economic Review*, vol. 4, no. 2, pp. 283–99.

——2007, 'The long goodbye: new establishments and the fall of union voice in Britain', *International Journal of Human Resource Management*, vol. 18, no. 7, pp. 1318–34.

Womack, JP, Jones, DT & Roos, D 1990, *The machine that changed the world*, Maxwell Macmillan, New York.

Wood, SJ & Wall, TD 2007, 'Work enrichment and employee voice in human resource management performance studies', *International Journal of Human Resource Management*, vol. 18, no. 7, pp. 1335–72.

Woolcock, E & Jerrard, M 2009, 'The role of employer associations in lobbying government: a cross-case comparison of the Australian Mines and Metals Association and the Australian Industry Group in 2007', *International Employment Relations Review*, vol. 15, no. 2, pp. 38–57.

Woolnough, R 2008, 'Get out of my Facebook', *Employment Law*, May, pp. 14–15.

World Economic Forum 2008, *The gender gap index*, World Economic Forum, Geneva.

World Health Organization (WHO) 2007, *Employment conditions and health inequalities: final report to the WHO commission on social determinants of health*, Employment Conditions Knowledge Network, WHO, Geneva.

Wright, C 1995, *Australian studies in labour relations: the management of labour – a history of Australian employers*, Oxford University Press, Melbourne.

——2006, 'The social dimension of the integration of Australian automotive manufacturing into global supply chains', *Employment Relations Record*, vol. 6, no. 2, pp. 47–60.

Wright, PM, Gardner, TM, Moynihan, LM & Allen, MR 2005, 'The relationship between HR practices and firm performance: examining causal order', *Personnel Psychology*, vol. 58, pp. 409–46.

Wright, PM, McMahan, G, Snell, SA & Gerhart, B 2001, 'Comparing line and HR executives' perceptions of HR effectiveness: services, roles, and contributions', *Human Resource Management*, vol. 40, no. 2, pp. 111–23.

Zumbansen, P 2005, 'The parallel worlds of corporate governance and labor law', *Indiana Journal of Global Legal Studies*, no. 13, p. 261.

■ Cases

Australian Municipal, Administrative, Clerical & Services Union v Ansett Australia Ltd [2000] FCA 441 (7 April 2000).

Automotive, Food, Metals Engineering, Printing and Kindred Industries Union v Visy Packaging Pty Ltd (No. 2) [2011] FCA 953 (31 August 2011).

Barclay v The Board of Bendigo Regional Institute of Technical and Further Education, 2011, FCAFC 14.

Batterham and Others v Dairy Farmers Ltd [2011] FWA 1230 (29 March 2011).

Christos v Curtin University of Technology [PR970172] AIRC (22 March 2006).

Construction, Forestry, Mining and Energy Union – Mining and Energy Division v Tahmoor Coal Pty Ltd, 2010, FWAFB 3510.

Construction, Forestry, Mining and Energy Union v Woodside Burrup Pty Ltd and Kentz E & C Pty Ltd, 2010, FWAFB 6021.

Doe v Unocal Corporation, 2002, United States Court of Appeals for the Ninth Circuit, <http://www.earthrights.org/files/Legal%20Docs/Unocal/0056603.pdf?>.

Electrolux Home Products Pty Ltd v Australian Workers' Union & Others, 2004, HCA 40.

Fair Work Ombudsman v Australian Shooting Academy Pty Ltd, FCA 1064.

Griffiths v Rose [2011] FCA 30 (31 January 2011).

Kenny v Epic Energy [PR S0947] AIRC (15 November 1999).

Narong Khammaneechan v Nanakhon Pty Ltd ATF, Nanakhon Trading Trust T/A Banana Tree Café, 2010, FWA 7891.

Owusu-Ansah v Danoz Direct Pty Ltd [2010] FWA 6340 (18 August 2010).

Queensland Rail v M Wake [PR 974391] AIRC (19 October 2006).

Re Minister for Tertiary Education, Skills, Jobs and Workplace Relations, 2011, Fair Work Australia Full Bench 7444.

Re The Manufacturing Grocers' Employees Federation of Australia & Another; Ex parte The Australian Chamber of Manufactures & Another, 1986, 160 CLR 341.

Willmott v Bank of Western Australia Ltd [2001] WAIRC 03013 (13 June 2001).

■ Legislation

Commonwealth

Age Discrimination Act 2004

Building and Construction Improvement Act 2005

Building and Construction Industry Improvement Amendment (Transition to Fair Work) Act 2012

Conciliation and Arbitration Act 1904

Copyright Act 1968

Disability Discrimination Act 1992

Equal Employment Opportunity (Commonwealth Authorities) Act 1987

Equal Opportunity for Women in the Workplace Act 1999

Fair Work Act 2009

Fair Work (Registered Organisations) Act 2009

Human Rights Act 2004

Independent Contractors Act 2006

Industrial Relations Act 1988

Industrial Relations Reform Act 1993

Paid Parental Leave Act 2010

Public Service Act 1999

Racial Discrimination Act 1975

Sex Discrimination Act 1984

Trade Practices Act 1974

Workplace Relations Act 1996

Workplace Relations Amendment (Work Choices) Act 2005

ACT
Workplace Privacy Act 2011

NSW
Workplace Video Surveillance Act 1998

Workplace Surveillance Act 2005

Victoria
Occupational Health and Safety Act 2004

Surveillance Devices Act 1999

Surveillance Devices (Workplace Privacy) Act 2006

United States
Alien Tort Claims Act 1789

Judiciary Act 1789

■ Index

United States, 5
  Alien Tort Claims Act 1789, 65, 75–7
  and Australian FTA, 31, 35, 37
  automotive industry, 239
  and Chile FTA, 35
  Congress, 66
  debt ceiling, 6
  employment regulation, 6
  failure to ratify Havana Charter, 66
  female employment, 34
  FTAs, 71, 72, 73
  GDP, 253
  GFC, 13
  global economic crisis (1970s), 12
  good-faith bargaining, 88
  HRM practices, 5
  ICFTU membership, 57
  ILRF, 75
  income inequality, 40, 42
  low-paid work, 30, 34, 35, 37, 274
  monitoring and surveillance, 164, 166, 167, 170
  neo-liberalism, 16, 44, 269
  nursing assistants, 30, 226
  OHS risks, 197, 203
  overseas-born workers, 179
  partnership unionism, 56
  productivity growth, 30
  Republican Party, 6
  retail and hospitality, 217
  Social Networking Regulation Pulse Survey, 162
  support for trade-labour linkage, 71
  trade agreements, 72, 73
  trade laws, 73
  unionised/non-unionised workplaces, 122, 123, 124
  wage spent on child care, 30
United States–Chile Free Trade Agreement, 72
United Voice, 218
unlawful dismissal, 91–2
Unocal Corporation, 77, 79–80
US Special Trade Representative (USTR), 73

Victoria
  AIRC unfair dismissal cases, 145
  ETU–BHP 2002 dispute, 55
  OHS issues, 205, 206
  OHS laws, 205
  surveillance laws, 165
  work-related stress, 200
Victorian Health Industry Association (VHIA), 231, 232
Victorian public hospitals

Bracks–Brumby government reforms, 230–3
  Casemix system, 227, 228, 229, 236
  cost-cutting policies, 226–7
  Diagnostic Related Groups (DRGs), 227, 228
  impact of reforms, 229–30
  Kennett government reforms, 227–8
  Key Performance Indicators (KPIs), 227, 232, 234, 236
  market-driven model, implementation of, 227–8
  nurses' work pressure, 233–6
Victorian Trades Hall Council, 62, 205
video surveillance laws, 164–6
violence, workplace, 60, 151, 199
visas, work, 50

wages
  accommodation and food services, 217
  AIRC concerns, 107
  APS model, 258–60
  BCA's vision, 140
  centrally fixed, 13, 15, 20
  dispersion and inequality, 40–3
  and labour market implications, 19–21
  National Minimum Wage, 88, 181, 218, 275
web cameras, 166
welfare capitalism, 27–9
Western Australian Industrial Commission, 159
'White Australia' policy, 86
white-collar jobs, 50, 193
Whitlam government, economic reforms, 15
Willmott v Bank of Western Australia Ltd, 159
Work Choices 2005
  abolition of, 85, 86
  AIRC, 141, 146
  amendments, 3, 20, 53, 108, 144, 145, 259
  AWAs, 93
  BOOT test, 87
  diminished unfair dismissal protection, 91
  elimination of awards, 91
  impact of, 84
  industrial action and secret ballots, 89
  introduction of, 82, 84, 141
  legislated safety net, 90
  and no disadvantage test, 50, 53
  non-union bargaining, 85
work intensification, 176, 194, 195, 230, 233–6
work organisation, 2, 30, 31, 114, 176, 238
  see also Victorian public hospitals

Printed in the United States
By Bookmasters